Immigrant Faiths

Immigrant Faiths

Transforming Religious Life in America

EDITED BY
KAREN I. LEONARD, ALEX STEPICK,
MANUEL A. VASQUEZ, AND JENNIFER HOLDAWAY

ALTAMIRA
PRESS

A Division of
ROWMAN & LITTLEFIELD PUBLISHERS, INC.
Walnut Creek • Lanham • New York • Toronto • Oxford

ALTAMIRA PRESS
A division of Rowman & Littlefield Publishers, Inc.
1630 North Main Street, #367
Walnut Creek, CA 94596
www.altamirapress.com

Rowman & Littlefield Publishers, Inc.
A wholly owned subsidiary of The Rowman & Littlefield Publishing Group, Inc.
4501 Forbes Boulevard, Suite 200
Lanham, MD 20706

PO Box 317
Oxford
OX2 9RU, UK

British Library Cataloguing in Publication Information Available

Library of Congress Cataloguing-in-Publication Data
Immigrant faiths : transforming religious life in America / edited by Karen I. Leonard ...
    [et al.].
        p. cm.
    Includes bibliographical references and index.
    ISBN 0-7591-0816-1 (alk. paper)
        1. United States—Religion. 2. United States—Religious life and customs.
    I. Leonard, Karen Isaksen, 1939-

BL2525 .I39 2004
200'.86'9120973 22   2004019150

Printed in the United States of America

 The paper used in this publication meets the minimum requirements of American
National Standard for Information Sciences—Permanence of Paper for Printed Library
Materials, ANSI/NISO Z39.48–1992.

Contents

1

Introduction

Karen Leonard

This volume shows the ways in which religious beliefs and practices are often central to immigrants' lives in the United States, confirming the failure of the secularization paradigm that informed recent decades of social science research and encouraged scholars of migration to overlook religion in their inquiries. Here, we highlight religion as a major force shaping and changing constructions of personal and community identity among immigrants. We also see religious beliefs and practices relating immigrants to the state and American civic life in various ways.

In the studies published here, religion plays multiple roles, facilitating mutual accommodations and adaptations on the part of immigrants and the state. The volume analyzes the broadening of national visions of religion and of state policy and the highly contextualized and diverse ways in which immigrants practice religion in old and new homelands. Religious commitments and practices can sustain a sense of identity and provide social capital as immigrants adapt to the new society. Sometimes religion helps immigrants to retain or establish transnational networks, and sometimes it helps to engage immigrants in American civic life. Transformation or retention of religious beliefs and practices in the new context can be seen as directly assisting immigrants to adapt by "becoming American," while, at other times, they can be seen as resistance to the new society.

What makes this volume different from others addressing similar themes? First, it integrates work by both new and established scholars from a range of disciplines (History, Sociology, Anthropology, Religious Studies) and on a variety of religions (Protestant and Catholic Christianity, vodou, Hinduism, Buddhism, Japanese spirit worship, and Confucian ancestor veneration). The volume features case studies (many by younger scholars) of particular immigrant groups framed by two powerful overviews by Alex Stepick and Manuel Vasquez, leading scholars of mi-

1

gration and religion. The overviews analyze the greater depth and changing emphasis brought to both migration studies and religious studies by bringing the two scholarly arenas together. Stepick opens the volume by outlining the contributions the field of religious studies makes to migration studies, and Vasquez closes the volume by summarizing the contributions the field of migration studies makes to religious studies. Both essays push the interdisciplinary study of religion, migration, and civic life forward, integrating the case studies as they make their analytical points.

A second distinctive feature of the volume is the questioning of conventional Western or European definitions of religion. This questioning comes, first, as Stepick, Vasquez, Marquardt, and Richman insist on placing Latin American immigrants and their religious lives squarely in the modern American arena, and, second, as our other authors highlight the religious lives of a range of non-Western, that is, Asian, immigrants. Studies of religion in the U.S. have responded slowly to the expanding religious landscape, moving from a focus on Protestantism to include Catholicism and Judaism and, in the last decade or so, to include Asian-origin religions, alternative religions, and new or transformed versions of Christianity and Judaism (Tweed 1997; Wuthnow 1988). The first scholarly treatments of these recent additions emphasized believers and practitioners who were indigenous, that is, not recent immigrants (Prebish 1979; Prebish 1999; Tweed and Prothero 1999), but the balance has changed (Iwamura and Spickard 2003; Yoo 1999; Min and Kim 2002; Prebish and Tanaka 1998; Yang 2000; Yang and Ebaugh 2001).[1] Attention has now shifted to the large numbers of post-1965 immigrants who are bringing long-established religions from their homelands to the U.S., primarily Asian-origin religions and ones that resist the standard Western definitions of religion in some respects.

If we look in an ordinary dictionary for the definition of religion (for example, my old Webster's 1960), we find the following: 1. Belief in divine or superhuman power or powers to be obeyed and worshiped as creator/s and ruler/s of the universe. 2. The expression of this belief in conduct and ritual. 3. Specific systems of belief, worship, and conduct, involving a code of ethics and philosophy. 4. A state of mind or way of life expressing love for and trust in God, and/or efforts to act according to the will of God, as in monastic orders. 5. The practice of religious observances or rites.

Some of the religions studied in this volume do not fit such a definition at all.[2] European and American scholars had constructed a canon of scholarship based on an ethnocentric or Eurocentric definition of religion (and Nakasone and Sered discuss the issue further). In the American context, other features have also been taken for granted, features like congregationalism, which I will discuss below when considering what is typically "American" about religion in the U.S.

The world, in fact, has many religions that are not well defined by Webster. Hinduism does believe in divine creation of the universe and in divinity, not just one version of creation but many, and not just one divinity but many forms of it. Buddhism, on the other hand, does not believe in a divine or superhuman power or powers as creators or rulers of the universe,[3] nor, many people hold, does Taoism. Then there is the complication of Confucianism.[4] In China, Vietnam, Korea, and Japan, religious thought has been closely intertwined with Confucianism, usually considered a philosophy of state rather than a religion and yet the strongest source of the ancestor veneration so often interwoven with Buddhism, Taoism, and Shintoism in Asia. In fact, Buddhism, Taoism, and Shintoism have developed, competed, and survived in homelands dominated by Confucian state systems for centuries. We might also expect Confucianism's dominance of the state and civic life, with its emphasis on the mutual responsibilities of ruler and ruled and on merit-based social mobility (recruitment of men by competitive examination to national civil services) to have interesting implications for the civic engagement of immigrants from many parts of Asia.

The volume questions Western definitions of religion by highlighting not only religions new to the U.S. but new ways of combining religious beliefs and practices in both private and public arenas. Many people in the world combine aspects of different "religions" in their spiritual beliefs and practices. As they did in their homelands, many of the new immigrants represented in this volume combine several "religions" in their spiritual lives.[5] Ancestor veneration is a continuing feature of immigrant life for the Okinawans, Koreans, Cambodians, and Chinese. Both ancestor veneration and spirit or *kami* worship (as in Japanese Shintoism) are practiced by Okinawan immigrants, Ronald Nakasone and Susan Sered find, and this helps explain the authors' discomfort with the concept of an Okinawan "religion." Kenneth Guest analyzes Chinese immigrants who continue to practice aspects of Buddhism, Taoism, and popular religions in New York but with vital transnational overtones, and Pyong Gap Min finds Korean Buddhists who become Christian after immigration but continue to commemorate their ancestors.[6] Thomas Douglas finds Cambodian immigrants who easily adopt Christianity or combine it in different ways with Buddhism and ancestor veneration.

It is not only the Asian immigrants who combine aspects of various religions. Karen Richman analyzes Haitian Catholics, with their syncretistic mix of African-Creole and European ideas and practices. She shows how vodou practices are drawn upon or discarded by both Catholic and Protestant Haitian immigrants in Florida, immigrants who relate to Christian institutions and congregations in the U.S. differently than in Haiti. In the U.S., she found Catholics becoming Protestants (and, she suggests, becoming American), thereby escaping from vodou-based family engagements in the homeland. Marie Marquardt's comparative analysis of two Mexican immigrant churches in Doraville, an edge-city in Georgia, also finds some Catholics becoming Protestants, perhaps more for reasons of the Protestant congregation's preparation for civic engagement than for reasons of family disengagement. In contrast, the Catholic congregation in Marquardt's study nurtures a pan-Latino identity that resists accommodation to American pluralism.

A third distinctive feature, following from the second, is the volume's emphasis on transnational religious networks and the creative interplay between immigrant and homeland beliefs and practices. In the contemporary cases here, non-

Christian as well as Christian religions are enabling immigrants to retain and transmit ethnic and transnational identities. Transnational sacred geographies and institutional networks (or the lack of them) play important roles. There are no sacred groves in the U.S. and Okinawan Buddhist and *kami* (Japanese spirit worship) priestesses have not migrated, so their followers must do without key formal rituals in Honolulu and Los Angeles and may acquire Christian or other religious affiliations new to them (Nakasone and Sered). A male leader of a Buddhist, Taoist, and Chinese popular-religion temple in New York's Chinatown ministers to a small, largely illegal immigrant group in the city but to a large and increasingly wealthy group back in the migrants' home village in southeastern China (Guest). Even as Cambodian refugees in Long Beach and Seattle try to sponsor Buddhist monks from home and establish monastic centers, they combine aspects of Buddhist, Christian, and ancestor veneration beliefs and practices. Their wide-ranging efforts seem related to their refugee status and to grounding themselves in the U.S. economy, but they are also rooted in a syncretistic religious heritage from Cambodia (Douglas).

Conversion to Christianity or the addition of Christian to homeland religious beliefs and practices occurs in several of these studies. Pyong Gap Min suggests that Korean immigrants to New York who had not been Christians[7] began to attend Christian churches or converted to Christianity in order to reinforce and transmit their ethnic identity. He shows that, while some structural features of congregational life continue as before (the system of units), new cultural tasks such as the teaching of the Korean language and etiquette characterize Korean immigrant churches. For Cambodian Buddhists, Thomas Douglas traces the conversion or semi-conversion to Christianity to experiences in the refugee camps or relationships with churches sponsoring migration or resettlement (see also McLellan 1999). I have already commented, above, on the movements among Christian denominations in the Haitian and Mexican cases studied by Karen Richman and Marie Marquardt.

The emphasis on transnational religious networks also offers new insights on the ways in which religious beliefs and practices relate to migration and civic life in both old and new homelands. The importance of textual or ritual religious specialists in the new homeland is clear. Cambodian Buddhist congregations are interacting with the Immigration and Naturalization Service to bring monks to the United States, Thomas Douglas shows; although Pyong Gap Min does not see Hindu temples as centers for congregational worship, Hindu temples are also sponsoring priests. However, Ronald Nakasone and Susan Sered did not find Okinawan priestesses and shamans migrating or being sponsored by Okinawan immigrants. Among Chinese Taoist/Buddhist/Confucians in New York, Kenneth Guest shows some religious leaders moving back and forth, using resources from the U.S. to strengthen their congregations in the old country and sustaining immigrants in the U.S. who are unable to participate in civic life because of their legal status or poverty. We see among them traditional Buddhist temples, innovative Buddhist temples, and Buddhist lay organizations (distinctions made by McLellan 1999:171-177), and it is the latter two types that participate more in American civic life. But in most of Guest's cases of Buddhist, Taoist, and popular religious practices, the homeland remains the more meaningful or accessible civic arena for the immigrants in New York's Chinatown; they seem to use religion to resist the homogenizing influences of global capitalism and the American labor market.

Finally, the volume addresses the changing relationships among the nation-state, religion, immigrants, and civic life over time. The American context of religious life and the national population have both changed dramatically. Immigration policies and trends have altered the national profile, in terms of nations of origin, ethno-racial, linguistic, religious, and other characteristics.[8] The changes in religious congregations and preferences in America are not always acknowledged, as Marie Marquardt's interview of Doraville's mayor well illustrates.

Although the secular nation-state still strives to separate religion and state, it has gradually expanded its civil religion beyond Protestant Christianity to include Catholics and Jews, and now it is being challenged to include Muslims, Buddhists, Hindus, and many other groups. The larger legal context and differential access to citizenship strongly shape religious institution-building in some cases. At the present time, the Republican party in power seems inclined to extend entitlements (such as resources for social and educational services) to faith-based groups.[9] Thus, immigrants' religious activities may or may not qualify them as "faith-based communities" for federal grants and services, a consideration that brings us back to how religion is being defined and to the state as the source of religious entitlements.

With studies ranging from the late-nineteenth century to the present, the volume shows both historical continuities and changes in state policy and the consequences for religion and civic engagement. In the earliest case, Derek Chang shows how the state's vision of a Christian nation helped incorporate African American and Chinese Christians while enabling them to gain educations, develop leadership roles, and stake claims to civic institutions in Raleigh, North Carolina, and Portland, Oregon. These movements to embrace and utilize the national norm of Christian citizenship were hindered by popular and legal constraints based on race and national origin, with both groups using religion to overcome such constraints. Then, Danielle Brune Sigler highlights the dynamic religious hybridities developing among African Americans and others in the early decades of the twentieth century as a creative immigrant from Cape Verde, Daddy Grace, built a new identity and a new religious movement. Coming from a Portuguese Christian African background, he worked chiefly with internal migrants moving north, African Americans seeking religious teachings free from the white-dominated Christian churches that had tolerated slavery. Daddy Grace's discourse and practice also used religion to erase or complicate racial issues.

Racial dynamics in the U.S., explicit in Chang's and Brune Sigler's discussions, are implicit in many of the other chapters. The continuing Christian-based national visions in North America encouraged immigrant Japanese Buddhists to become Christians in the early and mid-twentieth century (McLellan 1999), and conversion or partial conversion to Christianity affords similar material and psychological protection to some Asian immigrants today, as the contributions here by Min, Douglas, and Nakasone and Sered show.

Do we see, here, new immigrants "becoming American," or fitting into existing definitions of religion and religious life in the United States? As the national civil religion in the United States expanded to include Jews as well as Christians, as Jews became "white" (Brodkin 1998), the discourse about "Christian civilization" changed to "Western civilization" and the "Judeo-Christian tradition" (Segal 2002).[10] In this volume, particularly in the chapters considering Haitians and Mexicans who are affiliating with Christian congregations, we do see immigrants adapting to these concepts to some extent. And we see a further development (not represented in this volume), as many first-generation American Muslim immigrant leaders argue that Muslims are followers of one of the three Abrahamic religions and partners in Western civilization. For these new Muslim spokesmen in the U.S., it is "Western civilization" and the "Abrahamic tradition" as they claim a place in the national civil religious arena (Leonard 2003).

But how do the followers of non-Western, Asian or African, religions, followers prominent in this volume, fit into these evolving, expanding typologies? These studies offer some answers when we turn to religious structures and processes. There are certain characteristics attributed to religion in the U.S., perhaps most notably "congregationalism" but others as well. Social scientists hypothesize (or think they have established) that religious institutions and practices become "congregational" in the U.S. and that religious specialists take on a "pastoral role" that spans a wide, not narrowly religious, range of functions (Ebaugh and Chafetz 2000; Warner and Wittner 1998; Yang and Ebaugh 2001). They hypothesize that religious practices help maintain cultural, particularly linguistic, identities for immigrants and thus are a form of social capital that can strengthen immigrant self-confidence and possibly challenge adaptation to the U.S. They also speculate that the political potential for mobilization along religious lines is enhanced by location in the modern U.S. and that immigrants' diasporic religious interactions with home countries have strong ("Americanizing?") influences back home.

Congregationalism, often simply assumed to mean worshipping as a congregation in some religious setting, actually involves much more in the U.S. (Ebaugh and Chafetz 2000). It is generally taken to mean a formal decision-making structure, a defined membership, a hired clergyman, and regularly scheduled activities. These structures usually mean, in the U.S., legal incorporation to qualify as a tax-exempt religious organization and build up a dues-paying membership. This step involves new concepts of membership and of dues-paying for many immigrants, particularly those from religious traditions where one can worship at any temple (Buddhist, Hindu, Taoist, Confucian, or Shinto), and the preparation of constitutions and selection to boards or leadership positions can lead to conflicts and splits. As Pyong Gap Min points out, a mailing list for the Hindu temple in Queens is not a membership list, even though a temple has been built and Brahman priests have been imported and are being paid.

Gender is one of the important variables here, as in religious changes in America in general (Wuthnow 1988; Braude 1997). In Theravada Buddhism, for example (followed in Sri Lanka, Cambodia, Burma, and Thailand), monks were male and their social contacts with women were minimal, but in the U.S. contacts have increased and women are being temporarily or permanently ordained (Van Esterik 1992; Numrich 1998; Leonard 1997). Thomas Douglas proposes that Buddhist restraints on women's activities seem to be one reason for Cambodian refugee women to attend Christian churches or convert to Christianity. He, and Susan Sered and Ronald Nakasone, find some immigrant women assuming leading roles in Christian churches; in the case of the Okinawan women, this would be continuity with rather than change from the spiritual roles of women in the homeland. Marie Marquardt comments on women's leadership in one of the Mexican immigrant congregations, perhaps substituting for its minister's failure to take up a pastoral role (and material on pastoral roles can be found in other chapters). Kenneth Guest discusses a female spirit medium, who, unlike Nakasone and Sered's Okinawan priestesses, does come to the United States and continues her important role with respect to a Chinese village temple.

In this volume, we see religious, ethnic, and civic identities being clearly changed by migration but still at least partially shaped by attachments to the former homelands. The various religious or spiritual groups are following beliefs and practices that sometimes help to change and incorporate immigrants and sometimes work to preserve ethnic identities and/or resist an American identity. Some religious communities are preparing their members to be full participants in American pluralism, while others socialize their members into cultures of resistance. These cultures of resistance can be based on ethnic identity politics, as evidenced by Marquardt's Mision Catolica congregation (in contrast to the Sagrada Familia one), illegality and poverty, as evidenced by many of Guest's Chinese immigrants in New York, or, perhaps, on religious beliefs and practices that do not fit "normative" American religious beliefs and practices, as Nakasone and Sered suggest for Okinawans.

Some of the authors take account of specific local or regional contexts, showing that spatial patterns already set in American urban localities, rural churches, and house and apartment designs help determine how immigrants adapt their religious practices. At the same time, transnational or global networks are taken into account. Pyong Gap Min studied immigrant Korean Christian and Indian Hindu religious institutions in Queens, New York, and he found structural continuities in both the Korean Christian and Indian Hindu cases, in the former in congregational structuring to promote fellowship among residentially contiguous members and in the latter in continued reliance on domestic worship with only occasional visits to a temple (see also Mazumdar and Mazumdar). His Hindu informants frequently equated Hinduism with Indian nationalism, perhaps a feature of the current political landscape both in India and among diasporic Hindus, while his Korean informants related their religiosity to their cultural isolation in the U.S. and made no or scant reference to Korean nationalism. Also in New York, Kenneth Guest demonstrates strikingly that for his undocumented working-class Chinese immigrants, their status means reliance on their religious networks rather than American civic or economic institutions, and those networks stretch far beyond New York.

In other chapters, transnational or global networks and movements are also important parts of the analyses. Richman and Marquardt both show that congregationalism in the U.S. coexists with strong ties to the homelands and that sometimes movements originating in the homelands come to fruition in the U.S. Douglas compares Cambodian refugees in Long Beach, California, and Seattle, Washington, but also discusses developments in Cambodia. Nakasone and Sered's Okinawans moved from Hawaii to the mainland and also moved further from their Japanese-ruled historical roots, becoming "less Japanese" than in Okinawa. In the U.S., Okinawans seem to be accommodating themselves to new religious institutions, Buddhist or Christian ones, moving away from the Shinto-influenced *kami* or spirit worship of the homeland.

While all of the chapters deal thoroughly with religion and migration, patterns of civic engagement or non-engagement are less clear. It may be that longer studies, or longitudinal studies covering the next generation, are needed explore this issue more thoroughly.[11] As second and subsequent generations grow up in the U.S., will evolving ethno-religious identities and generational differences push or pull younger believers into new and different religious institutional contexts? Perhaps we will see ethnic churches or congregations merging with mainstream Christian or Buddhist churches or congregations as the languages of preaching and teaching change to English. Perhaps as more immigrant congregations organize as legal entities to take advantage of opportunities offered by the state, we will see increasing civic engagement. Important questions remain to be answered.

Notes

1. Thus Raymond Williams discusses "American cousins" only briefly in "Asian Indian and Pakistani Religions in the United States," *Annals of the American Academy of Political and Social Science* 558 (July 1998).

2. Even this introduction or preface illustrates the ethnocentric or Eurocentric culture of knowledge reflected in standard American dictionaries: in the same Webster's, above, the first meaning of "preface" refers to Christian liturgy, to the introduction to the Canon of the Mass.

3. At the Parliament of the World's Religions Centennial in 1993, Buddhists reminded the Parliament's council that Buddhists do not regard Buddha as a god and do not worship a creator; 100 years earlier Buddhists had also protested that the Parliament privileged Christianity and presupposed theism (Tweed and Prothero 1999:372-375).

4. For religions in China, see the *Journal of Asian Studies* 54:2 (May 1995), where Daniel Overmyer, Franciscus Verellen, Rodney Taylor, Gary Arbuckle, John McRae, and Stephen Teiser present discussions of these systems of thought and ritual.

5. The contrast is to the earlier pattern discussed by Derek Chang's chapter, where early Chinese immigrant Christians are shown adhering strictly to their Protestant denominational teachings.

6. For a concise overview of Korean religion, see Baker 2002.

7. Christianity, strong back in Korea, is the majority religion among Korean Americans and the largest religion among Chinese Americans (Yang 2000:253).

8. A 2001 study by the Graduate Center of the City University of New York found that

52% of American adults identified themselves as Protestant Christians, 25% as Catholic Christians, 1.3% as religious Jews, 0.5% as Muslims, 0.5% as Buddhists, and 0.4% as Hindus: *India-West*, Nov. 2, 2001, B22. This is controversial—for example, Muslims have claimed as many as 6 million followers in the U.S., not the 1.8 million estimated here. The study does show that the number of Muslims has doubled and the number of Hindus has tripled (to 766,000) from a similar survey in 1990.

9. Nakasone and Sered point out that such entitlements will not benefit groups like the Okinawans whose spiritual beliefs and practices do not seem to fit a "religious" definition.

10. Segal (2002) argues that Brodkin is talking about social mobility and class interests, not this shifting constellation of religious and civilizational identities.

11. Suggestive here is the religious scholar Bruce Lawrence's book-length essay, *New Faiths, Old Fears* (discussing Islam and various Asian religions in America) (2002); also, the forthcoming book by Janelle Wong, *Political Incorporation and the New Americans*, covers Latino and Asian immigrants and includes religion as one of the key topics.

References

Baker, Don. 2002. "Teaching Korean Religion." *Education in Asia* 7(3):33-35.

Braude, Ann. 1997. "Women's History Is American Religious History." In *Retelling U.S. Religious History*, ed. Thomas A. Tweed. Berkeley: University of California Press.

Brodkin, Karen. 1998. *How Jews Became White Folk and What That Says About Race in America*. New Brunswick, NJ: Rutgers University Press.

Ebaugh, Helen Rose, and Janet Saltzman Chafetz. 2000. *Religion and the New Immigrants: Continuities and Adaptations in Immigrant Congregations*. Walnut Creek, CA: AltaMira.

Iwamura, Jane Naomi, and Paul Spickard, eds. 2003. *Revealing the Sacred in Asian and Pacific America*. New York: Routledge.

Lawrence, Bruce B. 2002. *New Faiths, Old Fears: Muslims and Other Asian Immigrants in American Religious Life*. New York: Columbia University Press.

Leonard, Karen Isaksen. 1997. *South Asian Americans*. Westport, CT: Greenwood Publishing Company.

———. 2003. *Muslims in the United States: The State of Research*. New York: Russell Sage Foundation.

Mazumdar, Shampa, and Sanjoy Mazumdar. 2003. "Creating the Sacred: Altars in the Hindu American Home." In *Revealing the Sacred in Asian and Pacific America*, ed. Jane Iwamura and Paul Spickard. New York: Routledge.

McLellan, Janet. 1999. *Many Petals of the Lotus: Five Asian Buddhist Communities in Toronto*. Toronto: University of Toronto Press.

Min, Pyong Gap, and Jung Ha Kim, eds. 2002. *Religions in Asian America: Building Faith Communities*. Walnut Creek, CA: AltaMira.

Numrich, Paul David. 1998. "Theravada Buddhism in America: Prospects for the Sangha." In *The Faces of Buddhism in America*, ed. Charles S. Prebish and Kenneth K. Tanaka. Berkeley: University of California Press.

Prebish, Charles S. 1979. *American Buddhism*. North Scituate, MA: Duxbury Press.

———. 1999. *Luminous Passage: The Practice and Study of Buddhism in America*. Berkeley: University of California Press.

Prebish, Charles S., and Kenneth K. Tanaka. 1998. *The Faces of Buddhism in America*. Berkeley: University of California Press.

Segal, Daniel A. 2002. Review of *How Jews Became White Folks and What That Says About Race in America*, by Karen Brodkin, *American Ethnologist* 29(2):470-473.

Tweed, Thomas A., ed. 1997. *Retelling U.S. Religious History*. Berkeley: University of California Press.

Tweed, Thomas A., and Stephen Prothero. 1999. *Asian Religions in America: A Documentary History*. New York: Oxford University Press.

Van Esterik, Penny. 1992. *Taking Refuge: Lao Buddhists in North America*. Toronto: York Lanes Press.

Warner, R. Stephen, and Judith G. Wittner, eds. 1998. *Gatherings in Diaspora: Religious Communities and the New Immigration*. Philadelphia, PA: Temple University Press.

Williams, Raymond. 1998. "Asian Indian and Pakistani Religions in the United States." *Annals of the American Academy of Political and Social Science* 558 (July).

Wong, Janelle. 2003. "Political Incorporation and the New Americans." Unpublished book manuscript.

Wuthnow, Robert. 1988. *The Restructuring of American Religion: Society and Faith Since World War II*. Princeton, NJ: Princeton University Press.

Yang, Fenggang. 2000. "The Growing Literature of Asian American Religions." *Journal of Asian American Studies* 3(2):253.

Yang, Fenggang, and Helen Rose Ebaugh. 2001. "Transformations in New Immigrant Religions and Their Global Implications." *American Sociological Review* 66 (April): 269-288.

Yoo, David K., ed. 1999. *New Spiritual Homes: Religion and Asian Americans*. Honolulu: University of Hawai'i Press.

2

God Is Apparently Not Dead
The Obvious, the Emergent, and the Still Unknown in Immigration and Religion

Alex Stepick

Framing the Question

Over a century ago, Nietzsche declared that "God is dead." Nietzsche is dead wrong today, at least for immigrants.[1] The emerging literature discussed in this chapter documents the importance of religion to many immigrants. Nevertheless, immigration scholars are just beginning to appreciate this fact. *Immigrant America* (Portes and Rumbaut 1996) and the *Handbook for International Migration* (Hirschman, et al. 1999), two of the most widely read and fundamental volumes in immigration studies, do not mention religion at all. As the importance of immigrant religion has empirically emerged, since the mid-1990s, sociologists who study religion have hectored immigration specialists to pay attention to religion (e.g., Ebaugh and Chafetz 2000b; Warner and Wittner 1998). Beginning with doctoral dissertations, gradually expanding to include larger projects and now this volume, that call is being answered.

What, if anything, does the study of immigrants' religion add to an understanding of their experience? In response, this chapter reviews the past decade of research on immigration and religion and summarizes what has now become obvious, and what is emerging and what still remains unknown. The focus of this chapter is primarily on immigrants in the U.S., although it draws upon some research among European immigrants.[2]

At a metatheoretical level, scholars address the relationship between immigration and religion from different starting points that reflect their disciplinary backgrounds. Immigration specialists tend to be concerned with religion's impact on the perennial issues of immigrants' social and economic incorporation and assimilation into their adoptive society and its connection with ethnic and national identities. Religious studies specialists are more likely to focus on how relocation to a new land affects immigrants' religious beliefs and practices, along with the social organization of religious communities and institutions.

Scholars from specific disciplines approach immigration and its relationship to religion with varied objectives and foci. Sociologists tend to prefer mid-range generalizations that typologize empirical observations according to underlying similarities. Sociologists also tend to focus on social forces, particularly demographics and formal organizations (e.g., church congregations) as their principal variables. Psychologists tend to concentrate on issues particular to the individual, such as stress and depression, along with expressions of identity. Economists' main focus is on material issues, such as the costs of immigration to society and individual immigrants' desire to maximize income. Economists' focus on immigration has primarily examined the overall costs and benefits to a nation or taken for granted that individuals' fundamental motivations are economic. Not surprisingly, economic studies of the nexus of immigration and religion are rare. Political scientists tend to concentrate on the role of the state and the conflicting powers that constitute it. Thus, the focus of their work in the field of immigration is on how states do or should attempt to control immigrant flows or how immigrants affect politics, particularly electoral politics. As with economists, few political scientists have yet to examine immigration and religion, although church-state issues have been important in the U.S. since its founding. Anthropologists usually eschew both generalization and the identification of primary forces. Rather, anthropologists speak of cultures and societies as being holistic, that is, everything is related to everything else, so that primary causes are difficult or even impossible to distinguish. Instead, from the anthropological perspective, material forces are embedded in social and cultural webs that mutually constitute each other. For many, perhaps most, anthropologists, any generalizations that are abstracted from this web inherently distort empirical reality.[3] I am an anthropologist who has frequently collaborated with sociologists and who comes to religious issues from immigration studies. This review reflects those biases. I will attempt to describe mid-level generalizations while indicating the empirical complexity of the nexus of religion and immigration. I also am more interested in how religion affects immigrants and less interested in how immigrants affect religious beliefs, practices, and organizations.

This review of immigration and religion first summarizes what I believe may be viewed as obvious, that is, mid-level empirical generalizations. Later sections discuss emerging research and those areas still awaiting investigation, that is, what is still unknown. Topics that I address in these latter sections include religion's role in identity formation and maintenance, immigrants' use of religion to advance social capital, the impact of immigration on religious organizations, the relationship between religion and civic engagement, and finally a summary of religion and transnationalism.

The Obvious: What's Already Known

There are several generalizations regarding immigrants and religion that are now well established.

Religion Is Important for Many Immigrants

Numerous recent and historical studies have documented the important role religion holds in the lives of many immigrants. In the rapidly emerging literature on immigration and religion, Warner (Warner 1997; Warner 1998a; Warner 1998c; Warner and Wittner 1998) and Ebaugh (Ebaugh and Chafetz 1999; Ebaugh and Chafetz 2000a; Ebaugh and Chafetz 2000b; Ebaugh and Chafetz 2002; Ebaugh and Curry 2000; Ebaugh, et al. 2000) have been among the most visible and influential, but there are also a significant number of dissertations and an increasing number of other studies that will be referred to in this review. For Haitians, Richman in this volume indicates, "The church is the center of life outside of their (service) jobs." Similarly, I have documented via survey work the extraordinarily high church attendance rates among Haitians in south Florida. Bankston and Zhou (2000) have demonstrated similarly high church attendance among Vietnamese Catholics in New Orleans. Nationwide surveys of Presbyterians reveal that Koreans attend church much more frequently than native-born "Americans" (Kim and Kim 2001:82; Min and Kim 2002). As stated above, Nietzsche's famous declaration is dead wrong today. If he were still alive and visited various immigrant communities, he would observe that among immigrants, at least, God is very much alive.

Immigrant Religion Is Diversifying, Making the American Religious Landscape More Complex

Another clichéd truism in the sociology of religion is that immigrants diversify the religious landscape in their adoptive societies. In the U.S., for example, numerous Muslims, Hindus, Buddhists, and even Zoroastrians, along with others, pepper the traditional Judeo-Christian religious landscape. The terrorist attacks within the U.S. on September 11, 2001, brought sudden attention to the Muslim presence, but Muslims have been living in the U.S. for many years and have been at the center of public debates in Europe for more than a decade (see, e.g., Al Sayyad and Castells 2002; Haddad 2002; Soper 2001; Vermeulen 1997; Vertovec 2000).

Immigrants and Their Religious Practices Can Be Transnational

Unquestionably, for millennia people have cultivated religious ties across boundaries. Today, we speak of these ties as "transnational" for they span political as well as cultural borders. We know that many immigrants to the U.S. frequently advance religious ends transnationally. Among the more dramatic examples are Muslim terrorists who are a constant in contemporary journalism. Similar examples are offered by Hindu nationalists (Kurien 2002) and the Irish Republican Army who raise much of their funds from immigrant communities in the U.S. (Wilson 1998). Scholars of transnationalism, especially in the last five years, have gone beyond simply demonstrating that transnationalism exists. The term transnationalism and its dimensions have been more keenly defined and analyzed (e.g., Basch, et al. 1994; Guarnizo and Smith 1998; Mahler 1998; Morawska 2001; Portes 2001). Rather than simply documenting that it exists, we now have to demonstrate what difference transnationalism makes. Some scholars have begun to do that in the area of religion (Ebaugh and Chafetz 2002; Levitt 1998; McAlister 1998; Menjívar 1999; Rudolph and Piscatori 1997).

Besides these three well-documented generalizations, scholars of contemporary immigration and those of religion also should not forget the importance of learning from history. Religion was perhaps equally important among earlier waves of immigrants. One of the most important works on assimilation, Herberg's *Protestant, Catholic, and Jew* (1960) argued that religion was central to the identity and social structure of America. Moreover, as Min and Kim (2002) point out in their review of Asian immigrants and religion, Warner and Srole's classic study of assimilation emphasized the importance of the church in the organization of immigrants in the U.S. (Warner and Srole 1945).

To summarize, we know that religion is important to many immigrants, that immigrants have made the U.S. more religiously diverse, and that immigrants practice religion transnationally. Given these facts, researchers should look ahead to the question of what difference religion makes on our understanding of immigration. Some of the answers to that question are just beginning to emerge, while other answers are still completely unknown.

The Emergent and the Still Unknown

Identity Formation and Maintenance

Some immigrants, particularly adherents to Pentecostalism, emphasize Christianity as their primary identity. When asked who they are or how they identify, they respond, "Christian. We are all equal." While the ideal is admirable, virtually all immigrants recognize that society is riven by social, primarily racial and ethnic, divisions.

The traditional sociological assimilation literature usually posed immigrant identity as polar: an individual either sustained home country identity and loyalty or Americanized. Moreover, regardless of which end of the dichotomy, traditional assimilation models also tended to assume that identities were integrated into a single form. Recent research, however, has conceived identity as being more mixed, either a hybrid combination of home and host country loyalties or flexible identities with different components that vary according to context (see inter alia Levitt 1996; Stepick, et al. 2003). Flexible identities refers to individuals emphasizing some aspects of their cultural heritage in one context, but different aspects in another. Given that most immigrants are religious, the question is not if they have a religious identity, but how their religion articulates with alternative identities, with homeland versus adopted country, national versus ethnic identities.

Considerable immigration research has focused on the existence and impact of these divisions, and the emerging immigrant religion research confirms their importance in immigrants' religious lives, too. Most of the research on immigrant religious identities emphasizes religion's role in providing cultural continuity.

Religion and Cultural Continuity

Studies of immigrant religion frequently focus on how practicing religion, by tying immigrants to each other and symbolically to the homeland, helps mitigate the disruption and stress of migration (e.g., DeMarinis and Grzymala-Moszczynska 1995). Dolan (1992), for example, found that nineteenth-century letters of immigrants reflected an "understanding of the afterlife as a place of reunion" that mirrored the immigrants' separation from their loved ones in the homeland. Given the social and psychological conditions of separation and longing, at the turn of the twentieth century religious organizations provided a meaningful social identity to new groups of immigrants (Tiryakian 1991). A hundred years ago, the Catholic Church in the U.S. self-consciously created ethnic parishes precisely for this purpose. That is no longer the official policy, but the legacy often continues in both Catholic and Protestant congregations. Ebaugh et al. (2000) typologize congregations into neighborhood institutions, whose congregants come primarily from the surrounding area, and niche institutions, where congregants tend to be attracted from an extended geographic area on the basis of common identity such as nationality. They point out that many immigrant congregations follow the niche model, especially those that serve a widely dispersed immigrant national community.[4]

Regardless of whether neighborhood or niche, the emerging research emphasizes that immigrant religion maintains and reinforces immigrants' national or ethnic identity with their home country (Al-Ahmary 2000; Bankston

1997; Ebaugh and Chafetz 2000b; Lin and Jamal 2001; Min and Kim 2002; Warner and Wittner 1998; Warner 2000; Yang 2002; Yoo 2002; Zhou, et al. 2002).[5] Schrauf (1999) enthusiastically argues that religious practice is one of the few factors that preserves native language among immigrants and their offspring. Legge (1997) would agree as he found that more observant immigrant Jews in the U.S. are more likely to have maintained aspects of their home country culture. In this volume, Min argues that Indian Hindu immigrants maintain their cultural traditions and ethnic identity partially because the architecture of the temple, its interior furnishings, and other visual representations reproduce Indian culture (Min 2002).[6] Similarly, Korean churches help their members maintain Korean cultural traditions mainly because the members actively practice Korean cultural traditions, albeit within a religious context (See Chou 1991 for the same argument concerning Chinese). Tweed (1997) argues that the Miami shrine to Cuba's patron saint, *La Virgen de la Caridad del Cobre* (Our Lady of Charity), serves to unify an otherwise fractious exile community. Indeed, the festival in her honor annually fills the Miami Arena with around 15,000 participants (Hansing 2002b).

The social networks and organizational resources of religious organizations not only help immigrants define their identities, but they also combat prejudice and discrimination in their new society. The sermons and fellowship in Haitian congregations, for example, occasionally directly and almost always indirectly combat the extraordinary prejudice and discrimination that Haitians have faced in their journey and resettlement (Brodwin 2003; Stepick 1998).

Not all scholars agree that religious practice always promotes deepening ethnic and national identity among immigrants. Remennick (1998) argues that former Soviet Jews who have immigrated to Israel or the U.S. into local host communities that are more observant feel compelled to appear to be more religious after immigration, but their commitment to Judaism is superficial. This raises the general question: Even for those immigrants who are religious, are they more religious than they were before migrating? Does immigration have a role in enhancing their religious identity or is their practice of religion an unaltered continuation of homeland practices? Given that most are religious, how do their religious identities mesh or conflict with other identities, such as nationality?

Nationality and Ethnicity

Nationality and religion are obviously not the same. Not all Pakistanis, for example, are Muslim and certainly not all Muslims are Pakistani. What is the relationship between national identity and religion? The emerging literature indicates that immigration can emphasize religious identity at the expense of ethnic or national identity and that the two can conflict with each other. Gibb (1998), for example, argues that through immigration to Canada, Ethiopian Harari diminished their ethnic Harari identity but developed an increased collective Muslim identity. For people who come from regions with multiple religions, conflict can emerge between national or ethnic identities and religious identities. Leonard (2000) and Kurien (2001, 2002) address how religious differences between Hindu and Muslim South Asian immigrants produces conflict over the definition of Asian ethnic and national identities. Both Hindus and Muslims may seek to create a South Asian identity that unites them, but they disagree over the content of that identity. Many do not want to surrender their religious identity for a secular ethnic identity. Jeung (2002) describes a similar process among primarily East Asians in northern California who are constructing a pan-Asian identity. He finds that while everyone shares the pan-ethnic label Asian, the content is not singular. The label Asian embodies different meanings that reflect the diverse ethnic, occupational, and theological differences of the distinct congregations that participants gloss over, especially to outsiders. This emerging research leaves a number of questions to be addressed: Under what conditions do immigrants submerge their ethnic or national identity and prefer a religious one, such as the Ethiopian Harari have done? Under what conditions do pan-ethnic identities emerge that incorporate different religious traditions? What determines the degree of conflict versus cooperation concerning religion in these pan-ethnic groupings? What implications do these constructions of ethnic identities have for religious beliefs and practices? Conversely, what difference does religion make in the construction of ethnic groups?

Ethnically Mixed Congregations

Not all immigrants belong to religious organizations consisting solely of others from their home country. Many immigrants attend religious institutions that are multiethnic. How do congregations integrate those who are culturally different? Responses vary from the highly symbolic, such as hanging the flags of different congregants' home nations, to the more substantive that include having ethnic or national specific events. Often these celebrations emphasize home country culture, such as food and secular music, as much or even more than religious themes. Marquardt in this volume demonstrates that religious leadership may not only symbolically acknowledge national diversity, but also actively forge from this diversity a pan-ethnic identity among congregants. In her case, the identity is a politically charged Latino identity that is based upon the suffering that they have all suffered at the hands of immigration authorities, employers, and landlords.

Marquardt's case appears to be an anomaly. Many studies that focus on mixed congregations reveal that addressing the congregation's linguistic and ethnic diversity is a highly charged issue (Chappell 2000; Goode and Schneider

1994; Lawson 1998; Lawson 1999; Lawson 1981; Machacek 1999; Sanjek 1998; Zaidman 2000). The congregants debate how much public recognition minority members should receive. Should there be separate language services, simultaneous translation, or services only in English (Ebaugh and Chafetz 2000a)? Congregations tend to provide access to services in languages other than English if they have enough non-English speakers, but accommodation often ends there. Conflicts then brew over which group occupies preferred spaces and time slots for services. Mixed congregations clearly reveal that diversity introduces competing perspectives on a congregation's identity. Historical studies of the last great immigration wave reveal that conflict was seemingly inevitable between established religious leaders and immigrant newcomers (see, for example, the various chapters in Miller and Marzik 1977).

It is still unknown what determines the difference between Marquardt's example of forging a unity across nationalities and those more prevalent reports of divisions and difficulty. Is it solely because in Marquardt's case the congregants all speak the same language, Spanish? Does class play a role, that is, with the congregants all coming being socioeconomically similar? What role does leadership play? Does the theology of the leaders or congregants make a difference? All of these still unknowns can be addressed only by further research.

To this point, my discussion details how religion is one of the keys to solidarity along with identity maintenance, and transformation for many immigrants. It is not, however, the only basis for identity formation. A critical unknown is how religious identity articulates and probably often competes with identities based on gender and generation.

Changing Gender Roles

For twenty years, immigration research has demonstrated how immigration alters gender relations. Some general patterns have emerged: immigration frequently enhances women's status because of the common necessity and relative ease of entry women have into the U.S. labor market. Men often experience a comparative drop in status (Mahler 1999; Pessar 1995; Pessar 1999; Williams, et al. 2002; Zentgraf 2002).

The emerging literature indicates a parallel transformation of gender roles in immigrant religion. Women may become more religiously involved or empowered after migrating (Gibb and Rothenberg 2000). Women informally and occasionally formally assume greater roles in immigrant religious organizations than they had in their home countries.[7] While a congregation may remain strongly patriarchal with men dominating the formal and public roles, women's roles have grown (Boddy 1995; Detwiler-Breidenbach 2000; Kim and Kim 2001; Lee 2000).

What difference does this transformation of gender roles make? One of the common consequences is increased gender conflict as at least some males resent the increased visibility and social strength of women (Ayyub 2000; Ebaugh and Charfetz 1999). What is still unknown, however, are the factors that deter or enhance increased formal and political roles for women. Do men always remain publicly dominant? If not, under what conditions do women assume greater public responsibility? Does theology or religious leadership make a difference in how congregants respond to changing women's roles?

Generational Differences

Second-generation immigrants, that is, the children of immigrants, have become a central focus of recent studies of immigrants (Portes and Rumbaut 2001; Rumbaut and Portes 2001; Suárez-Orozco and Suárez-Orozco 2001). A seeming universal among the children of immigrants is intergenerational conflict or stress, principally between them and their parents. Immigrant parents want to protect their children from what they view as the dangers of American culture, such as early initiation into sex, a lackadaisical attitude toward schooling, and a lack of respect for authority. The youth seek to enjoy what they view as the freedoms of American society. In this struggle, youth frequently have an advantage over their parents as they usually speak better English and are more familiar with American ways. What differences do this generational divide make for immigrant religion?

Gans (1994) argues that second-generation immigrants are less religious, that their religious identity is more symbolic than real. Emerging empirical studies, however, paint a more complex picture. Bankston and Zhou (Bankston 1996; Bankston and Zhou 1995) have discovered that, at least among the Vietnamese youth they studied, those who have strong religious ties are more likely to be close to their ethnic community and do well in school than their less-religious peers. (My colleagues and I have witnessed the same among Haitian youth. See Stepick, et al. 2001.) More frequently mentioned in the literature, however, are the cases of immigrant youth who struggle with the religion of their parents. Second-generation immigrant youth usually prefer services in English, consider religious leaders as much out of touch with American culture as their parents, and view religion as an effort to limit their freedom and control them (Alumkal 2000; Chai 1998; Gibb 1998; Kim 1999; Lacoste-Dujardin 1994; Song 1999). In response, immigrant youth are more likely than their parents to shift religious affiliation or even reject religion all together.

How do immigrant congregations handle the second generation's challenges? We do not yet know. Perhaps as Tizon (1999) suggests, this religious generation gap is tied to the youth's development cycle and will disappear as the youth mature and create their own families. Alternatively, even after they mature, will immigrant and second-generation youth remain estranged from the religious traditions of their parents?

We also do not know if and how the second generation's struggle for a religious identity might relate to the emerging literature on segmented assimilation (Zhou 1997). Roof and Manning (1994) suggest that Latino second-generation immigrants are likely to adopt a multicultural or hybrid identity. Warner (1997) argues that immigrant congregations will evolve first into single language (e.g., Spanish), but multinational congregations (e.g., Spanish-speakers from different countries of origin) before further developing a hybrid or *mesitizaje* identity that combines elements of different traditions. The emerging research primarily among youth in school settings, however, indicates that adopting multiple identities is a more likely strategy (e.g., Stepick and Stepick 2001; Stepick, et al. 2001). As immigrant youth develop new religious identities, do they assimilate into one of America's ethnic/racial subgroups, that is to say African Americans, Latinos, or Asians? Or, are they as likely to assimilate into "mainstream," that is, non-Hispanic white, religious institutions and identities? Or, are their religious identities as complex and situational as those they develop in schools (Stepick, et al. 2001)?

Social Capital, Individual Instrumental Impacts

While the greatest proportion of the literature on immigrants and religion focuses on issues related to identity, a number of scholars have also focused on how immigrants instrumentally use religion in the process of their adaptation, primarily how religion affects economic success and social relationships. A number of scholars, for example, have addressed how Korean churches more than other institutions serve as focal points for the development of social networks and associated social capital. Korean immigrants meet at church where they develop and reinforce social ties that they self-consciously use for business purposes (Chai 2000; Hurh and Kim 1990; Kim and Kim 2001; Kwon, et al. 1997; Min 2000; Suh 2001; Yoo 1998).

Meeting in a religious organization means more than making and maintaining business connections. Ebaugh and Chafetz (2000) indicate how religious fictive kin provide a source of social capital for various ethnic groups. Fellow congregants often help each other with such things as finding housing and enrolling children in school.[8] Richman in this volume extends this argument of the material consequences of religion using Weber to partially address why Haitian immigrants are prone to convert to Protestantism. She describes how Haitian Protestants use the church as their primary social group through which they exchange food, loans, help, rides, job referrals, childcare, and other services. Through Protestantism, Haitians are also able to escape the transnational social obligations that are tied to the traditional religion of vodou. The Haitian Protestantism that she studied morally endorses individual pursuit of material self-interest. Richman's arguments are similar to earlier research that addressed why Latin American peasants were converting to Protestantism in recent decades (Annis 1987; Falla 2001; Garrard-Burnett and Stoll 1993; Junker-Kenny and Tomka 1999; Stewart-Gambino 2001). Using a complementary perspective, Brodwin (2003) demonstrates how the appropriation of Pentecostalism by Haitian migrants to Guadeloupe, French West Indies, defends them against denigrating stereotypes while also articulating sentiments of loss and remembrance of the Haitian homeland.

Some scholars have also noted how immigrants use religion to maintain the social class position they had in their homeland, but which migration has threatened. Buchanan (1979, 1983), for example, has described how upper-class Haitians in New York insisted on mass in French, as opposed to the more widely spoken Creole. Karpathakis (1994) similarly described how some Greeks in New York City pushed for increased religious orthodoxy that would concomitantly allow the most economically advantaged immigrants to protect their class status and prestige. How widespread is this link between religion, religious orthodoxy, and reinforcement of the homeland class structure? It would seem to depend on the class structure of the immigrant flow. If the vast majority of the immigrants are working class, the elite is likely to remain in the home country and will no longer be in positions of power within the immigrants' religious organizations. If so, do others use religion to reinforce a newly acquired class position? How is equality for immigrants actually manifested in religious organizations? Also remaining inadequately understood are the issues that Richman raises in her echoes of Weber: What is the relationship between immigrants' instrumental uses of religion and religion's moral discourse and context?

Structure of Religious Organizations

Ebaugh (Ebaugh and Chafetz 2000b; Yang and Ebaugh 2001) and Warner (1994, 1998b) have both argued that immigrant religious organizations in the U.S. move toward a congregational structure, regardless of their format in their home countries (also see Bankston and Zhou 2000). Becoming more congregational means, for example, that they become more likely to have professional religious leaders, lay involvement in administration, and a proliferation of non-religious, cultural activities and service provision. English-language classes and job training for the first-generation immigrants are often provided by religious organizations while home country language and cultural classes are added to serve the second generation. Suh (2001), for example, describes a Korean monk who has transformed a small Buddhist temple in Los Angeles into a renowned cultural center with a newspaper, radio show, television broadcast, Buddhist bookstore, and an art gallery. Congregational transformation is most obvious for non-Western religions, such as Buddhism and Hinduism, that do not have a congregational structure in their homelands, and in which worship is primarily domestic-based with the professional clergy little involved in people's secular lives. For many Catholics from Third World countries the shift is more to a different form of congregant participation than adaptation of a congregational structure. The key shift is financial. In the U.S., parishioners are expected to economically sustain their parishes whereas in their home countries they more often look to their parishes for aid as the church typically receives state support.

In this volume, Min (see also Min 2000) claims that the impact of immigration on religious organizations has been overemphasized. He points out that Korean Presbyterians had established a congregational structure well before immigration because of the influence of U.S. missionaries. Moreover, he argues that Hindu temples in the U.S. do not consider worshipers as members. Indian Hindus who come to a particular temple on a given day may go to another temple on another day.

The differences between Min and Warner may be more of emphasis than fundamental disagreement. Two trends appear to be emerging from the existing literature: (1). Non-Western religions become more congregationally organized in the U.S., (2). while Judeo-Christian ones preserve and possibly reinvigorate their congregational structures. Even if this revised hypothesis is true, there remain some unknowns: In what ways are Judeo-Christian congregations and non-Western religious institutions effective in responding to the adaptation needs of their congregants? Do non-Western religious organizations still develop activities to ease the immigrant adaptation process? Under what conditions do the latter feel particularly compelled to legitimize their religious beliefs?

Religion and Civic Engagement

In the wake of September 11, U.S. opinion leaders, including President Bush, pointedly avoided the "racialization" of religion. Bush explicitly proclaimed that the culprits did not represent all Muslims or Arabs and Islam should not be held responsible. Nevertheless, acts of violence against Muslims and mosques, and even non-Muslims from India and the Middle East, did occur. Muslims in the U.S. quickly organized to protect themselves by disavowing terrorist acts (Leonard 2002).

Reacting to prejudice and discrimination from the broader society is probably the most common form of immigrant religion civic engagement. One hundred years ago attacks that targeted "Jewish anarchists" and in the nineteenth century, "Irish papists," were more common than religious-tinged ethnic attacks at the turn of the twenty-first century. In fact, the emerging literature more frequently highlights religious organizations' positive responses to prejudice and discrimination than the attacks against religion or immigrants. Chang in this volume describes the racially inclusive vision of the American Baptist Home Mission Society in its missionizing among immigrants in the U.S. Similarly, Marquardt in this volume describes the role of a Catholic priest's liberation theology in a Mexican congregation in Atlanta. Additionally, liberation theology was present for the first fifteen years in the primary Haitian Catholic church in Miami, Notre Dame D'Haiti, which struck a visible pro-refugee and thus anti-Haitian government tone throughout the 1980s (Rey 2002; Stepick 1998). Similarly, the sanctuary movement for Central American refugees who made it into the U.S. was important both for the refugees themselves and in the broader political struggle over refugee rights (Aguilares 1985; Hammond 1993; Nackerud 1993).

Direct attacks on immigrant religion appear to be more common in Europe than the U.S. For at least twenty years, Europe has struggled to address immigrant religious diversity, most notably the increased presence of Islam (Gerholm and Georg 1988; Haddad 2002; Haddad and Smith 2002; Vertovec and Peach 1997; Zolberg and Long 1997). In Europe, religious intolerance remains part of the "legitimate" debate as religious diversity is assailed by right-wing and even a few moderate European politicians. European politicians who attack immigrants, including their religion, can win national elections in Italy, Austria, and Denmark and local elections in France and Germany. In the U.S., in contrast, while Jerry Falwell, Pat Robertson, and Franklin Graham, the son of Billy Graham, attacked the Muslim religion in the wake of 9/11, they were quickly condemned by the vast majority of religious leaders and politicians.

The constitutional protection of religion in the U.S.[9] and the absence of a state-supported religion may explain the greater religious tolerance in the U.S. Nevertheless, the intolerance of Jerry Falwell and others reflects a powerful minority of bigoted voices that were even stronger 100 and more years ago. For reasons beyond the scope of this chapter, religious and more generally racial and ethnic tolerance increased in the U.S. by the end of the twentieth century. As Nathan Glazer articulated, we have all become multiculturalists (Glazer 1997). It is no longer part of the dominant discourse to condemn different religions. Post-1965 immigrants have arrived at a time when pluralism has become an inescapable reality and an accepted ideology in American society, even in the wake of terrorist attacks under the name of religion.

Immigrant religion is notably absent in the public sphere on the hot-button, high-profile religiously infused issues that gather tremendous media attention. In spite of the constitutional church-state divide, religion thoroughly suffuses U.S. politics, including debates on abortion, homosexuality, school vouchers, and prayer in schools. Outside of formal politics, moreover, many American churches actively promote civic engagement through soup kitchens, Habitat for Humanity, and myriad other charitable works. African American churches, in particular, have been a focal point of leadership development and civic organization. However, the emerging literature gives little or even no evidence that immigrants are involved in these issues.[10] Why are immigrants invisible in these activities? Apart from their transnational ties, are immigrant congregations civically engaged beyond the church or mosque walls? Are they becoming incorporated into any of these religiously infused political issues? Do they become involved in electoral politics? Have researchers just missed them or are immigrants overwhelmingly consumed by other issues? Are they instead focused on politics in the homeland, or do they reject all explicit political involvement? Only further research can answer these questions.

Transnationalism

The world's dominant religions, such as Christianity, Islam, and Buddhism, became widespread because of transnational ties. They spread by spanning national boundaries. Though religious beliefs and religious organizations have been transnational for millennia, the transnational religious ties brokered by contemporary migrants are only beginning to be explored. Recent advances in transnational studies of religion have focused on (1). developing a typology for transnational religious ties and practices and (2). the relationship of transnational religious activities to the state.

Drawing upon the more general transnational literature (e.g., Guarnizo and Smith 1998), Levitt (1998, 2001) distinguishes between horizontal transnational ties, that is, those linking comparable local level groups, and vertical or extended transnational ties that form part of a vertically integrated system. In other words, transnational religious ties can be from below, that is, between individuals and local organizations, or from above, such as through the international Catholic Church. A local parish or congregation in Los Angeles or Garden City, Kansas, that pays to refurbish a specific church in El Salvador is a different kind of transnational flow than the Catholic Church organizing hurricane relief in Nicaragua.

For his part, Portes (2001) distinguishes not only transnational ties that are horizontal from vertical ties, but he also employs the locus of primary activity, that is, whether actions take place primarily in the home or host country. Portes argues, for example, that churches organizing binational exchanges of priests and pastors is primarily a host country activity, since priests and pastors mainly come from the home to the host country.

Hansing (2002a) has recently typologized the differences in the nature and content of transnational religious ties. She distinguishes between material, institutional, personal, media, and symbolic flows. Each of these types of flows has crosscutting distinctions by organizational level. Hansing distinguishes not only between macro and micro as in Levitt's and Portes's conceptualizations, but adds an intermediate level of analysis. More importantly, Hansing directs our attention to differences in the content of transnational religious exchanges including those which are symbolic or imagined. How useful are typologies? Do they categorize and capture important and relevant forms of immigrant transnational religion? If they do, what difference do they make? Does a macro versus micro transnational religious tie affect religious organization or immigrant adaptation? Do micro transnational religious ties, for example, impel larger organizations to respond to the needs of new immigrants or do they excuse organizations from responding to those needs? Do the costs involved in transnational religious exchanges at whatever level lessen the resources available among religious organizations to assist their congregant immigrant families and individuals? Do transnational ties provide social networks that lead to further immigration? These and other questions on the relationship between transnational religious ties and immigration have yet to be answered.

The other emerging area in the field of transnational religion and immigration is understanding the role that nation-states play in creating, maintaining, controlling, or at least influencing the nature of transnational religious ties. Historically, at least in the West, religion has been exported abroad as a key feature of colonialism and imperialism. The Spanish Empire is among the most obvious examples. The Vatican had a surprisingly small role in Spanish and Portuguese colonialism. Instead, Spain and Portugal directly controlled Catholic evangelization (Casanova 1997). The U.S. presence in the Pacific provides two other examples. In the nineteenth century, U.S. companies recruited Christianized Koreans, as opposed to the much more numerous Buddhists, to work in the sugar cane fields of Hawai'i. During World War II, the U.S. state often slandered Buddhism and used it as a justification for further restrictions on Japanese in the U.S. (Pierce, et al. 2001).

While many states promoted evangelization as a vehicle to economic and political domination, some transnational religious ties eventually produced challenges to the political structures of colonized lands. A mix of Christian teachings and American notions of democracy and individualism, for example, sparked the imaginations of young, reform-minded elites in Korea. In turn, these developments may have broader repercussions as once-colonized countries become immigrant-exporting countries. In the Korean independence movement against Japanese colonialism, the Korean immigrant population in the U.S., as well ongoing ties to U.S. church organizations such as Methodists, Presbyterians, and the YMCA, provided both material resources and ideological challenges to the Japanese presence (Pierce, et al. 2001). In a similar unintended consequence, Yang (1998) argues coerced modernization in the People's Republic of China impels immigrants to convert to Christianity. [11]

Mahler (2002) has recently compared how the different neo-colonial ties to the U.S. have affected immigrants' religious transnational ties in Cuba versus Nicaragua. Protestant churches in Cuba became integrated into the U.S. religious denominational structure because of ties established during the U.S.

occupation of the island between 1898 and 1902. After the Castro revolution, most Cuban religious leaders fled, a few stayed, but most importantly the institutional ties remained viable. The Pope's 1998 visit to Cuba helped reduce religious repression there, and U.S. religious organizations are rapidly reinvigorating extensive and intensive transnational ties.

In contrast, in Nicaragua the Catholic Church was dominant. Protestant churches were historically foreign, leaving missionary churches with lesser status and influence and far weaker ties to denominational institutions in the U.S. During the brief Sandinista period in the 1980s, U.S. religious, primarily Protestant, organizational involvement was likely to be initiated from the U.S. through what Mahler refers to as transnational religious tourism of progressives who came to Nicaragua to help construct a new society. After the defeat of the Sandinistas, the Catholic Church regained most of its political influence. Now, the Nicaraguan state confers duty-free treatment in importing material goods to the Catholic Church, whereas Protestant churches must pay duties. Although the transnational religious tourism of progressives has declined, the churches have stayed and many, especially the Pentecostal churches, are flourishing.

These examples suggest a broader pattern, that is to say, transnational ties to host country religious organizations are likely to produce challenges to political structures in developing nations. Such has been the case in Korea, China, Nicaragua, and perhaps will be in Cuba. On the other hand, the Catholic Church is a conservative influence in Nicaragua, but has long criticized political authority in Cuba. Is this because of more transnational ties in Cuba, or simply because the Catholic Church would rather challenge a socialist regime? What is the relationship between immigrant transnational religious ties and home country politics? Given that historical ties of colonialism and neo-colonialism have a contemporary effect on transnational religious ties, can we map and typologize these effects?

Addressing the Still Unknowns

We have reviewed the known that religion is important among immigrants, that immigrant religion has diversified the U.S. religious landscape, that many immigrants practice religion transnationally. Now that research has established those basic points, researchers need to move on to examine the implications of immigrant religion. The implications that interest us are likely to depend upon our pre-existing perspectives. Religious studies specialists are likely to address how immigration affects religion—the structure of religious organizations and beliefs. Immigration specialists are more concerned with how religion affects immigrant adaptation—social capital, identity, and civic engagement.

The overwhelming emerging consensus is that immigrant congregations maintain and promote home country identities, both religious and secular.

The unknown, however, is how these religiously based and promoted ideas interact with alternative identities, particularly those influenced by gender, generation, and "American" culture. There is emerging agreement that serious conflict over gender and generation identities persists within immigrant congregations, but it is still unknown how these conflicts are resolved and what impact they have on immigrants' broader lives.

A large number of studies have documented the development of social capital in immigrant congregations, especially among Korean Christians. It is possible that exploring the issue among other ethnic groups will reveal that other national groups or perhaps other religions do not so actively promote social capital among congregants. Largely unknown are the links between social capital and the moral discourse of religion. Do immigrants embody Weber's conclusions that Protestantism is better suited to capitalist societies and thus immigrant adaptation in developed countries?

The majority opinion argues that the social organization of immigrant religion tends to become more congregationalist in the U.S. Min in this volume, however, raises questions about whether some of this congregational form may have existed before immigration, particularly among Christians, and whether non-Christians have made significant moves toward congregationalism. Besides testing these hypotheses, the task remains for immigration specialists to determine what difference a congregational organizational structure has for immigrant adaptation.

We also know little about immigrant religious congregations' civic engagement. Do they consciously promote civic and political engagement within or beyond the congregation? Around what issues do they coalesce? When they engage in civic activities, do they cross classic sociological lines that have divided American society for generations or do they perform as ethnic, racial organizations or vehicles under the "cover" of religious legitimacy? In other words, how can focusing on immigrants' religious organizations and beliefs advance our understanding of how people negotiate their identities, social stature, legitimacy, and power in complex social arenas?

Analysis of transnational religious ties has barely begun. Typological frameworks have been suggested that need to be tested and refined. Research needs to address the significance of different types of transnational exchanges for both the organizational structure of religion and immigrant adaptation. For most immigrants, God is most decidedly alive. We researchers have learned this fact and but only begun to address its implications and the repercussion for the future of U.S. society.

Notes
This paper has benefited greatly from the thoughts and comments of my colleagues in the Miami Gateway Cities project. I have borrowed extensively from the ideas of especially Sarah Mahler, Katrin Hansing, and Terry Rey. Carol Dutton Stepick's editorial input sharpened the prose considerably. Karen Leonard, Sarah Mahler, Terry Rey, and Steven Warner all provided important feedback. All reviews are necessarily partial as new material is being published and some previous material is inadvertently overlooked. I apologize to those authors whose work I have failed to include.

1. Greeley argues that God and religion remain quite alive for most Americans, too, contrary to predictions of "modernization" theory. Greeley uses recent survey data to demonstrate that increasing numbers of Americans believe in an afterlife (Greeley and Hout 1999). His results do not distinguish between native and foreign-born respondents.

2. For a more thorough recent review of the European literature on diaspora and religion, see Vertovec 2001.

3. Of course, no discipline is monolithic. In anthropology, for example, Marvin Harris (1968) proposed cultural materialism, and many anthropologists who worked in the developing world have integrated political economy analysis into their work. Those researchers are not dominant within the American Anthropological Association, the primary graduate schools, or the principal journals.

4. In our current work as part of the Pew Immigrant Gateways Cities project (http://newimmigrants.org/ and http://www.fiu.edu/~iei/index/religion_imm.html) we have discovered, however, that neighborhood churches are often similarly divided by ethnicity. In one neighborhood we found two apostolic churches. One has overwhelmingly African American worshippers and the other has almost exclusively Jamaican immigrants.

5. These findings contrast sharply with more psychological approaches to immigration that generally emphasize immigration's disruptive psychological effects (inter alia Guarnaccia 1996; Suárez-Orozco and Suárez-Orozco 1994).

6. In a twist to this generalization, Sannella (1999) finds that changes in religious practices between the homeland and the host country led to increased stress.

7. The traditionally female-centered Okinawan religion described by Sered in this volume constitutes an important exception to this generalization, which may exemplify the possibility that the opposite trend may occur for women immigrants coming from female-centered religions.

8. By social capital we mean social ties that can be used instrumentally for other purposes, such as obtaining a job (see inter alia Bourdieu 1983; Coleman 1988; Edwards and Foley 2001; Portes 1998; Portes 2000) (Nee and Sanders 2001).

9. Religion is also accorded a privileged position in U.S. immigration policy as religious leaders can much more readily obtain visas than other immigrants to visit the U.S. According to INS statistics in 2000, over 1,000 ministers obtained visas to come to the U.S. (U.S. Department of Justice 2002: Table 5).

10. A Hispanic immigrant pastor, Eladio Jose Armesto, leads an organization, Take Back Miami, whose goal is to repeal a Miami-Dade County ordinance prohibiting anti-gay discrimination. There probably are other immigrant religious leaders and individuals

involved in similar political efforts, but they have not received attention in the academic literature.

11. Withol de Wenden (1998) has also demonstrated how French colonial policy influences the transnational ties and integration of Muslims in France.

References

Aguilares, Gilberto. 1985. "The Roots of the Sanctuary Movement: Witness of Refugees." *Church and Society* 75(4):7-15.

Al Sayyad, Nezar, and Manuel Castells, eds. 2002. *Muslim Europe or Euro-Islam : Politics, Culture, and Citizenship in the Age of Globalization.* Lanham, MD: Lexington Books.

Al-Ahmary, Abdullah Arib. 2000. "Ethnic Self-Identity and the Role of Islam: A Study of the Yemeni Community in the South End of Dearborn and Detroit, Michigan." Ph.D. diss., University of Tennessee.

Alumkal, Antony William. 2000. "Ethnicity, Assimilation, and Racial Formation in Asian American Evangelical Churches: A Case Study of a Chinese American and Korean American Congregation." Ph.D. diss., Princeton University.

Annis, Sheldon. 1987. *God and Production in a Guatemalan Town.* Austin, TX: University of Texas Press.

Ayyub, Ruksana. 2000. "Domestic Violence in the South Asian Muslim Immigrant Population in the United States." *Journal of Social Distress and Homeless* 9(3):237-248.

Bankston, Carl L., III. 1996. "The Ethnic Church, Ethnic Identification, and the Social Adjustment of Vietnamese Adolescents." *Review of Religious Research* 38(1):18-37.

———.1997. "Bayou Lotus: Theravada Buddhism in Southwestern Louisiana." *Sociological Spectrum* 17(4):453-472.

Bankston, Carl L., III, and Min Zhou. 1995. "Religious Participation, Ethnic Identification, and Adaptation of Vietnamese Adolescents in an Immigrant Community." *Sociological Quarterly* 36(3):523-534.

———. 2000. "De Facto Congregationalism and Socioeconomic Mobility in Laotian and Vietnamese Immigrant Communities: A Study of Religious Institutions and Economic Change." *Review of Religious Research* 41(4):453-470.

Basch, Linda, Nina Glick-Schiller, and Cristina Blanc-Szanton. 1994. *Nations Unbound: Transnational Projects, Postcolonial Predicaments, and Deterritorialized Nation-States.* Amsterdam: Gordon and Breach Science Publishers.

Boddy, Janice. 1995. "Managing Tradition: 'Superstition' and the Making of National Identity among Sudanese Women Refugees." In *The Pursuit of Certainty: Religious and Cultural Formulations,* ed. J. Wendy. London: Routledge.

Bourdieu, Pierre. 1983. "The Forms of Capital." In *Handbook of Theory and Research for the Sociology of Education,* ed. J. G. Richardson. New York: Greenwood Press.

Brodwin, Paul. 2003. "Pentecostalism in Translation: Religion and the Production of Community in the Haitian Diaspora." *American Ethnologist* 30(1):85-101.

Buchanan, Susan. 1979. "Language Identity: Haitians in New York City." *International Migration Review* 13(2):298-313.

Buchanan, Susan Huelsebusch. 1983. "The Cultural Meaning of Social Class for Haitians in New York City." *Ethnic Groups* 5:7-30.

Casanova, José. 1997. "Globalizing Catholicism and the Return to a 'Universal' Church." In *Transnational Religion and Fading States*, ed. S. H. Rudolph and J. Piscatori. Boulder, CO: Westview Press.

Chai, Karen Jung Won. 1998. "Competing for the Second Generation: English-Language Ministry at a Korean Protestant Church." In *Gatherings in Diaspora: Religious Communities and the New Immigration*, ed. R. S. Warner and J. Wittner. Philadelphia, PA: Temple University Press.

———. 2000. "Protestant-Catholic-Buddhist: Korean Americans and Religious Adaptation in Greater Boston." Ph.D. diss., Harvard University.

Chappell, David W. 2000. "Socially Inclusive Buddhists in America." In *Global Citizens: The Soka Gakkai Buddhist Movement in the World*, ed. D. Machacek and B. Wilson. New York: Oxford University Press.

Chou, Shi-Deh Chang. 1991. "Religion and Chinese Life in the United States." *Etudes Migrations* 28(103):455-464.

Coleman, James S. 1988. "Social Capital in the Creation of Human Capital." *Journal of American Sociology* 94:S95-S121.

DeMarinis, Valerie, and Halina Grzymala-Moszczynska. 1995. "The Nature and Role of Religion and Religious Experience in Psychological Cross-Cultural Adjustment: Ongoing Research in the Clinical Psychology of Religion." *Social Compass* 42(1):121-135.

Detwiler-Breidenbach, Ann M. 2000. "Language, Gender, and Context in an Immigrant Ministry: New Spaces for the Pastor's Wife." *Sociology of Religion* 61(4):455-459.

Dolan, Jay. 1992. *The American Catholic Experience: A History from Colonial Times to the Present*. Notre Dame and London: University of Notre Dame Press.

Ebaugh, Helen Rose, and Janet Saltzman Chafetz. 1999. "Agents for Cultural Reproduction and Structural Change: The Ironic Role of Women in Immigrant Religious Institutions." *Social Forces* 78(2):585-613.

———. 2000a. "Dilemmas of Language in Immigrant Congregations: The Tie That Binds or the Tower of Babel?" *Review of Religious Research* 41(4):432-452.

———, eds. 2000b. *Religion and the New Immigrants: Continuities and Adaptations Immigrant Congregations*. Walnut Creek, CA: AltaMira Press.

———. 2002. *Religion across Borders: Transnational Religious Networks*. Walnut Creek, CA: Altamira Press.

Ebaugh, Helen Rose, and Mary Curry. 2000. "Fictive Kin as Social Capital in New Immigrant Communities." *Sociological Perspectives* 43(2):189-209.

Ebaugh, Helen Rose, Jennifer O'Brien, and Janet Saltzman Chafetz. 2000. "The Social Ecology of Residential Patterns and Membership in Immigrant Churches." *Journal for the Scientific Study of Religion* 39(March 1):107-116.

Edwards, B., and Michael W. Foley. 2001. "Much Ado about Social Capital." *Contemporary Sociology* 30: 277-231.

Falla, Ricardo. 2001. *Quiché Rebelde: Religious Conversion, Politics, and Ethnic Identity in Guatemala*. Translated by P. Berryman. Austin: University of Texas Press.

Gans, Herbert J. 1994. "Symbolic Ethnicity and Symbolic Religiosity: Towards a Comparison of Ethnic and Religious Acculturation." *Ethnic and Racial Studies* 17(4):577-592.

Garrard-Burnett, Virginia, and David Stoll, eds. 1993. *Rethinking Protestantism in Latin America*. Philadelphia, PA: Temple University Press.

Gerholm, Tomas, and Yngve Georg, eds. 1988. *The New Islamic Presence in Western Europe*. London and New York: Mansell.

Gibb, Camilla. 1998. "Religious Identification in Transnational Contexts: Being and Becoming Muslim in Ethiopia and Canada." *Diaspora* 7(2):247-269.

Gibb, Camilla, and Celia Rothenberg. 2000. "Believing Women: Harari and Palestinian Women at Home and in the Canadian Diaspora." *Journal of Muslim Minority Affairs* 20(2):243-259.

Glazer, Nathan. 1997. *We Are All Multiculturalists Now*. Cambridge, MA: Harvard University Press.

Goode, Judith, and Jo Anne Schneider. 1994. *Reshaping Ethnic and Racial Relations in Philadelphia: Immigrants in a Divided City*. Philadelphia, PA: Temple University Press.

Greeley, Andrew, and Michael Hout. 1999. "Americans' Increasing Belief in Life after Death: Religious Competition and Acculturation." *American Sociological Review* 64 (6):813-835.

Guarnaccia, Peter J. 1996. "Social Stress and Psychological Distress among Latinos in the United States." In *Ethnicity, Immigration, and Psychopathology*, ed. Ihsan Al-Issa and Michel Tousignant. New York: Plenum.

Guarnizo, Luis Eduardo, and Michael P. Smith. 1998. "The Locations of Transnationalism." In *Transnationalism from Below*, ed. M. P. Smith and L. E. Guarnizo. New Brunswick: Transaction Publishers.

Haddad, Yvonne Yazbeck, ed. 2002. *Muslims in the West: From Sojourners to Citizens*. Oxford and New York: Oxford University Press.

Haddad, Yvonne Yazbeck, and Jane I. Smith, eds. 2002. *Muslim Minorities in the West: Visible and Invisible*. Walnut Creek, CA: AltaMira Press.

Hammond, John L. 1993. "War-Uprooting and the Political Mobilization of Central American Refugees." *Journal of Refugee Studies* 6(2):105-122.

Hansing, Katrin. 2002a. "Mulas, Medicina y mucho mas: Transnational religious connections between the Archdiocese in Miami and the Catholic Church in Cuba." Paper presented at the Cuban Research Institute Conference, Florida International University, Miami, Florida.

———. 2002b. *So What Colour is the Virgin, Really? Historical and Contemporary Representations of La Virgen de la Caridad del Cobre*. Nassau, Bahamas: Caribbean Studies Association.

Harris, Marvin. 1968. *The Rise of Anthropological Theory: A History of Theories of Culture*. New York: Crowell.

Herberg, Will. 1960. *Protestant, Catholic, Jew: An Essay in American Religious Sociology*. Garden City, NY: Anchor Books.

Hirschman, Charles, Josh DeWind, and Philip Kasinitz, eds. 1999. *The Handbook of International Migration: The American Experience*. New York: Russsell Sage Foundation.

Hurh, Won Moo, and Kwang Chung Kim. 1990. "Religious participation of Korean immigrants in the United States." *Journal for the Scientific Study of Religion* 29:9-34.

Jeung, Russell. 2002. "Asian American Pan-Ethnic Rormation and Congregational Culture." In *Religions in Asian America: Building Faith Communities*, ed. P. G. Min and J. H. Kim. Walnut Creek, CA: Alta Mira Press.

Junker-Kenny, Maureen, and Miklós Tomka, eds. 1999. *Faith in a Society of Instant Gratification*. Maryknoll, NY: Orbis Books.

Karpathakis, Anna. 1994. "'Whose Church Is It Anyway?' Greek Immigrants of Astoria, New York, and Their Church." *Journal of the Hellenic Diaspora* 20(1):97-122.

Kim, Jason Hyungkyun. 1999. "The Effects of Assimilation within the Korean Immigrant Church: Intergenerational Conflicts between the First- and the Second-Generation Korean Christians in Two Chicago Suburban Churches." Ph.D. diss., Trinity Evangelical Divinity School.

Kim, Kwang Chug, and Shin Kim. 2001. "Ethnic Role of Korean Immigrant Churches in the United States." In *Korean Americans and Their Religions: Pilgrims and Missionaries from a Different Shore*, ed. H.-Y. Kwon and K. C. Kim. University Park, PA: Pennsylvania State University Press.

Kurien, Prema. 2001. "Religion, Ethnicity and Politics: Hindu and Muslim Indian Immigrants in the United States." *Ethnic and Racial Studies* 24(2):263-293.

———. 2002. "'We are Better Hindus Here': Religion and Ethnicity among Indian Americans." In *Religion in Asian America: Building Faith Communities*, ed. P.G. Min and J. H. Kim. Walnut Creek, CA: AltaMira Press.

Kwon, Victoria Hyonchu, Helen Rose Ebaugh, and Jacqueline Hagan. 1997. "The Structure and Functions of Cell Group Ministry in a Korean Christian Church." *Journal for the Scientific Study of Religion* 36(2):247-256.

Lacoste-Dujardin, Camille. 1994. "Religious Transmission and Migration: Islamic Identity among Daughters of North African Immigrants to France." *Social Compass* 41(1):163-170.

Lawson, Ronald. 1998. "From American Church to Immigrant Church: The Changing Face of Seventh-Day Adventism in Metropolitan New York." *Sociology of Religion* 59(4):329-351.

———. 1999. "Internal Political Fallout from the Emergence of an Immigrant Majority: The Impact of the Transformation of Seventh-Day Adventism in Metropolitan New York." *Review of Religious Research* 41(1):21-47.

Lawson, Tony. 1981. "Paternalism and Labor Market Segmentation Theory." In *The Dynamics of Labor Market Segmentation*, ed. F. Wilkinson. London: Academic Press.

Lee, Suezan Cho. 2000. "Women in Leadership in the Korean-American Church." Ph.D. diss., Boston University.

Legge, Jerome S, Jr. 1997. "The Religious Erosion-Assimilation Hypothesis: The Case of U.S. Jewish Immigrants." *Social Science Quarterly* 78(2):472-486.

Leonard, Karen. 2000. "State, Culture, and Religion: Political Action and Representation among South Asians in North America." *Diaspora* 9(1):21-38.

———. 2002. "American Muslims, Before and After September 11, 2001." *Economic and Political Weekly* 37:24 (June 15):2293-2302.

Levitt, Peggy. 1996. "Social Remittances: A Conceptual Tool for Understanding the Relationship Between Migration and Local Development." Unpublished paper.

———. 1998. "Local-level Global Religion: The Case of U.S.-Dominican Migration." *Journal for the Scientific Study of Religion* 37(1):74-89.

———. 2001. *The Transnational Villagers*. Berkeley: University of California Press.

Lin, Ann Chih, and Amaney Jamal. 2001. "Muslim, Arab, and American: The Adaptation of Arab Immigrants to American Society." Paper presented at the meeting of the Social Science Research Council Working Group on Religion and Immigrants, Seattle, WA.

Lin, Irene. 1996. "Journey to the Far West: Chinese Buddhism in America." *Amerasia Journal* 22(1):107-132.

Machacek, David. 1999. "The Appeal of Soka Gakkai in the United States: Emergent Transmodernism." *Research in the Social Scientific Study of Religion* 10:57-75.

Mahler, Sarah J. 1998. "Theoretical and Empirical Contributions Toward a Research Agenda for Transnationalism." In *Transnationalism from Below*, ed. L. E. Guarnizo and M. P. Smith. New Brunswick: Transaction Publishers.

———. 1999. "Engendering Transnational Migration: A Case Study of Salvadorans." *American Behavioral Scientist* 42(2):690-719.

———. 2002. "Mapping Transnational Religious Ties for Analysis: Preliminary Lessons from a Comparison of Cuban & Nicaraguan Research." Paper presented at the second biennial Allen Morris Conference on the History of Florida and the Atlantic World, 'Immigration, Migration, and Diaspora,' Florida State University, Tallahassee, FL.

McAlister, Elizabeth. 1998. "The Madonna of 115th Street Revisited: Vodou and Haitian Catholicism in the Age of Transnationalism." In *Gatherings in Diaspora: Religious Communities and the New Immigration*, ed. R. S. Warner and J. Wittner. Philadelphia, PA: Temple University Press.

Menjívar, Cecilia. 1999. "Religious Institutions and Transnationalism: A Case Study of Catholic and Evangelical Salvadoran Immigrants." *International Migration Review* 12(4):589-611.

Miller, Randall M., and Thomas D. Marzik, eds. 1977. *Immigrants and Religion in Urban America*. Philadelphia: Temple University Press.

Min, Pyong Gap. 2000. "Immigrants' Religion and Ethnicity: A Comparison of Korean Christian and Indian Hindu Immigrants." *Bulletin of the Royal Institute for Inter-Faith Studies* 2(1):121-140.

———. 2002. "Religion and Ethnicity: A Comparison of Indian Hindu and Korean Protestant Immigrants in New York." Paper presented at Social Science Research Council Fellows Conference on Immigration Religion and Civic Life, University of Texas at Arlington.

Min, Pyong Gap, and Jung Ha Kim, eds. 2002. *Religions in Asian America: Building Faith Communities*. Walnut Creek, CA: AltaMira Press.

Morawska, Ewa. 2001. "Immigrants, Transnationalism, and Ethnicization: A Comparison of This Wave and Last." In *E Pluribus Unum? Immigrants, Civic Life, and Political Incorporation*, ed. G. Gerstle and J. Mollenkopf. New York: Russell Sage Foundation.

Nackerud, Larry Glenn. 1993. *The Central American Refugee Issue in Brownsville, Texas: Seeking Understanding of Public Policy Formulation from within a Community Setting*. San Francisco: Mellen Research University Press.

Nee, Victor, and Jimy Sanders. 2001. "Understanding the Diversity of Immigrant Incorporation: A Forms-of-Capital Model." *Ethnic and Racial Studies* 24(3):386-411.

Pessar, Patricia R. 1995. "On the Homefront and in the Workplace: Integrating Immigrant Women into Feminist Discourse." *Anthropological Quarterly* 68(1):37-47.

———. 1999. "Engendering Migration Studies: The Case of New Immigrants in the United States." *American Behavioral Scientist* 42(4):577-600.

Pierce, Lori, David Yoo, and Paul Spickard. 2001. "Religion and Race: Korean and Japanese American Religions, 1890-1945." Paper presented at a meeting of the Social Science Research Council Working Group on Religion and Immigration, Seattle, WA.

Portes, Alejandro. 1998. "Social Capital: Its Origins and Applications in Modern Sociology." *Annual Reviews in Sociology* 24:1-24.

———. 2000. "The Two Meanings of Social Capital." *Sociological Forum* 15(1):1-12.

———. 2001. "Introduction: The Debates and Significance of Immigrant Transnationalism." *Global Networks* 1(3):181-193.

Portes, Alejandro, and Rubén Rumbaut. 2001. *Legacies: The Story of the Immigrant Second Generation*. Berkeley and New York: University of California Press and Russell Sage Foundation.

Portes, Alejandro, and Rubén G Rumbaut. 1996. *Immigrant America: A Portrait*. Berkeley: University of California Press.

Remennick, Larissa I. 1998. "Identity Quest among Russian Jews of the 1990s: Before and after Emigration." *Sociological Papers* 6:241-258.

Rey, Terry. 2002. "Marian Devotion at a Haitian Catholic Parish in Miami: The Feast of Our Lady of Perpetual Help." Unpublished manuscript.

Roof, Wade Clark, and Christel Manning. 1994. "Cultural Conflicts and Identity: Second-Generation Hispanic Catholics in the United States." *Social Compass* 41(1): 171-184.

Rudolph, Susanne Hoeber, and James Piscatori, eds. 1997. *Transnational Religion and Fading States*. Boulder, CO: Westview Press.

Rumbaut, Rubén, and Alejandro Portes, eds. 2001. *Ethnicities: Children of Immigrants in America*. Berkeley: University of California Press.

Sanjek, Roger. 1998. *The Future of Us All: Race and Neighborhood Politics in New York City*. Ithaca, NY: Cornell University Press.

Sannella, Alessandra. 1999. "Migration, Transculturation, Discomfort, and Religion." *La Critica Sociologia* 131-132 (Oct-Dec):74-89.

Schrauf, Robert W. 1999. "Mother Tongue Maintenance among North American Ethnic Groups." *Cross-Cultural Research* 33(2):175-192.

Song, Minho. 1999. "Patterns of Religious Participation among the Second-Generation Koreans in Toronto: Toward the Analysis and Prevention of 'the Silent Exodus.'" Ph.D. diss., Trinity Evangelical Divinity School.

Soper, J Chrostopher. 2001. "Tribal Instinct and Religious Persecution: Why Do Western European States Behave So Badly?" *Journal for the Scientific Study of Religion* 40(2):177-180.

Stepick, Alex. 1998. *Pride Against Prejudice: Haitians in the United States*. Boston: Allyn & Bacon.

Stepick, Alex, et al. 2003. *This Land Is Our Land: Interethnic Relations in Miami*. Berkeley: University of California Press.

Stepick, Alex, and Carol Dutton Stepick. 2001. "Power and Identity: Miami Cubans." In *Latinos: The Research Agenda*, ed. M. Suarez-Orozco and C. Suarez-Orozco. Berkeley: University of California Press.

Stepick, Alex, et al. 2001. "Shifting Identities and Inter-Generational Conflict: Growing Up Haitian in Miami." In *Ethnicities: Children of Immigrants in America*, ed. R. Rumbaut and A. Portes. Berkeley: University of California Press.

Stewart-Gambino, Hannah W. 2001. "Religious Consumers in a Changing Religious Marketplace." Review. *Latin American Research Review* 36(1).

Suárez-Orozco, Carola, and Marcelo M. Suárez-Orozco. 1994. "The Cultural Psychology of Hispanic Immigrants." In *Handbook of Hispanic Cultures in the United States: Anthropology*, ed. T. Weaver. Houston: Arte Publico Press.

———. 2001. *Children of Immigration*. Cambridge, MA: Harvard University Press.

Suh, Sharon A. 2001. "Buddhism, Rhetoric, and the Korean American Community: The Adjustment of Korean Buddhist Immigrants to the U.S." Paper presented at a meeting of the Social Science Research Council Working Group on Religion and Immigration, Seattle, WA.

Tiryakian, Edward. 1991. "The Exceptional Vitality of Religion in the United States: A Rereading of Protestant-Catholic-Jew." *Social Compass* 38(3):215-238.

Tizon, Orlando P. Esguerra. 1999. "Congregation and Family: Changing Filipino Identities." Ph.D. diss., Loyola University.

Tweed, Thomas. 1997. *Our Lady of the Exile: Diasporic Religion at a Cuban Catholic Shrine in Miami*. New York: Oxford University Press.

U.S. Department of Justice, Immigration and Naturalization Service. 2002. *2000 Statistical Yearbook of the Immigration and Naturalization Service*. Washington, DC: Superintendent of Documents.

Vermeulen, Hans, ed. 1997. *Immigrant Policy for a Multicultural Society: A Comparative Study of Integration, Language, and Religious Policy in Five Western European Countries*. Brussels: Migration Policy Group (MPC) & IMES.

Vertovec, Steven. 2000. "Religion and Diaspora." Paper presented at the New Landscapes of Religion in the West conference at the University of Oxford, England.

———. 2001. "Religion and Diaspora." Working Paper no. WPTC-01-01. Oxford, England: Institute of Social & Cultural Anthropology.

Vertovec, Steven, and Ceri Peach. 1997. *Islam in Europe: The Politics of Religion and Community*. London: MacMillan Press, Ltd.

Warner, R. Stephen. 1994. "The Place of the Congregation in the Contemporary American Religious Configuration." In *American Congregations: New Perspectives in the Study of Congregations*, vol. 2, ed. J. P. Wind and J. W. Lewis. Chicago: University of Chicago Press.

———. 1997. "Religion, Boundaries, and Bridges." *Sociology of Religion* 58(3):217-238.

———. 1998a. "Approaching Religious Diversity: Barriers, Byways, and Beginnings." *Sociology of Religion* 59(3):193-215.

————. 1998b. "Immigration and Religious Communities in the United States." In *Gatherings in Diaspora: Religious Communities and the New Immigration*, ed. R. S. Warner and J. G. Wittner. Philadelphia: Temple University Press.

————. 1998c. "Religion and Migration in the United States." *Social Compass* 45(1):123-134.

Warner, R. Stephen, and Judith G. Wittner, eds. 1998. *Gatherings in Diaspora: Religious Communities and the New Immigration*. Philadelphia: Temple University Press.

Warner, Stephen. 2000. "Religion and New (Post 1965) Immigrants: Some Principles Drawn from Field Research." *American Studies* 41(Summer/Fall):267-286.

Warner, W. Lloyd, and Leo Srole. 1945. *The Social Systems of American Ethnic Groups*. Westport, CT: Greenwood Press.

Williams, L. Susan, Sandra D. Alvarez, and Kevin S. Andrade Hauck. 2002. "My Name Is Not Maria: Young Latinas Seeking Home in the Heartland." *Social Problems* 49(4):562-584.

Wilson, David A. 1998. *United Irishmen, United States: Immigrant Radicals in the Early Republic*. Ithaca: Cornell University Press.

Withol de Wenden, Catherine. 1998. "How Can One Be Muslim? The French Debate on Allegiance, Intrusion, and Transnationalism." *International Review of Sociology* 8(2):275-288.

Yang, Fenggang. 1998. "Chinese Conversion to Evangelical Christianity: The Importance of Social and Cultural Contexts." *Sociology of Religion* 59(3):237-257.

————. 2002. "Religious diversity among the Chinese in America." In *Religion in Asian America: Building Faith Communities*, ed. P. G. Min and J. H. Kim. Walnut Creek, CA: AltaMira Press.

Yang, Fenggang, and Helen Rose Ebaugh. 2001. "Transformations in new immigrant religions and their global implications." *American Sociological Review* 66(April): 269-288.

Yoo, David. 2002. "A religious history of Japanese Americans in California." In *Religions in Asian America: Building Faith Communities*, ed. P. G. Min and J. H. Kim. Walnut Creek, CA: AltaMira Press.

Yoo, Jin-Kyung. 1998. *Korean Immigrant Entrepreneurs: Network and Ethnic Resources*. New York and London: Garland Publishing.

Zaidman, Nurit. 2000. "The Integration of Indian Immigrants to Temples Run by North Americans." *Social Compass* 47(2):205-219.

Zentgraf, Kristine. 2002. "Immigration and Women's Empowerment: Salvadorans in Los Angeles." *Gender and Society* 16(5):625-646.

Zhou, Min. 1997. "Segmented Assimilation: Issues, Controversies, and Recent Research on the New Second Generation." *International Migration Review* 31(4):975-1008.

Zhou, Min, Carl L. Bankston III, and Rebecca Y. Kim. 2002. "Rebuilding Spiritual Lives in the New Land: Religious Practices among Southeast Asian Refugees in the United States." In *Religions in Asian America: Building Faith Communities*, ed. P. G. Min and J. H. Kim. Walnut Creek, CA: AltaMira Press.

Zolberg, Aristide R., and Litt Woon Long. 1997. "Why Islam Is Like Spanish: Cultural Incorporation In Europe and the United States." Paper presented at Inclusion and Exclusion: International Migrants and Refugees in Europe and North America, a meeting of the International Sociological Association, New School for Social Research, New York City.

3

"Brought Together upon Our Own Continent"
Race, Religion, and Evangelical Nationalism in American Baptist Home Missions, 1865-1900

Derek Chang

In late May 1863, members of the American Baptist Home Mission Society (ABHMS) assembled in Cleveland, Ohio, for the organization's thirty-first annual meeting. As delegates pondered the opportunities created by the Emancipation Proclamation of earlier that year and the increased immigration from Europe and China, the group's executive board boldly described an inclusive vision of America: "It is Europe, it is Asia, it is Africa, it is all of these brought together upon our own continent" (Executive Board of the ABHMS 1863:19). The nation remained mired in a bloody and protracted Civil War and, as a result, missionary labors and resources had declined precipitously. Nonetheless, the society had recently begun its first forays among ex-slaves in the Union-controlled territories of the U.S. South. Moreover, although Baptist evangelical activities among the growing Chinese population in California had reverted completely to local control, the ABHMS anticipated this to be only a temporary condition. As the society considered its charge—"North America for Christ"—it recognized the growing diversity of the American populace and envisioned a nation transformed not just by African American freedom and Chinese immigration but by evangelical Christianity.

The executive board's declaration proved at least geographically prescient. By the close of the decade, the ABHMS, the denomination's principal organization for domestic proselytizing, would direct missionaries in thirty-three states and territories, stretching from the eastern seaboard to the Pacific Coast and from the upper Midwest to the deep South. It supervised missionaries working among ex-slaves in the nine states of the former Confederacy, as well as in Tennessee, Kentucky, and Washington, D.C. Furthermore, the group had recently appointed three missionaries to work exclusively among the Chinese in

California, and white Baptists in Portland, Oregon, would soon petition the society to support a mission to that city's growing Chinese population (Executive Board of the ABHMS 1870:48).

This impressive expansion took place during a critical period in the development of American national identity. Even as the breadth of American Baptist mission fields reflected the growing diversity of the nation's population, movements to narrow the definition of the polity along racial lines gathered momentum. The Civil War had resulted in the emancipation of four million African-American slaves and in their new status as citizens. And—until the Exclusion Act of 1882—the rate of migration from China rapidly escalated, and numerous Chinese communities formed along the Pacific Coast and throughout the Western states (Daniels 1994:69).

Black claims to equality and Chinese desires to live in the U.S. directly challenged the historical link between whiteness and American national identity. As the nineteenth century came to a close, emancipation and Reconstruction led to white redemption and the savagery and intimidation of lynch law and Jim Crow. Moreover, increased immigration led to anti-Chinese vigilantism, discriminatory legislation, and, finally, exclusion. By the end of the century, white Americans had successfully, if temporarily, reinforced the racial bounds of citizenship.

This process did not occur without opposition. Segregation and disfranchisement did not flow inevitably from a reaction to emancipation. Nor was the movement from immigration to exclusion inexorable. Through the institutional footholds established by its missions to African Americans and Chinese immigrants and its commitment to those groups, the ABHMS played a vital—if often overlooked—role in late-nineteenth-century debates over race and national identity. In contrast to the restrictive measures proposed by advocates of Jim Crow and immigration exclusion, the ABHMS offered a vision of a racially inclusive Christian nation. Significantly, its mission programs, institutions established by white evangelicals and black and Chinese proselytes, became critical bases for the development and sustenance of alternative meanings of race and the national polity.

This chapter addresses three related aspects of the ABHMS and its work. The first section analyzes the comprehensive, national mission of the evangelical group, examining its historical roots and late-nineteenth-century discourse. It focuses on the intersection of the group's religious and nationalist beliefs and argues that the ABHMS must be understood as a spiritual *and* civic entity. The second considers a fundamental tension in ABHMS discourse between inclusion and hierarchy, a tension that exposes the challenges of using religion as a basis for civic incorporation. The third section examines the implementation of American Baptist projects in two locales, one among African Americans in Raleigh, North Carolina, and the other among Chinese immigrants in Portland, Oregon. These local perspectives provide details about ABHMS programs in action and the reception of those programs by blacks and immigrants. They reveal evangelical labors as two-way interactions between missionaries and proselytes, and they foreground contests over alternative meanings of religious conversion and civic belonging.

The ABHMS and "Evangelical Nationalism"

An ideology best described as "evangelical nationalism" lay at the center of ABHMS work. Grounded in a belief in the exceptional, providential destiny of America as a Christian nation, fueled by the evangelical mandate to convert more souls, and buttressed by the geographic and demographic expansion of the U.S., this ideology blurred the lines between "religious" and "civic." The ABHMS envisioned its evangelical nationalism as a blueprint for the settlement of the American West and, in the late-nineteenth century, the integration of "alien" elements, especially African Americans and Chinese immigrants.

From its very founding in 1832, the ABHMS understood the nation's spiritual and secular concerns to be inextricably linked. The group had been troubled by the social, civic, and moral uprooting which appeared to accompany westward migration, and it judged migrants to be "lamentably destitute of that Gospel which can alone bestow on the energy of individual communities a wise direction and happy issue" (Executive Committee of the ABHMS 1832a:246). One of the group's founders, Jonathan Going, warned that "a mighty effort must be made, and by the body of evangelical Christians in the United States, and made soon, or ignorance and heresy and infidelity will entrench themselves too strongly to be repulsed." If ignorance, heresy, and infidelity prevailed "our republic will be overturned and our institutions, civil and religious, will be demolished" (Morehouse 1883:317-18). For Going and others like him, there was little difference between America's spiritual welfare and its civic well-being.

Significantly, this link between sacred and secular found a parallel compatibility in the consonance between territorial and demographic expansion on one hand and the evangelical impulse to spread the Gospel on the other. The ABHMS, at its founding, was to be "the providential agency for the concentration of efforts of the denomination, in the contesting with irreligion and error the possession of this land, in supplying destitute regions with Gospel privileges, and in laying religious foundation for the populous future of the continent" (Morehouse 1883:300). If the geographic and religious growth of America was the engine driving the ABHMS, then national salvation was the destination. In its first annual report, the society made the aims of its evangelical nationalism clear by "summoning men to the support of this work, by every principle of enlightened patriotism and of Christian salvation" (Morehouse 1883:324). This vision of what religious historian Martin E. Marty has called the "righteous empire" still pervaded ABHMS ideology in the post-Civil War period (Marty 1970:1).[1] In 1883, Indiana minister and home mission advocate Lemuel Moss declared, "Every missionary of this Society has been an apostle of freedom; every preacher of this Society has been a spiritual agent of our great Government, carrying everywhere thoughts of civil freedom" (Moss 1883:101). American Baptists believed home missions to be the primary instrument of evangelical Christianity, and, thus, the keys to safeguarding American civilization and society.[2]

Yet while the ABHMS remained committed to evangelical nationalism, slave emancipation and the increased immigration of the Chinese tested the limits of the society's definition of the nation. The society never questioned its ministry to either group, but the fears of civil chaos and religious degradation that had fueled the original home mission movement took on a racial cast during the last third of the nineteenth century. Chinese immigrants and African Americans—considered culturally alien, religiously heathen or unorthodox, and, increasingly, biologically distinctive—posed new problems for the evangelical organization. The Reverend William M. Haigh, for example, warned that the end of slavery and the ratification of the Fifteenth Amendment had created "1,000,000 of illiterate voters" and that "the balance of power in this nation is thrown into the hands, not of the intelligent and wise, but the degraded, the ignorant." (Haigh 1879:107). According to Haigh, a new battle had been joined for national well-being and religious conversion, and nothing less than "the safety and perpetuity of our beloved land" was at stake (Haigh 1879:107).

The work among the Chinese was no less urgent. As early as 1846, denominational newspapers had alerted readers to the possibility of a flood of immigration from China (*Religious Herald* [Richmond, VA], 26 March 1846). After 1850, as immigration increased, American Baptists welcomed the evangelical opportunities provided by the arrival of so many souls in need of conversion, but they also turned a cautious eye toward the possible religious and civil effect of so many non-Christians. A report of the society fretted about evangelical efforts on the Pacific Coast: "These States face Old-World paganism. . . . [A]lready they have invited one hundred thousand Chinese to furnish cheap labor to their ever-increasing industries" (Executive Board of the ABHMS 1873:12).

The anxiety of the native-born whites who led the ABHMS was shared by many European Americans. Yet, rather than moving to *exclude* African Americans and Chinese immigrants from the polity—a view which gained prominence especially during the 1880s and 1890s and which, by 1900, was predominant among white Americans—American Baptists sought to *include* these two groups. To be sure, this support of the Chinese and blacks might be attributed to broader political trends and affiliations. Indeed, the ABHMS had a strong connection to the Republican Party, which for a time supported the efforts of federal Reconstruction in the South and immigration in the West (Chang 2002:36, 92).[3] However, it is more likely that the influence worked in the opposite direction—that American Baptists' commitment to evangelical nationalism inspired their political affiliations.

In fact, the ABHMS project reflected what historian Susan Thorne has called the "egalitarian promise of inclusion" at the core of evangelicalism (Thorne 1999:147). In this formulation of Christianity, individual agency, not predestination, was the key to salvation, and all were equal in sin and redemption.[4] Although this egalitarian ideological trajectory often fell well short of the mark in practice, it nonetheless provided a foundation for some of the society's public pronouncements on matters of race. In the 1840s, for instance, several leading members established the American Baptist Antislavery Convention (ABASC), which helped precipitate the schism between northern and southern Baptists (Chang 2002:57-71). They argued that slavery undermined the evangelical belief in all people as "free moral agents" (Galusha 1850:46). This antebellum example hints at a significant strand of American Baptist ideology which would continue after the Civil War: The ABHMS would place religion, not race, at the heart of its criteria for national inclusion.

During the late nineteenth century this foundation of inclusive ideology found expression in the society's ambitious goals for freedpeople and Chinese immigrants. In 1865, the organization forthrightly offered its vision of the place of newly emancipated blacks in America: The ABHMS was committed to the "elevation of the liberated bondmen" and believed it to be a matter of national importance that freedpeople "be invested with the *elective franchise*, and with all the privileges of whatever kind belong to American citizenship" (Executive Board of the ABHMS 1865:44). Central to this belief was a recognition of the "full, absolute, equal humanity" of African Americans (Executive Board of the ABHMS 1882:12). And, although a smaller focus for the society, the growing number of Chinese on the Pacific Coast had a place in this imagined nation.[5] In 1873, the organization's Committee on the Chinese announced its belief "that the Chinese are destined to become before long a large and worthy portion of our adopted American citizenship; and that special missionary labor among them . . . is one of the most imperative duties of the hour" (Executive Board of the ABHMS 1873:12).

The society's commitment to an inclusive vision of evangelical nationalism carried significant weight, for the ABHMS had never been bashful about its role as a *public* entity. Despite its incorporation as a private enterprise and its private sources of funding, the organization believed its mission to be singularly important to the civic welfare of the nation. American Baptists accordingly took vocal, public positions on a whole host of issues. In addition to the often vituperative and ultimately divisive debate over slavery and the formation of the ABASC, Baptists were among the earliest groups to come to the defense of Chinese immigrants. Thus, in response to an anti-Chinese diatribe by California Governor John Bigler, the Baptist *Home and Foreign Journal* published a rejoinder by Chinese merchants as well as editorial comments accusing Bigler of "betray[ing] a mass of ignorance in regard to the character of that people" (*Home and Foreign Journal* 1852:1).

Moreover, the society's officers, as well as local Baptists affiliated with the group, often had strong links to state power. George N. Briggs and John K. Griffin, for instance, not only served as two of the society's original vice presidents, but also won election to Congress from Massachusetts and South Carolina, respectively, as Whigs (Executive Committee of the ABHMS 1832b:5; *The Tribune Almanac for the Years 1832-1868* 1868:12,13). As American Baptists began their work in the South in 1861, Ira Harris became the society's president. Later that year, he would become a U.S. senator from New York. Even before the war ended, the ABHMS used its influence to prevail upon the Office of the Adjutant General, giving the organization's missionaries the authority to take control of Baptist churches in occupied territories of the Confederacy (Executive Board of the ABHMS 1864:15).

Locally, the links between Baptist mission advocates and civic power were equally clear. The Failing family, which helped provide financial support and leadership for the Chinese Mission School in Portland, Oregon, exemplified this dynamic. The Failings were active civic leaders in business, government, and philanthropy, who, not coincidentally, helped to found the city's First Baptist Church (Chang 2002:257-62). American Baptists not only articulated a connection between civic and religious missions in their rhetoric, but they acted as public figures, using the society, individual churches, and their positions as politicians to advocate for and implement evangelical nationalism.

This vision of inclusion espoused in official pronouncements and advocated by powerful men took shape in specific ABHMS programs. A committee devoted to assessing the work in the South declared that the goal of the society should be "the entire reorganization of the social and religious state of the South" (Executive Board of the ABHMS 1862:50). Indeed, the group would organize congregations, establish churches, staff schools, and found universities and seminaries for former slaves, thus playing a central role in the spiritual *and* civil reconstruction of the region.[6] Similarly, the ABHMS understood conversion to Christianity to be critical to its work among Chinese immigrants, but also believed that this spiritual transformation was inextricably linked to a civic goal. In the words of the major ABHMS publication, all proselytizing among the Chinese on the Pacific Coast was designed "to make of these populations American citizens" (*Baptist Home Mission Monthly* 1879:102).

Hierarchy in Evangelical Nationalism

Yet, in practice, the implementation of egalitarian—or even inclusive— programs proved more elusive than in religious rhetoric. In fact, the inclusive discourse and practices of evangelical nationalism often masked a countervailing trajectory. Because American Baptist efforts coupled spiritual and worldly concerns, they sought a comprehensive transformation of African Americans and Chinese immigrants. Samuel Haskell, chairman of the organization's Committee on the Work for the Freedmen hinted at this total conversion when he noted that evangelical programs should address African Americans' "body, mind, and spirit" (Executive Board of the ABHMS 1864:33). This material, ideological, and religious endeavor, however, was based on an assessment of fundamental and hierarchical differences between missionaries and their potential proselytes.

Thus, when Lemuel Moss articulated the ABHMS vision of inclusive evangelical nationalism, he argued that evangelical Christianity played a specific and critical role: "[A] free people will never be constituted or held together by any iron band. They must be held together by something that is powerful enough to assimilate and purify and elevate and unify all those discordant elements that may come within its range" (Moss 1883:101). In this formulation of inclusion, uplift and assimilation formed the foundation of any "positive" change in proselytes assessed by missionaries. Indeed, the goal of "elevating" target communities assumed their lesser condition and implied a sense of hierarchy. Inclusion could only come after conversion, manifested not only by a profession of faith but by attendant social transformations as well. For American Baptists, this meant a thorough inculcation in the beliefs of evangelical Christianity *and* middle-class values.

The methods for uplift reveal the class and gender hierarchies shaping American Baptist standards for national inclusion. Among African Americans, for instance, the ABHMS decided in 1866 not only to devote resources to the education of adults but also to make the training of a black elite a particular area of concentration (Executive Board of the ABHMS 1866:31-35). Thus, the society withdrew much of its support from common schools and focused its attention on instructing black ministers and teachers, believing them to be "the leaders of all social movements among the freedmen" (Executive Board of the ABHMS 1866:17). "If we can lead and elevate them," American Baptists reasoned, "we may through them hope to elevate the mass of the people" (Executive Board of the ABHMS 1866:17). This strategy underscored the central position of elitist evangelical nationalist schemes and harkened back to an antebellum Whig heritage that emphasized the leadership of a chosen class who assumed responsibility for others and for an orderly society (Chang 2002:37-42; Maffly-Kipp 1994:26; Howe 1979:31, 34, 150-80).

For the mission to the Chinese, the focus on training community leaders echoed the organization's practical concerns and ideologies of social change espoused in the South. To be sure, the ABHMS recognized the cost effectiveness of concentrating on educating potential Chinese preachers, ministers, and missionaries. As was the case in the South, mission officials believed that the most efficient way of reaching the most souls was to convert a few select leaders. Chinese Christians might have greater access to more potential proselytes and could aid missionaries with language and translation difficulties.

Significantly, these practical considerations cannot be separated from American Baptist social theories (and evangelical practices) calling for the development of a leadership class of proselytes. In 1875, the Reverend E. Z. Simmons made this clear to the executive board when he argued "that intelligent converts should be educated in this country, with a view to their better preparation for effective church work among their countrymen here and in China." (Executive Board of the ABHMS 1875:19) Not coincidentally, that same year the society's annual report noted that several converted Chinese had returned to China to preach the Gospel (Executive Board of the ABHMS 1875:19). Chinese evangelicals were thus envisioned by the ABHMS as a trans-Pacific Christian elite, poised to lead the Chinese at home and abroad from heathenism to salvation.

Perhaps even more than its strategy, the society's educational tactics exposed class-bound understandings of uplift. In its mission in the South, American Baptist tactics hinged on inculcating black leaders—ministers and teachers in particular—with European-American middle-class values of industriousness, temperance, discipline, and, of course, piety. In addition to basic literacy skills and academic subjects, including theology, ABHMS schools emphasized "morality." The organization of student-based temperance organizations, for example, became a point pride for American Baptist missionaries (Tupper 1885; Executive Board of the ABHMS 1887:33). As an item from the society's principal publication explained, the ministers and teachers educated in ABHMS institutions were positioned to become community leaders not only because of their superior schooling but also because, in these schools, they learned the essential elements of civilization (*Baptist Home Mission Monthly* 1878:18-19).

On the Pacific Coast, also, the inculcation of missionaries' definitions of morality also became the goal. In fact, the education provided by mission schools for the Chinese emphasized not just religious principles or secular learning, but "Christian civilization" (Chinese Mission School Records). White Baptists in Portland, Oregon, for example, established the Chinese Mission School as a first step toward the development of a "permanent college for Chinese instruction to be used for bringing the wayfarers into contact with the best culture and purest morals of our land" (Chinese Mission School Records).

In both mission fields, the specific class content of the comprehensive curricula was evident in the focus on industriousness. Well before it became popular to espouse the virtues of "industrial education" for black Southerners, Henry Martin Tupper's mission in Raleigh relied on bricks manufactured by students "to lessen the cost of construction" and to defray other costs (Hartshorn 1910:89). This labor and its resulting commodities played more than a merely fiscal role for the Raleigh mission. For Tupper—and his northern missionary brethren—productive labor was an essential part of the curriculum. The push to create black free laborers during the Reconstruction period is a well-known story, and the ABHMS contributed in its own way to this project (Saville 1994; Foner 1983; Anderson 1988). For these free-labor advocates, servitude had obliterated the incentives of upward social and economic mobility, helping to perpetuate the lowly status of slaves. Tupper and others like him sought to inculcate ex-slaves with what they believed to be the core values of a free-labor society, especially work discipline, to transform them into good, productive, and independent citizens. Their purpose was best summed up by the society's 1874 pronouncement: "Self-help is the best help" (Executive Board of the ABHMS 1874:36).

Among the Chinese "self-help" was equally important. Although American Baptists never established their planned industrial school, the everyday pedagogy of mission schools underscored the themes of industriousness. In Portland, for example, the Chinese Mission School was not free. Rather, students paid for books and were expected to contribute money during monthly collections taken in their classes (Chinese Mission School Records). Soon after the school opened, administrators began requiring students to pay teachers directly for each class taught (Chinese Mission School Records). Teachers, almost exclusively local white women, earned one dollar per month per student. However, they did not depend on these salaries for their livelihood and donated them directly to the school (Chinese Baptist Church Records.) Why, then, have the students go through the ritual of paying teachers? Although the extant record provides no clear answer, it is likely that the reason lies in the lessons administrators and teachers hoped to instill in their Chinese students. Like "industrial education" in the South, the insistence upon students paying teachers directly for services may have been a part of that more extensive curriculum, with the fee-for-use payment structure representing a prime example of basic market relations.

Significantly, the acceptance of class-bound *gender* prescriptions represented a central marker of success in the endeavor to transform black and Chinese leaders. In the South, missionaries expressed the political and economic condition of freedmen in gendered terms, setting "manhood" at the opposite extreme of slavery. One official commented, for example, that the goal of American Baptist ministerial education was to "lead freedmen to act, not as though slaves, but upon the responsibility of their manhood" (Executive Board of the ABHMS 1866:33). An annual report from the society's Richmond Institute proclaimed, "It has been the aim of the instructors not simply to insist on studious habits in the students, but they have also striven to develop every manly quality; they have aimed to make *men* of their pupils—God-fearing, self-denying men" (Executive Board of the ABHMS 1869:40). In the post-bellum recalculation of the equation of "blackness" and "servitude," the society sought to instill the "manly" quality of independence in ex-slaves. This was the aim of ABHMS self-help programs and the ultimate goal of evangelical nationalist education.

Moreover, like other white, middle-class evangelicals of the time, American Baptists believed women to be the central purveyors of piety and purity within the home (Pascoe 1990). Black women thus became a special focus of the society which began providing curricula for the training of female teachers in 1869 (Executive Board of the ABHMS 1869:39; Higginbotham 1993).

The society hoped these teachers would be the female equivalent of ministers, transmitting the values and knowledge they learned in missionary schools to greater numbers of African-American women, men, and, especially, children (Higginbotham 1993:19-46). As ABHMS officer Henry Lyman Morehouse observed some years later, "A well-qualified Christian teacher for the common school is, as facts show, a great power for good in the community—second only to the educated preacher of the Gospel" (Morehouse 1883:415).

African-American teachers' roles, as envisioned by the ABHMS, consisted of more than pedagogy. The very same report that announced the admission of women to the academic department of Wayland Seminary added, "Their influence has been salutary, besides exciting a healthy degree of emulation, refining manners, and conversation" (Executive Board of the ABHMS 1869:54). American Baptist theories of educated black female leadership considered behavior and academic learning equally important. As the organization's commitment to training African-American women became more focused in the mid-1870s and, especially after 1880, reports alternately emphasized book learning and the manners and skills of respectable domestic womanhood as featured elements of ABHMS curricula. In 1874, when the society boasted that "all the seven [ABHMS theological] schools admit [women] except one," it also expressed an important facet of its philosophy behind this commitment: "Any intelligent person can see at once, that if we educate young men for the ministry, and leave them to make marriages with heathen women, we practically nullify all our efforts to elevate the race, by leaving young minds to be molded by ignorant, superstitious women. Our young men will lose half the benefit of their culture by such alliances" (Executive Board of the ABHMS 1874:34).

In missions to the Chinese, gender considerations played a central role in programs as well. The overwhelmingly male immigrant population raised the specter of sexual threat to white women while popular European-American images of Chinese women depicted them as immoral, unclean, and enslaved prostitutes (Almaguer 1994:160-62; Chan 1991:94-146; Takaki 1998:121-23). The missionary project of assimilation to Christian morality and behavior was thus deemed critical. Missions to Chinese men, while couched simply in terms of conversion, specifically targeted social and cultural practice. While their sexuality was never explicitly mentioned, religious transformation would result in the disciplining of sexual appetite. Noted missionary Jesse B. Hartwell, "It can be easily demonstrated that the Christian religion can and does elevate, purify, and ennoble the Chinese character, that it practically lifts the Chinaman up to a new plane of life, enlarging his powers, strengthening his mind, purifying his morals, and fitting him to live in the midst of a cultivated Christian community" (*Baptist Home Mission Monthly* 1885:93-94).

Although Baptists never engaged in the rescue missions for Chinese prostitutes that their Presbyterian and Methodist counterparts established, their work with Chinese women reflected a desire to teach them the values of purity and piety central to women's missionary discourse (Pascoe 1990). Through the same methods that missionaries used in the South—home visitation and teaching in Sunday schools and day schools—Baptist evangelical women hoped to transmit Christian morality and lead women away from lives the missionaries deemed degrading.

The American Baptist project of national inclusion, then, depended upon a religious and social transformation of proselytes that undermined the egalitarian possibility of a civic order based on evangelical nationalism. The elevation envisioned by American Baptists assumed the lower social, cultural, and religious status of blacks and Chinese. As a standard for inclusion, conversion required not just a profession of faith but the adoption of middle-class social and religious practices exemplified by "proper" gender roles and behavior. The national mission of the ABHMS was thus constrained by a definition of racial meaning inextricably linked to class and gender relationships.

The ABHMS in Local Perspective

The task of resolving the central tension between evangelical nationalism's inclusive and roughly egalitarian trajectory on the one hand and its tendency toward hierarchy and uplift on the other fell to missionaries working in the field. In practice, American Baptist evangelicals were met by proselyte populations who, contrary to theorists' expectations, actively engaged the missionaries and offered their own ideas for mission programs. Moreover, the hostile climate toward African Americans and Northerners in the South and Chinese immigrants on the Pacific Coast provided an element of hardship which home mission theorists had not anticipated. In fact, it was in the specific, local interactions between missionaries and proselytes that evangelical nationalism—and its racial implications—played out. The deployment of evangelical nationalism is thus revealed not as a one-way process of evangelization but as a dialectic in which proselytes, though often ignored by missionaries and left out of the official record, articulated an alternative vision of America.

Two of the most important local missions affiliated with the ABHMS were established in Raleigh, North Carolina, and Portland, Oregon. The mission in Raleigh was initiated by Henry Martin Tupper, an Andover Theological Seminary-trained minister and Union Army veteran. Tupper had been commissioned by the executive board of the society to begin evangelizing among the freedpeople of North Carolina. He helped found an African-American congregation and developed what would become Shaw University, a centerpiece of the society's nineteenth-century educational efforts among black Southerners. In Portland, local Baptists and community leaders established a mission school for the Chinese of that city and later received financial and moral support from the national body. Sponsored by the city's First Baptist Church, the Chinese Mission School (CMS) was led, in part, by a converted evangelical from China.

Although preceded by efforts in northern California, the CMS was the longest continuously running American Baptist institution among the Chinese in the U.S. (Chang 2002).

While the American Baptist missions in Raleigh and Portland developed in significantly different ways, the two projects offer important insights into the structural limits as well as the egalitarian promise engendered by local manifestations of evangelical nationalism. Perhaps the most important institutional difference was that the call for the Raleigh mission was initiated by the ABHMS executive board in New York City while the Portland project began at the behest of local white Baptists.[7] This difference reflected the priorities of the central executive board for whom the Civil War and four million freedpeople took precedence over tens of thousands of Chinese emigrating to the Pacific Coast.[8]

The two projects were situated in very different regions. Raleigh was a governmental and administrative city located in a state of the former Confederacy. Even as Tupper arrived in North Carolina, the state was in the process of establishing the proper credentials for formal reunion with the North. Portland was the major commercial city of the Pacific Northwest and sat some 3,000 miles west of ABHMS headquarters in New York. Yet, from the perspective of the executive board dominated by Northeasterners, the two regions were bound together as part of a common evangelical nationalist project emanating west and south from the eastern seaboard.[9] Both projects were part of a larger attempt to bring evangelical nationalism to the religious, social, and political periphery. The society hoped not only to continue its antebellum project of connecting the western reaches of the continent to the social, cultural, and religious norms of the Northeast but also to play a central role in the re-union of North and South (Maffly-Kipp 1994:35; Executive Board of the ABHMS 1865:9-10).

More significantly, the two missions are also comparable as local articulations of the society's national civic endeavor. Indeed, the Raleigh and Portland missions stemmed from similar social, demographic, and political dynamics. In the decade preceding the establishment of American Baptist missions in both locales, the non-European-American population had increased greatly, and these demographic shifts became the focal point of ABHMS labors. Although the total populations of both cities and their respective counties had grown, the increase in the number of African Americans in Raleigh and surrounding Wake County and the number of Chinese in Portland and surrounding Multnomah County far outstripped the growth of the white populations in both areas.[10] These increases attracted much attention from white observers. Historian Howard N. Rabinowitz writes of the South, "[B]oth visitors and residents were struck by the numbers of new Negroes in the cities. Whatever the actual count, it seemed to observers that the cities were teeming with blacks" (Rabinowitz 1996:21; Litwack 1980:314.) On the Pacific Coast, the increase in Chinese immigration also fueled responses out of proportion to the actual number of immigrants arriving.[11]

The rapid influx of blacks and Chinese into cities throughout the South and the Pacific Coast, respectively, threatened to disrupt assumptions of white citizenship and privilege. Whites feared the concentration of non-whites and worried that these new populations would not be as easy to control through state and local institutions. Historian Leon F. Litwack writes that, in the South, whites saw "a once productive labor force, released from proper supervision, [filling] the cities and towns as vagrants, thieves, and indigents" (Litwack 1980:314). In California, the state senate held hearings concerning the "social, moral, and political effect of Chinese immigration" in general, but a large majority of the testimony centered on the role of immigrants in San Francisco's "Chinese quarter" (California Senate Special Committee on Chinese Immigration 1876). Like black Southerners, the Chinese were characterized as dishonest, unclean, and a drain on public resources.

The ABHMS project is perhaps best understood as a response to this climate of white anxiety. Missionary officials in the North and northern missionaries laboring in the South expressed alarm over the potential political power of four million illiterate ex-slaves. Among the Chinese, national concerns were mentioned but usually subordinated to the more immediate anguish over heathenism. Despite these differences in emphasis, both ABHMS missions were direct responses to this racial phenomenon. In fact, in Rev. M. B. Anderson's assessment, the most important element in the South was "colored brethren from whom the light of the cross of Christ has been shut out by the pall of slavery" and, in a veiled reference to the Chinese, the westward extension of evangelical Christianity to the Pacific Coast was most significant so "we shall soon have 'flanked' heathenism and be able to attack it in the rear" (Executive Board of the ABHMS 1865:9-10).

Missionaries and officials were also troubled by the increasingly vituperative opposition to both groups. For the missionaries who welcomed emancipation and immigration, such "un-Christian" behavior seemed to pose an even greater challenge to social stability than the freeing of slaves or the settling of Chinese. On the Pacific Coast, American Baptists, chagrined by white outrage and violence directed toward the Chinese, called for the end of such "barbarous treatment." (Executive Board of the ABHMS 1880:37) Missionaries in the South, often dependent upon local whites, were more circumspect with their criticism. Nonetheless, subtle characterizations of white opposition to black citizenship rights made the ABHMS position clear. In 1870, for example, the society's executive board quoted a southern minister as saying, "I have not conversed with an intelligent man since the close of the war, whose opinion was not decidedly in favor of educating the colored people" (Executive Board of the ABHMS 1870:21). At the very moment, then, that emancipation and immigration offered the greatest opportunity for the society's evangelical nationalist goal of inclusion, local realities pushed missionaries and their sponsors toward an agenda of social control and hierarchy.

Nevertheless, in-depth investigations of the responses of local blacks and Chinese to American Baptist efforts in Raleigh and Portland, respectively, reveal countervailing pressures to push missionaries to fulfill the democratic possibilities of evangelical nationalism. In the years following the Civil War, Afro-North Carolinians struggled to define the meaning of freedom on *their* terms, and the American Baptist Home Mission Society's project in Raleigh became a vital staging area in this fight. The ostensible aims of the school initiated and supervised by ABHMS missionary Henry Martin Tupper matched well with the freedpeople's emphasis on education as a key in establishing equal citizenship rights in the post-war nation. Although less obviously than in North Carolina and the South where emancipation and the direct applicability of the Fourteenth and Fifteenth Amendments brought the definition of freedom to the fore, similar concerns accompanied immigrant participation in the CMS. The history of discriminatory law and practice in Oregon, supported by the 1790 prohibition against the naturalization of non-whites, soon combined with a national movement to circumscribe the rights of the Chinese further. Denied the protection of civil rights, they sought acceptance, community, and refuge in local institutions such as the mission school.

For many blacks in Raleigh and Chinese in Portland, American Baptist evangelical labors provided material resources that had previously been beyond their means. Both groups embraced the educational opportunities provided by mission schools, and the enthusiasm evinced by African-American and immigrant mission participants extended well beyond a desire to learn. They availed themselves of American Baptist resources and made significant monetary contributions from their modest incomes, thus helping to establish lasting mission institutions. In so doing, they created vital social, cultural, and political space for themselves. The primary locations for assembly in these missions—the classroom, the Sunday school class, the chapel—all became crucial sites for social and religious congregation among proselytes.[12] As black Baptists and Chinese Christians began community-building, they made their case for participation and inclusion in American religious and civic life using the institutions and rhetoric of evangelical nationalism.

In Raleigh and Portland, African-American and Chinese immigrant proselytes, respectively, publicly asserted their belonging in various ways that drew on evangelical nationalist ideas, institutions, and resources. These practices, in part, reflect a desire by blacks and immigrants to take advantage of ABHMS philanthropy, but the actions also reveal a deeper set of motivations. Afro-North Carolinians, for example, sought Henry Tupper's services to perform religious rites, such as marriage ceremonies (Tupper 1865). African-American couples wanted to exercise this newly won basic civil right. Under slavery, the illegality of slave marriages, the forced conjugality between non-consenting partners, and the disruption of marital and other family ties through slave sales marked the choice of freedpeople to marry as a poignant counterpoint to the unfreedom of bondage and made such decisions assertive political acts (Edwards 1997:45-57). Even after the North Carolina legislature, as part of the state's Black Codes, passed a law which required ex-slaves to register marriages with county clerks or justices of the peace, the high level of compliance, as documented by historian Herbert Gutman, can be seen as a choice made by freedpeople to formalize marital bonds and reaffirm ideas of marriage that had been held during slavery (North Carolina 1866:99; Gutman 1976:414-18). Moreover, the confirmation of marriages by the civil government held great practical value, for legal sanction legitimized freedpeople's children, qualified spouses for soldiers' pensions, and qualified couples for the possible reapportionment of land (Litwack 1980:240).

Yet, ex-slaves, by specifically seeking a missionary or minister, such as Tupper, to sanctify new or existing matrimonial bonds and conduct funeral rites also indicated their religiosity. The religious devotion that inspired them to call for a public ceremony officiated by a Christian clergyman, too, served as a declaration of hard-won freedom. In the antebellum era, slaves had developed and practiced a religion that fused African traditions with the Christianity propagated by evangelical plantation missions (Raboteau 1978). Shaped by the punishing oppression of servitude, the emancipatory faith and egalitarian spirit of African and Old Testament theology, and the relentless zeal for freedom of the slaves themselves, this religion, according to Albert J. Raboteau, "was both institutional and noninstitutional, visible and invisible, formally organized and spontaneously adapted" (Raboteau 1978:212). This "invisible religion" constituted a site of significant, though usually clandestine, resistance to the slave regime. Thus, the public expression of religious faith, especially those marking crucial moments in the lifecycle such as marriage or death, represented powerful expressions of emancipation (Raboteau 1978:227; Edwards 1997:47).

This religiosity was linked in significant ways to freedpeople's new political standing. Laura Edwards has persuasively argued that, as white North Carolinians sought ways to limit the rights, control the freedom, and compel the labor of African Americans in the wake of emancipation, the state's interest in marriage became central (Edwards 1997:35-38). "To keep freedpeople from threatening civil society," writes Edwards, "they had to be brought into it. To be brought into it, they had to be married" (Edwards 1997:37). Although providing an opportunity for blacks to gain increased authority within the state, marriage laws and conservative white leaders tended to emphasize the "obligation, not the rights, of marriage" (Edwards 1997:37-38). Nevertheless, by choosing a minister to represent the state rather than a secular official such as a justice of the peace or county clerk, the freedpeople invoked a higher authority than the state. Their choices reflected an understanding of civil power tempered by the emancipatory and redemptive qualities of Christianity.

In Oregon, perhaps the most dramatic—and certainly the most public— examples of Chinese assertions of belonging came in the form of open concerts. These concerts performed a supremely practical function—to raise money for mission institutions. They also provided a platform for Chinese participation in civic and religious society. By simultaneously displaying the positive influence of missionary work and presenting the audience with a glimpse into what was deemed unique Chinese culture, these concerts exemplified the constant tension in missionary work between assimilating proselytes and delineating difference. Using this tension to their advantage, Chinese participants—and other community members—could imbed a "hidden transcript" within these public performances and convey not only forms of Christian expression but ideas about the meaning of freedom and belonging through a white-sanctioned event.[13]

On April 26, 1875, Chinese students and their teachers presented a full program of twenty-four songs, prayers, reports, recitations, and addresses in a public concert (Chinese Baptist Church Records). It was the first of several CMS events held in Portland during the 1870s. The nearly full house at First Baptist Church paid twenty-five cents each, and the proceeds were "applied for the payment of the organ now used by the Chinese church" (Chinese Baptist Church Records). At these events and others like them, Chinese students who were training for Christian conversion demonstrated their grasp of religious songs as well as American secular learning, such as English and geography. Moreover, students also sometimes performed recitations and songs in their native tongue.

For the white sponsors of the school, the concerts demonstrated the power of evangelical Christianity to re-shape the Chinese. In the midst of increased anti-Chinese agitation, white advocates of the mission school hoped these presentations would demonstrate that the Chinese could be transformed through the power of Christianity. Noted the *Oregonian* after the initial exhibition, "The house was pretty well filled and the evening's exercises passed off with credit to the scholars, and showed that the efforts put forth to teach the Chinese were not all in vain" (Chinese Baptist Church Records). Thus, when students sang, "I Will Sing for Jesus" or "The Morning Light is Broken" or "All to Christ I Owe," and performed exercises in reading and speaking English and in geography, they indicated to the audience of advocates, potential supporters, and even skeptics that they were capable of making the transformation from heathen aliens to Christian residents. In short, the religious context diminished the perceived threat of Chinese immigration to white residents.

For Chinese participants, the exhibitions demonstrated their spiritual and social transformation to mission teachers, sponsors, and audience members. Although this function overlapped with and even endorsed the assimilationist desires of white evangelicals, for the Chinese in Portland, the necessity of overcoming the social obstacles imposed by perceptions of cultural and racial difference seems to have outweighed the desire to confront directly the ethnocentric assumptions of evangelical Christianity.

Participants also used the opportunity presented by these concerts to demonstrate their fellowship with white, evangelical Portland, and Chinese neophytes asserted their membership within the larger Christian community. The

April concert, in particular, symbolized this sense of congregation. For the first ten Chinese baptized by First Baptist Church, the performance was the first public recognition of their baptism the day before (First Baptist Church Records).

Finally, such performances exemplified the connections students had formed with each other. The singing of hymns and recitation of lessons and scripture together confirmed bonds which forged in classes and religious meetings and during worship. This sense of community was critical for the Chinese in Portland who, due to skewed sex ratios, white hostility and violence, discriminatory legislation and hiring practices, and itinerant housing situations, found it increasingly difficult to establish stable families and other institutions.

This feeling of community echoed beyond the walls of First Baptist Church. Although the audiences were probably composed almost entirely of Portland's white residents, the concerts sent a message to the larger Chinese population. The mission's concerts represented the largest—and most peaceful—interactions between the city's Chinese and white inhabitants. Although dozens—even hundreds—of interactions between immigrants and European Americans most certainly occurred without incident each day, numerous episodes of harassment and violence set the tone for race relations in the city. In addition, Portland's major newspaper regularly publicized the growing anti-Chinese animosity in San Francisco and added to the ominous climate. The embrace of Chinese Christians by the city's elite who supported the mission signaled a refuge from the growing storm over the immigrants' presence in the U.S. and in Portland itself.

Beyond the assertion of their public belonging, black North Carolinians and Chinese Oregonians found ways to demonstrate what their idea of civic inclusion should look like. Individual achievements provided models of education, citizenship, and aspiration for others throughout proselyte communities. As historian Kevin Gaines noted of the early twentieth century, the example of educated blacks "represented the struggle for a positive black identity in a deeply racist society" (Gaines 1996:3). Thus, when Caesar Johnson became one of Shaw University's first graduates, it signaled more than merely an individual accomplishment. Born into slavery in 1840, Johnson had been identified by American Baptist officials as an important evangelical in the early 1870s, earning a commission to work in Warren County (U.S. Bureau of the Census 1880; Executive Board of the ABHMS 1872:119; Executive Board of the ABHMS 1873:66). In 1872, he entered Shaw to hone his theological knowledge. After graduating, Johnson remained in Raleigh where he gained prominence as a minister and activist within the African-American Baptist State Convention. He proved to be an inspiration for his sibling who followed in his footsteps (U.S. Bureau of the Census 1880; Shaw University 1882:4). Men like Johnson, through their educational and professional accomplishments, provided models for others in the years after emancipation.

In Oregon, the example of individuals educated at the CMS sent a clear message to fellow Chinese about the possibilities engendered by the mission project. Of the first ten Chinese converts of the CMS, Song Sam Bo appears in the extant record most fully. In 1875, the same year that he was baptized, Song expressed interest in continuing his studies beyond the mission school (Chinese Mission School Records). Three months later, "It was unanimously agreed to send Bro. Song Sam Bo to McMinnville College" (Chinese Mission School Records). The mission's commitment to Song continued for more than two years while he completed his studies (Chinese Mission School Records). Song's ambition and the opportunities provided by the school must have illuminated a world of possibility to his fellow students.

Those individuals who came to represent upward striving also helped to establish formal and informal networks and institutions in both regions. Shaw-trained ministers and educators helped to lay the groundwork for a loosely connected group of schools, churches, and denominational institutions, even as the hope of emancipation and Reconstruction gave way to the despair and violence which led to Jim Crow. Noted one Shaw graduate, "We have sent out hundreds of teachers who are now doing service in our public schools, scores of ministers who are now preaching the gospel, and dozens of men in other walks of life" Hartshorn 1910:489). As students, the men and women who attended the Raleigh school often took to the North Carolina countryside during summer vacations to preach the Gospel and organize educational and religious meetings for more isolated populations. Upon graduation, some became missionaries commissioned by the ABHMS to preach and build institutions. Others were called to the pulpit in autonomous black churches, becoming leaders of perhaps the most important institutions within African-American communities.

These ministers also helped to organize larger regional and state denominational associations, such as the North Carolina State Convention (Colored), which lay outside the authority not only of local white Baptist organizations but of the ABHMS as well. The black state Baptist convention came to be dominated by students and former students of Shaw. Caesar Johnson and N. F. Roberts, who would eventually become acting president of the school, both held elected posts within the organization while maintaining close ties with the Raleigh school (*Proceedings of the First Annual Session of the General Association of Colored Baptists* 1868; *Proceedings of the Eleventh Annual Session of the Baptist State Convention of North Carolina* 1878:1). And they were but two examples of a common phenomenon (Jones 1940:13; Simmons 1968:280).

Finally, educators—women and men—who trained at the Raleigh university established, managed, and taught at other schools for African Americans. These schools, like the Waters Normal Institute in Winton, North Carolina, became critical institutions as public resources for black education diminished. Shaw graduate C. S. Brown established the school and staffed it with fellow Shaw alumnae ("Waters Normal Institute, Winton, N.C." n.d.; Hartshorn 1910:488).

Connections such as these were nurtured at the Raleigh mission institution and became an organizing device for activists. Students who attended Shaw

spent time together in classes, religious services, prayer meetings, and dormito-
ries, and the personal relationships and sense of fellowship fostered by congregation passed beyond Shaw's physical boundaries to create formal and informal
networks of black Baptist educators. The significance of these bonds and the
institutions that grew out of them can hardly be overemphasized. The establishment, maintenance, and proliferation of autonomous institutions implicitly repu-
diated missionary contentions that blacks were not yet ready to take over leadership of the project and undermined the very basis of the ABHMS notion of
uplift. Moreover, mission participants helped to create vital institutional space.
Their active leadership of individual congregations and schools placed them at
the center of two of the most important institutions within black communities.
As the gains and expectations of emancipation and Reconstruction were turned
back by a bloody and repressive tide of white supremacy, churches and schools
led and established by educated blacks became critical sites for spiritual succor,
social services, community development, and education.

The Chinese who participated in the mission school in Portland also
used the mission programs as launching pads for autonomous and semi-
autonomous institutions and networks. Chinese missionary Dong Gong, like
many of his black counterparts in the South, was directed to minister not only to
his fellow countrymen in Portland but to the Chinese throughout Oregon and
Washington Territory, as well (Executive Board of the ABHMS 1882:150). He
thus ministered to significant but isolated Chinese populations in rural and min-
ing settlements while helping to establish Chinese congregations in towns other
than Portland.[14]

These labors were part of a much larger, transnational network of Chinese Christians. Students and leaders linked the Chinese Mission School in Portland to other churches, schools, and missions throughout the Pacific Coast of the
U.S. and across the ocean to China. Dong Gong, for example, had been converted as a migrant in San Francisco by ABHMS evangelical John Francis and
returned to China where he studied under the direction of Baptist missionary R.
H. Graves (*Baptist Home Mission Monthly* 1880, 15; Executive Board of the
ABHMS 1873:25). He returned to the U.S. at the urging of Francis, and he
worked in northern California before moving to Portland to minister to Chinese
in the Pacific Northwest (Executive Board of the ABHMS 1873:25; First Baptist
Church 1906:15-16). When Dong returned to southern China to be reunited with
his family, he continued his evangelical work and called upon his Chinese
Christian brethren in Portland to contribute "several hundred dollars" for his
mission project and chapel across the Pacific (Executive Board of the ABHMS
1881:46; *Baptist Home Mission Monthly* 1881:60). Dong's successors at the
Portland mission school continued and elaborated this transnational network of
Chinese converts.[15]

The significance for Chinese Christian leaders and converts went well
beyond the establishment of a church or a school in a single locale. Each institution became an important point of reference for immigrants and migrants. Carrying a letter testifying to former membership in the Baptist mission or church in

Canton or part of the U.S. assured Chinese Christians a warm welcome into the Portland community.[16] And, if they chose to leave Portland, the converts at the mission received a similar letter they could present to Baptist institutions wherever they eventually settled (First Baptist Church Records).

Moreover, immigrant converts who met one another through mission projects created their own meetings and societies independent from white-run evangelical organizations. As Wesley Woo has shown, Chinese Christians—led by Baptist converts—organized the interdenominational Youxue Zhengdaohui in 1871 (Woo 1991:226). Based in San Francisco, it was a posthumous tribute to Baptist convert and ABHMS-commissioned missionary Fung Seung Nam (Woo 1991:226; Executive Board of the ABHMS 1872:19, 99-100).

To be sure, Chinese immigrants and migrants had other institutional resources upon which to draw during their travels between south China and the United States, among which family and district organizations remained perhaps the most important. Nevertheless, the connection to an explicitly Christian organization with links to the city's powerful gave immigrants and migrants a claim to protection from white patrons. In 1875, for example, First Baptist church member Captain Nathaniel Ingersoll convinced his fellow congregants to send a letter to an acquaintance of his who captained a steamship bound for China (First Baptist Church Records). The letter asked Ingersoll's friend to look after one of the mission school's converts who was returning home aboard the vessel—to "hunt up our Brother and give him words of cheer and comfort while on his voyage" (First Baptist Church Records).

With the formation of these transnational links, Chinese Christians offered an alternate vision of the connection between religion and civic belonging. American Baptists used their understanding of evangelical nationalism to make conversion, not race, the standard for inclusion in the nation. For them, Christianity was an essential component of national identity and belonging. For Chinese converts, however, membership or participation in mission-based networks articulated a more cosmopolitan version of evangelical Christianity in which the nation mattered less than religious fellowship. As part of a transnational migration that negotiated the economic, political, and social structures of two countries, Chinese Christians used the rhetoric and programs of the ABHMS to moderate the power of the nation and emphasize the communal, congregational nature of evangelical Christianity.

Conclusion

African Americans in Raleigh and Chinese immigrants in Portland actively participated in the institutional life of their respective ABHMS missions. They contributed generous amounts of money from their relatively small incomes and committed tremendous energy and labor to the establishment of programs. Although the evangelical projects themselves were the cooperative creations of white missionaries and sponsors in conjunction with black or Chinese prose-lytes, African Americans and immigrants already understood the missions to be theirs. Through their hard work, sacrifice, and active participation they staked their claim to institutions within both cities.

Their efforts, in fact, resulted in the formation of critical social, cultural, and political space. Although not entirely free from the gaze of white Baptists, the mission were important sites for social and religious congregation. Moreover, African-American and Chinese proselytes used the religious and civic implications of evangelical nationalism to their advantage by asserting their right to secular inclusion through religious conversion. In this sense, they not only claimed the missions as their own but also promoted a vision of an inclusive civic polity. Finally, black Baptists and Chinese Christians also helped to establish autonomous institutions beyond the supervision of white evangelicals. These loosely connected networks became crucial in the struggle to sustain and protect black and Chinese communities as the nineteenth century closed with a maelstrom of white supremacist violence, agitation, and legislation. Indeed, by the end of the century, the society's vision of evangelical nationalism had been eclipsed by a narrower conception of America and its polity. Jim Crow and immigration exclusion had reinforced the historic link between whiteness and national identity.

Yet, even as the nation entered what has been famously called the "nadir of American race relations" in the 1890s, black Baptists and Chinese Christians continued to work aggressively through American Baptist networks not only for national inclusion but for a transformation of the fundamental meanings of citizenship and civic belonging (Logan 1954).[17] Fung Chak, an outspoken Chinese-born ABHMS missionary in Oregon, persisted in his denunciations of the ill treatment of immigrants. Many black Baptists in the South expressed their dismay over racial hierarchy within American Baptist institutions by splitting from the white-dominated organization and forming the National Baptist Convention in 1895. These actions were emblematic of the late-nineteenth-century contest over the link between race and national identity. That these events occurred within an evangelical Christian organization was no coincidence, for religion, as well as race, played a pivotal role in questions of national identity and belonging in the late nineteenth century.

American Baptist work among African Americans in the South and Chinese immigrants on the Pacific Coast exposed both the promise and the limits of the Baptist project. For white evangelicals, the desire to create a Christian America had led it to a conclusion full of radical possibility. Despite the recent model of black slavery and the long-standing 1790 Naturalization Act which restricted citizenship rights only to those immigrants who were "free whites," the ABHMS believed that its evangelical nationalist project should be expanded to include freedpeople and the Chinese in America not just as co-religionists but as fellow citizens. Yet, internal ideological contradictions and, more especially, external opposition limited the application of this belief. Nevertheless, ABHMS labors and institutions provided critical resources for African Americans and Chinese immigrants as they sought to dismantle the hierarchy of race by fulfilling their aspirations for freedom, inclusion, and equality.

Notes

I wish to thank Dennis Cordell and Karen Leonard for their thoughtful comments on an early presentation of the research for this essay. Research was conducted with the support from a Religion and Immigration Fellowship from the Social Science Research Council.

1. Marty argues that American evangelicals, especially between 1776 and 1877, "set out consciously to create an *empire*. They set out to attract the allegiance of all the people, to develop a spiritual kingdom, and to shape the nation's ethos, mores, manners, and often its laws" (1970:1).

2. The belief in the connection between America's spiritual and civic fates was not unique to the ABHMS, and the organization's founders were part of a broader, multidenominational home mission movement (Maffly-Kipp 1995).

3. The national Republican Party was not wholly supportive of Chinese immigration (Gyory 1998).

4. The home mission movement in America during the 1830s and the founding of the ABHMS in 1832 grew, in large part, from the religious fervor of the Second Great Awakening during which the "voluntary principle" gained theological popularity. In a reversal of the Calvinist concept of the elect, the voluntary principle held that anyone could "come to Christ" through prayer (and contact with those who already had experienced "new birth") and be saved. Home missionary associations developed as mechanisms to disseminate the Great Revival's religious, cultural, and social ideas over time and space, thus institutionalizing the era's spiritual passion (Miller 1965:36-72).

5. The term "imagined nation," as I have used it here, has two meanings. First, it refers to the nation that American Baptists hoped to establish. The second sense of the phrase is drawn from Benedict Anderson's analysis of nationalism and the nation. He defines "nation" as "an imagined political community" in which links among citizens are "conceived as a deep, horizontal comradeship" (1991:6-7).

6. Historian Daniel Stowell has pointed to the contested "process by which southern and northern, black and white Christians rebuilt the spiritual life of the South in the aftermath of the disruptions wrought by the Civil War" as *religious* reconstruction. For Stowell, the competing visions of what reconstruction entailed included the restoration of the old order for southern whites, evangelization and Christianization for northern whites, and the establishment of a "new and separate religious life" for freedpeople (1998:7).

7. The Portland CMS began when seventy-five Chinese men assembled in the Good Templar's Building for the first time on November 13, 1874, after more than a year of planning by the leaders of First Baptist Church (First Baptist Church Records).

8. The work among the Chinese on the Pacific Coast, for both the Southern Baptist Convention and the ABHMS, ceased during the Civil War and reverted to local control by individual congregations. Both groups re-entered the field only slowly after the war, and, by the end of the 1870s, the Southern Baptists had withdrawn completely from the field, leaving its work among Chinese immigrants to the ABHMS (Chang 2002:145-151).

9. In 1870, for example, twenty-one of the twenty-two officers and managers of the ABHMS (excluding three field secretaries) hailed from New York, New Jersey, Massachusetts, or Pennsylvania. Contributions to the society from individuals in New York, Massachusetts, Rhode Island, Pennsylvania, and New Jersey predominated, making up nearly 75% of the $179,689.32 donated in 1870 (Executive Board of the ABHMS 1870:3, 43).

10. The black population in Raleigh and Wake County increased 96.2% and 32.6%, respectively, between 1860 and 1870, compared to white increases of 18.1% for Raleigh and 37.2% for Wake County. The Chinese population in Portland and Multnomah County increased almost 2000% and 2200%, respectively, for the same time period. Author's calculations from the U.S. Census. The Chinese were not enumerated in the published 1860 Federal Census. This figure was compiled by the author from the manuscript schedules of the 1860 Federal Census (U.S. Bureau of the Census 1860).

11. In Portland, for example, a city census in 1862 recorded a mere 87 Chinese, but the city's newspaper still remarked upon the inundation of immigrants (McCormick 1864:9; *Oregonian* [Portland] 24 March 1864). Interestingly, it is likely that the enumeration of the Chinese in the directory is low, for the same survey of the city includes 700 people among the "Floating Population, estimated from calculations made from Registrars of Hotels and Boarding Houses." Because many Chinese lived in boarding houses, it is probable that many were included in that figure. Still, even if the Chinese improbably consisted of one half of the "floating population," they would have made up less than 10 percent of the total population of the city.

12. My use of "congregation" relies heavily upon historian Earl Lewis's discussion of the Jim Crow South. He writes that "congregation was important because it symbolized an act of free will, whereas segregation represented the imposition of another's will." He adds that although blacks in Norfolk "adroitly" reversed the language of oppression, they "discovered, however, that congregation in a Jim Crow environment produced more space than power" (Lewis 1991:92).

13. James C. Scott uses the term "*hidden transcript* to characterize discourse that takes place 'offstage,' beyond direct observation by powerholders. The hidden transcript is thus derivative in the sense that it consists of those offstage speeches, gestures, and practices that confirm, contradict or inflect what appears in the public transcript." In the case of the Portland concerts (and their counterparts in the South), the discourse of proselytes occurred quite literally "onstage" (1990, 4-5, 202-203).

14. In 1877, for instance, Dong helped the white-run Baptist Church in Salem establish a thriving Chinese mission school (*Oregonian* [Portland], 17 November 1877; *Oregonian* [Portland], 23 November 1877; *Oregonian* [Portland], 25 January 1879; *Oregonian* [Portland], 8 November 1879).

15. Dong's most notable successor was Fung Chak, who began his evangelical career at the ABHMS mission in San Francisco. Fung became an outspoken critic of anti-Chinese measures before returning to China. He would return to Oregon in 1887 (Executive Board of the ABHMS 1875:63; Chang 2002:338).

16. Fung Chak, for example, noted in 1881 that the mission school and First Baptist Church had "received three Chinese by baptism [and] two by letter" (*Baptist Home Mission Monthly* 1881:172).

17. Although Rayford Logan's work only focuses on African Americans, his characterization could also well be applied to Chinese-white relations.

References

Aarim-Heriot. 2003. *Chinese Immigrants, African Americans, and Racial Anxiety in the United States, 1848-1882.* Urbana: University of Illinois Press.

Almaguer, Tomás. 1994. *Racial Fault Lines: The Historical Origins of White Supremacy in California.* Berkeley and Los Angeles: University of California Press.

Anderson, Benedict. 1991. *Imagined Communities.* New York: Verso.

Baptist Home Mission Monthly. 1878. 1 (August): 18-19.

Baptist Home Mission Monthly. 1879. 1 (January): 102.

Baptist Home Mission Monthly. 1880. 2 (January): 15.

Baptist Home Mission Monthly. 1881. 3 (March): 60.

Baptist Home Mission Monthly. 1885. 7 (April): 93-94.

California Senate Special Committee on Chinese Immigration. 1876. *Chinese Immigration: The Social, Moral, & Political Effect of Chinese Immigration; Testimony Taken Before a Committee of the Senate of the State of California.* Sacramento: State Printing Office.

Chan, Sucheng, ed. 1991. *Entry Denied: Exclusion and the Chinese Community in America, 1882-1943.* Philadelphia: Temple University Press.

Chang, Derek. 2002. "'Breaking the Shackles of Hierarchy': Race, Religion, and Evangelical Nationalism in American Baptist Home Missions, 1865-1900." Ph.D. diss., Duke University.

Chinese Baptist Church Records. Portland, Box 2, MSS 1560, Oregon Historical Society, Portland.

Chinese Mission School Records. Portland, 1873-85, Baptist Church Records, MSS 1560, Oregon Historical Society, Portland.

Chinese Mission School Records. Portland, Financial Records, October 1874-July 1885 and Misc. Loose Papers, 1882-86, MSS 1560, Oregon Historical Society, Portland.

Daniels, Roger. 1994. *Asian America: Chinese and Japanese in the United States Since 1850.* Reprint. Seattle: University of Washington Press.

Edwards, Laura F. 1997. *Gendered Strife and Confusion: The Political Culture of Reconstruction.* Urbana and Chicago: University of Illinois Press.

Executive Board of the ABHMS. 1862. *Thirtieth Annual Report of the ABHMS.* New York: American Baptist Home Mission Rooms.

———. 1863. *Thirty-first Annual Report of the ABHMS.* New York: American Baptist Home Mission Rooms.

———. 1864. *Thirty-second Annual Report of the ABHMS.* New York: American Baptist Home Mission Rooms.

———. 1865. *Thirty-third Annual Report of the ABHMS.* New York: American Baptist Home Mission Rooms.

———. 1866. *Thirty-fourth Annual Report of the ABHMS.* New York: American Baptist Home Mission Rooms.

———. 1869. *Thirty-seventh Annual Report of the ABHMS.* New York: American Baptist Home Mission Rooms.

———. 1870. *Thirty-eighth Annual Report of the ABHMS.* New York: American Baptist Home Mission Rooms.

———. 1872. *Fortieth Annual Report of the ABHMS.* New York: American Baptist Home Mission Rooms.

———. 1873. *Forty-first Annual Report of the ABHMS.* New York: American Baptist Home Mission Rooms.

———. 1874. *Forty-second Annual Report of the ABHMS.* New York: American Baptist Home Mission Rooms.

———. 1875. *Forty-third Annual Report of the ABHMS.* New York: American Baptist Home Mission Rooms.

———. 1880. *Forty-eighth Annual Report of the ABHMS.* New York: American Baptist Home Mission Rooms.

———. 1881. *Forty-ninth Annual Report of the ABHMS.* New York: American Baptist Home Mission Rooms.

———. 1882. *Fiftieth Annual Report of the ABHMS.* New York: American Baptist Home Mission Rooms.

Executive Committee of the ABHMS. 1832a. Address. *American Baptist Magazine.* 12:8 (August): 246.

First Baptist Church, Portland, Oregon. 1906. *Manual & Directory of the First Baptist Church, The White Hall Temple, Portland, Oregon.* Portland: F.W. Baltes & Company, Printers.

First Baptist Church Records. Portland, Oregon, Minutes, 1854-1906, Baptist Church Records, MSS 1560, Oregon Historical Society, Portland.

———. 1832b. *First Annual Report of the ABHMS.* New York.

Foner, Eric. 1983. *Nothing But Freedom: Emancipation and Its Legacy.* Baton Rouge: Louisiana State University Press.

Gaines, Kevin. 1996. *Uplifting the Race: Black Leadership, Politics, and Culture in the Twentieth Century.* Chapel Hill: University of North Carolina Press.

Galusha, Elon. 1850. Address to Southern Baptists, delivered 30 April 1840. *Facts for Baptist Churches,* ed., A. F. Foss and E. Mathews. Utica, NY: American Baptist Free Mission Society.

Gutman, Herbert G. 1976. *The Black Family in Slavery and Freedom, 1750-1925.* New York: Vintage.

Gyory, Andrew. 1998. *Closing the Gate: Race, Politics, and the Chinese Exclusion Act.* Chapel Hill: University of North Carolina Press.

Haigh, W. M. 1879. Address. *Baptist Home Mission Monthly.* 1:7 (January): 107.

Hartshorn, W. N., ed. 1910. *An Era of Progress and Promise, 1864-1910: The Religious, Moral, and Educational Development of the American Negro Since His Emancipation.* Boston: Priscilla Publishing Co.

Harvey, Paul. 1997. *Redeeming the South: Religious Cultures and Racial Identities Among Southern Baptists, 1865-1925.* Chapel Hill: University of North Carolina Press.

Higginbotham, Evelyn Brooks. 1993. *Righteous Discontent: The Women's Movement in the Black Baptist Church, 1880-1920.* Cambridge, MA: Harvard University Press.

Home and Foreign Journal. 1852. 2:3 (September): 1.

Howe, Daniel Walker. 1979. *The Political Culture of the American Whigs.* Chicago: University of Chicago Press.

Jones, Calubert A. 1940. "A Brief Sketch of the History of Shaw University." In *Shaw Bulletin.* Raleigh, NC.

Lewis, Earl. 1991. *In Their Own Interests: Race, Class, and Power in Twentieth-Century Norfolk, Virginia.* Berkeley: University of California Press.

Litwack, Leon F. 1980. *Been in the Storm So Long: The Aftermath of Slavery.* New York: Vintage Books.

Logan, Rayford. 1954. *The Negro in American Life and Thought: The Nadir, 1877-1900.* New York: Dial Press.

Maffly-Kipp, Laurie F. 1995. *Religion and Society in Frontier California.* New Haven, CT: Yale University Press.

Marty, Martin E. 1970. *Righteous Empire: The Protestant Experience in America.* New York: Dial Press.

McCormick, S. J. 1864. *The Portland Directory for the Year 1864.* Portland, OR: S. J. McCormick.

Miller, Perry. 1965. *The Life of the Mind in America: From the Revolution to the Civil War.* New York: Harcourt, Brace & World, Inc.

Montgomery, William E. 1993. *Under Their Own Fine and Fig Tree: The African-American Church in the South, 1865-1900.* Baton Rouge: Louisiana State University Press.

Morehouse, H. L. 1883. "Historical Sketch of the American Baptist Home Mission Society for Fifty Years." In *Baptist Mission Homes in North America; Including a Full Report of the Jubilee Meeting, & a Historical Sketch of the American Baptist Home Mission Society, Historical Tables, Etc., 1832-1882.* New York: Baptist Home Mission Rooms, 1883.

Moss, Lemuel. 1883. "Results of Home Mission Work." *The Baptist Home Mission Monthly.* 5:5 (May): 101.

North Carolina. 1866. *Public Laws of the State of North Carolina, Passed by the General Assembly at the Session of 1865-66.* Raleigh: Wm. E. Pell.

Pascoe, Peggy. 1990. *Relations of Rescue: The Search for Female Moral Authority in the American West, 1874-1939.* New York: Oxford University Press.

Proceedings of the Eleventh Annual Session of the Baptist State Convention of North Carolina, 1877. 1878. Raleigh, NC: Edwards, Broughton & Co., Printers and Binders.

Proceedings of the First Annual Session of the General Association of the Colored Baptists of North Carolina, Held with the Church at Goldsboro, N.C., October 17-19, 1867. 1868. Raleigh, NC: Mills & Hughes, Printers.

Rabinowitz, Howard N. 1996. *Race Relations in the Urban South, 1865-1890.* Athens: University of Georgia Press. Original edition, 1978.

Raboteau, Albert J. 1978. *Slave Religion: The "Invisible Institution" in the Antebellum South.* New York: Oxford University Press.

Saville, Julie. 1996. *The Work of Reconstruction: From Slave to Wage Laborer in South Carolina, 1860-1870.* New York: Cambridge University Press.

Scott, James C. 1990. *Domination and the Arts of Resistance: Hidden Transcripts.* New Haven, CT: Yale University Press.

Shaw University. 1882. *General Catalogue of the Officers and Students of Shaw University, 1875-1882.* Raleigh, NC: Edwards Broughton & Co.

Simmons, William J., ed. 1968. *Men of Mark: Eminent, Progressive, and Rising.* New York: Arno Press.

Stowell, Daniel W. 1998. *Rebuilding Zion: The Religious Reconstruction of the South, 1863-1877.* New York: Oxford University Press.

Takaki, Ronald. 1998. *Strangers from a Different Shore: A History of Asian Americans.* Rev. ed. Boston: Back Bay Books.

Thorne, Susan. 1990. *Congregational Missions and the Making of an Imperial Culture in Nineteenth-Century England.* Stanford, CA: Stanford University Press.

The Tribune Almanac for the Years 1838 to 1868, Inclusive, Volume 1. 1868. New York: New York Tribune.

Tupper, Henry Martin. 1865. Diary. Henry Martin Tupper Manuscript Collection, James E. Cheek Learning Resource Center, Special Collections and Archives, Shaw University, Raleigh, NC.

———. 1885. Shaw University Annual Report for 1885. Henry L. Morehouse Correspondence Files, Group 4, Box 8, Folder 2, Archival Collection, Board of National Ministries, American Baptist Historical Society, Valley Forge, PA.

U.S. Bureau of the Census. 1860. Manuscript Schedules of the 1860 Federal Census. Multnomah County, Oregon.

———. 1880. Manuscript Schedules of the Population Census. Wake County, North Carolina.

"Waters Normal Institute, Winton, N.C." n.d. Henry L. Morehouse Correspondence Files, Box 9, Folder 14, Archival Collection, Board of National Ministries, American Baptist Historical Society, Valley Forge, PA.

Woo, Wesley. 1991. "Chinese Protestants in the San Francisco Bay Area." In *Entry Denied: Exclusion and the Chinese Community in America, 1882-1943,* Sucheng Chan, ed. Philadelphia: Temple University Press.

4

Daddy Grace: An Immigrant's Story

Danielle Brune Sigler

Most recent works in the field of religion and immigration have focused on specific immigrant communities in the United States and the trends that occur within these communities, with particular attention to assimilation, syncretism, and the maintenance of religious traditions.[1] While this chapter also seeks to understand the relationship between religion and immigration in America, it takes as its subject not an immigrant community, but a single immigrant: Charles Manuel "Sweet Daddy" Grace.[2] A focus on one man—and a highly original man at that—may seem to have limited applicability. Yet Grace's life and his church, the United House of Prayer for All People of the Church on the Rock of the Apostolic Faith, offer a particular glimpse into America in the early twentieth century and its toleration of and attraction to difference in the religious sphere of life.

While much of Grace's life is rather extraordinary, his early experiences in America read like a fairly conventional immigrant story. Marcelino Manuel deGraca left Brava, one of the Cape Verde Islands off the west coast of Africa, and arrived in the United States in 1904. DeGraca, like many other Cape Verdean immigrants, anglicized his name to Charles M. Grace[3] and settled in New Bedford, Massachusetts, where his father, mother, and other family members were already living. Grace was part of a growing Cape Verdean immigrant community seeking a better life in southeastern Massachusetts.[4] Cape Verdeans had first arrived in New Bedford via the whaling trade, and settled in the area. During the early twentieth century, they left the Portuguese-controlled islands in growing numbers and sought out economic opportunity in the U.S. Once there, however, Cape Verdeans often encountered racial discrimination because the range of their skin tones made it impossible for Americans to pinpoint their race or ethnicity.

During his first fifteen years of residence in the United States, Grace worked a number of jobs in and around southeastern Massachusetts. He spent time in the cranberry bogs, a common occupation for Cape Verdeans. He also worked in sales in a number of different locations and made an effort at free-lance work, selling items he could buy wholesale. Here the conventional aspects of Grace's story end. Disenchanted with the limited options available to him as an apparently non-white immigrant, Grace ultimately turned outside of his community for support and to the pulpit as his calling. He created an original ministry with a basis in the Holiness and Pentecostal religions that were blossoming around him.

The Holiness movement had its origins in American Methodism; John Wesley had instructed early Methodists about the need for a second religious experience, or sanctification, that occurred after conversion. In the 1880s as ministers and other Methodists saw "sanctification" lose importance within the denomination, they left and began forming new organizations, with an emphasis on recapturing and maintaining "holiness." Holiness religion and its outgrowth, Pentecostalism, followed in the tradition of Methodism in the United States by giving men and women who had not received a conventional religious education the opportunity to lead. Holiness and Pentecostal religion generally rejected educated clergy in favor of religious leaders who demonstrated their merit through their own experience of sanctification and their ability to lead others to it. This helps to explain Grace's attraction to and success in this religious tradition.

As Ebaugh and Chafetz explain in their anthology of "continuities and adaptations in immigrant congregations," "the role of religion in the mainte-nance and reproduction of ethnic identity was a major—arguably *the* major—theme throughout our entire project" (2000:18). While Grace did not apparently turn to religion as a tool for the *reproduction* of his ethnic identity in successive generations, he certainly saw it as a tool for the *maintenance* of his ethnic iden-tity—though not perhaps in the manner to which Ebaugh and Chafetz refer. To understand Daddy Grace, one must understand that his status as an immigrant from Cape Verde and as an outsider generally was *fundamental* to his success as the head of a religious organization that continues today, over eighty years after its inception and over forty years after his death. Grace relied on his accent, skill with language, and his status as "other" to set himself apart from other popular religious leaders of the day as well as to challenge accepted categories of race. His difference helped to substantiate his religious authority within his church. Grace, however, did not seek to extend this celebration of difference (or, in other words, to reproduce this ethnicity) to other Cape Verdeans or among them. In-stead, he sought out populations that would be less familiar with his ra-cial/ethnic/national/cultural identity—populations that would view him as an original.

In understanding Grace's life and the lessons it can offer scholars of re-ligion and immigration, two questions are of particular importance: Why would a man from a predominantly Catholic island who had been consistently excluded from full economic participation on the basis of his skin color, accent, and national background turn to an American, Protestant form of religion as a means of seeking success and acceptance? And why would that man then champion and celebrate the very things that had been a liability in his everyday life?

In addition to addressing these issues, Grace's life is illuminating because it is an exception that proves the rule. The choices he made and the criticism he received throughout his life offer valuable insight into why many immigrant communities function in the ways that they do. His life illustrates the advantages and liabilities of focusing his ministry on populations outside of his own immigrant community as well as the role that fame and notoriety can play in acceptance of otherwise rejected ethnic/racial identities.

From employment opportunities to residential options, Grace's life in and around southeastern Massachusetts was constrained by the color line. In New Bedford, Cape Verdeans established themselves along the waterfront; they were generally unwelcome in the "white" areas of town and uninterested in the primarily African American "West End." Cape Verdeans did not fit comfortably into the black/white dichotomy that dominated thinking about race in the northeastern United States.

Writing in the *Evening Standard* in 1905, journalist Cooper Gaw devoted a lengthy article to explaining just who these "Cape Verders" were. His article offers insight into the situation in which Grace and other Cape Verdeans found themselves. Gaw delineated their branch of the "human family" tree as being "Africans with an admixture of Portuguese blood." And though he later went on to explain that immigrants from Cape Verde were "black," they did not seem to fit the racial stereotypes Gaw and others attributed to African Americans who fell under this same broad category. In fact, Gaw explained that

> The only object [of this article] has been to relate some facts about a people whose presence in communities which were hot beds of abolitionism 35 years ago, has stirred up among the white inhabitants a prejudice comparable to that which exists in the south against the southern negroes, with whom the Cape Verder has little in common except color and ancestry. (Gaw 1905:12)

This final line is particularly compelling, as it not only highlights the difficulty of identifying the race of Cape Verdean immigrants, but also the increasing racism that Cape Verdean immigrants like Grace faced in New Bedford.

In addition to the experience of racism, another factor shaped Grace's life and future in the United States. He and other Cape Verdeans witnessed first-hand the Holiness awakening spreading across the country. Beginning in November 1896, the Reverend George Noble, a member of one of these Holiness organizations, turned his missionary eye toward Cape Verdean immigrants, the "Portuguese" of New Bedford, Massachusetts. The Portuguese immigrant community to which Noble brought his Pentecostal testimony was a unique one, battling to assert its own national and ethnic identity in a country that rejected such assertions. Reverend Noble, however, accepted the Portuguese on their own terms, and it is perhaps owing to this acceptance that his mission was so successful among them. Noble embraced the national identity to which the immigrants themselves adhered. He offered them a place of worship, in marked contrast to other established churches including the Portuguese Catholic church, which found Cape Verdeans a liability to their own tenuous status in the community. Following a tradition of mission work in immigrant communities, Noble met a "sanctified Portuguese" who offered him an entrance into the community. Over ten years later, Noble fondly recalled the origins of his work and explained, "praise, God, the blessed work begun on South Water Street, New Bedford is still going on" (1909:7-8). John J. Diaz,[5] a Cape Verdean and Noble's "son in the Gospel," took up Noble's message and carried it not only to his fellow immigrants, but back to the islands themselves, establishing a mission on the island of Brava.

Thus, Reverend Noble had endeavored to bring the gospel to an immigrant community in New Bedford at the turn of the century. Diaz then attempted to spread the Gospel to his homeland. Both of these moves have precedents—immigrant communities were often the targets of missionaries, and immigrants would then in turn carry new religious beliefs and practices home with them. Noble faced the additional challenge of overcoming his outsider status and finding a "son in the gospel" to help with his work. Diaz faced the trials of trying to spread a Protestant faith throughout the predominantly Catholic islands—work that he was qualified to do on the basis of his own sanctification experience. Grace's story, however, flies in the face of these standard narratives.

Given the merging of a relatively new form of religion with a relatively new immigrant population facing increasing discrimination, it is little wonder that southeastern Massachusetts produced a new religious leader who would confound and confuse racial boundaries and embrace a faith that allowed him to express himself freely and give him the opportunity to lead. Unlike Diaz, however, Grace turned his missionary zeal toward a broader audience, one that might admire and celebrate his difference. The religious forms he brought them would be familiar, but he, himself, would appear unique and original. Though he turned to his countrymen and women initially, Grace's greatest successes would be outside of the Cape Verdean immigrant community.

As previously suggested, Holiness and Pentecostal churches did not require formal training and they lacked central governing bodies. This gave both men and women of different races the opportunity for leadership. Pentecostalism, which emphasized glossolalia, or speaking in tongues as a sign of baptism of the Holy Spirit, had its foundations in the Azusa Street revival headed by William J. Seymour, a man the *Los Angeles Daily Times* described as "an old colored exhorter, blind in one eye."[6] Thus, this new form of American religion offered Grace a rare opportunity for leadership and financial success. Grace would not have been able to create his own Catholic parish[7] nor would he have been able to operate a church in most established denominations. He could, however, easily create his own church grounded in the Holiness and Pentecostal religion that was thriving around him. Another Cape Verdean, Theophilo Gonsalves, believed that the Pentecostal church would eventually make significant inroads among Cape Verdeans precisely because it "is more democratic in her government" (1908:2).

Grace took advantage of the democratic nature of the church, naming himself "reverend" or "bishop." Initially he preached in and around New Bedford, building his first church in Wareham, Massachusetts, and ministering primarily to other Cape Verdeans. In December 1921 Grace built a new mission in New Bedford next door to the former location of Reverend Noble's Nazarene mission. Grace called his church the "House of Prayer"—taking the phrase from Isaiah 56:7. Although "House of Prayer" also appears in Matthew, Mark, and Luke, Grace traced the derivation of the name of his church to Isaiah. This is significant because the full text of Isaiah reads, "for mine house shall be called an house of prayer for all people." Grace included this full statement in the name of his church: the United House of Prayer for All People of the Church on the Rock of the Apostolic Faith. His use of "all people" suggests an awareness of his and his fellow immigrants' status as outsiders, but it is also important to note that over the course of his life, "all" became ever more expansive. Grace aimed his ministry at *all* people, not *his* people.

The "apostolic faith" denoted a type of religion that had its roots in the Azusa Street revival, whose newspaper was called the *Apostolic Faith*. Throughout his life, however, Grace and his followers eschewed the terms Holiness or Pentecostal, which outsiders used both interchangeably and in opposition to each other when describing the movement in its early years. Grace's emphasis on "apostolic faith," though it suggested a connection with the theology of Azusa Street, including the practice of speaking on tongues, also indicated his desire to remain autonomous and not to be pigeonholed under a particular denominational umbrella beyond the House of Prayer itself. Apostolic faith may have had another significance for Grace as well; he saw himself in terms of the lineage of great prophets and apostles—an idea that played upon his status as a mysterious man from another land.

Ironically, given the emphasis on experience within the apostolic faith, Grace himself did not speak of a particular moment of conversion or a call to the ministry. He embraced a type of religion that would give him the freedom to make his mark without the authority of a governing body (which might have proved difficult for a Cape Verdean immigrant, generally regarded as black), but he also rejected the rhetorical strategy of many great evangelists of the era. Billy Sunday, for instance, whose rise to success predates Grace's, told of his moment of conversion outside a barroom. For Sunday, a former professional baseball player and self-described drunk, this was an integral part of his "common man" appeal. Grace, however, did not appeal to his congregations as "one of them" or as a "common man"—instead he consistently emphasized his difference.

Instead of talking about a shameful past or a moment of spiritual enlightenment, Grace substantiated his position by speaking in larger terms. In the later years of his ministry, Grace explained that he had brought God to America—thus immigrant experience, more than a moving conversion experience, held a significant place in establishing his authority as a religious leader. Given that Grace explained his mission not in terms of a defining moment of spiritual awakening but in terms of bringing the gospel to the United States, it is not surprising that he ultimately focused his ministry on a region of the country in which Cape Verdeans were virtually unknown. As Max Weber explains in his essay "Sociology of Charismatic Authority," the leader's sense of mission and its acceptance by his congregation is fundamental: "charismatic claim breaks down if his mission is not recognized by those to whom he feels he has been sent" (1968:20). Grace's claims of unique spiritual gifts that stemmed from his foreign past would have found a more impressionable audience outside of Massachusetts. Grace's followers outside New Bedford's Cape Verdean community would have been less familiar with the circumstances of his birth and subsequent migration and more likely to accept his claim of divine mission, unaware of the economically driven migration that typified the Cape Verdean experience.

Nevertheless, throughout his tenure as head of the House of Prayer, Grace consistently pursued the economic success he had failed to find in his early years in the United States. He demonstrated a remarkable capacity for financial planning and investment—one that supports the contention that discrimination played a significant role in his earlier failed attempts at business in the United States. Anthropologist Arthur Huff Fauset, who included Grace in his 1944 work *Black Gods of the Metropolis*, explained, "we have here a clear example of an organic urge which, because it is caught up in the paradoxes of the peculiar American dichotomy, seeks to find its way out through perhaps the only channel reserved to it, namely, the religious channel" (1970:89). Fund-raising was a fundamental part of the House of Prayer and the presentation of moneys raised even took on ceremonial status within the church. Congregations would present Grace with elaborate items—wishing wells, pumpkins—covered in dollar bills. Fundraising was not conducted undercover nor did Grace make any attempt to hide the real amount of funds raised from his followers. Houses of Prayer hung pictures of the buildings Grace had purchased, including one of his best known acquisitions—the El Dorado apartment building in New York; these images were symbolic of their collective economic might. Following his death, one journalist explained, "Had he been white, he might well have been able to employ [his assets] in business from a more conventional base. With luck, he could have been one of the great modern financial buccaneers" (Oberdorfer n.d.). Both this observation and Fauset's sixteen years earlier point to the unique opportunity that religion could present a man who, as an immigrant and racial "other," could not apply his business acumen in another area of American life.

Following his early success in and around New Bedford, Grace headed south in his "gospel car" and began to focus his ministry in the southeastern United States. As the name of his church implied, Grace sought out members of all races. Throughout his life, officials of the church would emphasize that the House of Prayer reached out to people "regardless of nationality, race, or creed." Nevertheless most of Grace's followers were African Americans—though he continued to maintain a somewhat racially mixed congregation throughout his lifetime. One possible reason for the predominance of African Americans is Grace's move to the American South. Many white Southerners may have perceived Grace himself as a "Negro" and rejected him as a religious leader. Indeed, as Grace become more and more well-known as a leader of a "black religion," whites may have been less inclined to join.[8] Perhaps because Grace was part of an immigrant community that had difficulty gaining acceptance and asserting its own racial identity, he created a religious organization in which religious belief more than racial identity formed the basis of union and solidarity.

Grace's role as a minister to a predominantly African American congregation was even more surprising given his Cape Verdean background. Many Cape Verdeans in the United States rejected associations with African Americans; they were well aware of the extent of racism in the country and did not wish to be aligned with African Americans. Additionally, Cape Verdeans were an immigrant population with more obvious cultural links to other Portuguese immigrants and peoples of Portuguese descent in the United States. Of course many Portuguese who considered themselves "white" rejected association with Cape Verdeans to avoid any negative implications themselves. Cape Verdeans consistently found that they did not fit in America's racial schema. Grace, however, in embracing religion and creating his own ministry had created a platform from which he *could* assert and maintain any and all identities.

Given that Grace did not understand his organization as part of the "black church," it is not surprising that African American members found something new and different in the House of Prayer. He did not center the church on race or discussions of race. When he referred to differences between the House of Prayer and other denominations or the American public generally, he spoke primarily in terms of class and educational difference. Membership in the House of Prayer, not race, was the dominant category for Grace and his followers as he presided over his growing religious organization. His followers, in turn, embraced Grace as their "Daddy" and he often referred to them as his children. His family transcended racial, national, or ethnic difference. The members of the House of Prayer were his children; he was father to them all.

The House of Prayer was just one of many religious options available to African Americans of the era. In conjunction with the Great Migration, religious organizations and storefront churches were multiplying rapidly. While mainstream denominations continued to flourish, a host of new organizations came into being as well.[9] Father Divine offered his followers a "raceless" society—rejecting any racial category as artificial and socially constructed. Marcus Garvey had begun offering African Americans a quasi-religious black nationalism in 1918. Noble Drew Ali instructed his followers in the traditions of Islam, and William Crowdy had created an African American Jewish movement before the turn of the century. The options were varied and seemingly unlimited. Grace, who offered his followers a religious but not explicitly racial identification, found a significant African American following in the South and later in the North as he spread the House of Prayer to urban centers. His role as head of the House of Prayer and mysterious man of God was instrumental to his success.

Even as Grace's followers throughout the South accepted his unique but often vague and undefined identity, the press struggled to label him— dubbing him both a "Portuguese faith healer" and the "Black Christ." Note that while "Portuguese" refers to nationality, "black" refers to a racial category— thus emphasizing the inability of many Americans to talk in a coherent way about categories of race, nationality, and ethnicity. This struggle to claim a racial or national identity of his own choosing—in other words the maintenance of his ethnic identity—went on throughout Grace's life. In 1952 *Ebony Magazine* hailed Grace as "America's Richest Negro Minister" even as Grace proclaimed from the text of the article that he was "not a Negro." However, being the head of a major religious organization—and achieving a certain amount of fame— certainly made Grace's claims easier and more effective. By founding a new religious organization, Grace granted himself a unique status. He had discovered a realm in which his followers, and to a certain extent, the American public, tolerated and even celebrated his difference.

While his race continued to confound, he emphasized his noticeably foreign origins. As newspapers and government officials had difficulty in labeling Grace racially, they also struggled—outside of New Bedford—to identify his national origins. Part of their difficulty stemmed from comments Grace had made himself. In 1923, Grace had taken a trip to the Holy Land. The trip proved to be significant throughout his life and he often related stories of his travels abroad. Upon his return, Grace had been held at Ellis Island for violating restrictions on resident alien travel. The *New York Times* explained that Grace, a "Portuguese" and clergyman, had been out of the country for more than eight months. Grace was ultimately freed and he returned first to New Bedford to share his stories. He brought back a number of artifacts that he would use throughout his life. A recording of his sermons from 1926 labeled him "Bishop Grace from the Holy Land." His affinity with the Holy Land was so close that it became unclear to many observers whether he had visited the Holy Land or if, indeed, it was the land of his birth. Thus Grace strove to "maintain" his identity as an immigrant. His ambivalence about his ethnicity and nationality stemmed in part from his country of origin and ongoing battles within the Cape Verdean community about identity.

As Grace's ministry grew throughout the southeast, he built his headquarters in Washington, D.C. Nevertheless, New Bedford did remain an important place for Grace and the House of Prayer as the site of his initial successes. Grace also retained his ties to the Cape Verdean population through his family members—many of whom remained in New Bedford—and through charitable acts benefiting the islands. Grace and his followers donated clothing to send along with other remittances back to the islands. These events, however, were rarely covered outside of regional newspapers.

Grace used his abilities and unique appearance to set himself apart from other popular religious leaders of the first half of the twentieth century. The rise of celebrity culture and an emphasis on personality combined with the increasingly diverse religious climate of the 1920s and 1930s to create celebrity religious leaders.[10] Evangelists like Aimee Semple McPherson and Father Divine set themselves apart from others by emphasizing their unique attributes. McPherson—an attractive divorcée—created pageants and plays to attract followers to her missions. Father Divine offered his followers massive banquets and a doctrine of positive thinking and racelessness. Each of these major players on the American religious scene offered something unique—not only in terms of religious worship and practice but in their own personalities and appearances.

Grace learned from these other evangelists and their successes. He had emphasized his originality from the beginning—his mission did not begin in a barroom or a church, but could be traced back to a foreign land. He presided over mass baptisms, first in natural bodies of water and swimming pools, and later, as he moved into more urban environments, with fire hoses. In doing so, he became a favorite of newsreel cameras and still photographers. Nevertheless, throughout his ministry, it was his appearance and the public's inability to definitively classify him—racially or ethnically—that attracted the most consistent attention.

His appearance was a constant source of comment from the press. Grace had always presented himself immaculately groomed, but as his ministry grew, he created his own unique style that further set him apart. He had long, flowing hair and grew out his fingernails on his left hand. He wore colorful cutaways. His own congregation commented on his appearance, one member memorialized "this peculiar looking man" (*Grace Magazine* 1960) after his death, and another explained that, "any man, regardless of how he looks to others, can wear what he pleases" (Long). Grace set himself apart, through his appearance, through the rituals and practices of the House of Prayer, and in doing so, also set an example to his followers of the value of originality.

Grace's speech and language also demonstrated to his parishioners and the American public that he was unique and had come from another land. He spoke with a thick accent and did so throughout his life. Dr. Robert Washington, who grew up in the House of Prayer, explained, "You know he was not one of those roaring preacher-types. We thought more of him as teaching than preaching. . . . he spoke deliberately. He had an accent so obviously he had to protect himself against his accent" (Washington 1999). As evidenced by recordings of Grace from different periods of his life, Grace had a very deliberate manner of speaking. He often sounded more as if he were delivering a lecture than a sermon. Nevertheless, he rolled his r's theatrically and played up the unique qualities of his speech.

In addition to his accent, Grace "would tantalize the church sometimes by speaking foreign languages. If, for example, he saw a Spanish person in the audience then he would speak Spanish to that person and of course the congregation thought that he was pretty hot stuff" (Washington 1999). Grace's ability to speak many languages besides English, a skill groomed during his formative years on Cape Verde, was yet another tool that he used to impress his congregations and visitors. His linguistic abilities were probably particularly impressive to rural southern audiences who may have had less familiarity with foreign languages than audiences living in urban centers.

In spite of his many gifts as a minister, Grace's presentation was undeniably different from most Holiness/Pentecostal/apostolic ministers of the era. He did not speak with the same type of rising and falling cadences—and though his delivery was impassioned, it was not necessarily as compelling for his congregation. To fill any potential void, Grace's services and celebrations relied heavily on music. His unique style of preaching, based in his Cape Verdean heritage, actually appears to have given birth to a new form of religious music— the trombone shout band. The bands, which evolved over the course of Grace's ministry, centered on the instrument said to be most able to mimic the human voice. The comparison was so apt that James Weldon Johnson labeled his ode to ministers, *God's Trombones*.[11] The music of the trombone shout bands was (and is) truly unique—it mimics the rising and falling emotion of a sermon and is described as "spirit-filled." It stirred up congregations and encouraged them to "catch the spirit." Thus, Grace's difference not only attracted followers, but also resulted in a new, significant religious musical form.

Grace found tremendous success as a religious leader. He founded a new denomination that outlasted his death—a significant achievement for a religious organization based so heavily on charismatic authority. He was the subject of countless newsreels and magazine stories as well as the object of scrutiny at the hands of the FBI and the IRS. When Grace died on January 12, 1960, in one of his homes in Los Angeles, he continued to confound authorities as they attempted to assign him a particular racial category on his death certificate.

Under the guidance of Grace's successor, Bishop McCullough, members of the House of Prayer erected a monument to Grace in New Bedford's Pine Grove cemetery in his family's plot. Of the information that they decided to include on the tomb was Grace's place of this birth, listed as "Cape Verde Islands/Portugal." His foreign origins thus retained their significance even after his death. They also retained their complexity as both Cape Verde and Portugal comprised the description of his birthplace.

Grace's death marked the passing of a man who seems to fulfill the requirements of the immigrant rags-to-riches story. However, Grace excluded himself from that narrative. He focused on his status as an original, a man with spiritual gifts that he brought to this country for the benefit of its citizens. His authority and his value to his congregation rested in this fact. Thus, Grace created a ministry primarily outside his own immigrant community where his difference and immigrant past set him apart. Grace, with the support and authority of his religious position, challenged conventional American labels of race and ethnicity. Throughout his life he consistently rejected the label "Negro" and explained instead, as did countless other Cape Verdeans of his era, that he was a white man from Portugal. Grace, however, had the power to make such assertions and the power to make people at least consider them. Grace the immigrant found success by moving out beyond his community into the broader American society, but he succeeded in that society by retaining and even championing his immigrant identity.

Notes

1. See, for example, the collections of essays in *Religion and the New Immigrants*, edited by Helen Rose Ebaugh and Janet Saltzman Chafetz (New York: AltaMira Press, 2000).

2. This chapter is based on research I conducted for my dissertation, "Sweet Daddy Grace: The Life and Times of a Modern Day Prophet" (University of Texas, May 2002). Grace did not leave behind a significant collection of papers, nor is there an extensive amount of scholarly work about Grace. My work has relied on a variety of government documents, published reports, publications, and memories from the House of Prayer and its members.

3. In contrast to religious leaders who adopt new "spiritual" names in conjunction with their ministries, Grace had anglicized his name as early as 1910—at least nine years before beginning his ministry.

4. See Marilyn Halter's work *Between Race and Ethnicity* (Urbana: University of Illinois Press, 1993) for the most in-depth treatment of Cape Verdean immigration in the United States.

5. Also referred to as Joao J. Dias in other Nazarene and non-Nazarene sources.

6. "A Weird Babel of Tongues," *Los Angeles Daily Times,* 18 April 1906, 1.

7. For that matter, Cape Verdeans struggled for years to create their own Catholic parish in New Bedford.

8. It is important to note, however, that Grace himself did not view the House of Prayer as a "black church" or himself as a black man. For more on this discussion, see "Beyond the Binary" in *Race, Nation, and Religion in the Americas*, Elizabeth McAlister and Henry Goldschmidt, eds. (New York: Oxford University Press, 2004).

9. For more on this, see Milton Sernett, *Bound for the Promised Land* (Durham: Duke University Press, 1997).

10. See Warren Susman's work for more on the rise of celebrity culture (Susman 1984).

11. See Nick Spitzer's discussion of the shout bands in liner notes, Saint's Paradise, Smithsonian Folkways Recordings, SFW CD 40177, 1999.

References

"America's Richest Negro Minister." 1952. *Ebony* (January): 8-19.

Brune, Danielle. 2002. "Sweet Daddy Grace: The Life and Times of a Modern Day Prophet." Ph.D. diss., University of Texas, Austin.

"Daddy Grace, A Peculiar Looking Man." 1960. *Grace Magazine* (September): 4.

Dorsett, Lyle W. 1991. *Billy Sunday and the Redemption of Urban America*. Grand Rapids, MI: Wm B. Eerdmans Publishing, Co.

Ebaugh, Helen Rose, and Janet Saltzman Chafetz. 2000. *Religion and the New Immigrants*. New York: AltaMira Press.

Ellis, William T. 1914. *"Billy" Sunday, The Man and His Message*. N.p.: L. T. Myers.

Fauset, Arthur Huff. 1970. *Black Gods of the Metropolis*. Reprint. New York: Octagon Books.

Gaw, Cooper. 1905. "Cape Verde and the Cape Verdean Immigration." *New Bedford Evening Standard* (July 29):10,12.

Goldschmidt, Henry, and Elizabeth McAlister, eds. 2004. *Race, Nation, and Religion in the Americas*. New York: Oxford University Press.

Gonsalves, Theophilo. 1908. "The Gospel in Cape Verde Islands." *Beulah Christian* (July 4):2.

Grace, Charles Manuel. "Bishop Grace From the Holy Land." In *Preachers and Congregations*, Volume 4: 1924-1931. Document Records. DOCD-5548.

———. *Saint's Paradise*. Smithsonian Folkways Recordings. SFW CD 40177, 1999.

Halter, Marilyn. 1993. *Between Race and Ethnicity*. Urbana: University of Illinois Press.

Long, Elder James. Unpublished draft. Private Collection.

Noble, Rev. George. 1909. "History of the Work Among the Portuguese in New Bedford, Mass. and Providence, R.I.." *Beulah Christian* (May 1):7-8.

Oberdorfer, Dan. n.d. "Evangelist's multi-million dollar Kingdom on Earth." *Afro-American*.

Poinsett, Alex. 1960. "Farewell to Daddy Grace." *Ebony* (April):25-28, 30, 32, 34.

Sernett, Milton. 1997. *Bound for the Promised Land*. Durham: Duke University Press.

Susman, Warren. 1984. *Culture as History*. New York: Pantheon Books.

Washington, Dr. Robert. 1999. Interview by the author. New Orleans, LA.

Weber, Max. 1968. *Max Weber on Charisma and Institution Building*. Edited by S. N. Eisenstadt. Chicago: University of Chicago Press.

5

Ritual Transformations in Okinawan Immigrant Communities

Ronald Nakasone and Susan Sered

Introduction

In the United States, "religion" generally refers to the theistic faith traditions of Judaism and Christianity, their attendant rituals that stem from notions of a transcendental divinity, and doctrines that are "believed in" or "adhered to." In the normative American view, while religion is a highly personal experience, it is often identified with a congregation, a "faith based organization" that people "join" or "belong to" (see Wuthnow 1994; Ellwood 1973; Porterfield 2001).

This model is assumed to be universally applicable. Yet our research on Okinawan (*Uchinanchu*)[1] Americans in Hawai'i, California, Washington, D.C., New York, and Boston makes it clear that what Americans commonly understand to be "religion" is quite foreign to Okinawan Americans and their ancestral spiritual tradition, as it is to other newly American populations. The Okinawan immigrants and their children, grandchildren, and great grandchildren whom we interviewed speak English and are familiar with the normative American understandings of "religion," yet few embraced "religion" as a useful category when speaking about their spiritual[2] beliefs, experiences, and practices, which cannot be meaningfully separated from other aspects of Okinawan life and culture.

The following discussion explores several important questions regarding the spiritual lives of Okinawan Americans: In what terms do *issei* (first generation), *nisei* (second generation), *sansei* (third generation), and *yonsei* (fourth generation) men and women describe their current identities, world-views, moral choices, and spiritual paths? To what extent, and in what ways, have traditional ritual practices been preserved, transformed, or reduced? To what extent, and in what ways, have traditional cosmological and moral notions and emphases been preserved, transformed, or reduced? To what extent have traditional Okinawan values, such as *yuimaaruu* (communal or mutual assistance), been chipped away at by American valuation of individual entrepreneurship or Western notions of individual religious "belief"? What do *issei, nisei, sansei,* and *yonsei* men and women mean when they speak about the "Okinawan spirit"? What role do the *kenjinkai* (prefectual association) and cultural clubs and classes play in the spiritual life of Okinawans?

We will begin with a brief history of Okinawa, its modern immigration, and its spiritual culture, with special attention to the experiences of Okinawan Americans. The second half of the chapter highlights the voices of Okinawan Americans on their perceptions of "religion." We conclude with some reflections on the poor fit between normative American understandings of "religion" and the spiritual culture of Okinawans, and their implications for research and for public policy.

Methodological Reflections

The two authors of this essay come to this project from very different backgrounds, both personal and scholarly. Nakasone is a *sansei* Okinawan American, born and raised in Hawai'i. A Buddhist scholar and cleric, whose maternal grandmother was a *yuta* (shaman), he is interested in Okinawan spirituality and culture.[3] Sered is an anthropologist of religion specializing in the study of gender and religion. From 1994 to 1995 she lived in the Okinawan village of Henza, conducting fieldwork among the *kaminchu* (priestesses), *yuta,* and other spiritual practitioners. During 2000 and 2001 Sered traveled around the U.S., meeting with Okinawan individuals and communities in Hawai'i, California, and New York. She interviewed several dozen men and women, and participated in a variety of rituals, cultural activities, and social gatherings of Okinawan *kenjinkais.*[4] We also draw on newsletters (past and present) of various *kenjinkai,* books, poems, articles, and essays written by Okinawan Americans, and several works of fiction by an Okinawan American author.

Background

Okinawa[5] has shared a common political identity with Japan only since 1879, when the independent Ryūkyū Kingdom was forcibly annexed by the emerging Japanese empire. The largest of 160 islands of the Ryūkyū Archipelago, which stretches from the southern Japanese island of Kyushu to the island of Taiwan, Okinawa Island was a major commercial center that linked East, North, and Southeast Asia. As a result of these extended contacts, Okinawa is not, as it has often been suggested, a provincial Japanese outpost, but possesses a distinct culture that reveals varying degrees of affiliation with China, Japan, Korea, Indonesia, and Thailand. Okinawans speak a language quite different, though related to, Japanese.

The current imagining of an Okinawan identity is still colored by the efforts of the early Meiji Period (1968-1912) government to solidify Japanese authority over nearby island territories and to create a modern nation-state to counter Western imperial designs (Peattie 1988:2). The incorporation of these territories confronted the Japanese with two intertwined issues: how to integrate the indigenous inhabitants and how to clarify what it meant to be Japanese. The process of crystallizing the modern "Japanese self" required the creation of an "other self" that would clearly underscore the uniqueness of the Japanese people. *Seiban* or "aborigine" referred to the growing empire's newly subjugated people who were at the margins of Japanese identity (Nakasone 2002:18). For the Okinawans the label, *seiban* was not simply epistemological. As "aborigines" the Okinawans were to be civilized, and civilization meant becoming "Japanese" (Tomiyama 1990:1-19). Consequently, the Meiji government initiated a series of measures intended to extinguish "uncivilized" Okinawan customs, including the language and "irrational" shamanic practices, and to modernize the newly acquired territory. Okinawans, on the margins of Japanese identity and culture, were subject to intense discrimination.[6] The Okinawan subjects' position vacillated between being "Okinawan" and being "Japanese."

The first-large scale exodus from Okinawa occurred during the first forty years of the twentieth century. Prefectural archives show that between 1899 and 1911, 13,335 Okinawans left their homeland. Of this number 10,250 settled in Hawai'i and only 863 migrated directly to the continental U.S. Between 1927 and 1940 larger numbers of Okinawans migrated to South and East Asia (21,047) and to South America (31,243). By 1940, 75,318 persons, approximately 15 percent of the population, had migrated overseas (cited in Tamamori and James 2000:75).

The modern history of Okinawan migration was shaped by the demand for cheap labor after the demise of the African slave diaspora (R. Arakaki 2002:30) and Japanese imperial expansion after World War I (Tomiyama 2002:57-61). Japanese entrepreneurs enlisted Okinawan labor to populate and work in the newly acquired League of Nations mandate territories in the southeast and northeast Pacific once held by the Germans. Migration was also the result of the disastrous colonial policies of the Japanese government that forced the Okinawans to plant vast fields of sugar cane. The great dependence on sugar as the primary cash crop exposed the Okinawa economy to worldwide economic fluctuations. When sugar prices fell in 1920, many Okinawans lost their livelihood and were forced to consume *sotetsu* (poisonous sago palm). Cycles of economic depression, population pressures, and lack of farmland forced many to migrate.

World War II decimated the Okinawan population and devastated Okinawan farmlands. Approximately one quarter of the island's population was killed. Prime farmland was forcefully requisitioned by the U.S. military. In addition, after 1946 more than 180,000 out of an estimated 332,000 Okinawans and their descendants living abroad were repatriated back to war-shattered Okinawa (Nakasone 2002:17). This large influx of people resulted in a lack of employment opportunities and forced a second wave of migration, not unlike the earlier exodus. Between 1948 and 1993 most of the 17,714 Okinawans who left ventured to South America (Tamamori and James 2000:75). Many Okinawan women also left as brides of servicemen, who were stationed on Okinawa; their numbers are not recorded in the prefectural census. Interest in emigration waned after the late 1960s with the growing prosperity of Japan and as overseas immigrants began returning to Japan and Okinawa. Of the estimated 200,000 foreigners of Japanese descent living in Japan, approximately 60,000 are Okinawans (Tamamori and James 2000:74).

At the present, the two largest concentrations of Okinawans in the U.S. reside in Hawai'i and Los Angeles, where approximately 55,000[7] and 15,000 people, respectively, claim to be Okinawan. These communities include first, second, third, fourth, and even fifth generation of Okinawan descent, each with varying degrees of affiliation with their ancestral homeland. These communities were established during the pre-World War II migration wave.

Okinawans in Hawai'i have in many ways re-created the traditional social and cultural life of their ancestral homeland. The United Okinawan Association, the umbrella organization, consists of a number of *sonjinkai* (village associations). Brought together by shared memories and a common place, these "locality" clubs were a source of fellowship and support, and served as an extended family for the early immigrants. The sentiment of *yuimaaruu* (mutual assistance), nurtured in the ancestral villages and brought to Hawai'i, subsequently evolved into a pan-Okinawan identity when the "locality" clubs banded together to coordinate relief efforts for their war-devastated homeland (M. Arakaki 2002:133-134). The *yuimaaruu,* compromise, and deference to community that motivated early and post-war assistance efforts remain principal features of the Okinawan American ethos.

Nostalgia and pride in their cultural heritage have also spawned a fair number of music and dance studios, and in fact it is common to hear Okinawans in Hawai'i explain that Okinawan culture has been preserved better in Hawai'i than in Okinawa, where Japanese policy and cultural dominance have (sometimes forcibly) eliminated parts of the traditional Okinawan cultural repertoire.[8] In an effort to assert their identity, comparisons are made between Okinawan and Japanese culture: "Art, music, and dance that is Okinawan identity. Japanese identity—weapons." This informant associates the Japanese with the martial spirit of the samurai warrior in contrast with the former Ryūkyū Kingdom, which as a matter of national policy did not have a standing army (Kerr 1958:258-259).

Like the Okinawan community of Hawai'i, the numerically fewer and geographically scattered Okinawans in the greater Los Angeles area continue to struggle with defining themselves against the Japanese. However, unlike the Hawai'ian Okinawans, they did not establish "locality clubs," but rather formed a more comprehensive *kenjinkai* (prefectural association). Approximately 2,000[9] of the estimated 15,000 Okinawans in the area belong to the Okinawan Prefectural Association,[10] which sponsors annual events and gatherings. There are also a number of Okinawan music, dance, and karate studios. Okinawans in California share with their Japanese neighbors memories of internment camps during World War II. And, having forcibly been scattered during that time, the Okinawan community has not returned to its pre-war level of internal social integration. However, as for their Hawai'ian co-ethnics, *yuimaaruu* continues to be a respected and central moral and cultural value among Uchinanchu in California.

Okinawans in other parts of the United States comprise small communities, often energized by the ongoing arrival of Okinawan women who come as wives of American servicemen. In some instances the small numbers have precluded any sort of organized Okinawan cultural life, and Okinawan identity has little group salience. In other instances, small communities have enlarged their numbers by welcoming non-Okinawans who love Okinawan culture.

As part of the Japanese immigrant community, Okinawans are double minorities (Kobashigawa 1996:29-44) in the United States. As such, they have been the target of "double discrimination"—racism and suspicion from European Americans and prejudice and scorn from Japanese who saw Okinawans as *seiban,* "primitive" and "backward." This double discrimination is a mirror image of the present double occupation of Okinawa by Japan and by the American military. While many Okinawan Americans speak about experiences of discrimination with sadness, for the most part people say that it has made them "stronger" or "more flexible" rather than bitter or angry. Okinawan Americans diverge widely in their opinions regarding the Japanese and American (or the Japanese versus American) presence in Okinawa,[11] yet there is great consensus regarding the uniqueness of Okinawan culture, identity, and history. Neither annexation of Ryūkyū by Japan nor the subsuming of Okinawan Americans into the category of Japanese Americans has eliminated a clear sense of Okinawan cultural identity and a unique Okinawan spirit.[12]

Traditional Spiritual Culture

The present Okinawan American spiritual experience is rooted in *utaki* spirituality. *Utaki,* or "sacred grove," is the focal point of the indigenous spiritual culture of Okinawa. While it has been transformed by Buddhism, Shintoism, Taoism, and Confucianism, *utaki* spirituality exhibits elements—orality, place, and ancestral veneration—that are associated with primal faith traditions. Though *utaki* spirituality lacks written documents, its metaphysical support can be vaguely extrapolated from the *Omoro sōshi*, an anthology of 1553 ancient songs and poems that were sung by shamans and villagers.[13] These songs and poems reflect the deep feelings the ancient Okinawans have toward their island home, toward their ancestral *kami* (deities), and for *niraee kanaee*, a place of abundance and the home of the *kami* who bring happiness and treasures when they visit this world.

Like primal traditions, *utaki* spirituality is embedded in a place. Located in the hills or forest, the focal point of an *utaki* is a grassy clearing where the village priestess(es) performs rites of thanksgiving and asks for a bountiful harvest and health in front of an *ibi*, a stone representing the *kami*, ancestral spirits, and a censer.[14] On appointed days of the year, the *kami* journeys from *niraee kanaee* to the *utaki*. The village *utaki* is associated with the burial site of the founding family-*niiya* or root house of the village. The veneration of the earliest ancestors is a prominent feature of *utaki* spirituality. Human ancestors are thought to be prolongations of the village's and a family's earliest progenitors, who are believed to be divine. Ancestors are thus a bridge between the current generation and their first ancestor, and pioneers are revered over their descendents—a sentiment that is evident in the memorial observances sponsored by the *kenjinkai* to honor the earliest immigrants.

The founding family assumed the highest secular and spiritual authority in the village. The root-house provided political and administrative leadership through the root man, *nichu,* and the spiritual authority through the root deity, *nigan.* A female member of the house, usually the sister, took charge of the ritual observances. Male and female shared equal prestige and authority. The reference to brother and sister sovereignty is found in the *Omoro sōshi* and served as the model for administering the Ry\ky\an Kingdom. The position of the national priestess, *chifijin*, eroded with the growing influence of patriarchal Confucianism, and her authority was systematically eradicated after the Japanese formally annexed the kingdom. The last chief priestess died in 1944 (Lebra 1966:121).

Reverence to the ancestral spirits is also found in a traditional Okinawan home. The *fii nu kang,* the hearth or fire *kami*, represents the most distant ancestor; it symbolizes the continuity of the household and its relationship to higher *kami* (Lebra 1966:184). In the past the hearth, constructed by three stones, was focus of worship; more recently three small stones are placed in a box of ashes close by the stove, a practice that has largely disappeared in the U.S. The other ubiquitous *kamis* are the *futuki,*[15] or deceased spirits of parent, grandparent, or sibling who reside in their respective *ifee* or memorial tablets that are placed in the *ubutidan* or *sochyan udan* (ancestral shrine) located in the main room of the house. From this most advantageous location, the deceased ancestors observe the daily activities of their descendents. They are informed of the family weddings, deaths, visitors, births, promotions, and other minor and major family happenings. The ancestral shrine serves as a daily reminder of their ancestral presence.

The Okinawans believe that with the end of corporeal life a person commences a spiritual life that matures into ancestorhood. This process is aided by a cycle of memorial observances sponsored by the living descendents and grounded in gratitude and inclusion in their daily lives. Traditionally, the oldest female officiates at family observances. The thirty-third year memorial service is the last service dedicated specifically to the memory of an individual, unless the person is especially noted, and marks the person's complete transition to an ancestral spirit. After the completion of the service, the individual's memorial tablet is ritually burned and the deceased's name is placed in the ancestral shrine and is honored with all other ancestors. The Okinawans believe that misfortune may visit the family if the ancestral shrine and/or tomb are neglected or if memorials and other rituals are not observed. Rituals are therefore performed partly to placate and appease the ancestral spirits.

Equally important is the family crypt, where the living can commune with the deceased. However, since family tombs are usually located in out-of-the way places on mountain sides, they are visited on special occasions such as New Year's and *shiimee*, the spring equinox. The memorial tablet, memorial observances, and gravesite visits are important parts of the Okinawan American experience.

The *kaminchu*[16] and *yuta* are the two principal ritual functionaries. Both roles are usually assumed by women since the Okinawans believe that women possess spiritual powers superior to those of men. The *kaminchu* is a hereditary position and refers to the priestess in charge of mortuary, memorial, and celebratory rites. Once organized nationally, the chief priestess of each village would travel to Seefa Utaki, the national shrine, and together with the national priestess offer prayers on behalf of the nation. The *yuta*, in contrast, functions as a medium through whom the human and spirit worlds can communicate. Possessing paranormal powers of clairvoyance and prognostication, *yuta* are consulted when misfortunes occur, to interpret dreams, and about matters related to the ancestral spirits and proper rituals. Outside the formal ritual structure, *yutas* are persons who possess shamanic powers.

Immigrant Spiritual Culture

While many key elements of the traditional Okinawan culture and moral ethos have been preserved in the United States, most of the formal rituals and ritual leaders have not made the trip across the ocean. Why some ritual practices and beliefs are retained while others are transformed or abandoned is a complex question. To be sure, the emigrants tended to be young people who were not expected to be actively involved in or particularly knowledgeable about spiritual beliefs or ritual practices. But more fundamentally, we surmise that many of the rituals are unknown to most Okinawan Americans[17] because the *kaminchu* and *yuta* who performed them did not migrate.[18] Further, as noted above, many of the rituals are embedded in specific sites in Okinawa. Interestingly, the names of roles such as *kaminchu* and *yuta* are familiar to first- and second-generation Okinawan Americans, although there often is some confusion regarding the difference between them and some tendency to translate both as "fortunetellers"—a disparaging description probably picked up from Christian missionaries.

The *kaminchu*, the most respected ritual experts, are associated with particular geographic locations. Stories circulate of priestesses who "tried" to leave their villages and go to mainland Japan or to the United States, but found themselves plagued by illnesses, misfortunes, or uneasiness that reminded them that they need to stay physically close to the ocean, mountains, clans, villages, and sacred groves with which they are identified. Thus the dearth of *kaminchu* has meant the demise of women's religious leadership. Interestingly, among the small number of Okinawan American Christian pastors there are at least several women, a fact that perhaps does continue to reflect traditional egalitarian and gynocentric patterns.

While the traditional female spiritual leadership may have significantly eroded,[19] men's secular leadership, reinforced by both Japanese and American norms, has carried over from Okinawa. Men are almost always the heads of the *kenjinkai*, an arrangement that fits traditional Okinawan patterns of male secular leadership. However, women are credited with preserving Okinawan domestic culture (especially food), and it is common to hear that Okinawan women are especially "strong." Typically, this means they worked hard both outside and inside the home and that they are resilient under pressure. Indeed, when Sered asked a group of women participating in an Okinawan dance class in Hawai'i why so few men were involved, the answer was identical to those she received when she asked similar questions in Okinawa: men go away and women stay put.

Continuing the tradition of openness and eclecticism,[20] Okinawan Americans engage "religion" in diverse ways by participating in a variety of Christian, Buddhist, and ancestral rituals. Okinawan American families often include members of both Buddhist temples and Christian churches; Christian or Buddhist identity generally does not preclude devotion to the ancestors; and individuals typically say that "all religions are good" rather than claim that only one religion is right or true. Thus Okinawan Americans often turn to Buddhist temples for mortuary and memorial services. In Hawai'i, a significant number of Okinawans are part of a Jikoen, which is affiliated with the Jōdō Shinshū Honganjiha lineage established by the Japanese Buddhist cleric Shinran (1173-1262). The Jikoen temple is identified as an Okinawan temple. Others are members of Christian denominations. A small number are members of a new faith called Ijun.[21]

As the victims of double discrimination and the target of missionaries, Okinawans in the U.S. quickly learned that others (Japanese and Euro-Americans) viewed their *yuta* and *kaminchu* as "superstition." In order to erase this stigma, some Okinawan families made (and make) pragmatic decisions to send their children to Christian schools. Other Okinawans became Christian because of perceived opportunities for social mobility. Nakasone remembers that there was a great deal of coercion to be Christian. "My father told me that there was pressure to be Christian if you wanted to be on the managerial staff of the plantations [in Hawai'i]." Still others associated with the Buddhist temple that represented what they believed to be part of their past and as a refuge from racism. However, those who steered clear of both Christian churches and Buddhist temples did not seem more likely than other families to know or practice much of the traditional Okinawan ritual repertoire.

Demands that everyone profess the same beliefs or engage in identical ritual practices are not part of Okinawan spiritual culture. When asked about "religion" in a general way (for example, "In your village/community, what do people believe about this?"), typical responses began: "Speaking for myself," or "In my case." There is no one formal "Okinawan belief system," nor is there any one person (or category of people)—in Okinawan villages or in U.S. *Uchinanchu* communities—who speaks for or represents the whole community in terms of belief. Individuals' comments quoted in this paper may echo thoughts expressed by others as well, but should not be seen as expressing universally agreed upon religious opinions, choices, practices, or perspectives.

The Okinawan Spirit

Like American Jews, Okinawan Americans, for the most part, have not remapped sacred space (such as the *utaki*) in the U.S.[22] In a gradual way, as *issei* and *nisei* die, local cemeteries are becoming more important, yet the deep spiritual ties between people and place have not been recreated here. On the other hand, for many Okinawan Americans *all* of Okinawa has been transformed into a sacred place. When second-, third-, and fourth-generation Okinawan Americans make a trip to Okinawa (often in the context of an organized group or event), the preeminent feeling seems to be of spiritual homecoming, of "somehow" being able to communicate with people despite not speaking fluent Japanese, and of "somehow" easily finding their way around despite little previous knowledge of Okinawan geography.

Okinawan communities in the U.S. arrange events that celebrate their heritage. A member of the California community told us that he is, "Proud of Okinawa and its culture! We are active in keeping the culture alive." He reminisces, "We had picnics every summer and women made lots of food. Maybe the picnics were in place of *Obon*.[23] The program had Okinawan dances. Other people would come too. Okinawans would make plates of food and give it to spectators." In addition to events connected to traditional festivals (like New Year's), the California community holds a golf tournament, an annual bazaar, and other "fun, cultural events."

These organized activities of Okinawan communities in the U.S. highlight the limitations of a term like "religion" that grew out of a particular sort of Euro-Christian historical experience and belief system. Okinawan Americans who clearly state that they have no "religion," often actively participate in events that might be construed to be "religious." Two comments are in order here. First, the Okinawan language has no word that translates as "religion." The Japanese expression, *shukyō*, created in the late nineteenth century and commonly referring to Buddhism or Christianity, denotes a formal institutional structure and codified beliefs. In contrast, Okinawan beliefs and rituals are simply "what we do" or the "Okinawan way." Second, it is sometimes the case that explicitly spiritual (*kamisama* or deity-related)[24] content from traditional Okinawa events is abandoned in the U.S. because it is felt to be "superstitious," and because (for the most part) the appropriate community-wide ritual experts (priestesses and shamans) are not here to lead the events, or because members of the communities have seen that in the U.S. "religion" tends to be a contentious issue. Mrs. Shizuko Akamine, a former president of the Hui Okinawa organization who was appointed goodwill ambassador from Hawai'i to Okinawa by the former Governor Masahide Ōta, explains that as a community they do "culture *only* " because each person has his or her own religion. "So this way there are no fights."

Rather than speaking about "religion," many Okinawan Americans prefer to identify an "Okinawan spirit" that characterizes their personalities and communities. This "spirit" is *yuimaaruu*. "Ninety-eight percent of the time I can recognize Okinawan people by the spirit." Another informant remarked, "Okinawans are more open, warm, tell jokes tell more jokes than Japanese. I don't think that Japanese tell jokes!" As several women in Hawai'i explained the Okinawan spirit: "That there is one big *ohana* [clan (Hawai'ian expression)]— family. People take care of each other." "The family takes care of each other." "The same thinking as in Okinawa." "People share food with each other. We are always giving things."

One young man further explained, "Uchinanchu [Okinawan] spirit is generosity and connection. Okinawan identity. Emigrants send much money back to Okinawa." Some Okinawan Americans express pride that Okinawa has a stronger ongoing relationship with emigrant communities than do other Japanese prefectures with their emigrants. "Other Japanese immigrants feel abandoned [in the United States], not Okinawans."

While some stress generosity, sharing, an easy-going nature and warmth in interpersonal relationships as the essence of the "Okinawan spirit," others stress that the "Okinawan spirit" lies in concrete expressions of Okinawan aesthetic and material culture. Thus we were told:

> Okinawan spirit is preserved in the performing arts. Okinawans are very proud of it. Dancing, singing, drinking!

> The *issei* (first generation) in Hawai'i survived because of music, the *sanshin* (three-string plucked lute).

> You have to give Okinawan immigrants credit for being proud and upholding the truth of their culture and being so active even to the third and fourth generation.

If this essay were to truly reflect the priorities of the people with whom we spoke in the course of this research, it would include pages of descriptions of cultural events in various communities. At Okinawan community events around the United States, groups of children and adults perform traditional Okinawan *sanshin*, *kutu* (a thirteen-string lute), *teku* (drum), *uta* (song), *uduui* (dance), and *eisaa* (a type of folk dance). In Hawai'i and California there are numerous schools and studios of Okinawan music and dance. While most of the instructors live in the United States, the teaching of Okinawan arts is enriched by visits from Okinawan teachers and study trips to Okinawa.

One consultant explained,

> One way of keeping the community together is the annual Uchinanchu Mensore.[25] Many go to this convention of emigrants in Okinawa. So the Okinawan government seems to have a role in encouraging the preservation of Okinawan identity in the diaspora. People here are concerned with preserving Okinawan culture, but only dancing and singing have been inherited, not the language. We need a place to meet to preserve cultural heritage. This is something we learned from the Jews who have community centers everywhere.

That Okinawan communal identity tends to be defined in terms of "culture" rather than "religion" indicates the ability of aesthetic and material culture to keep the community strong and to preserve the Okinawan spirit. Yet, in light of the valorization of religion that characterizes American society in general, having "only" culture and not religion tends to demean the importance, significance, or sacrality of the acts or events that do not resemble mainstream Euro-Christian religion. Bifurcation into "culture" versus "religion," which reflects Western categories, is not authentically or traditionally Okinawan and does violence to the integrity of Okinawan ways and worldviews.

Ancestors

Veneration of the ancestors is the abiding feature of *utaki* spirituality that has been retained by the immigrant community. Many Okinawan Americans who define themselves as having "no religion" do in fact honor their ancestors and carry out ancestor rituals including visits to graves on New Year's, Memorial Day, the anniversary of the death, and other occasions that are important to the spiritual life in Okinawa. Many of these observances no longer follow the traditional Okinawan ritual cycle, but are now in tune with the U.S. calendar. Annual memorial services and regular visits to the places of burial of first-generation grandparents or parents are commonly observed in summer and coincide with the traditional Buddhist *Obon* observance. Families often will share a meal at the cemetery or at a nearby restaurant or park, a carryover of the traditional ritual of sharing a communal meal at the family grave site. Respect for and remembering one's ancestors are embedded in Okinawan American life, and comments like these are typical:

> There is no Okinawan church. We only honor the ancestors.

> We teach our children a sort of religion—our God is not Jesus, we are not Christian. Our god is ancestors—grandpa, grandma. They are our guardians. That is the best religion. We don't kill each other like Jews and Christians. Our ancestors protect us, a direct relationship, closer to our god. More relieve my pain and solve my problems; my father raised me, not Jesus. Ancestors helped me to grow up healthy, survive, become a man.

> When I would ask my parents about religion they would say what's important is what is in your heart. Be kind, respect people, respect your grandparents, respect us.

Some Okinawan Americans are attracted to Christian or Buddhist denominations that emphasize ancestors or ancestor veneration. For example, a number of Okinawan women in the New York area have joined the Shinnyo-En Buddhist sect because it is "similar to Okinawan religion, with attention to the ancestors." Reverend Shinsuke Uehara, the Okinawan pastor of the mostly Okinawan congregation of the Iesu no Mitama Kyokai (Spirit of Jesus Church) on the outskirts of Honolulu, preaches that full body immersion baptism on behalf of one's ancestors is the only way that the living can help their ancestors in return for the concern that the ancestors have for them. Reverend Uehara acknowledges that baptism for the dead is relatively unusual in Christian denominations, and that this is one of the reasons that the Iesu no Mitama Kyokai is popular among some Okinawans. He explains: "Many Okinawans come because they worry about ancestors, and we baptize for the dead. So they can relax here. . . . Some members used to have *fii nu kang*—hearth deity—shrine and *butsudan*,[26] and after they were baptized for their ancestors they felt secure without those things."

Even Okinawan Americans who identify strongly with mainstream Christian denominations continue to pray to the ancestors. As one man explained to me: "It is important for kids to go back to Okinawa to the grandparents' house to sit at the *butsudan* and grandma teaches them. We never tell them [our kids] that other religions are wrong." Within the larger Okinawan American communities, the first generation of immigrants has taken on some of the role and aura of ancestors. At a conference celebrating 100 years of Okinawan immigration to Hawai'i held in the summer of 2000, speakers reiterated that their speeches and the various festivities were "in honor of the *issei* generation who struggled so hard and whose legacy has made it possible for Okinawans in the United States today to thrive."

The Los Angeles Okinawan Kenjinkai held a memorial service in 1999 at Evergreen Cemetery where a prominent Okinawan is buried.[27] While there, many took the opportunity to visit the graves of relatives. Mr. Sadao Tome, chair of the Memorial Service at Evergreen Cemetery for the 1999 ninetieth anniversary celebration of the Okinawan community, explained that: "We honored *issei*—pioneers. We invited two churches—Christian and Buddhist—Japanese Buddhist. Because some people are Buddhist and some are Christian.[28] We want to be equal. Each led a service. The Lt. Governor from Okinawa came."

In communities with smaller or newer Okinawan populations, ancestor veneration in the form of visits to cemeteries is not yet possible. Still, people continue to honor elderly members of the community. At communal New Years parties around the country the elderly are invited up on stage where they receive tribute and applause. In some communities special festivities (*kajimaya*, a late life ritual celebrating 97 years of age) are held for people reaching certain landmark ages in their 80s and 90s.[29]

"All religions are good!"

Okinawan Americans generally express a great deal of flexibility regarding religion. As one woman explained,

> When my husband died they did a Christian service at 49 days and one year after the death. That is the Okinawan way, but the service was a Christian memorial service. [Combining Okinawan and American customs] is typical.[30] This is because of the history of being conquered by various people. Okinawans had to go with what prevailed at the time. Japan. China. Okinawans became very flexible people to survive. In Hawai'i there was prejudice and Okinawans had to merge their native culture with Hawai'i.

Another man had a similar experience:

> I am *chonan* [eldest son] and have a *butsudan*. For memorial events
> on the third, seventh year, and so on a priest comes over to pray with
> us. A Buddhist priest. The priests are very accommodating about do-
> ing this. In Okinawa a *yuta* would have done this, but here we don't
> have a choice, there is only Buddhism and so Buddhist priests are
> happy to come over for this.

While some Okinawan Americans assimilate Okinawan ways with
Christianity or Buddhism, other Okinawan Americans celebrate rituals of a variety of faith traditions. One man explained, "My wife is Jewish. We celebrate
Japanese holidays and Jewish holidays and Christian holidays." A number of
men and women told us that they have chosen to explore a variety of faith traditions. For example, "I always have been interested in religion. I was not blessed
with blind faith. I have to understand." One woman explained, "When I was a
girl it bothered me that my family had no religion. I would go to church, various
churches, with my friends. Still today I go to various churches and temples and
shul [*sic*. '*Shul*' is the Yiddish word for synagogue] and Buddhist temple for
New Year's."

Another theme expressed by many Okinawan Americans is the validity
or beauty of all faith traditions and the absence of any coercion to follow only
one tradition. One woman told me, "My husband is Italian. I was baptized at St.
Catherine's church so we could get married, but I believe in Catholicism. Actually, partly. Partly in all religions. All religions have good inspiration." Another
woman explained,

> My mother wanted us to have some religion, so we joined congrega-
> tions wherever we lived. First Christian, and then Buddhist. We were
> always a bit Buddhist with *butsudan* and *Obon*. Now I am [a member
> of] Ijun. Ijun leaves Sundays open for other churches, and Mr. Taka-
> yasu [Rokuro Takayasu, the founder of Ijun] encourages people to go
> to other churches.

Religious coercion is anathema to Okinawan Americans. "My parents let us
choose our religion. This is America and you should be American. We'd have
lots of discussions comparing different cultures. We did Christian and Buddhist
things. But now I am hungry for Asian culture."

Over the past decade or so there has been an awakening and strengthening of interest in Asian and Okinawan identity and culture among Okinawan
Americans for several reasons. A new affluence has allowed the leisure time and
resources to explore things Okinawan and to travel back and forth between the
U.S. and Okinawa. The first generation of immigrants has now also become
ancestors and the second generation is finding its way as elders. At the same

time, world and ethnic music and dance in general are increasingly popular throughout the U.S., while on a more controversial note, Okinawa has been in the news recently because of the presence of American military bases and violent crimes committed by American servicemen in Okinawa.

Conclusion

As of this writing, "religion" (as opposed to "Okinawan culture," "the ancestors," and "the Okinawan spirit") remains inappropriate to the endeavor of capturing Okinawan identity and heritage. Robert Ellwood, a noted observer of American religion, writes that "A *religion* means a group centrally concerned with the 'means of ultimate transformation,' which has simultaneous expression in three areas: *theoretical* or *verbal* (myth and doctrine); *practice* or *worship* (ritual, cultus, and other special behavior); and *sociological* (a structure of interpersonal action which enables a continuing group life)" (1973:4). Other scholars have drawn attention to some of the key features of American religion: concern with "spiritual formation" (that is, "deepening or maturing of an individual's faith" [Wuthnow 1994:6]); "pragmatism" (that is, the idea that religion should make one into a better person, help one cope with tragedy, and build character [Porterfield 2001:5]); "the priority of internal experience over external authority" (Porterfield 2001:19); and a "congregational model of religious organization" (that is, religion as "a voluntary gathered community") (Porterfield 2001:19).

The spiritual tradition of most Okinawan Americans clearly differs from the parameters set forth by Ellwood and other scholars, clergy, policy makers, and laity. Ellwood's notion of "ultimate transformation," for example, is something quite different from Okinawan spirituality, where an individual's "spiritual formation" is achieved gradually over thirty-three years of memorial observances and involves family effort.

These ancestral veneration rituals typically reflect the same attitude and behavior one extends to living elders and so are not easily detected. Highly pragmatic and relishing the here and now, doctrines are vague; myths tend to be fluid, variable from village to village, and not particularly widely known. Okinawan spiritual culture manifests itself in the community and family (both alive and deceased) far more than in a formal organized congregation or set of doctrines, but it helps one cope with tragedy and misfortune.

It is crucial to clarify that this analysis is not purely an intellectual exploration of competing epistemologies. Worldviews, and the practices associated with them, are valorized or demeaned, respected or disrespected, and rewarded or not rewarded according to their fit with normative values and political agendas and government policies and regulations. The poor fit between Okinawan experience and the highly ethnocentric Euro-Christian paradigm of "religion" has problematic implications: A number of people with whom we spoke in carrying out this project described feeling "inferior" or discriminated against because they grew up "without religion." Others reported joining Buddhist or Christian churches because they felt that they were expected to "belong" to some "religion," because they were targets of missionaries, or because they needed a religious affiliation in order to receive particular services such as funerals or weddings.

In the U.S. "religion" generally is seen as something good and positive, and religious individuals receive respect—a major form of social capital. As federal government agencies (including the Immigration and Naturalization Service) consider moving toward increasing funds for faith-based organizations and the services they provide, communities whose practices do not fit the Euro-Christian "religion" paradigm stand to lose out not only in terms of social recognition (as has been the case for Okinawan Americans), but also in terms of access to economic resources, while those who fit normative American congregational-institutional models stand to gain a great deal. This has important implications for all immigrant populations (and indeed for all Americans) who do not "affiliate with," "join," or "have membership in" a government-recognized religious institution. As this research demonstrates, both researchers and policy makers need to give greater attention and recognition to spiritual beliefs and practices that do not fit into these standard criteria, and expand their notions of faith traditions in order to support non-normative groups.

Notes

We are indebted to the many people who shared their thoughts and experiences with us in the course of the fieldwork on which this essay is based. We wish to particularly thank Professor Shingi Kuniyoshi and Jane Kuniyoshi for patiently reading and commenting on drafts of the essay. All errors are solely our own.

1. *Uchinanchu*, derived from *Uchina* (Okinawa), and *chu* (person) refers to persons born in Okinawa or of Okinawan ancestry. The expression, however, is often used in contrast to *Yamatonchu*, the people of Japan. *Yamato* refers to the ancient name of Japan, circa eighth century; *chu* refers to person. Used in this later sense, *Uchinanchu* has a political edge. Okinawans use the expression to assert their difference from the Japanese and to recall their former political and cultural independence. While an Okinawan is simultaneously an *Uchinanchu* and "Japanese," a Japanese person can never be an *Uchinanchu*.

2. "Spirituality" is preferable to "religion" when speaking of the Okinawan faith tradition. Derived from the Latin *religiō,* a bond between humanity and the gods, "religion" implies a belief in a transcendental being who created and guides the universe. Such a definition is not appropriate to non-theistic faith traditions such as Buddhism, Taoism, and Confucianism; nor to the faith tradition of the Okinawan people. The more universal expressions "spiritual" and "spirituality," which refer to the non-material inner core

where a person is open to the transcendental and touches ultimate reality, are more appropriate. Persons in more structured religious organizations can experience reality through their faith tradition; similarly, persons who belong to the more loosely structured elemental traditions of the Native Americans and Okinawans, or persons who commune with the beauty of nature, can also experience ultimate reality.

3. His most recent book, *Okinawan Diaspora*, is a collection of studies that examine how Okinawan identity was constructed in the various countries to which Okinawans migrated, and how these experiences were shaped by the Japanese nation-building project, globalization, and the large U.S. military presence on the island.

4. Most of the interviews were conducted in English, with a scattering of Okinawan and Japanese words and phrases. A few interviews were conducted in Japanese with the help of bilingual assistants. The methodological difficulties of conducting research in a geographically scattered community were somewhat offset by the ease of communication via telephone, email, and letters.

5. In this text, "Okinawa" refers to the entire Ryukyuan cultural sphere.

6. In an effort to assimilate Okinawa, the Japanese government worked to shift Uchinanchu loyalties from the Ryukyuan royal family and sentiment for their recent loss of independence to Emperor Meiji in Tokyo and to the Japanese nation. Early in 1880 the Japanese began the task by revamping the educational curriculum to suit Japan's needs and by opening new schools that offered instruction in Japanese. Ten years after the end of the kingdom, portraits of the Japanese emperor and empress were placed in every school in Okinawa. The Temporary Land Readjustment Bureau was created in 1898 to convert 76% of the total land area from communal holding to private ownership. This land reform effectively dismantled the powers of the state and community ritual functionaries who were supported by communal land grants. Japanese nationalists established the Shinto shrine of Nami-no-ue in 1924 and enshrined the four kings of Ryukyu to encourage Okinawans to think of their own royal house as a branch of the Japanese imperial line.

7. Estimate made by Dr. Albert Miyasato, President of the HUOA.

8. Probably the most egregious attempt by the Japanese was the prohibition of *uchinaguchi*, their mother tongue. To achieve absolute unity and full mobilization, Japanese officials intensified their efforts to encourage Okinawans to speak standardized Japanese. Okinawa could not be fully modernized, they argued, unless the Ryūkyūan dialect was completely eradicated. See David Coates, "Pure Land of Beauty," pp. 121-122.

9. This estimate was made by Ms. Yoko Maeda.

10. Unlike Hawai'i, the Okinawan community did not formerly organize around village associations (*sonjinkai*). Few in number and widely scattered they coalesced around the larger prefectual association (*kenjinkai*). This pattern is not novel: the Japanese community was organized around such prefectual associations as Hiroshima *kenjinkai*, Shiman *kenjinkai*, Kagoshima *kenjinkai*, Wakayama *kenjinkai*, and Fukushima *kenjinkai*.

11. During the past decade a growing number of younger Okinawan Americans has been organizing to protest the presence of American bases in Okinawa.

12. On the *Uchinanchu* spirit, see Arakaki Makoto's essay noted in the bibliography (2002).

13. The collection spans approximately six centuries—from the time Okinawa was an island of villages until the island kingdom was invaded by the Japanese in 1609. Scholars have suggested various meanings for "*omoro*": divine song; songs sung in the sacred woods; and to think, thoughts, or reflections.

14. An incense vessel.

15. *Futuki* is the Okinawan pronunciation of *hotoke*, which originally referred to Siddhartha Gautama, the historical Buddha. The popular understanding of *hotoke* has now also come to mean the deceased who are born in the Pure Land located somewhere beyond the western horizon.

16. This is a generic term that includes *nuru, negami*, and *watigami*.

17. On the work of *nuru, kaminchu*, and *yuta* in an Okinawan village see Sered's book *Women of the Sacred Groves* noted in the bibliography.

18. In the Hawai'ian community a small number of *yuta* do continue to function in a very quiet way.

19. To a lesser extent this is happening in some parts of Okinawa as well, as village and town dignitaries (usually men) take public roles in new rituals imported from Japan.

20. Nakasone notes that current Okinawan ritual is an eclectic blend of indigenous, Confucian, Daoist, and Japanese Buddhist traditions (Nakasone 2002:153-155).

21. Ijun was founded by Rokuro Takayasu. While similar to Japanese new religions in many ways, the core of Ijun is the revitalization of traditional Ry\ky\an (Okinawan) spirituality.

22. The exception is the Hawai'ian Ijun group for whom certain places in the volcano of the island of Hawai'i are understood to be *utuusi*, "go through places," in which prayers are transmitted to sacred sites in Okinawa.

23. *Obon*, a Buddhist service of gratitude for the deceased, is observed on the fifteenth day of the seventh month of the lunar calendar.

24. *Kami* means deity, *sama* is an honorific.

25. We believe this informant is referring to the Worldwide Uchinanchu Festival sponsored by the Okinawa Prefectural Government, held every five to six years.

26. *Butsudan* refers to Buddha altar. Okinawans generally do not enshrine images of the Buddha in these altars, but rather the *butsudan* functions as their household ancestor shrine. "*Butsudan*" is pronounced "*butidang*" in the Okinawan language.

27. This seems to be Mr. Nishime Tokuta, the first president of the Los Angeles-area Okinawan *kenjinkai*. Nakamura Gongoro, the first Okinawan to graduate from USC Law School, is another dignitary buried at the cemetery.

28. The Christian minister is Reverend Haruko Iwata. She is a pastor of the Foursquare Gospel Church.

29. A number of consultants told us that Okinawans in the United States are not as long lived as in Okinawa (Okinawa has the longest life expectancy of any contemporary society). The reasons offered for the traditional longevity include living closer to nature in Okinawa, eating natural and healthy food, and an atmosphere of mutual assistance in Okinawan villages.

30. The forty-ninth day and one year memorial services are part of the Buddhist memorial ritual cycle that many Japanese American Christian churches have had to adopt because of pressure from their members.

References

Arakaki Makoto. 2002. "Hawai'i *Uchinanchu* and Okinawa: *Uchinanchu* Spirit and Formation of a Transnational Identity." In *Okinawan Diaspora,* ed. Ronald Nakasone. Honolulu: University of Hawai'i Press.

Arakaki, Robert. 2002. "Theorizing on the Okinawa Diaspora." In *Okinawa Diaspora,* ed. Ronald Y. Nakasone. Honolulu: University of Hawai'i Press.

Coates, David A. 1996. "Yanagi Soetsu and the Pure Land of Beauty." In *The Okinawan Experience,* ed. Ronald Y. Nakasone. Fremont, CA.: Dharma Cloud Publishers.

Ellwood, Robert S. 1973. *Religious and Spiritual Groups in Modern America.* Englewood Cliffs, NJ: Prentice-Hall, Inc.

Higa, Kei, ed. 1983. *Okinawa daihyakka jiten* [Okinawa Encyclopedia]. 4 vols. Naha: Okinawa Times.

Hokama Shūzen, ed. 2000. *Omorosōshi.* 2 vols. Tokyo: Iwanami bunko.

Hokama Shūzen and Saigo Nobutsuna. 1978. *Omorosōshi.* Tokyo: Iwanami shoten.

Kerr, George H. 1958. *Okinawa, The History of an Island People.* Rutland, VT: Charles E. Tuttle.

Kobashigawa, Ben. 1996. "Okinawa Issei Identity: Pride and Shame." In *Reflections on the Okinawan Experience,* ed. Ronald Y. Nakasone. Fremont, CA: Dharma Cloud Publishers.

Kubo Noritaka. 1993. *Okinawa no minkanshinkō, chugoku bunka kara mita* [Okinawan folk religion, as seen from Chinese culture]. Hirugisha, Naha.

Lebra, William P. 1966. *Okinawan Religion: Belief, Ritual, and Social Structure.* Honolulu: University of Hawai'i Press.

Mauricio, Michael. n.d. "Thousand Mile Eyes." In *Waipahu: Its People and Heritage,* ed. Michael Mauricio. Waipahu, Hawai'i: Waipahu Centennial Committee.

McDermontt, John F., et al. 1980. *People and Cultures of Hawaii: A Pychocultural Profile.* Honolulu: University of Hawai'i.

Nakasone, Ronald, ed. 1996. *Reflections on the Okinawan Experience.* Fremont, CA: Dharma Cloud Publishers.

———. 2002. *Okinawan Diaspora.* Honolulu: University of Hawai'i Press.

Okinawa Club of America. 1989. *History of the Okinawans in North America.* Translated by Ben Kobashigawa. Los Angeles: UCLA Asian American Studies Center Press.

Peattie, Mark R. 1988. *Nan'yō: The Rise and Fall of the Japanese in Micronesia, 1885-1945.* Honolulu: University of Hawai'i Press.

Porterfield, Amanda. 2001. *The Transformation of American Religion: The Story of a Late-Twentieth-Century Awakening.* New York: Oxford University Press.

Sakihara, Mitsugu, ed. 1981. *Uchinanchu: A History of Okinawans in Hawaii.* Honolulu: University of Hawai'i/United Okinawan Association of Hawai'i.

Sakihara, Mitsugu. 1987. *A Brief History of Early Okinawa Based on the Omoro Soshi.* Tokyo: Honpo Shoseki Press.

Sered, Susan. 2000. *Women of the Sacred Groves: Divine Priestesses of Okinawa.* New York: Oxford University Press.

Takayasu, Rokuro. 1993. *Beyond Eternity: The Spiritual World of Ryukyu.* Translated by Christopher A. Reichl. Michigan City, IN:. Reichl Press.

Tamamori, Terunobu, and John C. James. 2000. *Okinawa: Society and Culture.* 2nd ed. Naha: Bank of Ryukyus International Foundation.

Tomiyama Ichirō. 1990. *Kindai nihon shakai to "Okinawajin"* [Modern Japanese society and the Okinawans]. Tokyo: Nihon keizi hyōronsha.

———. 2002. "The 'Japanese' of Micronesia: Okinawans in the Nan'yō Islands." In *Okinawan Diaspora,* ed. Ronald Y. Nakasone. Honolulu: University of Hawai'i Press.

Wuthnow, Robert, ed. 1994. *"I Come Away Stronger": How Small Groups are Shaping American Religion.* Grand Rapids, MI: William B. Eerdmans Publ. Co.

6

Religion and the Maintenance of Ethnicity among Immigrants
A Comparison of Indian Hindus and Korean Protestants

Pyong Gap Min

L ike many other Korean immigrants, I was not a Christian prior to immigration to this country. However, I began to attend a Korean immigrant church mainly for the benefits of meeting Korean friends and teaching my children the Korean language and customs. While attending the church, I realized how effective Korean churches were in helping Korean immigrants maintain their ethnicity and, in the late 1980s, I decided to conduct research on the "ethnicity functions" of Korean immigrant churches using survey research in New York City. In reviewing the sociological literature on religion and ethnicity for this project, I found many studies focusing on the Judeo-Christian ethnic groups—Italian, Irish, Jewish, and Greek—at the turn of the twentieth century that emphasized participation in religious congregations as the major mechanism for maintaining ethnicity (Dolan 1975; Du Bois 1967; Greeley 1972; Ostergren 1981; Rosenberg 1985; Tomasi and Engel 1971; Warner 1994; Warner and Srole 1945). My own 1989 survey of 131 Korean immigrant churches in New York City demonstrated that Korean churches contributed to the preservation of ethnicity among Korean immigrants by helping them to increase their co-ethnic fellowship and to maintain Korean cultural traditions (Min 1991, 1992).

Many other studies of post-1965 immigrant groups have also supported the hypothesis that there is a relationship between participation in an ethnic congregation and the preservation of ethnicity (Bankston and Zhou 1995; Fenton 1988; Hurh and Kim 1990; Kurien 1998, 2002; Lin 1996; Williams 1988). For example, based on a survey of Vietnamese high school students, Carl Bankston and Min Zhou (1995:530) concluded: "religious participation consistently makes a greater contribution to ethnic identification than any of the family or individual

99

characteristics examined, except recency of arrival." Although non-Judeo-Christian religions such as Hinduism and Buddhism do not consider participation in a congregation a major component of religious practice, many Buddhist and Hindu immigrants in the United States do participate in temples, albeit less regularly than Christian groups, and this also contributes to maintenance of their ethnicity. Irene Lin describes how the process works at a Chinese Buddhist temple in California (Lin 1996): "Hsi Lai Temple offers Mandarin, Taiwanese, and Cantonese classes, mainly to 1.5 and second generation Chinese Americans. Special classes on Chinese culture are offered, as well, including Chinese art, folk dance, music, cooking, and tai-chi, classes that help overseas Chinese to keep in touch with their ancestral roots."

In 1997 and 1998, I conducted a survey of Chinese, Indian, and Korean immigrants in Queens, New York City, and compared patterns of ethnic attachment among the three groups. One of my major findings was that Korean Protestant immigrants participate in a congregation far more frequently than Indian Hindu immigrants (Min 2000). While 83 percent of Korean Protestants participate in the Sunday worship service every week, only 22 percent of Indian Hindus go to a temple every week. Assuming participation in a congregation is the only mechanism through which religion can contribute to the preservation of ethnicity, I concluded that Korean Protestant immigrants have a huge advantage over Indian Hindu immigrants in maintaining ethnicity through religion.

However, my subsequent conversations with Indian Hindu immigrants, including faculty members and priests, informed me that Hinduism is not a congregation-oriented religion and that Hindus practice religion mainly through family rituals. I also learned that Indian Hindu immigrants can maintain their ethnic traditions through religion effectively because their religious values and rituals are inseparably tied to ethnic customs (including funerals and weddings), values, holidays, food, music, and dance (see Min 2000).

Because they focused exclusively on congregations, scholars of the earlier European immigrant groups overlooked the significance of religious rituals practiced at home and/or in small groups and the association between religious rituals and ethnic culture for the preservation of ethnicity. However, the influx of immigrants from Third World countries in the post-1965 era has led many researchers to pay special attention to the effects of so-called "domestic religion" on the preservation of ethnicity (Brown 1991; Ebaugh and Chafetz 2000:391-393; Orsi 1996; Stepick 1998:92; Stevens-Arroyo and Diaz-Stevens 1994; Wellmeier 1998).

Post-1965 immigrant groups serve as good cases for examining the effects of "domestic religion" on ethnic preservation for two reasons. First, many of these groups have brought with them non-Western religions, such as Hinduism, Islam, and Buddhism, which involve more family and small-group rituals than participation in a congregation. Second, their religious rituals and faiths are inseparably tied to their weddings, funerals, food, holidays, music, dance, and other elements of folk culture. This close connection between religious rituals and ethnic culture is apparent even among many Latino and Caribbean Catholic immigrant groups, who have incorporated much of their folk culture into Roman Catholicism brought over by their European colonizers. In fact, almost all the studies cited above that have examined "domestic religion" or "folk religion" focus on Latino or Caribbean Catholic immigrant groups.

Protestantism was introduced to Korea at the turn of the twentieth century and popularized only over the last thirty-five years.[1] Thus, its religious tenets and rituals are not directly related to the Korean language, traditional food and dress, national holidays, or music and dance, although it has incorporated shamanistic and Confucian elements of Korean culture (Baker 1997). But Korean Protestant immigrants are very active participants in an ethnic congregation, and this can help them to maintain their ethnicity. By contrast, Indian Hindu immigrants participate in congregational worship much less frequently, but they intensively practice family rituals that are deeply connected to Indian cultural traditions. Thus, Korean Protestants and Indian Hindus seem to represent extreme cases of using either participation in a congregation or family/small group rituals to preserve their ethnicity.

This chapter examines the fundamentally different ways in which Korean Protestant and Hindu immigrants use religion to preserve their ethnicity. Gordon (1964:38) and other researchers (Kim and Hurh 1984:78-82; Reitz 1980; Yinger 1994:3-4) have used ethnicity or ethnic attachment to indicate three interrelated ethnic phenomena: retention of ethnic subculture (cultural), involvement in ethnic networks and interaction (social), and group self-identification (psychological). This chapter examines how and to what extent participation in religious institutions and the practice of religious rituals at home contribute to one or more of the three components of ethnicity for the two Asian immigrant groups.

Research Methods

Traditionally, social scientists interested in immigrants' religious practices conducted ethnographic research on a selected congregation. Two major studies of contemporary immigrants' religious practices (Ebaugh and Chafetz 2000; Warner and Wittner 1998) have largely taken the traditional congregational approach, although the latter study asked some members of congregations about practicing religion at home. However, since many contemporary immigrant groups practice religions that focus on family or small-group rituals, it is important to combine ethnographic research on congregations with personal interviews with selected informants in a non-congregational setting. Interviewing outside the place of worship was especially important for this study, because Indian Hindu immigrants practice religion mainly through family rituals. Thus, this chapter is based on ethnographic research on a Korean church and a Hindu temple and personal interviews with fifty-six Korean Protestant and fifty-nine Indian Hindu immigrants in New York.

Ethnographic research was conducted at a Korean Protestant church and a Hindu temple located in Queens, New York City, between February 2001 and December 2001. Queens is an ideal place for a comparative study involving Korean Protestant and Indian Hindu immigrants because the vast majority of both Korean and Indian immigrants in New York City reside in Queens.[2] As of 2000, there were approximately 600 Korean churches in the tri-city area, which has a Korean population of about 200,000. Most Korean churches are small, with fewer than 200 members. The selected Korean church (hereafter referred to as the Queens Korean church) is a large Presbyterian church with about 3,700 members in 2001. Established in 1973, it is one of the oldest Korean churches in New York City.[3]

There are approximately twenty-five Indian temples in the tri-city area, and about 450,000 people of Asian Indian ancestry. The selected temple (hereafter referred to as the Queens Hindu temple) is probably the second largest and oldest Hindu temple in New York City, established in 1977. Hindu temples do not have membership, with the exception of executive committee members, but according to a staff person, about 3,000 devotees attend the temple over three weekend days. The temple accommodates a range of devotees of mainly southern Indian regional subcultures who speak five different languages (Hindi, Telugu, Kannada, Tamil, and Malayalam). About 90 percent of the participants in the temple are Indian immigrants and their children, with Bangladeshi and Guyanese Indians, and white American Hindus making up the rest. Depending upon the region and/or sect, Hinduism has many faces in terms of deities, sacred texts, institutions, and cultural practices (Williams 1988:39). Thus, the results of research on a Hindu temple would differ depending upon which temple were chosen. The Queens Hindu temple was selected for this study partly because it is comparable in history and size to the Queens Korean church, but mainly because it is ecumenical in organization, incorporating many different regions and sects.

Ethnographic research involved three components: participant observation of services and other socio-cultural activities in the two selected congregations, personal interviews with religious leaders and congregation members, and a review of documents. In spring 2001, a Korean student took notes on Sunday services, the dining room, Korean language classes, and other socio-cultural activities in the Queens Korean church. She also interviewed five staff members and several other members of the church, and gathered documents pertaining to the church. In summer 2001, I made similar observations in the Korean church and personally interviewed a pastor, two other staff members, and several lay members of the church. Between summer 2001 and fall 2002, I also observed worship and socio-cultural activities in the selected Hindu temple, including language and dance classes, wedding ceremonies, and devotees eating in the dining hall. I also personally interviewed five staff members of the temple and several lay participants.

Next, we conducted fifty-six tape-recorded personal interviews with Korean Protestant immigrants and another fifty-nine interviews with Indian Hindu immigrants in New York between December 2000 and November 2001. I conducted interviews with fifteen Korean Protestants and twenty Indian Hindus, while two Korean and two Indian students, all perfectly bilingual, conducted the other eighty personal interviews. The interviewees were located through personal channels, and we tried to maintain a good representative sample in terms of socioeconomic status, age, and sex.[4] In order to examine how they taught their children religious and cultural values at home, we made efforts to interview Koreans and Indians with one or more children. It turned out that the vast majority of Indian (N=55/59) and Korean (N=52/56) interviewees were married, with most having one or more children in school.

We asked the informants about their backgrounds, their participation in congregational worship and cultural and fellowship activities at their church or temple, observance of religious faith and rituals at home, teaching religious and cultural values to children, and the relative importance of religion versus ethnic background for their identity. Indian Hindus were interviewed using the English questionnaire, while Korean Protestants were interviewed using the Korean language questionnaire. To capture family practice of religious rituals and religious decorations, we tried to interview a significant proportion of the informants at home. Forty-nine percent of Indian and fifty-four percent of Korean interviewees were interviewed there, while others spoke to us in a church/temple, a store, or an office. The interview took approximately thirty to ninety minutes to complete.

Ethnographic Research on a Korean Church and a Hindu Temple

Ethnographic research on the Korean church generally confirmed the previous findings regarding the ethnic fellowship and cultural retention functions of Korean immigrant churches (Hurh and Kim 1990; Kim 1981:187-207; Kim and Kim 2001; Min 1992). A small church consisting of dozens of families provides its members with the opportunity for face-to-face, family-like primary social interactions, and this explains why there are so many small Korean churches. By contrast, large churches are at a disadvantage in terms of offering such opportunities (Min 1992). Despite being larger than the average Korean immigrant church, the Queens Korean church has organized several social activities to enhance fellowship and networks among its members. First, the church helps members to enjoy fellowship after the Sunday service by providing snacks and lunches. There are four separate services for Korean immigrants on Sunday, beginning at 8:30, 10:00, 12:00, and 2:00. Most immigrant members attend the ten or twelve o'clock service and afterward eat a Korean lunch for $2 at the cafeteria with their relatives or friends. Often they can eat excellent Korean dishes free because they have been donated by a family that celebrated a wedding or a birthday on the previous Saturday. Many of those who attend the early morning or afternoon service chat with their friends afterward with bagels and coffee offered free. Other members often go to a Korean restaurant in Flushing with their kin members or friends.

Kim, a fifty-five-year-old man who had been a member of the church for seven years, emphasized fellowship as an important component of his participation.

> Q: How important do you think fellowship is in a Korean church?
> R: Of course, praying and listening to sermons are the most important reasons that I regularly participate in a church. But I am not honest if I say fellowship is not an important reason I choose to come to this church every week. From the beginning, I chose this church because two of my friends asked me to join their church. Since I joined this church I have made more friends here. After the 10 a.m. Sunday service, my wife and I usually eat with two or three Korean couples in the church cafeteria. Often, we go to a Korean restaurant in Flushing together after the Sunday service. We do it because it is very convenient to do it.

The church has twenty-two functional committees and many other organizations, including three choirs, the Korean school, and the missionary committee. Many church members belong to two or three organizations, and most belong to at least one organization. Their participation in (weekly or monthly) committee meetings and involvement in their committee activities also enhances their fellowship and personal networks. Since members of each organization work for common goals within the church and have extended formal and informal social interactions, they can make friends with one another easily. The church has also divided its members into age-specific groups for missionary activities.[5] This grouping by age facilitates informal networks because the members of a particular age group have similar life experiences. This forty-three-year-old Korean woman explains how age-based group activities foster informal friendship networks:

> Q: Can you tell me about your church group activities?
> R.: My husband and I belong to the 41- to 45-year-old missionary group. About fifteen couples in our group actively participate in church missionary activities. In addition to an official monthly meeting held at the church, we have one or two unofficial meetings at a member's home with dinner. We spend a lot of time together.
> Q: Do you maintain strong friendship ties with other members because of your common involvement in church activities?

R: Of course. Our frequent formal and informal meetings, our common Christian belief, and the same life stage with school-attending children have solidified our friendship ties. Three couples from the group are among the five best friends of ours. We usually take family trips together with the couples.

Other church activities that facilitate fellowship for subgroups within the congregation include a three-day family summer retreat in Upstate New York, separate retreats for male and female members, a full-day of athletic competitions on Memorial Day, and an annual *hyodo kwankwang* (a "filial tour") for elderly members. But the most important arrangement through which the large church provides its members with the opportunity for face-to-face, small-group interactions is the *gooyuk yebae* (district services) or "cell ministry" (see Kwon et al. 1997; Min 1992). This practice, which was transplanted from South Korea, is emphasized by pastors in Korean immigrant churches mainly as a means to increase the membership in the church. But it is also effective in fostering Korean immigrants' friendship networks. The Queens Korean church has divided its members into six major areas and subdivided them into 112 districts or cells based on the location of members' households. Each cell usually consists of thirteen households. Each district holds a two-hour service once a month in the evening under the guidance of the head of the district at a district member's home. After a short service, the participants usually eat dinner prepared by the host family and enjoy fellowship, talking about children's education, small businesses, politics in Korea, and other matters of mutual interest. The church's central office assigns new members to particular districts based on their addresses, and new members receive various kinds of assistance from the head and other members of the cell that help them adjust to American society. As a result of these frequent meetings in each other's homes, members of the same district often become close friends, exchanging informal dinner invitations and helping each other.

In 1988, the Queens Korean church established a school for the elderly, which offered free classes in English, Bible study, music, aerobics, and seminars on health every morning. About 130 elderly members were enrolled in the school in 2001. Fellowship, as well as education, is an important goal of the school. The elderly participants take two overnight trips out of the city each year. More significantly, after eating a free lunch, many of them go together to Korean bakeries in Flushing. One such small group, called *Baeknyonhe* (the Association for the Age 100, in order to express their hope of living to a hundred), consists of about twelve elderly men eighty years old and over. The group's leader described their activities:

Every afternoon between two and five, we meet at Kanaan Korean Bakery in Flushing and enjoy talk over a Korean tea. When we leave for home, we wish one another a safe night to see all others the next day again. Each member invites other members for his birthday party. That means we celebrate one birthday almost every month. A sixty-year-old elder, who had attended the church for more than fifteen years, told me that many other members are involved in such small groups, and that they make it easy to establish informal networks with other church members.

Korean churches also help Korean immigrants to retain their cultural traditions and preserve their ethnicity in several different ways. First of all, the church celebrates two major Korean traditional holidays: New Year's Day and *Chooseok* (the Korean Thanksgiving Day) with Korean food served and many women wearing traditional Korean dresses (*chimajogori*). The church also organizes special services to observe two major national holidays, the March 1 Independence Commemoration Day and the August 15 Independence Day. On these occasions, the pastor emphasizes Korean patriotism in his sermon by connecting the Korean independence movement or independence from colonization with a phrase from the Bible, while the church members sing the March 1 independence day song and loudly exclaim *daehandongip manse* (long live Korean independence) three times.

Reverent Chang, who had served as the main pastor since the foundation of the church, emphasized "helping second-generation Koreans learn the Korean language and culture as an important mission of a Korean immigrant church." Only three years after its foundation, the church established the Korean school to give Korean children ethnic education. The Korean school is open three hours (between 9 A.M. and 12 P.M.) on Sunday for basic classes and five hours (between 9 A.M. and 2 P.M.) for extension classes. It offers various courses related to the Korean language, etiquette, history, and music for kindergarten through college students. For Korean language classes, the school uses textbooks adopted by public schools in South Korea. The kindergarten program given on Tuesday and Thursday between 10 and 12 teaches Korean as well as English. The church also tries to teach children Korean etiquette and Korean customs through other educational programs, including the Bible study meeting on Friday. Teachers emphasize "filial piety" as the central element of Korean etiquette. Twice a year, children have joint services with their parents. At one such service for junior high school students and their parents in May 2001, a pastor gave a sermon emphasizing the obedience of children to their parents: "just as Jesus Christ obeyed God, children should obey their parents." In services celebrating Parent's Day in May, young members pin carnations on middle-aged and elderly members. On Parents Day, teachers in elementary and high school classes help students to write letters of appreciation to, and to buy gifts for, their parents.

One major difference between the Hindu temple and the Korean church in their social and cultural functions lies in the different degree of importance attached to fellowship and ethnic social networks. Compared to the Korean church, the temple does not serve much as a place for fellowship and social networks. First of all, although it has a mailing list, the temple does not consider its participants to be its members. Indians who visit the Queens Hindu temple also visit other temples. All the Hindus with whom I talked in the temple told me that they also attended one or two other temples. While participants are referred to as *sungdo* (sacred friends) in the Korean church, they are called "devotees" in the temple. These two different terms suggest that the Korean church puts more emphasis on the fellowship aspect of the congregation than the Hindu temple.

Moreover, the style of worship at the temple does not provide much opportunity for fellowship and primary social interactions. Korean Protestants usually go to church once a week on Sunday (although more than one-third of them also go to a mini-service on Friday) and have services as a group. By contrast, the temple is open from eight in the morning to nine in the evening for seven days a week. Indian Hindus visit the temple at different times on different days (although most participate on weekends because of convenience) and worship particular deities of their own choice individually or as a family unit. Although some devotees eat snacks or vegetarian food at the temple canteen, they usually do not consider meeting with their friends and/or relatives for fellowship important, as many members of the Queens Korean church do.

In addition, unlike the Korean church, the temple does not organize group activities, like summer retreats or athletic competitions that might foster social networks and fellowship among its devotees. Apart from health workshops given twice a year, the temple also has fewer programs to provide social services for its devotees. Given that the temple does not consider its devotees to be its members, it is not surprising that it has not organized such social activities and programs.

While the Hindu temple does not contribute much to building fellowship or social connections among its devotees, it does help Indian Hindus to retain their Indian cultural and sub-cultural traditions and ethnic/sub-ethnic identities in other ways. As earlier noted, the Korean church helps its members to maintain Korean cultural traditions mainly because the members actively participate in it and practice "Korean" cultural traditions (rather than "Christian" cultural traditions). By sharp contrast, the temple helps Indian Hindus to maintain their cultural traditions and ethnic identity mainly because of the association between the Hindu religion and Indian cultural and sub-cultural traditions.

Religious practices helped white Catholics to reproduce ethnic culture partly because their churches were similar in architectural design to those in the home countries (Dolan 1975; Ebaugh and Chafetz 2000:386-390). The Indian temple also contributes to the preservation of Indian culture and identity because the architecture of the temple, its interior furnishings, and other visual representations reproduce Indian culture. When the temple was built in the early 1970s, eight architects from southern India were invited to make it resemble Tirupati Devasthanam, a large temple in the state of Andhra Pradesh. Some statues of deities were sent from southern India. Because of the physical reproduction of the architectural design, the temple reminds Indian immigrants of their home country. Some devotees told me, "I like to come to this temple regularly because here I feel like I am in little India." According to an usher, Indian immigrants from all over the tri-city areas visit the temple on the weekend to see "Little India."[6] Many middle-aged Indian immigrants from Connecticut, Philadelphia, and even as far as New Hampshire make family visits to the temple a few times a year to get this "feeling of being at home."[7]

Second, the temple helps Indian Hindus maintain their cultural traditions and ethnic identity because it celebrates major Hindu holidays. The temple celebrates all major Hindu holidays, which are also Indian national holidays, with various cultural activities. Most Hindu devotees attend the temple several times a year to celebrate major holidays, often dressed in traditional costumes (*sari* for women and *dhoti* for men). The biggest cultural event is an annual parade on the last day of the Ganesha Chaturthi festival week in August or September. To celebrate his birth, the devotees parade Lord Ganesha's statue in a beautifully decorated chariot through the major streets of Flushing, accompanied by a singing and dancing group of devotees. At the 2001 festival, I witnessed about 3,000 Indian Hindus, many of whom had come from New Jersey and Pennsylvania, participating in or watching the event. I realized how powerful the parade was in displaying Indian cultural traditions to the American public in the heart of Flushing. The Queens Korean Protestant church also celebrates two major Korean cultural holidays, but it cannot present Korean holidays to the public in this way because Protestantism does not represent Korean culture.

Third, the temple enhances Indian cultural traditions by offering various language and cultural classes and programs for Hindu immigrants and the second generation. It also has a class on yoga and meditation on Sunday in which white Americans, as well as Indian Hindus, participate. For second-generation children, it offers several Indian language classes, including Sanskrit and Hindi, and Indian music/dance on Saturday or Sunday. Several Indian dance teachers at the center often participate in intercultural programs, performing traditional Indian dance and music for New Yorkers. About seventy second-generation Hindu children and adolescents meet regularly on the second and fourth Saturdays each month for religious education and cultural activities. Most importantly, the temple has organized a monthly lecture on Hindu religion by gurus or professors from India and other parts of the United States. I attended a lecture given at the temple's auditorium in December 2002 attended by about 200 people. The lecture by a well-known Hindu scholar was entitled "The Face of Hinduism in America: Threats and Opportunity." The lecturer discussed the "pervasive biases against Indianness and Hinduism by higher education institutions, high schools, and the media" and suggested strategies to enhance the influence of Hinduism and Indian culture in the United States. After the lecture, participants engaged in hot debates about how to present Hinduism and Indian culture to Americans accurately and positively. My participation in the lecture has helped me to understand how much Indian Hindu immigrants approach Hinduism as an Indian religious and cultural heritage.

Finally, the temple helps to preserve Indian cultural traditions by performing various rituals for Indian Hindu families. In 1997 it established the Community Center next to the temple's main building to be used for various cultural and social activities. The Community Center includes a wedding hall, a canteen and dining hall, and an auditorium. In the wedding hall, the nine priests who work for the temple perform wedding ceremonies, birthday parties, and many other life-cycle rituals for Hindu families, usually on weekends. They also perform a number of rituals, including weddings and funerals, at Hindu homes, hotels, and crematoria.[8] The temple charges fixed fees for performing these rituals, which are an important source of its revenue. A gift shop inside the canteen and dining hall sells pictures of deities, idols, coins, veda and prayer books, audio tapes of special bhajans, video tapes of celebrations, and Sanskrit and Hindi music tapes.

In September 2001, I watched a Hindu wedding ceremony for an Indian bride and a white American groom performed in the center's wedding hall. I was deeply impressed by the fact that not only the white groom but also his parents and relatives observed the Hindu style of wedding ceremony presided over by a Hindu priest, wearing traditional Hindu dresses and following Indian music and dance. After the ceremony, all white participants ate vegetarian food. When I asked the groom's parents whether they were converts to Hinduism, they told me that they were Christians but that they simply followed Hindu rules for their son's wedding because the bride's parents insisted on having a Hindu wedding. A Hindu priest told me that only a small proportion of Indian-white weddings are performed at a Hindu temple.[9] Nevertheless, I realized what a powerful cultural influence Hinduism has on American society because it is a religion indigenous to India. I have also witnessed a Christian wedding ceremony performed in a Korean church for a Korean bride and a white groom, but there was not much Koreanness about the ceremony other than the Korean food served afterwards.

As previously noted, the Queens Korean church, too, contributes to the preservation of Korean culture mainly because its members use the congregation to practice Korean customs and values and to teach them to their children. But it is less effective for the retention of ethnic culture than the Queens Hindu temple because Korean Protestantism has not incorporated much Korean folk culture. But the Hindu temple is very effective for the preservation of Indian culture because the architecture of the building, the form of worship, and many rituals practiced there symbolize Indian, especially southern Indian culture.

Findings from Personal Interviews about Participation in a Church or a Temple

Personal interviews confirm the observations noted above about the different ways in which the Korean church and the Indian Hindu temple reinforce ethnicity. Personal interviews with Korean Protestants revealed that they attend church very frequently; 89 percent of them attended church at least once a week, 35 percent twice or more. Eight interviewees (14 percent) said that they attend the church every morning, in addition to the Sunday and Friday evening services.[10] They usually spend two to five hours just for the Sunday service and fellowship and an average of 8.3 hours per week if voluntary activities are included. Seven respondents reported that they spent 20 or more hours weekly for church activities. They held eldership and/or other important positions, or belonged to a choir in their church, and thus spent a lot of time participating in committee meetings, visiting sick members, cooking in the kitchen, and/or performing other voluntary activities.[11]

As expected, the Indian Hindus went to a temple much less frequently than Korean Protestants go to church; 24 percent of them go once a week or more, and two-thirds said they attended only once a month or once a year.[12] As noted above, while most Korean Protestant immigrants consider participation in church essential to practicing their religion,[13] Indian Hindus do not share this belief. They feel they can practice religion at home without going to the temple, as reflected by their popular phrase that "god is everywhere." Nonetheless, many Hindus agreed that they could concentrate on their worship inside the temple more effectively than they could at home.

Asking the Hindu respondents how many hours per week they usually spent for temple activities proved to be an irrelevant question because only a small proportion of them go to temple every week. Most respondents reported that they spent half an hour to a few hours on each visit to the temple. It takes less than half an hour for their religious service alone, but they spend one to three hours when they participate in a lecture and/or other cultural activities. Far fewer Indian Hindu respondents than Korean Protestant respondents were found to participate in voluntary services for their congregation. Instead, Hindu temples, usually large in size, depend mainly upon employees for their operation rather than upon voluntary work by devotees. This finding is not surprising at all, given that Hindu devotees usually do not have membership in a particular temple, while all Korean Protestants have an exclusive membership in their church.

The analysis above shows that Korean Protestants participate in an ethnic congregation far more frequently and spend far more time on each visit than Indian Hindus. Korean Protestant immigrants spend more time in the Korean church because they put far more emphasis on co-ethnic fellowship as an important reason for their participation in a Korean congregation.

We asked the respondents to list the important reasons why they participate in a Korean church or a Hindu temple regularly. The majority of both Korean (57%) and Hindu (66%) respondents cited religious or psychological purposes, such as "to worship God," "to glorify God," "to enhance my religious belief," "for peace of mind," and "to cope with my personal difficulty," as the most important reason for their participation in the place of worship. But there is a big difference between the two groups in the emphasis placed on co-ethnic fellowship. Forty-two percent of the Korean respondents cited co-ethnic fellowship and other related factors, such as "to belong to a Korean group," "to maintain ethnic networks," "to enjoy a family-like atmosphere," and "to cope with the alienation deriving from American society," as the primary reason for their participation in a Korean congregation. Another 20 percent cited them as the second most important reason.

The following response by a Korean male retailer in his mid-forties is typical:

> Although I live in a white neighborhood, I do not talk much with my neighbors. For six days, I serve black customers and get stressed. I need an outlet to express my feeling with fellow Koreans. That is a Korean church. When I talk and eat lunch with my friends in my church on Sunday, I feel at home and relaxed. A Korean church is a Korean community. I don't know how other Korean immigrants who don't go to a Korean church can survive in this country.

The overwhelming majority of the Korean respondents reported that after the Sunday service they spend an hour or two eating there and talking with their friends. Husbands and wives often eat separately with their own friends, and so do their children. Fifteen of the fifty-six Korean respondents (27%) were either Buddhists or atheists in South Korea and have become Christians in the United States. They emphasized co-ethnic fellowship as the main reason for their initial decision to participate in a Korean church. A sixty-two-year-old Korean man who came as a foreign student thirty-one years earlier said: "I had no religion in Korea, but I started to attend a Korean church in New York City because there was no major Korean organization other than a few Korean churches at that time. To learn about the Korean community, I had to go to a Korean church." Another female respondent who was a Buddhist in Korea reported: "When I came here, I had a severe barrier in English. I needed to make friends with Koreans. My friend's mother was serving as a Bible woman. She asked me to come to her church and I followed her."

By contrast, few Indian Hindu respondents emphasized co-ethnic fellowship as a major reason for their participation in a Hindu temple. Only two of the fifty-eight Hindu respondents cited fellowship as the main reason for going to a temple regularly, and another nine of them listed it as the second most important reason. Asked, "How long do you stay in the temple for fellowship after service?" only nine respondents said they ate Indian food after service, talking with their friends. Many Hindu respondents said, "I chat with my friends after service," but they do not spend much time. About half of the Hindu respondents said they ate at the temple after service, but they usually ate with their family members rather than with their friends. This is in strong contrast with Korean Protestants who usually eat lunch with their friends, often with same-sex friends. This difference is partly due to the fact that Korean Protestants have services together, but separately from their children. This makes it easy for them to eat lunch with their friends after the service. But although most Indian Hindus visit the temple on the weekend, they can worship any time on any given day individually, as a family unit, or in a small group. This makes it hard for them to meet friends and enjoy worship and fellowship together unless they make a special arrangement in advance.

While fellowship is not an important reason why Indian Hindus attend the temple, the preservation of ethnic culture and identity is a major reason for their participation. The majority (58%) of the Hindu respondents chose retention of ethnic culture and identity for themselves and their children as the most or second most important reason for their participation in the temple. Given that a Hindu temple and Hinduism symbolize much of Indian culture, this is not a surprising finding at all. Asked the major reasons why she went to the temple, a forty-year-old Hindu woman said: "We are from India. Helping our children to learn about their root is the main reason for going to temple. Have them know about Hindu gods and goddesses." Another informant, a thirty-five-year-old man with two children, put it this way: "I think the main reasons are for my own peace of mind and my children's development. We want our kids to know as much as possible about their religion and culture." Many respondents reported that they went to temple with their children a few or several times a year to celebrate religious holidays, to observe cultural activities, and/or to have ritual performed for their children and/or other family members.

We asked the Hindu respondents whether they "think attending an Indian Hindu temple is helpful in maintaining Indian cultural traditions." With a few exceptions, all of them said yes. The following statement by a male Hindu with twelve years of residence in the United States is typical: "Yes, it definitely is. Temple reinforces the teachings of the holy book. It helps us to follow the customs and so on and to keep our faith, even though our society is different from India. It's a place where we feel that we belong, plus we get to associate with people of the same beliefs and culture at the temple." A forty-six-year-old Hindu woman, who worked as a bank teller, associated participating in a temple with Indian identity and culture: "I think by going to temple, my Indian identity is made stronger. Hinduism and Indian culture are linked, so by going to temple I am reminded of my roots and I bring this home with me."

We asked the Hindu respondents with one or more children a related question, "Do you think attending a temple is helpful to teaching your children

Indian cultural traditions? In what ways?" Again, all respondents who were parents agreed that it is definitely helpful. A forty-year-old biological researcher with one child gave the following response: "Yes it is. My daughter was born in the U.S. So taking her to temple is a good way of teaching her the rituals, customs, and beliefs of her people. She will learn how to make the proper sacrifices to the Gods and how to perform their pujas." These responses offer indisputable evidence that Indian Hindu immigrants' participation in a temple is inseparably tied to their intent to maintain and transmit their cultural traditions. When Korean Protestant respondents were asked the same questions regarding the relationship between participation in a church and cultural retention, the vast majority of them did not consider cultural retention as a major reason. Only twelve of the fifty-six Korean respondents (21%) chose cultural preservation for themselves and/or their children as the most or the second most important reason for their participation in a Korean church. However, an overwhelming majority of the respondents agreed that their participation was helpful in maintaining Korean cultural traditions (75%) and teaching their children the Korean language and culture (89%). Many respondents, however, emphasized that cultural retention was the result rather than an objective of their membership in a Korean church.

It is interesting to see how they feel participation in a Korean church helps them to preserve Korean culture. Many respondents said that they and their partners were too busy with their work to prepare food to celebrate traditional Korean holidays (the Lunar New Year's Day and the Korean Thanksgiving Day), but that they could celebrate the holidays with traditional Korean food in their churches. Some also pointed out that without going to a Korean church they could never observe Korean national holidays in the United States. Their responses to other related questions suggest that many of the respondents' churches celebrate the Korean traditional and national holidays in a more authentic way than the Queens Korean church, the object of my ethnographic research, does. Several respondents indicated that their participation in a Korean church helped them maintain Korean values of "group orientation and filial piety" in a space away from the "American value of individualism." Three respondents reported that participation in a Korean church rather than an American church enabled them to hold memorial services for their deceased parents, the Christian version of ancestor worship, with the main pastor and close church members invited to their homes.[14]

The Korean Protestant respondents consider participation in a Korean church more important for the intergenerational transmission of Korean culture than for their own maintenance of it. Many indicated that they could not lose Korean cultural traditions no matter how long they live in the United States, but that they have difficulty teaching their children Korean cultural traditions by themselves at home. They feel that, as a mini-Korean community, a Korean church is effective for teaching the Korean language and culture. Several respondents reported that they participated in a Korean church, especially for their children's ethnic education, as did this sixty-five-year-old Korean man who lived in the United States for forty years:

> It is almost impossible for us to teach our children the Korean language, customs, and identity individually through instructions. The children can learn Korean cultural traditions and identity effectively in a group setting. A Korean church is an ideal place they can learn "Korean" things naturally. Korean children who participate in a Korean church can learn the Korean language and history in a Korean program there. They can also learn about Korean holidays and Korean etiquette in interaction with other Koreans, especially with Korean adults.

As his comments reflect, what Korean Protestants mean by ethnic education is teaching children the Korean language, Korean culture, and ethnic identity. But many respondents emphasized that participation in a Korean church is particularly helpful in enabling their children to learn the "Korean etiquette" of showing respect for their parents and other adults. A thirty-seven-year-old Korean woman with two children explained how a Korean church can do this:

> Korean etiquette places emphasis on children showing respect when they talk and interact with adults. American children say "you" when they talk to parents, just like when they talk to their friends. But Korean children should not say "you" to parents. They are supposed to say "Yes, father" or "Yes, Mother." And they give a greeting to an adult by giving a deep bow instead of saying "hello." This kind of Korean etiquette I cannot teach at home. Children can learn it naturally in a Korean church from their friends and Sunday school teachers. We have asked Sunday school and Friday Bible study teachers to teach Korean etiquette as well as Christian values.

Some respondents reported that for the Parent's Day in May their churches organized activities similar to the Queens Korean church to show children's appreciation to their parents, and that the "filial" activities had positive effects on their children. Two respondents pointed out that they could not teach their children "filial etiquette" effectively at home because they did not live with elderly parents, but that their children could learn it in their church because of the presence of elderly members there.

As previously noted, Indian Hindu respondents consider that participation in a Hindu temple facilitates their children's learning mainly because of religious rituals, including chanting *mantras* in Sanskrit and celebrating religious holidays, which are, to them, the central elements of Indian culture. By contrast, Korean Protestant immigrants emphasize a Korean congregation as the context for teaching their children "Korean" rather than "Christian" etiquette. They cannot emphasize Christian values and rituals as the content of their children's ethnic education because the Christian religion itself does not include many Korean cultural elements.

Findings from Personal Interviews on Religious Practices at Home

Personal interviews with Korean Protestant and Indian Hindu immigrants provided information about their religious practices at home that is not available from ethnographic research on the two selected congregations. As expected, the personal interviews reveal that Indian Hindus practice religious rituals extensively at home regardless of how often they go to a temple and that they spend far more time practicing religious rituals at home.

While only 24 percent of Indian Hindu respondents reported that they went to a temple once a week or more, all respondents but one were found to have set up a shrine at home to practice Hinduism. A family shrine or altar for a Hindu consists of religious statues and/or pictures of gods of goddesses and saints, incense stickers, and lamps. Respondents generally prayed at least once per day, usually in the morning after a bath, often offering food, flowers, and/or money. Many prayed twice or more each day and practiced other Hindu rituals at home, such as reciting a few *mantras*, meditating, and reading scriptures from the holy book. All but three respondents reported that they fasted at least once a year, usually once a month or once a week. Many Hindu respondents said that it is difficult to remain vegetarian in the United States because few American fast food and restaurant menus do not include meat. But the majority of them said that they did not eat any beef or pork at home and they tried not to eat any meat products at least for one day a week. More Americanized Hindus made it a rule not to eat meat at least on important Hindu holidays. Also, all but one respondent said that they regularly listened to tapes of Hindi songs, with most listening on a daily basis whether at home or at work.

All respondents celebrated Indian religious holidays at home, preparing Indian food and inviting relatives. Many celebrate a religious holiday almost every month, as this forty-eight-year-old Indian woman described: "We have almost one Hindu holiday every month. We do a puja at home and go to the temple and sing *bhajans*. We make food for offerings, it's called prasad. And everybody gets together to celebrate." By contrast, few celebrate non-Hindu Indian holidays at home (even though several indicated that they participated in the Indian Independence Day parade in Manhattan). One respondent said: "Indian culture is so much based on Hinduism that there is no non-religious Indian holiday." Her statement is factually wrong, but it reflects many Indian immigrants' perception that Hindu rituals constitute the central elements of Indian culture. The majority of the Hindu respondents indicated *Dwali* as the most important religious holiday on which they prepare special foods and light candles to welcome Lord Ram. I visited an Indian Hindu home on *Dwali* in September 2001 and saw the host couple celebrating the holiday with many relatives invited. The husband was using an entire room as a shrine, housing several statues of gods and goddesses. Many of the visitors were watching an Indian television program that aired the celebration of *Dwali* from India. The host offered me vegetarian food.

In addition, all informants said that they put up decorations signifying Hindu religion and identity at home, such as pictures, statues, idols, and woodcrafts of gods and goddesses. Some have Hindu symbols all over their houses, as did this thirty-nine-year-old woman with two children:

> Q: What decorations do you put at home to signify your Hindu identity?
> R: Yeah, all over. I have a big statue of Lord Ganesh in my living room, so you can see it as soon as you enter. Then I have another one in my party room. Then I have a temple upstairs. And in my foyer I have a Lord Krishna statue. Then I have a little temple in my kitchen. Almost in every room I have something.

The personal interviews indicate that, to celebrate special days for their family members, Hindu immigrants more often have religious rituals performed at a temple than at home. But more than two-thirds of the respondents said that they invited a Hindu priest to their home at least once a year to perform special rituals for their family members.

Asked about their religious practices at home, about 45 percent of Korean Protestant respondents said that they read the Bible a few times a week or more, each time spending about fifteen to thirty minutes. About 40 percent of the respondents reported that in addition to praying routinely three times before meals they prayed twice a day, usually when they get up in the morning and before they go to bed at night. About 35 percent said they sang hymns and/or gospel songs a few times a week or more at home. But many respondents indicated that their long hours of work gave them little time to sing hymns at home, while others commented that it is difficult to sing hymns alone at home. But most of them did regularly listen to tapes of hymns or gospel songs, and to Korean Christian radio programs at home, while driving, or at work. These figures suggest that Korean Protestant immigrants probably spend more or at least as much time as Indian Hindus in practicing religious faith at home, reading the scriptures, praying, and singing or listening to hymns.

However, while Korean Protestant immigrants remain very religious at home in terms of reading the Bible and praying regularly, they do not engage in religious practices at home that are directly related to Korean cultural traditions. The personal interviews reveal that most Korean Christian immigrants celebrate or observe Easter in a church rather than at home. Also, they celebrate the white

American version of Christmas in a Korean church with lots of religious activities but no Korean cultural activities, while at home they usually give gifts to their family members. Given that there is no Korean version of Christmas comparable to Hanuka or Kwanzaa, this is quite natural. Even when they celebrate traditional Korean holidays, most Korean Protestant immigrants do not do much at home; instead, they usually celebrate them in a church, eating traditional Korean food and playing traditional games with their co-ethnic church members. This proves once again that Korean Protestant immigrants use their participation in a Korean congregation rather than the content of their religion to maintain their cultural traditions. Moreover, Korean Protestants do not put up religious decorations at home as Indians do. Nine of the fifty-six Korean respondents reported that they had no religious decorations at home at all. The other respondents had one or more of the following items: a framed picture of Jesus Christ, one or two framed Biblical phrases (*sunggu*), and a statue of cross (*sipjaga*).

Probably the most significant difference between Indian Hindu and Korean Protestant immigrants in retaining their ethnicity through religion lies in their practice of ethnic culture through religion at home. As noted above, Indian Hindu immigrants engage in many religious rituals, such as celebrating several holidays with traditional Indian food every year, eating vegetarian food, and fasting on many religious days, that can be considered reproductions of Indian cultural traditions. By sharp contrast, Korean Protestant immigrants' religious practices at home, although extensive in their religious terms, do not contribute to the retention of Korean cultural traditions. As already indicated, since Hinduism is a religion indigenous to India, Hindu rituals are closely related to the holidays, food, music, and other elements of Indian folk culture. But Protestantism has such a short history in Korea that the religious rituals have no connection with comparable elements of Korean folk culture.

Furthermore, the radical difference between Indian Hindu and Korean Protestant immigrants in the maintenance of ethnicity through religious practices at home is partly due to the differences in the style of worship particular to the two religions. Different forms of Hinduism have developed gradually in Indian states in a natural way over centuries by incorporating local cultural traditions. Thus, observing religious holidays and performing ceremonies on auspicious family occasions with *puja*, traditional food, and flowers is central—more important than reading and interpreting sacred texts—to practicing Hinduism. Given this, it is quite natural that most Indian Hindu respondents reported practicing these rituals at home. But Protestantism puts far more emphasis on reading the Bible and listening to the pastor's sermons than on practicing informal rituals at home. Regardless of whether it would help to maintain Korean cultural traditions or not, Korean Protestants, like other Protestants, do not practice religious rituals much at home.

Conclusion

All religious immigrant/ethnic groups use both mechanisms—participation in a congregation and practice of religious rituals at home—to preserve their ethnicity to some extent. But, because of different styles of worship and the different levels of association between religion and culture, some groups depend upon one mechanism to a far greater extent than the other. Accordingly, in examining the two ways in which immigrant or ethnic groups preserve ethnicity through religion, it is helpful to compare two groups that are distinctive in using the two mechanisms.

Indian Hindu and Korean Protestant immigrants present two such extreme cases. Korean Protestant immigrants are known to be most active in participation in congregations, but they practice a religion that was not indigenous to Korean society. Thus, they maintain Korean ethnicity primarily by increasing their fellowship and social interactions, and by practicing Korean culture through their active participation in an ethnic congregation. Indian Hindu immigrants participate in a religious organization much less frequently than Korean Protestant immigrants because Hinduism is not a congregation-oriented religion. But their moderate participation in a Hindu temple contributes to their ethnic preservation as much as Korean Protestant immigrants' active participation in a church because the architecture of the temple and the religious faith and rituals practiced there symbolize Indian culture and identity. Moreover, Indian Hindus perform religious rituals at home that are deeply embedded in Indian cultural traditions while Korean Protestants rarely practice religious rituals related to Korean folk culture. This research has shown not merely that Korean Protestant and Indian Hindu immigrants use religion for ethnic preservation in fundamentally different ways, but also that Indian Hindu immigrants have advantages over Korean Protestant immigrants in maintaining their ethnicity through religion because their religious faith and rituals are closely related to Indian culture and identity.

Theoretical discussions of the ethnicity function of religion are based on the earlier congregation-oriented Judeo-Christian groups. As a result, researchers have emphasized the role of immigrant and ethnic congregations in the preservation of ethnicity for immigrant and ethnic groups. While the other important mechanism for maintaining ethnicity has been recognized, it has not been fully examined. Yet, even some non-Protestant white ethnic groups at the turn of the twentieth century, such as the Irish and Jews, may have preserved their ethnic culture and identity through religion mainly because their religious rituals are inseparably tied to their cultural traditions. For example, Rosh Hashana and Yom Kippur, the two major Jewish religious holidays, have become Jewish ethnic holidays, while St. Patrick's Day, a national holiday in Ireland, has turned into an ethnic holiday for Irish Americans.

Since religious rituals are more often practiced in family and community settings than in congregations, the exclusive focus of earlier studies on congregations has not captured the effects of religious rituals practiced outside the congregation on ethnic retention. By combining personal interviews with Indian Hindu and Korean Protestant immigrants conducted in non-congregational settings with ethnographic research on two selected religious institutions, this study has captured the effects of religious practices at home and in religious institutions among Indian Hindu and Korean Protestant immigrants. It also demonstrates the methodological advantages of a combination of ethnographic research on congregations with personal interviews, especially for non-Judeo-Christian groups.

Notes

1. In 1962, Protestants composed only 2.8 percent of the population in South Korea (Park and Cho 1995:119).

2. According to 2000 U.S. Census data, 72 percent of Korean and 64 percent of Indian Americans are settled in the Borough of Queens.

3. It was natural to select a Presbyterian church because Presbyterian churches comprise more than half of all Korean immigrant churches in the United States (Min 1992). As a result of American Presbyterian missionary activities in Korea beginning at the end of the nineteenth century, about 55 percent of churches in both South Korea and the United States are Presbyterian.

4. As a result, the Korean interviewees consisted of equal numbers of men and women, while the Indian interviewees consisted of thirty-two men and twenty-seven women. Seventy-one percent of Indian and 66 percent of the Korean interviewees had completed four years of college.

5. These are separate from the Missionary Committee that specializes in overseas missionary activities. Thus, all church members belong to a missionary group, although only a small proportion of its members regularly participate in missionary activities.

6. By contrast, the physical characteristics of the Queens Korean church and other Korean immigrant churches never reflect a Korean architectural design. Most Korean immigrant churches rent space from a white American church or share a church with white American Christians. Many small Korean immigrant congregations use private homes or commercial buildings for their services. Moreover, even those large Korean churches that have their own buildings cannot boast that these physical structures are culturally unique because the church buildings in both South Korea and the Korean community in the United States generally follow the Western (Gothic) style of architecture.

7. The temple's annual calendar that includes information about daily and hourly religious activities lists addresses and phone numbers of several hotels in the Flushing area for Hindu visitors from other states.

8. Indian Hindus cremate bodies when people die. In the United States, Hindus priests usually perform funerals at crematoria.

9. According to a Hindu priest, when second-generation Indians marry white American partners, the majority of them have two wedding ceremonies, one following the Hindu ritual and the other following the other ritual. Even when they perform the Hindu wedding, a Hindu priest more often presides over the wedding in a hotel than at a temple.

10. In fact, respondents in this study attend church a little more frequently than Korean immigrant samples in other studies, which suggests that they may be a little more religious than the average. Eighty-five percent of the respondents to the 1997-1998 telephone survey of Korean immigrants in Queens attended a Korean church at least once a month (Min 2000), while 78 percent of the Korean respondents to the 1997 racial and ethnic panel study regularly attended the Sunday service (Kim and Kim 2001:82).

11. The 1997 racial and ethnic panel study by the Research Center of the Presbyterian Church (USA) revealed that Korean Presbyterians devoted more time and donations to their own church than other Presbyterian groups, but that they devoted less for non-church community activities (Kim and Kim 2001:83).

12. This finding from the personal interviews is similar to that of the 1997-1998 telephone survey of Indian immigrants in Queens (22% participated once a week or more often) (Min 2000).

13. In the 1997 racial and ethnic panel survey, 67 percent of the Korean Presbyterian sample regarded "attending church regularly" as an essential quality of a good Christian life. Much lower proportions of Latino, African American, and white Presbyterian samples considered regular participation in a congregation as essential to a good Christian life. See Kim and Kim 2000:82.

14. Ancestor worship is the ritual of family members and relatives gathering and praying before the household altar where ancestral tablets and food offerings are placed on traditional Korean holidays and on the days before ancestors died. Considered probably the most important Confucian value in commemorating deceased ancestors, it is still widely practiced in South Korea. As Roman Catholicism has allowed local people to practice the religion without giving up their local culture, Korean Catholics have preserved the practice of ancestor worship. Korean Protestants have stopped the practice, but instead hold memorial services in church in memory of their ancestors.

References

Abramson, Harold J. 1973. *Ethnic Diversity in a Catholic America*. New York: John Wiley.

Baker, Donald. 1997. "Christianity." In *An Introduction to Korean Culture*, ed. John H. Koo and Andrew C. Nahm. Elizabeth, NJ: Hollym.

Bankston, Carl, III, and Min Zhou. 1995. "Religious Participation, Ethnic Identification, and Adaptation of Vietnamese Adolescents in an Immigrant Community." *Sociological Quarterly* 36:523-534.

Brennan, Patrick J. 1990. *Re-Imagining the Parish: Base Communities, Adulthood, and Family Consciousness*. New York: Crossroad.

Brown, Karen McCarthy. 1991. *Mama Lola: A Vodou Priestess in Brooklyn*. Berkeley: University of California Press.

Dolan, Jay. 1975. *The Immigrant Church: New York's Irish and German Catholics, 1815-1865.* Baltimore: Johns Hopkins University Press.

Du Bois, W. E. B. 1967. *The Philadelphia Negro.* New York: Schoken Books.

Ebaugh, Helen Rose, and Janet Saltzman Chafetz. 2000. *Religion and the New Immigrants: Continuities and Adaptations in Immigrant Congregations.* Walnut Creek, CA: AltaMira Press.

Fenton, John. 1988. *Transplanting Religious Traditions: Asian Indians in America.* New York: Frager.

Gordon, Milton. 1964. *Assimilation in American Life: The Role of Race, Religion, and National Origin.* New York: Oxford University Press.

Greeley, Andrew. 1972. *The Denominational Society: A Sociological Approach to Religion in America.* Grenview, IL: Scott Forseman.

Hurh, Won Moo, and Kwang Chung Kim. 1984. *Korean Immigrants in America: A Structural Analysis of Ethnic Confinement and Adhesive Adaptation.* Rutherford, NJ: Fairleigh Dickinson University Press.

———. 1990. "Religious Participation of Korean Immigrants in the United States." *Journal for the Scientific Study of Religion* 29:19-34.

Kim, Illsoo. 1981. *New Urban Immigrants: The Korean Community in New York.* Princeton, NJ: Princeton University Press.

Kim, Kwang Chung, and Shin Kim. 2001. "The Ethnic Role of Korean Immigrant Churches in the U.S." In *Korean Americans and Their Religions,* ed. Ho-Youn Kwon, Kwang Chung Kim, and Stephen Warner. University Park, PA: Penn State University Press.

Kurien, Prema. 1998. "Becoming American by Becoming Hindu: Indian Americans Take Their Place at the Multicultural Table." In *Gatherings in Diaspora: Religious Communities and the New Immigration,* ed. Stephen Warner and Judith Wittner. Philadelphia, PA: Temple University Press.

———. 2002. "'We Are Better Hindus Here': Religion and Ethnicity among Indian Americans." In *Religions in Asian America: Building Faith Communities,* ed. Pyong Gap Min and Jung Ha Kim. Walnut Creek, CA: AltaMira Press.

Kwon, Victoria Hyunchu, Helen Rose Ebaugh, and Jackqline Hagan. 1997. "The Structure and Functions of Cell Group Ministry in a Korean Christian Church." *Journal for the Scientific Study of Religion* 36:247-256.

Lin, Irene. 1996. "Journey to the Far West: Chinese Buddhism in America." *Amerasia Journal* 22:106-132.

Min, Pyong Gap. 1991. "Cultural and Economic Boundaries of Korean Ethnicity: A Comparative Analysis." *Ethnic and Racial Studies* 14:225-241.

———. 1992. "The Structure and Social Functions of Korean Immigrant Churches in the United States." *International Migration Review* 27:1370-1394.

———. 2000. "Immigrants' Religion and Ethnicity: A Comparison of Indian Hindu and Korean Christian Immigrants in New York." *Bulletin of the Royal Institute of Interfaith Studies* 2:121-140.

Orsi, Robert Anthony. 1996. *Thank You, St. Jude: Women's Devotion to the Patron Saint of Hopeless Causes.* New Haven, CT: Yale University Press.

Ostergren, Robert. 1981. "The Immigrant Church as a Symbol of the Ethnic Community and Place in the Upper Midwest." *Great Plains Quarterly* 1:225-238.

Park, In-Sook, and Cho, Lee-Jay. 1995. "Confucianism and the Korean Family." *Journal of Comparative Family Studies* 26:117-134.

Reitz, Jeffrey. 1980. *The Survival of Ethnic Groups.* Toronto: McGraw Hill.

Rosenberg, S. 1985. *The New Jewish Identity in America.* New York: Hippocrene Books.

Stepick, Alex. 1998. *Pride against Prejudice: Haitians in the United States.* Boston: Allyn and Bacon.

Stevens-Arroyo, Anthony M., and Ana Maria Diaz-Stevens, eds. 1994. *An Enduring Frame: Studies on Latino Popular Religiosity.* Vol. 1. New York: Bildner Center for Western Hemisphere Studies.

Tomasi, S. M., and M. H. Engel. 1971. *The Italian Experience in the United States.* Staten Island, NY: Center for Migration Studies.

Warner, Stephen. 1994. "The Place of the Congregation in the American Religious Configuration." In *American Congregations: New Perspectives in The Study of Congregations,* vol. 2, ed. James Wind and James Lewis. Chicago: University of Chicago Press.

———. 1998. "Immigration and Religious Communities in the United States." In *Gatherings in Diaspora: Religious Communities and the New Immigration,* ed. R. Stephen Warner and Judith Wittner. Philadelphia: Temple University Press.

Warner, Stephen, and Judith Wittner, eds. 1998. *Gatherings in Diaspora: Religious Communities and the New Immigration,* ed. R. Stephen Warner and Judith Wittner. Philadelphia: Temple University Press.

Warner, W. L., and Leo Srole. 1945. *The Social System of American Ethnic Groups.* New Haven, CT: Yale University Press.

Wellmeier, Nancy J. 1998. "Santa Eulalia's People in Exile: Maya Religion, Culture, and Identity in Los Angeles." In *Gatherings in Diaspora: Religious Communities and the New Immigration,* ed. R. Stephen Warner and Judith G. Wittner. Philadelphia: Temple University Press.

Williams, Raymond Brady. 1988. *Religions of Immigrants from India and Pakistan: New Threads in the American Tapestry.* New York: Cambridge University Press.

Yinger, J. Milton. 1994. *Ethnicity: Source of Strength? Source of Conflict?* Albany: State University of New York Press.

7

Changing Religious Practices among Cambodian Immigrants in Long Beach and Seattle

Thomas J. Douglas

Introduction

K hmer Buddhism is traditionally viewed as a syncretic religion, absorbing, modifying, and incorporating pre-Buddhist Cambodian beliefs and practices such as Brahminism, the Vaishnavite cult of kings, Shaivite worship, and folk magic.[1] Yet Khmer Buddhism also remained resistant to the influences of both Islam[2] and Christianity. Despite being ruled as a French Protectorate from 1863 to 1954, Buddhist Khmer were very resistant to European attempts to convert them as part of the French "civilizing" mission.[3] A large percentage of the neighboring Vietnamese did convert to Catholicism under French tutelage, but Cambodian resistance to Christian mission activities continued in Cambodia's post-colonial period up to the notorious Pol Pot period from 1975 to 1979, the time of the "Killing Fields."

During the post-Pol Pot crisis, when hundreds of thousands of Cambodians fled into refugee camps along the Thai-Cambodian border, Christian relief agents in the camps found many refugees willing to engage in Christian prayer groups, Bible studies, worship services, and baptisms. Critics of these new converts claimed that the neophytes were simply "rice-bowl Christians," refugees who hoped to gain greater access to the social services and immigration assistance offered by Christian aid organizations. Yet many of these converts continue to engage in Christian practices today, two decades after their initial exposure to Christian religious beliefs and practices. Furthermore, after immigration to the U.S., many Cambodian refugee parents have permitted their children to become involved in Christian organizations and churches, even though the parents themselves are not

123

converts to Christianity.

In Aihwa Ong's recent work, *Buddha is Hiding*, she demonstrates persuasively that Christianity is part of the systematic reconfiguring of Cambodian immigrant subjectivity in the U.S. (Ong 2003). She argues that Christianizing immigrants is a major way of disciplining Cambodians to become "good American citizens," teaching them to adopt American standards of morality and work ethics, to replace "Asian" patriarchy with a more Westernized and egalitarian style of child rearing. Yet, Ong's Oakland Bay-area informants are largely cut off from traditional Khmer Buddhist practices, other than those they can continue in the privacy of their homes. Her inner-city subjects are unlikely to attend traditional Cambodian religious events since, at the time of her study, the nearest Cambodian temple or *wat* was located in Stockton, California, at least an hour's drive away.

At both of my research sites, Long Beach, California, and the Seattle-Tacoma area of Washington,[4] the relationships involving Cambodian immigrants, Christianity, and Buddhism are more complex than those that Ong describes. At both sites, several Khmer Buddhist wats have been in operation for many years, and since the late 1980s Buddhist community organizations, monks from the *sangha* (Buddhist monastic order), and lay leaders or *achaas* have been in place. Despite the fact that large numbers of Cambodian immigrants have converted to Christianity, a powerful interest in building traditional Khmer religious institutions remains in these new Cambodian immigrant communities.

In both Long Beach and Seattle, Cambodian Christian institutions thrive alongside the Buddhist ones. The impoverished districts in which Cambodians live at both sites have numerous Khmer Christian organizations, ones I initially assumed to be in competition with Buddhist beliefs and practices. I soon learned that competition was an inappropriate way to conceive of the situation. Instead, Buddhism and Christianity both contributed to dialogues about morality, gender, and power and prestige; the immigrants' access to social services helped structure these dialogues. Considering Christianity and Buddhism to be complementary, most of my informants were engaged in both Christian and Buddhist practices. Cambodian immigrants claimed that Buddhist and Christian philosophies, moralities, and subjectivities were not at odds, and they maintained this in the face of pressures from Christian leaders who asserted that a synthesis between the two religions was at best unlikely and at worst an anathema.

Such dialogues among religions can be seen as a consequence of migration and globalization. In today's postmodern, global context the Third World is imploding into the first (Rosaldo 1988:85). Or, putting it another way, there is no longer a simple division between core and peripheral countries; the periphery can be viewed as colonizing the core itself (Sassen-Koob 1984). Michael Kearney noted the arrival of Southeast Asian refugees in the U.S. after the Vietnam War as an example of this type of global implosion (Kearney 1995:554). Thus, Cambodian identity is being reconfigured and re-imagined in the context of the Cambodian refugee community settings in the U.S.

Cambodian refugee identity is bound up with the religious reconfigurations occurring in the refugee communities. These feature close relationships with

Christianity and Christian institutions, complex and sometimes ambivalent relationships with Buddhist monks, and attempts to relate a new religious life to urban post-industrial settings. The complex and apparently contradictory religious affiliations and practices of Cambodian immigrants speak to their efforts to create new meanings in the context of their experience as refugees and their insertion into a particular form of American capitalism at the turn of the millennium.

The Socio-Historical Background of Cambodian Immigrant Communities

May Ebihara, the only American anthropologist to work in Cambodia prior to Pol Pot's infamous regime, had written that "To be Khmer (Cambodian) is to be Buddhist" (Ebihara 1971). Yet, at the Long Beach center where I worked I found Cambodians dedicated to their community who did not, at least at first glance, support Ebihara's claim. Many Khmer staff members said that they were Christians now or had been practicing Christians in the past. This Cambodian agency was devoted to preserving Cambodian culture and identity among Cambodian immigrants, and yet most of the staff had significant links with Christian groups. However, I soon realized that religion and religious identity played multi-faceted roles. While I agree with Ong that Christianity plays a powerful role as a Western hegemonic disciplinary tool in Cambodian immigrant communities (Ong 2003:195-228), Buddhism clearly also plays a powerful role in the communities I studied. Buddhism sometimes subverts, sometimes complements, and sometimes appropriates Christian values, practices, and subjectivities.

After surveying briefly the events that produced the Cambodian refugee communities in the U.S., I survey, also briefly, traditional Cambodian religious beliefs and practices. Then I present ethnographic data about refugee Cambodian wats in Long Beach and Seattle and, through descriptions of two community events revolving around Cambodian religious traditions, I illustrate the interweavings of Buddhism and Christianity. Finally, I turn to interviews with Cambodian immigrants about their religious experiences, interviews that reveal the significant and changing place of religion in their lives. The immigrants all invoked key words associated with Western subjectivity: *choice, freedom, self-identity*, and *personal responsibility*, reflecting not only their evolving religious beliefs but their induction into American society as refugees.

Before looking at the two sites of my research, it is first necessary to understand the socio-political background that contributed to the formation of the Cambodian refugee communities. In 1975, the U.S. forces left South Vietnam, contributing to the collapse of the U.S.-supported Cambodian government and the victory of the communist Khmer Rouge forces.[5] Taking over in the spring of 1975, the Khmer Rouge began systematic destruction of all those associated with the old regime. People with some education, people who had worked for the former government, or people who simply wore glasses were killed, even secretaries and other holders of minor governmental positions. Not even Buddhist monks were spared, and, as we shall see, Buddhism suffered in many ways. Perhaps two million Cambodians died in the holocaust (Welaratna 1993:1).

The great outpouring of Cambodian refugees, many of whom ended up in the U.S., began in January 1979, when Vietnamese invaders overthrew the Khmer Rouge. The long-standing animosity between the Cambodian and Vietnamese governments produced widespread fear, and hundreds of thousands of Cambodians sought refuge in Thailand.[6] As the new Vietnamese-controlled "People's Republic of Kampuchea" tried to restore order, many refugees escaped to the U.S. Prior to 1980, there were only about 14,000 Cambodians in the U.S. Between 1980 and 1990, 103,796 documented Cambodian refugees arrived; according to the 1990 U.S. Census, 147,411 Cambodian refugees lived in the United States (Shinagawa 1996:103). California was home to almost half of these, with some 68,190 Cambodians.

The largest concentration of Cambodians outside of Cambodia is in Long Beach, my first research site, which had an estimated 30,000 to 50,000 Cambodian residents in the 1990s (Bunte and Joseph 1992; Lee 1996:211; Shaw 1989:16). In Long Beach, Cambodians are heavily concentrated in the area known as the Anaheim Corridor, one of the poorest sections of the city and home to African Americans and Latinos before the arrival of Cambodians (Shaw 1989:16; Riposa 1995). The low rents were one of the reasons Cambodians settled there. In 2002, a two-bedroom apartment could be rented for about $400 a month. Some Cambodian college exchange students had settled in Long Beach in the 1960s, attracting the first wave of Cambodian refugees being processed at Camp Pendleton (Lew and Sugiyama 1995:4). California's mild weather, allowing people to plant bananas, sugar cane, and fruit trees in the tiny yards of their apartment complexes, was another reason for the choice of Long Beach.

Those immigrants from the first wave, called "The '75 People" by the refugees who came later, and the Cambodian organizations the first wave immigrants established attracted later Cambodian arrivals. About one-half of the refugees in Long Beach had originally been placed outside of California (Selden 1989:A-12), but Long Beach became a secondary migration destination as word of the community there spread. Today, several key Cambodian non-profit agencies operate in Long Beach, the two most prominent being the United Cambodian Community (UCC) and the Cambodian Association of America (CAA). At least five Cambodian Buddhist wats (three of them relatively small "house" temples) and numerous Cambodian Christian churches and fellowship groups are also located in Long Beach. Finally, there is the Cambodian Business Association (CBA), its many members with businesses located in the Cambodian business district centered on Anaheim Street.

Seattle, Washington, my second research site, has a much smaller Cambodian community, with an estimated 5,000 Cambodian immigrants and their families. The Office of Refugee Resettlement had designated the Puget Sound area as a Southeast Asian immigration destination point, and many Khmer immigrants were initially placed there.[7] The Khmer Guided Placement Project (KGPP) was created by the

Office of Refugee Resettlement (ORR) in 1980 to place "free cases," or Cambodian refugees without sponsoring relatives, in clusters of 300 to 1,000 people in twelve different project sites, diverting them from "impacted" areas like Long Beach, California. These new Cambodian communities were to become self-sufficient and reduce secondary migration to the impacted areas (Bruce 1982:iii; Ratliff 1995:4).

Seattle and Long Beach are similar in many ways. Like Long Beach, Seattle has a large military-industrial complex, a harbor with good anchorage facilities, and an aviation industry. In both sites, a flexible labor supply was needed to accommodate the changing demands of the harbor and aerospace industries, and some Cambodian refugees found low-skilled, relatively low-paid employment connected to these industrial complexes.[8] Seattle's weather is also milder than that of many other locations in the Pacific Northwest.

There are some organizational connections between the two sites. The Cambodian Association of America (CAA) headquartered in Long Beach was called in to assist the KGPP and to provide satellite CAA entities in each of the new cluster communities, including Seattle (Bruce 1982:11-14). Although the number of Cambodian immigrants in the Seattle area has declined as immigrants have moved on (some to Long Beach), Cambodian community leaders maintain that the Seattle-Tacoma area is currently the third-largest settlement of Cambodians in the U.S., and I observed some Cambodians still immigrating there.

In Seattle, too, the Cambodians have settled in the poorer sections of the city, and social service agencies, wats, and businesses serving Cambodians are located there. In West Seattle, the Park Lake public assistance housing complex, a former military base, is home to many low- income Cambodians as well as other impoverished groups, and other Cambodian families are clustered in the adjacent White Center area, a relatively low-income district nearby. Another low-income area on the east side of Seattle, Rainier Valley, has numerous Cambodian families. Two Cambodian non-profit agencies and other community service organizations assist the residents of these areas. There are two Cambodian wats in Seattle, one serving Cambodians in the Rainier Valley and the other near the White Center area of West Seattle, and there are at least ten more wats in the greater Seattle-Tacoma area. The White Center and Rainier Valley areas are home to many Cambodian businesses.

Traditional Cambodian Religious Practices

Religious beliefs and practices in the Long Beach and Seattle Cambodian communities interweave Khmer Buddhism brought from Cambodia with Christianity learned in the refugee camps and the new sites. To assess the changes in the immigrants' religious lives, we need to review aspects of traditional religions in Cambodia. Theravada or Hinayana Buddhism, the dominant religion of Cambodia (Bagdasar 1993:57; Ebihara 1985:131; McLellan 1999:133; Numrich 1996:xvi; Smith-Hefner 1999:21), is mixed with spirit worship, Brahminism, and other pre-state forms of Khmer worship (Bagdasar 1993:58; Ebihara 1971:364, McLellan 1999:148; Needham 1996:86; Welaratna 1989:73-75). Shamans known as *Khmer kru*[9] use magic rituals and worship ancestral spirits, and these features are regularly combined in Cambodian religious practice with Theravada Buddhist ritual. In Cambodia, Theravada Buddhism became closely allied with the royal state, supporting hierarchal Khmer social distinctions between royalty, *sangha* (monastic orders), and peasants (Bagdasar 1993:67-68).

Theravada Buddhism, the oldest of the major Buddhist traditions, is also called "the Way of the Elders." It emphasizes earning merit in this life in order to influence one's karmic destiny in the next incarnation. In the Cambodian tradition, the king was considered the rightful Khmer ruler because he had acquired exceptional merit in his previous life. Buddhist wats, staffed by monks, dotted the Cambodian landscape, and all young Cambodian men were expected to spend time as monks in the local wats, where they received both religious and temporal training before marriage. The role of the laity is to produce merit through proper behavior or dharma, whereas the role of the monks is to channel and transfer merit to those, both living and dead, who need more merit in order to improve their karma (McLellan 1999:14).

The concept of merit is central to Cambodian Buddhist beliefs (Ebihara 1974:313; Welaratna 1989:72-73) and is invoked to explain class and gender differences. The elderly often spend a great deal of time in the temples, earning merit to improve their status in their next life. Good works produce *bon* (merit) and bad works produce *bap* (evil or sin). Authority and social power are linked to morality, to proper moral behavior in a previous life. According to this philosophy, those with authority, like the Khmer aristocratic classes, must have accumulated a lot of bon in past lives to have achieved their current status.(Bagdasar 1993:67-68). Cambodian Buddhists are enjoined to avoid five things: lying, immoral sexual behavior, stealing, killing (save for insects, fish, and small animals), and alcohol. Monks and others seeking merit may apply more stringent rules than these to their everyday lives (Hopkins 1996:88).

Any member of the ruling class, especially the king, must have been very deserving in past lives to earn his position in this life. Furthermore, because men are viewed as moral superiors to and authorities over women, according to this principle men must have earned more merit than women in their previous incarnations. Women's behavior is believed to reflect bon or bap onto their male kin, enhancing or detracting from the men's reputations.

Bon and bap can also be accumulated by groups of people, such as entire families or communities. Merit can be passed on to others, by women to men and by the living to the dead, the latter especially by ritual acts performed by monks to assist deceased souls. Surviving family members can also engage in activities that will accumulate merit, such as fasting or chanting, and monks can send this merit to the deceased to help them in the afterlife. The influence of bad deeds can be passed on as well.[10]

Buddhism in Cambodia suffered under the Khmer Rouge. During Pol Pot's years in power (1975-1979), the practice of Buddhism was forbidden. Sacred sites were desecrated and made into places of imprisonment and torture (Welaratna 1989:78-80). In Theravada Buddhism, the state of one's mind ought to be pure when one dies in order to facilitate re-incarnation—an unsettled mind at the time of death can lead to years of wandering as a lost soul. Converting a wat, symbol of tranquility and harmony, into a scene of violence was a double sacrilege, against Buddhism and against the souls of those murdered there. Buddhist temples became sites where souls were condemned to wander in dark and troubled states, where no rituals could be performed to redeem them. Cambodians feared dying during the Khmer Rouge reign of terror. The dead could not die as they should and could not be treated by the living as they should; their souls wandered the earth as ghosts rather than being reborn (Welaratna 1989:309-310). One monk told me that during this time he could not risk chanting or engaging in any display of piety because he would have been immediately killed.

Buddhism was slowly rebuilt in Cambodia in the years that followed the Pol Pot regime. During the decade-long Vietnamese occupation (1979-1989), the state permitted Khmer Buddhist wats to be reopened and built, and Buddhism was officially declared the state religion of Cambodia (Chandler 2000:236). By the time the new Cambodian constitutional monarchy was instituted in 1993, Buddhism was fully reinvigorated in the Khmer homeland.

In overseas refugee communities, too, Cambodian Buddhism was being reconstituted. In both Long Beach and Seattle, Khmer wats were established in the immigrant communities. These wats were being built at approximately the same time that temples were reopening in Cambodia. This might be seen, then, as a reflection of what was happening in the homeland. However, unlike those Cambodians who stayed in the mother country, Khmer refugees formed new and often continuing relationships with Christian organizations through their experiences in the refugee camps, relationships that did not end with the opening of Buddhist wats in the immigrant communities. New Cambodian churches and congregations were also being established and recruiting members assertively.[11]

In both Long Beach and Seattle, the establishment of wats and the importation of monks or *Bhikku* from Cambodia reflected class and political differences in the refugee communities to some extent. In the Long Beach area, the large wat on Willow Street was associated with some of the earliest arriving Cambodian immigrants, many of whom had been powerful in Cambodia before the rule of Pol Pot. The smaller Twentieth Street Long Beach temple was associated with the later arriving, less economically successful Cambodian immigrants, people often of rural origin and with limited if any formal education. The two Long Beach wats competed for followers and for status in the community, and it was not unusual to hear rumors about corruption in a wat or unscrupulous behavior by its monks.[12]

The two wats in Seattle and the others in the greater Seattle-Tacoma area seemed less rivalrous than those in Long Beach, perhaps reflecting the lack of an earlier and wealthier group of immigrants. The monks throughout the Puget Sound area often visited each other, even spending the nights at each other's wats. The Seattle wats also drew monks from outside of the area, including regular visitors from Southern California, New England, Laos, and Australia. The wat near the

White Center district, *Wat Khemarak Pothiram,* was often referred to simply as the "New Temple" (the Rainier Valley wat in Eastern Seattle had been built first and was known as the "Old Temple"). The New Temple maintained strong ties with a nearby non-profit Cambodian agency, where I worked as a volunteer and observed that the monks were on close terms with its executive director.[13]

Like some other wats in Tacoma and Long Beach, Seattle's New Temple had once been a large single family home. Its lawn now featured an outdoor shrine used for community events, and the home's conversion into a religious center provided upstairs sleeping rooms for monks, an internal worship area with a large shrine, a kitchen, and downstairs sleeping rooms for women known as *duan chee.* These elderly women, often widows, helped care for the temple and its monks, but they were not nuns.[14] Monks were generally recruited from the rural areas of Cambodia where they were trained.[15] Monks from the Cambodian countryside were regarded as more pure and authentic than monks trained in urban settings; the latter are considered more likely to have given in to avarice or the temptations of the flesh.[16] Besides the monks and the *duan chee,* senior laymen known as *achaas* also served in the wat. *Achaas* or lay leaders acted as liaisons between the monks and the secular world. This important role was both traditional, because monks are supposed to limit their engagement with the world beyond the wat, and a result of migration, since most monks have come recently to the U.S.

Achaas, although laymen, can and do serve as Buddhist ritual specialists. To gain their special ritual knowledge, they must have served as monks in the past.[17] Though ritual chants are available in written form, most achaas learned the appropriate chants and rituals through oral repetition and observation of other achaas. The achaas were usually important members of the local lay Cambodian Buddhist Association, and they presided over small religious ceremonies, such as death anniversaries, and participated with monks in larger ceremonies for major religious holidays, funerals, and weddings. Elderly people often seek the help of achaas to increase their merit for their next life. The achaas are paid for their ritual services. The achaas in Seattle had tremendous influence within the Cambodian community and they could make or break a community member's reputation; they also exercised influence regarding the reputations of agencies serving the community.[18] At the West Seattle temple, the achaas as well as the monks were on good terms with the young executive director of the nearby non-profit Khmer agency.

The temples in Seattle and Long Beach were sponsored and maintained by local Buddhist community organizations, on whose boards many achaas held powerful positions. They not only served in the wats but could strongly influence the goals and development of the wats, along with the other laymen serving as board members. According to the charters of the sponsoring Cambodian Buddhist organizations in Long Beach and Seattle, monks were not permitted to serve as board members and had no voting power. These regulations, people told me, were new and arose in the U.S. context.[19] In Cambodia it is the monks, not the laity, who control the wats. One monk in Seattle had repeatedly urged the board members of his wat to grant voting powers to the monks, but they refused. This monk finally left Seattle and relocated to Pennsylvania, where the monks had the authority to direct their wats as they saw fit.

The Cambodian Buddhist lay organizations in Long Beach and Seattle raised money to build wats and then sponsored monks from Cambodia to staff them. Requests had to be formally submitted to the INS to sponsor Khmer monks to serve the Cambodian-American Buddhist communities. Thus, the Buddhist sponsoring bodies considered themselves patrons and the monks their clients, clients completely dependent on the sponsors for their migration and subsequent welfare.[20] If these monks had remained in Cambodia, they would have other institutional support from their own kin, from the state, and from other wats. But in the U.S. they are almost totally dependent on their wat boards. While patron-client relationships are a traditional part of Khmer culture (cf. Chandler 2000:105-106; Ong 2003:30,32), this situation is unique, clearly representing a changed relationship between monks and laity. Patrons are traditionally viewed as having moral authority over their clients, yet monks should be morally superior to lay people. This partial reversal of moral authority puts a strain on social relations between monks and laity within Khmer communities.

Monks had the mission of reintroducing Khmer Buddhist practices that had been "lost" from the Cambodian cultural repertoire, practices aggressively eliminated by the Khmer Rouge. Most Khmer refugees had not engaged in Buddhist practices for some years, and there had been no Buddhist organizations in the refugee camps, only Christian ones. When large numbers of Khmer arrived in the U.S. in the early 1980s, there were no wats in place, and Buddhist immigrants were limited to whatever domestic practices they could recreate easily. The children initially gained formal religious training exclusively from Christian groups. But the reintroduction of wats and the monastic order in some U.S. communities in the late 1980s changed this situation. Major Khmer Buddhist holidays could once again be celebrated with appropriate rituals, funerals and death anniversaries could be held with the proper blessings of monks. Sunday schools, an American institution, were organized to teach Khmer-American children about Buddhist dharma, and afterschool and summer classes were organized at wats to teach children Khmer language and literature.

Wats in California try to follow Cambodian traditions. The New Temple in Seattle had a well-known chief monk, Uch Seng,[21] and three other monks staying at it in 2000 (though more came in following years). Uch Seng explained that, ideally, a wat ought to have a chief monk and three "right-hand" monks and three "left-hand" monks, along with several achaas. Together, the monks and the achaas form the core staff of the wat. Because it was difficult and expensive to bring monks from Cambodia and monks were seldom recruited from Cambodian-American communities, this Seattle wat, like many others, suffered from a shortage of manpower. Any man may become a monk, but he must give up sexual relations to do so; thus a married man can become a monk, ideally only with the agreement of his wife. A man can also leave his monk's position at any time.[22]

Traditional Khmer Buddhist customs and commemorations were being observed in the American wats. At Seattle's New Temple, I witnessed monks undergoing the period of seclusion called Chol Vassa (the "Buddhist Lent" or the "Rains

Retreat"), scheduled in Cambodia during the three-month rainy season. Buddha's disciples once ventured out during the rainy season and damaged the newly planted rice paddies of the farmers, so the Buddha ordered all monks to stay in their temples for the months of July through September. Today, Khmer monks remain in the U.S. wats for learning and meditation during this period, and fasting is common. Chol Vassa is also the preferred initiation time for Khmer men to become monks, especially for those undertaking a temporary period of service.[23]

The end of the Chol Vassa usually overlaps with a major Khmer festival known as Prachum Ben (or Pchum Ben), an autumn commemoration of the dead that takes place in Cambodian wats and homes and traditionally lasts two weeks. However, because of time pressures in the U.S., this honoring of the dead (like all major Cambodian observances) was usually compressed into a two-day weekend. During Prachum Ben, families make offerings to the dead, visit the wats, and make gifts to the monks.

Prachum Ben feasts are also held in private homes to honor the dead, and one such event well illustrated the changing nature of Cambodian religious practices. Sponsored by a prominent member of the Seattle Cambodian community, one who gave lots of money to a local wat, the event was attended by several hundred guests. In the front yard of the sponsor's home were rows of empty chairs and tables where the monks, arriving later than most guests, would sit. Tarps and carpets were set up in the backyard and patio to shelter a temporary altar and the guests. An outdoor kitchen had been set up and Cambodian women prepared the food, drawing from large plastic vats of uncooked chicken and other meats, tubs of rice and pots of broth, and cartons of fruits and vegetables.

An elderly achaa oversaw the Prachum Ben commemoration, and the guests, after initially greeting the host and his family, went straight to the achaa and presented him with money. The achaa was dressed in the traditional white shirt and black pants that is customary for Khmer achaas. Taking the money, the achaa blessed it in Pali, then recorded the names of the givers and the amount donated; the money was to be shared between the achaa and his wat and its monks.

Near the achaa was a temporary outdoor shrine, incense burning and bundles of gifts wrapped in colored cellophane lying there for the monks. The gifts included coffee, sugar, toothbrushes, and other personal items, the standard package given to monks during Prachum Ben. Those donating the gifts are earning merit or good karma, and the monks would later chant and sprinkle blessings of rose water over them and the other guests. Though this event lasted all through the night and into the next day, most people came and visited for an hour or two before leaving. Only the achaa and the host were present for the entire event.

This privately hosted Prachum Ben was both a religious event and a social gathering, and the atmosphere was not somber. People ate and talked freely and children played with little supervision. Though participants were paying their respects to the deceased as well as to the Buddha, there was an air of celebration and not all attendees considered themselves Buddhists. Cambodian refugees, Khmer-American Buddhists and Christians alike, attended this and other such events.

Another Prachum Ben festival was sponsored by the Seattle non-profit

Cambodian agency where I was based. This event was scheduled for the afternoon of the last day of the Prachum Ben two-week period so that the monks would be free to attend. The biggest obstacle was finding a building large enough for the expected attendees. The executive director of the Cambodian agency finally rented a local Salvation Army gymnasium, persuading the reluctant pastor of the Salvation Army to allow a Buddhist event in his Christian facility. He was helped by the pastor's assistant, who, determined to maintain good relations with the Cambodian community, intervened to assure the pastor that this was really not a religious but a cultural festival.

The day before this religious or cultural festival, the agency's executive director, his wife, several children from the agency's after-school program, and I decorated the gymnasium by inflating balloons and putting up streamers. On the afternoon of the festival, an achaa, dressed in the usual white shirt and black pants, and four monks from the New Temple came to the Salvation Army gymnasium. A few hundred Cambodian-Americans were already there, along with the food and drink they had prepared for distribution. A large stage was erected under the basketball hoop at one end of the gym, on which the monks were seated on pillows before a small Buddhist altar with statue, incense, and candles. Carpets were laid on the floor for worshipers to kneel and chant. The agency's executive director invited everyone, both Christian and Buddhist, to come forward and participate. Many attendees did kneel and chant, but others simply sat in the folding chairs and waited for the religious part of the festival to be over. The achaa opened the chanting and the monks followed in turn, burning incense and sprinkling rosewater to bless the worshipers. After about thirty minutes of chanting, the monks ate and returned to the wat.

At Khmer religious events, no one is supposed to eat before the monks, but this tradition is changing. Women serve the monks first, and other guests start their meals only after the monks have finished eating. However, many people at this agency-sponsored Prachum Ben festival did not follow the rule and ate their noon meal before the monks arrived. Those who broke with tradition justified their behavior by pointing out that the monks arrived an hour later than expected and that the monks might not have shown up at all. Many of those who had eaten before the monks later felt embarrassed, feeling that they had lost face when the monks did arrive. One woman, the wife of a community leader, defensively said that she was hungry and "it was the monks' own fault that they were late," but her husband had refrained from eating until after the monks had come and had their meal.

At this agency-sponsored Prachum Ben event, the food was accompanied by live Cambodian music, singing, and dancing. First, Cambodian youth performed what they called "ethnic Cambodian dances." The girls wore sparkling pink veils revealing only the ovals of their faces, with pink tunics covering their bodies. The boys wore white shirts and loose white pants with wide blue and white plaid sashes tied around their waists. These dances were those of the minority Cambodian Muslim community known as the *Cham*. The dancers were not Muslims, the director told me, but the organizers wanted to represent Cambodian ethnic traditions as part of the celebration. After the Cham dances, a live band played traditional and contemporary Cambodian songs. Male and female Khmer singers entertained the crowd as people of all ages danced together, colored lights and a fog machine adding to the ambience. The Salvation Army gymnasium had become a Cambodian nightclub for the final evening of Prachum Ben.

Questions of Religion, Gender, and Moral Authority

Whether or not one should eat before the monks was part of an emerging and lively dialogue about the role of monks in Cambodian refugee communities. Monks are traditionally the repository of moral authority, yet I heard accusations that one wat or another had succumbed to corruption or that certain monks were not keeping their vows. Cambodians questioned the personal integrity of monks as well as the value of the entire monastic system. This concern over the sangha's morality was not limited to monks in the U.S., for informants often told stories about monks in Cambodia who were also failing to lead virtuous lives. Monks were said to be lazy, corrupt, or "no longer helping the community." Monks and their wats were said to be secretly growing rich. Monks were accused of changing their clothes and visiting brothels by night, in both Cambodia and the U.S., and some were accused of engaging in homosexual behavior. I heard frequent complaints that monks "just sit in the temple and don't work," complaints from both self-identifying Buddhist and Christian Cambodian immigrants; some of the accusers were leaders in their Cambodian-American communities who said that monks were no longer concerned about the common people.

Accusations about the morality of Buddhist monks referred back to the conspicuous lack of Buddhist aid in the refugee camps. Most Cambodian immigrants had spent months or even years in refugee camps in the 1980s before coming to the U.S., camps that were key sites for missionary as well as humanitarian activities by American and European Christian groups. Most immigrants had received assistance from one or more Christian groups and felt that Buddhism had failed them in the camps. One man had spent nearly ten years being moved between various refugee camps and, while pleased to receive aid from the Christians, had frequently wondered "where are the monks, where are the Buddhists?" Cambodians' closest Buddhist neighbors, the Thai, were ambivalent about Khmer refugees, and Khmer refugees were robbed, beaten, raped, and murdered by Thai camp guards.

After their introduction to Christianity in the refugee camps, many Cambodian immigrants continued to engage in Christian practices. In both Long Beach and Seattle, numerous Khmer Christian churches thrive in the hearts of Cambodian communities.[24] Cambodian churches can be Baptist, Lutheran, Methodist, Mormon, Nazarene, or other denominations, but those I attended could all be considered evangelical or fundamentalist. Religious services at these churches followed a similar format. An hour or so of "Sunday School" was followed by another hour or two of the main service. The Sunday Schools were actually designed for adults, and only occasionally did children have their own services; usually, children ran freely in and out of the church during services, receiving only rare expressions of disapproval from adults.

In the Khmer Christian churches, the gender patterns were very different from those in the Buddhist wats. Women outnumbered men in the churches by about three to one. While this is partly due to the fact that more Cambodian women than men survived the Khmer Rouge death squads, in the Buddhist wats the women only slightly outnumbered the men. Men were the designated pastors and elders, the leaders in the churches as in the wats, yet women were noticeably more active and contributed conspicuously to the church services. Women always sang hymns, in trios, quartets, or small choirs, and often a woman read a Bible passage to the congregation. In the Sunday School services, women were especially active, leading the congregation in prayers, singing, and question-and-answer sessions. In the formal worship service, women let the men lead except for the singing. At one Seattle evangelical church, I thought that this gender line had been crossed when a Khmer woman, the wife of a Caucasian missionary, provided Bible instruction to the entire congregation during the formal service. But her "talk," people said, was "only a Sunday School lesson," and a male member of the church gave the "real sermon."

Cambodian women were well aware of the fact that they had more public roles in Christian churches than in the wats. One Long Beach woman told me she enjoyed the relative freedom she found in Christian churches. She had become a youth leader at a Nazarene church and had even been sent out of state for formal leadership training. A Seattle woman told me that while living in a refugee camp as a teenage girl, she had been allowed to participate freely in Christian religious events, much more than her Buddhist upbringing had prepared her for, and she had also liked attending Christian camp services because she could meet and interact with members of the opposite sex there, something forbidden by her parents. Since immigrating, this woman has been heavily involved in a Seattle Cambodian-American church, participating in prayer, singing, and Bible study groups. Although most evangelical Christian churches grant official leadership positions only to men, many Khmer women have found that Christian churches offer them greater opportunities for religious participation than the Khmer Buddhist wats.

Khmer women participating in Christian churches did not necessarily abandon Buddhism. Many Cambodian immigrant women and men engage with both Buddhism and Christianity. Participation in one religion did not bar people from participating in another religion.[25] For many immigrant Khmer and their families, religious identity was clearly very fluid, even when, at first encounter, they self-identified as belonging to only one religion. One Cambodian man in his mid-thirties at a Tacoma Buddhist wat told me, "I [am] Christian like you, I believe in both."[26] He believed that Buddha and Jesus are the same, that both Buddhism and Christianity have the same moral system, "don't kill, don't steal, be honest, be respectful, and so on."

Other interviewees spoke similarly about their involvement with both Buddhism and Christianity. A teenager in Seattle suddenly started wearing a cross, although he had told me that his entire family was Buddhist. When asked about this, he said that his mother had recently given it to him, and his sister added that their mother sometimes went to a Christian church. In their family, they considered both Buddha and Jesus to be good. "Buddha and Jesus, it's the same thing," she said. Shortly afterward, the young man replaced the cross with a Buddhist pendant, again a gift from his mother and given on the occasion of the Prachum Ben festival. Another man, a Khmer photographer at a funeral ceremony in a Seattle wat, told me that he had become a Jehovah's Witness after his arrival in the U.S., but he thought that Buddhism also had many good things to offer. In fact, the photographer still attended events at the wat and engaged in Buddhist practices when not at the Kingdom Hall. The leaders of the Jehovah's Witnesses condemned multi-religious participation, but he himself believed that there was nothing wrong with it. To be a good person, he said, one did not have to limit oneself to only one religion.

Like the photographer, many Cambodians had undergone a Christian conversion either in the refugee camps or shortly after their arrival in the U.S. These conversions often took place while they were teenagers or young adults and were sometimes accompanied by a total disassociation from all things Buddhist. Such converts initially refused to go to the wat or to participate in the death anniversaries of relatives and ancestors, but after a number of years, the same individuals found that they were drawn back into traditional Khmer religious observances. In Long Beach, one woman had regularly attended services at three different Christian churches each Sunday before settling on one evangelical church where she trained to be a youth lay minister. As a young woman, she said, she had struggled to believe that only Christians would receive salvation, but she questioned why God would send Buddhists and other non-Christians to Hell if they were good people. She is still active in a Cambodian-American church but has rejected the belief that Christianity is the only path to salvation; she now attends Buddhist celebrations and observes death anniversaries with other family members.

Generational conflicts within families often resulted from children's attendance at Christian churches and youth groups, permitted and even encouraged by parents eager to help their children become American. One Long Beach Cambodian man spent many years serving as a lay minister in a local Christian church but became disillusioned by these generational conflicts. Often Cambodian children attending churches began insisting that their parents would go to Hell unless they converted. Such "Christian" children asserted that Buddhist religious beliefs were wrong and, in particular, "ancestor worship" was a sin. Parents who once feared that gangs or violence would destroy their families found their families being pulled apart by religious differences instead. Christianity, this man felt, was causing children to challenge the moral authority of their parents. For many Khmer parents, the realization that religion could turn their children against them was an unwelcome shock. They had agreed to let their children attend church because they thought it would reinforce morality and family values.

Christian churches did target Cambodian young people in both Long Beach and Seattle, offering economic and social opportunities otherwise unavailable to Cambodian immigrants such as educational support and field trips. The Cambodian youth pastor in Long Beach cited above stated that his church's motto was: *If you can't reach the old, then reach the young.* The church looked to Cambodian children as potential converts even when their parents were seen as a "lost cause." Cambodian young people "accepted" Jesus because they had no other options, the youth pastor said, and he criticized the local Buddhist wat for not providing the kinds of social support that was available in the Christian churches. He said, "We wanted to save the young people, but did we tear the family apart? We were not taking all the elements of their life into consideration. We were working in a tunnel." This man eventually disassociated himself from his church because of the generational conflicts and because he could not accept that people like his father, killed in Cambodia, and his mother, who practices Buddhism, would go to Hell. He still claims that Cambodian children who go to Christian churches will be more successful in American society and is ambivalent about the religious education and affiliation of his own two sons.

Khmer monks, unexposed to Christianity and confident about their own religion, did not criticize Christianity and frequently claimed there were many routes to salvation. Many stated that if a person lived a good life, it did not matter to what religion that person belonged (one monk did tell me cheerfully that Buddhism was the "express route"). The monks, like many other Cambodians, believed that both Christianity and Buddhism had positive things to offer, that the Buddha and Jesus had taught similar codes of morality. Monks told me that occasionally Cambodian funeral services were performed incorporating both Christian and Buddhist rites, with a Christian minister and Buddhist monks both attending and officiating.

Marriages across religious lines occurred and sometimes caused conflicts, but usually they served as another illustration of Cambodian notions of complementarity between Buddhism and Christianity. One woman had experienced great conflict with her family, attending Christian meetings in the refugee camp against her parents' will. She converted and threatened her family members with Hell unless they converted, but despite this strong stance, she eventually chose to marry a Buddhist. She married a Khmer immigrant with American citizenship, a move that facilitated her own acquisition of a green card. Her Buddhist husband is not bothered by the fact that she is a Christian and does not prevent her from attending regular church services. The couple has a school-aged son whom the mother has raised in the Christian church, and the wife and son pray daily for the husband's conversion. Another Cambodian woman, brought over as a bride for her American-raised husband and in the U.S. for only one year when I interviewed her, said that since coming to the U.S. she enjoyed going to both Buddhist wats and Christian churches; she wanted to experience it all. She considered it important to "see what is good about both," an attitude characteristic of most Cambodians discussing their religious choices in the U.S.

Migration, Religion, and the Economy

David Harvey, in his 1989 work *The Condition of Postmodernity*, posits a rise in fundamentalist religious activities as a result of the postmodern crisis and the economic pressures of globalization. The Cambodian refugees clearly do not fit that model. They are not rejecting an old religion in favor of a new one or becoming "fundamentalist" in their commitments to either Buddhism or Christianity. They are subject to new economic pressures and they are reconfiguring their religious beliefs and practices in the U.S.

Life is far from easy for Cambodian-Americans. This essay has focused on their religious life, but the refugee communities have not recovered from the devastations inflicted upon them in Cambodia and in the camps. In Los Angeles County, California, the United Way reported that Cambodians have the highest unemployment (65%) of any ethnic group (United Way of Los Angeles 1996), and in Seattle over 54 percent of Cambodian families live below the federal poverty level, the highest level reported for any group (Seattle Human Services Department Report June 25, 2001). Drugs, alcoholism, spouse abuse, youth gangs, violence, low literacy, depression, post-traumatic stress disorder, and gambling addictions all plague Cambodian-American communities.

Many Cambodians did make connections between their changing religious views and their insertion into a modern capitalist economy. Sometimes they spoke as though well-grounded in Durkheim and Weber,[27] speculating about their changing religious worlds and the relative values of Buddhism and Christianity to their working lives in the U.S. One man stated that Buddhism could not survive in America because in the U.S., a person had to be aggressive, and Buddhism taught passivity. He connected religion to the success or the lack of it among refugee children in American classrooms. Describing non-Christian Cambodian children, he said, "We don't raise hands (in the classroom). We don't chase after what we want." Christianity, in his view, did teach aggression, and he quoted Mark 16:15 from the Bible, "Go ye into all the world and preach the Gospel to every creature." Christianity, unlike Buddhism, instructs people to "go out into the world," and thus being Christian was an advantage in the American socio-economic context. He spoke favorably of the discipline of Christianity and likened it to the discipline required for success in a capitalist world (Foucault 1977; Rose 1990). Yet this man was unhappy with Christianity and did not want Cambodian American children to be "mono-religious." He strongly wanted them to grow up experiencing both Buddhism and Christianity, seeing what was good about both.

Cambodian immigrants are under explicit pressures to conform to a Westernized work ethic. Christian churches introduce many Cambodian youth to work, encouraging them to raise funds for summer camp by holding car washes or bake sales. At one Long Beach church, the predominantly white congregation with whom Cambodians shared the facilities was asked by the pastor to hire Cambodian church youth to do odd jobs in their homes so that the youth could do summer missionary work in Cambodia.[28] This contrasts with the Cambodian Buddhist model of giving young monk initiates rice bowls for the purpose of begging at this same stage in life.

Furthermore, the adoption of the capitalist work ethic leads to questioning of the purpose and value of wats and the monks. Negative or ambivalent views about the Cambodian monastic system could reflect the acceptance of a Westernized work ethic by Khmer immigrants. Cambodians in the U.S. do not witness the years of Buddhist discipline, the training of the monks they bring from the homeland; they see the monks here as the beneficiaries of their sponsors' support. These monks, as one Khmer immigrant put it, "just sit in the temple and eat." The work of the Buddhist monks is commonly devalued and the monks are characterized as greedy, lazy, and corrupt. Are monks a boon or a parasite on Cambodian communities? This is one of the questions with which Cambodian-Americans struggle as they interweave old and new religious beliefs and practices.

Conclusion

Cambodian-Americans fled a holocaust and years of hostile and repressive regimes in their homeland.[29] Arriving in the U.S. as refugees, most of them impoverished, they have little certainty in their lives. They are reconstituting Buddhism in their new settings and often mixing with it Christian beliefs and practices learned in the refugee camps and the new American sites of settlement. The ethnographic data shows Cambodian immigrants searching through religious traditions, as one informant put it, to "find what is good in both." Men, women, and children are experiencing constraints and opportunities as they explore both religions, and sometimes generational if not gender conflicts disrupt families and come to the attention of the refugee communities. Cambodian parents tend not to force their children into one religion, but, as exemplified by the Seattle mother who gave her son both a cross and a Buddhist pendant, encourage their children to explore the possibilities of the religions available to them. As one Cambodian father said, "Let [the children] choose their way."

Cambodians continue the tradition of hybridity and mixture characteristic of religious life in the homeland, but new Christian elements are being incorporated. Cambodian holidays and community events in the U.S. are never simply Buddhist activities. Christian and Buddhist Cambodians both attend these events, and dance from Cambodia's Muslim minority *Cham* community can be included as well. Some Christian churches in Long Beach and Seattle allow Cambodians to use their auditoriums to perform traditional Khmer classical dances, dances based on Hindu mythology. Cambodian Americans are making efforts to maintain Buddhism, but there is a consensus that strict boundaries between Christian and Buddhist beliefs and practices are not necessary, that Cambodian-American religious identities can draw on both traditions. Clearly, one cannot claim, for Cambodians in the U.S., that to be Khmer is to be Buddhist. Rather, to be a Cambodian in the U.S. is to be seeking and reconfiguring religious identities in a capricious and insecure world.

1. Khmer refers to ethnic Cambodians, who make up 94% of the population of Cambodia. The Cambodian immigrants to whom I spoke used the term "Brahminism" to refer to all pre-Buddhist Khmer practices, regardless of whether or not these practices were, strictly speaking, of Brahmin or Indian origin. Vaishnavism refers to the worship of Vishnu and Shaivism to the worship of Shiva, both Hindu gods.

2. One Khmer king converted to Islam in the mid-seventeenth century after taking a Malaysian wife, but he was deposed by rival Khmer princes who resented his conversion and asked for assistance from Vietnam in overpowering him. He was deposed and died a prisoner of the Vietnamese in the 1650s. See Chandler 2000 for Khmer religious history.

3. One of the conditions of the French Protectorate was that France had the right to proselytize for Roman Catholicism (Chandler 2000:140).

4. I first worked as a volunteer at a Long Beach Cambodian non-profit agency in 1995 in their tutoring and mentoring program, dealing with the issues facing Cambodian youth, such as high drop-out rates, poor academic performance, gangs, drugs, alcohol, violence, and teen pregnancy. I went on to do my dissertation field work there from 1998 and in Seattle from 2000.

5. Cambodia's Prince Sihanouk had tried to maintain his country's neutrality in the Vietnam war. A U.S.-supported coup of March 28, 1970, ousted him, created the Cambodian Republican, and elevated Lon Nol to the position of prime minister with strong American economic and military support. Cambodia's peasant population, unhappy with the coup and considering Prince Sihanouk to be a sacred ruler, rioted against Lon Nol's government, leading to brutal retaliations that caused the growth of the Khmer Rouge. By 1974, the Khmer Rouge, led by the infamous Pol Pot, controlled about half of the Cambodian countryside, and on April 17, 1975, the Khmer Rouge entered Phnom Penh and took control of Cambodia (Welaratna 1993:19-23). Sihanouk fled to China during Lon Nol's rule and then was installed as a nominal leader by the Khmer Rouge. Then in 1976 Sihanouk protested the violence and resigned his position, remaining basically a prisoner of the Khmer Rouge until the Vietnamese invasion of Cambodia in 1979 (when he again took refuge in China). Returning again, Sihanouk was crowned king of Cambodia on September 24, 1993, though he holds only very limited power.

6. In 1979, about 100,000 Cambodians fled to Thailand, and a famine then sent another 500,000 refugees there. In 1979 and 1980, approximately one-tenth of the entire population of Cambodia was in refugee camps. Although the Thai government initially sought to prevent the entry of these "illegal immigrants," it eventually bowed to international pressure and established refugee camps with international assistance and on condition that countries, including the U.S., would accept refugees (Welaratna 1993:186; Shaw 1989:11-13).

7. Seattle's "International District," near downtown, is known for its many Vietnamese businesses.

8. In 2000, when I arrived to do my research, the Seattle Boeing Aerospace Plant was cutting back on employment, and many Cambodians found jobs as card dealers at one of the many local casinos in the Seattle-Tacoma area. Such employment has recently become popular among Cambodians in the Long Beach area as well. Though no card casinos exist in Long Beach, there are some in nearby cities such as Hawaiian Gardens, where a Khmer-style altar sits at the entrance to a casino.

9. Cambodian Buddhist monks are also often simultaneously *Khmer kru*, with knowledge of magic, astrology, talismans, and the spirit world.

10. Some Cambodians, including monks, suggested that the intense sufferings of the

Cambodian people under Pol Pot were due to a kind of collective Khmer karma (cf. Ebihara, Mortland, and Ledgerwood 1994:80). One man told me that when he was a child living under the Khmer Rouge regime his father, a military leader in the Lon Nol government, told him that Cambodia was being punished for its corruption and greed, and that the Khmer people, the father included, deserved the treatment they were receiving at the hands of Pol Pot. Some Christian groups supported this by telling Cambodian immigrants that their country had suffered so badly because they believed in the wrong god.

11. I have described the Christian churches and fellowships and their aggressive efforts to attract and retain Cambodian members more fully in another article (Douglas 2003).

12. Similarly, in Janet McLellan's study of Toronto Cambodians, the Khmer community was highly fractured and politically weak (McLellan 1999:141).

13. An important distinction between the Long Beach and Seattle communities concerned this relationship between wats and social service agencies. Although the Long Beach community agency where I volunteered was dedicated to promoting traditional Cambodian values, its employees were closely allied with Christian organizations, and this may have contributed to tensions between the wats. In Long Beach, the agencies pre-dated the wats, while in Seattle they were established at roughly the same time.

14. Women have not been ordained as *Bhikkuni* or nuns in Theravada Buddhism for over five centuries (cf. Hopkins 1996: 91, Ledgerwood 1990: 34 and Smith-Hefner 1994:27 for a further discussion of women's roles in the temples).

15. Though I did meet Khmer-American teenage boys who served in wats as lower-ranked monks for a few weeks or months, all of the higher, long-term monks were sponsored from Cambodia.

16. Ironically, the great desecrators of Buddhism, the Khmer Rouge, were mostly of rural origin.

17. One monk asserted that women could serve as achaas, but that this was unlikely because in recent centuries only men had been trained as members of the sangha or Buddhist order.

18. The director of my non-profit Khmer organization in Seattle tried to maintain the approval of the local achaas, two of whom often came by the agency; the director told me that his friendship with them had been very beneficial for the overall acceptance and success of his organization.

19. Institutional control by laity is apparently not true of all wats in the U.S., as I heard of some Khmer-American wats controlled by the monks themselves.

20. In fact, the relationship mirrored the experiences of most Cambodian refugees with their sponsors for immigration to the U.S.

21. Uch Seng had survived the Pol Pot reign of terror, when there were no practicing monks at all in Cambodia; he said that during the Vietnamese occupation temples were reopened and many new monks were trained. He had been a monk for twenty years, ten of them in the U.S.

22. One Seattle monk left his position at the wat and got a job working at a car rental agency, remaining on good terms with the monks and frequently visiting the wat.

23. Monks could spend not more than one night at a time away from the temple during the three-month Vassa (the Pali word for "retreat"). In exceptional circumstances a monk could leave his "rains retreat" for a maximum of seven days.

24. Cambodians usually rented space from or shared a facility with another Christian congregation, meeting at the same time but separately in another part of the church or meet-

ing in afternoons instead of mornings.

25. McLellan's study in Toronto and Ong's study in Oakland describe similar attitudes among Cambodian immigrants (McLellan 1999:133-158; Ong 2003:205,209).

26. The man apparently assumed I was Christian because I was white.

27. Emile Durkheim saw religion as a reflection of social values (Durkheim 1915:420-421), theorizing that as new socio-cultural values were explored and incorporated, there would be accompanying changes in a group's religious practices and beliefs. Max Weber linked the development of capitalism to the rise of the Protestant work ethic (Weber 1930).

28. In contrast, at this same church white young adults were also raising money for their participation in a short-term summer mission project in Eastern Europe. Yet, they solicited donations from the congregation and did not have to "earn" it through working for church members.

29. In Cambodia, French colonialism was followed by a brief period of self-rule, U.S. intervention during the Lon Nol years, the genocidal rule of the Marxist Khmer Rouge, and Vietnamese invasion and control. Currently, a short-lived democratic government has given way to a military coup d'etat directed by a former Khmer Rouge party member and Vietnamese political puppet, Hun Sen.

References

Bagdasar, Craig B. 1993. "Khmer Conflict Style: Cultural Foundations and Forms of Resolution." Ph.D. diss., The Union Institute.

Bruce, Robert G. 1982. *A Preliminary Assessment of the Khmer Cluster Resettlement Project: Final Report.* Washington D.C.: Office of Refugee Resettlement.

Bunte, Pamela A., and Rebecca M. Joseph. 1992. "The Cambodian Community of Long Beach: An Ethnographic Analysis of Factors Leading to a Census Undercount: Final Report for Joint Statistical Agreement 89-31." In *Ethnographic Evaluation of the 1990 Decennial Census Report; no. 9.* Washington D.C.: Bureau of the Census.

Chandler, David. 2000. *A History of Cambodia.* Boulder, CO: Westview Press.

Chung, Rita Chi-Ying, and Marjorie Kagawa-Singer. 1993. "Predictors of Psychological Distress among Southeast Asian Refugees." *Social Science Medicine* 36(5):631-639.

D'Avanzo, Carolyn, Barbara Frye, and Robin Froman. 1994. "Culture, Stress, and Substance use in Cambodian refugee women." *Journal of Studies on Alcohol* 55(4):420-426.

Douglas, Tom. 2003. "The Cross and the Lotus: Changing Religious Practices among Cambodian Immigrants in Seattle." In *Revealing the Sacred in Asian and Pacific America*, ed. Jane Naomi Iwamura and Paul Spickard. New York: Routledge.

Durkheim, Emile. 1915. *The Elementary Forms of the Religious Life.* Translated by J. W. Swain. London: Allen and Unwin.

Ebihara, May. 1971. " Svay, A Khmer Village in Cambodia." Ph.D. diss., Columbia University (1968).

———. 1974. "Khmer Village Women in Cambodia: A Happy Balance." In *Many Sisters*, ed. Carol J. Matthiason. New York: Free Press.

———. 1985. "Khmer." In *Refugees in the United States: A Reference Handbook*, ed. David W. Haines. Westport, CT: Greenwood.

Ebihara, May M., Carol A. Mortland, and Judy Ledgerwood, eds. 1994. *Cambodian Culture since 1975: Homeland and Exile.* Ithaca: Cornell University Press.

Foucault, Michel. 1977. *Discipline and Punish: The Birth of the Prison.* New York: Vintage

Books. (1995 ed.)

Geertz, Clifford. 1973. *The Interpretation of Cultures.* New York: Basic Books.

Harvey, David. 1989. *The Condition of Postmodernity.* Oxford: Basil Blackwell.

Hing, Bill Ong, and Ronald Lee, eds. 1996. *Reframing the Immigration Debate.* Los Angeles: LEAP Inc. and UCLA Asian American Studies Center.

Hopkins, Mary Carol. 1996. *Braving a New World: Cambodian (Khmer) Refugees in an American City.* Westport, CT: Bergin and Garvey.

Kearney, Michael. 1995. "The Local and the Global: The Anthropology of Globalization and Transnationalism." In *Annual Review of Anthropology,* vol. 24, ed. William H. Durand, E. Valentine Daniel, and Bambi Schieffelin. Palo Alto, CA: Annual Reviews Inc.

Ledgerwood, Judy. 1990. "Changing Khmer Conceptions of Gender: Women, Stories, and the Social Order." Ph.D. diss., Cornell University.

Lee, Gen Leigh. 1996. "Chinese-Cambodian Donut Makers in Orange County: Case Studies of Family Labor and Socioeconomic Adaptations." In *Reframing the Immigration Debate,* ed. Bill Ong Hing and Ronald Lee. Los Angeles: LEAP Inc. and UCLA Asian American Studies Center.

Lew, Gena A., and Brandom Sugiyama. 1995. "Focus On: The Cambodian Business Community in Long Beach." *LEAP* 8(2):4-5.

McLellan, Janet. 1999. *Many Petals of the Lotus.* Toronto: University of Toronto Press.

Needham, Susan Anne. 1996. "Literacy, Learning, and Language Ideology: Intracommunity Variation in Khmer Literacy Instruction." Ph.D. diss., University of California, Los Angeles.

Numrich, Paul D. 1996. *Old Wisdom in the New World.* Knoxville: University of Tennessee Press.

Ong, Aihwa. 2003. *Buddha is Hiding: Refugees, Citizenship, and the New America.* Berkeley: University of California Press.

Ong, Paul, Dennis Arguelles, Susan Castro, Bruce Chow, Chanchanit Hirunpidok, Tarry Hum, Winnie Louie, Erich Nakano, and Roderick Ramos. 1993. *Beyond Asian American Poverty.* Los Angeles: Leap.

Ratliff, Sharon Kathleen. 1995. "Caring for Cambodian Americans: A Multidisciplinary Resource for Helping Professionals." Ph.D. diss., Ohio State University.

Rezowalli, Gary James. 1990. "Acculturation and Distress among Cambodian Refugees." Ph.D. diss., Pacific Graduate School of Psychology.

Riposa, Gerry. 1995. "Urban Empowerment: The Cambodian Struggle for Political Incorporation in California." *Texas Journal of Political Science* 16(2):5-21

Rosaldo, Renato. 1988. "Ideology, Place, and People without Culture." *Cultural Anthropology* 3(1):77-87.

Rose, Nikolas. 1990. *Governing the Soul: The Shaping of the Private Self.* New York: Routledge.

Rouse, Roger. 1991. "Mexican Migration and the Social Space of Postmodernism." *Diaspora* 1(1):8-23.

Sassen-Koob, Saskia. 1984. "The New Labor Demand in Global Cities." In *Cities in Transformation,* ed. M. P. Smith. Beverly Hills, CA: Sage.

Selden, Nadine. 1989. "Cambodians in Long Beach." *Long Beach Press-Telegram* (December 10): A;1, 14-17.

Shaw, Scott. 1989. *Cambodian Refugees in Southern California: The Definitive Study.* Hermosa Beach, CA: Buddha Rose Publications.

Shinigawa. Larry Hajime. 1996. "The Impact of Immigration on the Demography of Asian Pacific Americans." In *Reframing the Immigration Debate*, ed. Bill Ong Hing and Ronald Lee. Los Angeles: LEAP Inc. and UCLA Asian American Studies Center.

Smith-Hefner, Nancy. 1994. "Ethnicity and the Force of Faith: Christian Conversion among Khmer Refugees. *Anthropological Quarterly* 67(1): 24-38.

———. 1999. *Khmer American: Identity and Moral Education in a Diasporic Community*. Los Angeles: University of California Press.

United Way of Greater Los Angeles. 1996. *Asian Pacific Profiles: Los Angeles County*. Los Angeles: United Way of Greater Los Angeles.

Walters, Tali Karin. 1994. "Acculturative Stress, Social Support, and Trauma in a Community Sample of Cambodian Refugees." Ph.D. diss., Boston College.

Weber, Max. 1930. *The Protestant Ethic and the Spirit of Capitalism*. Los Angeles: Roxbury Publishing Co. 1996 edition.

Welaratna, Usha. 1989. "Cambodian Refugees in California: After the Holocaust." M.A. Thesis: San Jose State University.

———. 1993. *Beyond the Killing Fields: Voices of Nine Cambodian Survivors in America*. Stanford, CA: Stanford University Press.

———. 1998. "The Presence of the Past in Conflicts and Coalitions among Cambodians, African-Americans, and Hispanics in Central Long Beach (California)." PhD. diss., University of California, Berkeley.

8

Religion and Transnational Migration in the New Chinatown

Kenneth J. Guest

Manhattan's Chinatown exists in the American popular imagination as one of the signature sights of New York City, spoken of in the same breath with the Statue of Liberty, the Empire State Building, the Brooklyn Bridge, Wall Street, Central Park, Little Italy, and the New York Yankees. The name, Chinatown, evokes images of crowded streets, curbside fish and vegetable markets, firecrackers on the Chinese New Year, cheap Chinese restaurants with whole roasted ducks dangling in the window, narrow alleyways, incomprehensible Chinese signs and sing-song Chinese language, mysterious gang violence, old ladies telling fortunes by the park, and old men playing dominos and mahjong. Tourists from across the United States and around the world flock to Mott Street to buy Chinese trinkets and sample Chinese food. New Yorkers brave the throngs on Mulberry and Grand Streets to buy fresh vegetables, seafood, and meat. Overwhelmed visitors crowd under the golden arches of the Canal Street or Bowery McDonalds, oases of Americana in a sea of foreignness. These powerful stereotypes of Chinatown accentuate the exoticism of this ethnic enclave on New York's Lower East Side. They play upon the strongest Orientalist tendencies of American cultural discourse, reinforcing the notion of Chinatown's marginalized otherness and setting this area and its inscrutable people apart from the rest of New York City and even the rest of U.S. culture.

These stereotypes tend to obfuscate and mystify the complex internal dynamics of Chinatown, dynamics which often pit Chinese against Chinese based on differences of regional origin, language, educational background, economic resources, political persuasion, and legal status. The new Fuzhounese immigrants who labor in the restaurants, construction sites, and hundreds of garment factories run by Chinese in the area and across the country are the most vulnerable to this intense stratification. For while Chinatown is a gateway into

America for most Fuzhounese and the beginning of their pursuit of the American dream, for many Chinatown is also a trap, an ethnic enclave manufactured by the economic and political Chinatown elites to keep them isolated and thus vulnerable to labor exploitation. In the midst of this complicated economic and social context, Fuzhounese have succeeded in establishing a set of religious communities that serve as sites for recreating social and religious networks from China and enable transnational flows of ideas, resources, and people.

Religion and the Fuzhounese

Sitting in the temple on Canal Street in Chinatown is a young man, nineteen years old, casually yet neatly dressed and carrying a medium-sized-duffel bag. He has just arrived days before from Chang'an, a village on China's southeast coast. Like thousands of others from that area, he has been smuggled by Chinese snakeheads (human smugglers) into New York by often dangerous routes. The temple on Manhattan's Lower East Side is a way-station on his journey, and he is now waiting patiently for a van that will pick him up and drive him to a city in the U.S. Midwest. Others from Chang'an have preceded him, opening a Chinese restaurant there where he has been promised work.

> I finally made it to America on my third try. I was arrested twice and sent back to China—once in Japan and once in Thailand. I finally came through the Middle East, eastern Europe, and then on a plane to New York with a fake visa. I just want to make money. There's nothing for me at home in Chang'an. So I came out.

It is a sweltering June day. Inside, the small store-turned-temple is decorated in austere fashion. A few chairs line the walls. A list of temple contributors and leaders is mounted prominently just inside the door. On the far wall is a glass-encased altar holding twenty small statues arranged on five ascending levels. A dragon is painted on the back wall of the altar encasement. Huang Di, the emperor, sits on the uppermost level. Confucius, Lao Zi (representing Daoism), and the Buddha sit side by side on the second level. A long table extends from the altar back toward the front door, its surfaces covered with offerings of fresh fruit, ritual candles, and a few pots of burned incense.

A group of seven men and two women occupy the chairs lining the side walls of the temple. Mr. Li, one of the temple leaders, introduces the temple. "The members of the temple have all immigrated from the village of Chang'an or next door Dongqi Village." These two villages are located about thirty miles east of Fuzhou City on the north bank of the Min River. "Most all of them have been smuggled into the U.S. over the past few years." Asked if many more Chang'an villagers would be coming to New York, Mr. Li laughed and said, "Most of them are already in New York but more are coming all the time!

It's mostly just grandparents and small children in Chang'an now. The young people—men and women—have come to New York, most of them illegally, to find work."

Over the past fifteen years tens of thousands of mostly rural Chinese like the young man in the temple have arrived in New York's Chinatown to seek economic opportunities in below-mininum-wage jobs in restaurants, garment shops, and the construction industry. They come from towns and rural villages around Fuzhou, the capital city of Fujian Province on China's southeast coast, across from Taiwan. Many come illegally, pushed by the economic uncertainty of China's rapidly transforming economy, pulled by New York's ravenous labor market, and carried along by a vast Chinese human smuggling network.

Over the past fifteen years, these Fuzhounese immigrants have transformed the face of New York's Chinatown, supplanting the Cantonese as Chinatown's largest ethnic Chinese community and vying for leadership in the area's economics, politics, social life, and even language use. In many ways the Fuzhounese are to today's Chinatown what the Cantonese were before 1985. Cantonese first arrived in California in the 1840s and worked as low-wage farm laborers, prospecting for gold, and in railroad construction before spreading to the East Coast after the completion of the transcontinental railroad in 1869. The Cantonese have dominated life and work in Chinatown throughout much of its history. But since the 1980s the largest single source of Chinese migration to New York and the United States as a whole has been the area around Fuzhou.

Like the Cantonese who migrated to Chinatown before them, the Fuzhounese have brought with them their religious beliefs, practices, and local deities. Over the past fifteen years, Fuzhounese have established a number of their own religious communities, fourteen by the end of 2002. These include Protestant and Catholic churches as well as Buddhist, Daoist, and Chinese popular-religion temples. In the complex economic, political, and social environment of Chinatown's ethnic enclave, these religious organizations have become central locations for the transient Fuzhounese, enabling them to build a community; activate networks of support built on kinship, region, and faith; and establish links to their home temples, churches, and communities. In a context where many of these undocumented immigrants have no means for engaging the mainstream U.S. economy and culture, participating in transnational activities of these religious communities may, in fact, provide alternatives to incorporation.

Chinese Religion in Diaspora

Chinese have been migrating out of China for hundreds if not thousands of years to escape civil unrest, natural disasters, and poverty as well as to diversify their families' economic base. Where they have gone they have taken their religious practices with them. The Chinese religious community in New York City reflects the history of Chinese immigration and the diversity of the Chinese diaspora. Fuzhounese religious communities are but the latest edition. New York's Chinese temples and churches have been formed by ethnic Chinese immigrants from Taiwan, Hong Kong, Macau, Singapore, Burma, Malaysia, Indonesia, Thailand, and Vietnam as well as mainland China. The mainlanders include the earliest immigrants from the Taishan area of southern Guangdong Province; scholars, businessmen, and professionals from China's major urban centers; post-1989 Tian An Men political asylum seekers; Fuzhounese from towns and villages of China's southeast coast; and a small recent wave of undocumented workers from Wenzhou, a coastal city twelve hours north of Fuzhou by bus.

Each group brings a different set of linguistic and cultural traditions, economic resources, and religious beliefs and practices. Chinese immigrants speak Cantonese, Mandarin, Fuzhounese, the local Taiwanese minnan dialect, Wenzhounese, and English. They use these languages in different combinations, sometimes with separate religious services within the same institution, sometimes with simultaneous translation during the same services, and sometimes with a determined effort to stick to one language over the others. The religious institutions also represent different historical waves of immigration out of China and into New York. Early Cantonese immigrants and their grown children, who are often now established as middle-class professionals and business owners, congregate together in certain churches and temples. Hong Kong and Taiwanese who have come since the 1970s gather in others. Fuzhounese undocumented immigrant laborers form their own institutions. Second-generation Chinese may meet in the same building as their parents, but their English language congregations are often distinct ritual and programmatic entities.

Chinese established their earliest religious altars in family and village association halls that began to emerge in the Five Points area of lower Manhattan, starting on Pell, Doyer, and lower Mott Streets in the 1800s. The Methodist Five Points Mission, originally opened in 1848 to serve Irish immigrants, began its first work with Chinese in 1878, renting space at 14 Mott Street. Transfiguration Catholic Church, located at 29 Mott Street, began an outreach to Chinese in 1909. Two temples, referred to by non-Chinese as "joss houses" were constructed in the 1880s, the first an elaborate space on the third floor of 10 Chatham Square and later an even more magnificent hall at 16 Mott Street in the Consolidated Benevolent Association Building.[1] With the expansion of Chinatown in the 1890s, not only did tourists begin flocking to its restaurants, tea merchants, and gift shops but also to its temples. The oldest extant Buddhist temple in Chinatown, the Eastern States Buddhist Association, opened in 1963 (Yu 1995; Chin 1995; Anbinder 2001).

Today, churches and temples have expanded through a wide swath of the Lower East Side. In recent years, Chinese religious communities have also emerged in significant numbers as part of the economically diverse Asian communities in Flushing, Queens, and in the working-class Chinese neighborhood of Sunset Park, Brooklyn. A few other Chinese congregations are scattered throughout the five boroughs, including Chinese Christian fellowships on most major college campuses. A recent explosion of Chinese meditation groups related to China's persecuted Falun Gong movement gathers in public parks and members' homes throughout the city.

Eighty-four religious institutions were identified in this study in the Chinatown area, fifty-nine of which are exclusively Chinese. In addition, three Catholic churches have multiple congregations in one parish, combining Chinese and Italians or Chinese and Hispanics. The twenty-two non-Chinese institutions include a wide range of congregations: Protestant (Hispanic, African American, European American), 10; Jewish, 4; Roman Catholic, 4; Greek Orthodox, 1; Ukrainian Orthodox, 1; Jehovah's Witness, 1; Japanese Buddhist, 1. The sixty-two institutions with Chinese members include: Buddhist, 26; Protestant Christian, 23; Chinese popular religion, 8; Catholic, 3; Daoist, 2.

Fourteen congregations specifically serve the Fuzhounese population in Chinatown. Five are popular religious temples venerating local deities from the home village or region in China from which their adherents have come. Four congregations specifically identify themselves as Buddhist temples, although these may incorporate elements of Daoism or popular religion as well. Two independent Protestant Christian congregations have been established. One temple, the Temple of Heavenly Thanksgiving, identifies itself as Daoist but includes Buddhist and Daoist deities on its altar as well as the sage Confucius. The two Catholic churches with Fuzhounese constituents are multi-ethnic parishes including older groups of Italians along with Cantonese-speaking Chinese from south China and Hong Kong and more recent Fuzhounese arrivals. Excluding the two Catholic parishes, the other twelve Fuzhounese religious groups are independently established with no formal institutional association beyond their own local organization. Mirroring the Fuzhounese migration, these institutions are all recently established and as such fairly fragile. Only the He Xian Jun Buddhist Temple (1987) and the Protestant Church of Grace (1988) were founded prior to 1990. All of the others were established during the past decade.

One can easily count the number of religious organizations, but measuring the religiosity of New York's Chinese population is a complex task. A telephone survey of 164 Chinese residents of Queens in 1997 and 1998 recorded the following religious affiliation: Protestant, 13.4 percent; Catholic, 6.7 percent; Buddhist, 21.3 percent; Other, 1.8 percent; No Religion, 56.7 percent.[2] While this provides a broad sense of the religious preferences of Chinese in New York City, the analytic framework of the survey forced respondents to fit their beliefs into an institutional framework that does not reflect the religious experience of most Chinese, and certainly not the religious practices of recent immigrants from Fuzhou. Many studies of Chinese religion stress the intertwining of Buddhism, Daoism, and Chinese popular religious beliefs at the local level and their integration with family and village customs and activities (Weller 1987; Sangren 1987; Shahar and Weller 1996). As exemplified by the two Fuzhounese temples examined later in this chapter, most religious expression in mainland China's rural areas is not readily reduced to the formal categories of Buddhism or Daoism. Chinese popular religious expression, which includes funerals, weddings, veneration of ancestors, and festivals related to the Chinese lunar calendar, is vibrant and central to family and home village life. Such beliefs and practices do not disappear when immigrants arrive in New York, but continue in homes, stores, shops, restaurants, and temples, although they may be modified to fit a new cultural environment.

Unaffiliated institutions, regardless of size, are abundant but difficult to detect without street-by-street observation. Individual, family, and business oriented religious expressions are also difficult to document in a survey of institutions. In many Chinese homes, offerings are made to the Kitchen God, and Chinese restaurants, stores, and businesses often house small altars at which owners offer prayers. These religious practices, intimately intertwined with Chinese family and village culture, are not as readily identifiable out of context in the United States environment. Public processions and festivals also do not register on a map of religious institutions. Yet they play a distinct role in projecting an ethnic community's religious beliefs into the public domain in the most multicultural, multi-ethnic, multi-religious of global cities.

Survival and Solidarity in Chinatown's Ethnic Enclave

Chinatown provides a dramatic economic and social context for these emerging Fuzhounese religious communities. Fuzhounese immigrants utilize their social capital to mobilize family, village, ethnic, and religious networks in order to begin their journey in the United States and survive in Chinatown's ethnic enclave. But survival is no easy matter in what is essentially an unregulated free-enterprise zone operating within a globalized world economic system that successfully exploits disadvantaged Chinese immigrants. Fuzhounese immigrants come to New York seeking economic opportunities and a chance at a better life for themselves and families. But what many find is grueling toil and economic uncertainty. Garment shops and restaurants operate six days a week, ten to twelve hours a day, and pay as little as two dollars an hour, without benefits. Recent waves of illegal immigrants from Fuzhou have driven wages down further still. While these wages are higher than in mainland China's free-enterprise zones, and the working conditions somewhat better, most illegal immigrants only work for these wages and under these conditions because they have no options beyond the enclave. Many are under intense pressure and sometimes coercion to pay off debts of up to $60,000 to smugglers who brought them into the U.S. or to family and friends who provided the bridge loans.

Although the Chinatown economic and political elite who benefit from these exploitative labor relations often hide behind the rubric of "ethnic solidarity," a more genuine form of working-class ethnic solidarity does exist, and recent immigrants use it to mobilize the financial and social capital necessary for entering the United States and surviving in this highly stratified environment. Fuzhounese immigrants, particularly undocumented immigrants, are extremely creative actors working to manipulate a system stacked with disadvantages. In ingenious fashion, these newcomers to New York employ language and kinship affinities, and hometown and family networks, to find jobs, housing, health care, child care, and legal advice. As we shall see, Fuzhounese religious communities are central sites for constructing and reconstructing networks of ethnic solidarity and accessing available financial and social capital as immigrants make their way along an often precarious journey. At the same time, this isolated ethnic enclave is a trap for many Fuzhounese who, marginalized by language, culture, and class from both the mainstream U.S. economy and the Chinatown elites, have no way to escape.

An Immigrant's Story: Mr. Lu Jianguo

The story of Mr. Lu Jianguo from Fuqi Village is typical of many Fuzhounese who have been smuggled into the U.S. over the last decade. It is primarily a story of young people who, despite great ambition and adventurous spirit, have found their lives fragile and often broken.

> My name is Lu Jianguo. I'm thirty years old, married, and have two children. I'm from Fuqi village on the southern bank of the Min River just as it opens into the Pacific Ocean. Fuqi used to have 4,000 people, but now 2,000 are here in America. There aren't even enough people to work the farms. Now they're rented to outsiders from Sichuan Province [southwest China].
>
> Fuqi is a pretty poor village on the side of a hill. There's not much farm land. Most of the income comes from fishing. My family was always very poor. I've been eating bitterness since I was born. If you don't have money people can't stand you. There were times when we didn't really have enough to eat. I only went to school until I was ten. We were so poor I had to go to work. I can read a little bit but not too much. There's no way we could make it better there. My older brother left in 1986 and was smuggled into America. He got his green card in the amnesty in 1989 after Tian An Men Square/June 4th. I came in 1992. I paid the smugglers $20,000. I had to pay it off over time once I got here, plus a lot of interest. We spent sixty days on the boat coming. I'm not sure where we landed, because I don't speak any English. Maybe somewhere near Boston. Then the snakeheads brought us to New York.
>
> My wife came over around the same time as I did. She was also smuggled in. She's not from my village. I'm not sure where she's

from. I've never been there though I think it's nearby. I've never really been anywhere in China. We met here in New York and got married here. I couldn't have married in China. I was too poor. My wife is at home. She just gave birth. So she isn't working. I can't find any work right now either. We're living on our little bit of savings. She works in a garment factory. She's very brave and strong. She works until one or two o'clock every morning. Sixteen or eighteen hours a day. Most women do. She'll look after the baby for a while and then go back to work.

We live in a three-bedroom apartment, three families, each with one room. We're all from Fuzhou. We have to take care of ourselves. Nobody looks after us. If you get sick there isn't anybody to help. Each family pays $400 a month for the apartment.

Maybe when my daughter grows up my wife and I can go back to China and my daughter can petition for us to come legally. I have two children. One here in New York. One in China. The one in China is one year old and is being raised by my wife's parents. I paid someone I knew $1,000 to take her back to China. That's the way it works usually. A woman I knew took her back. The baby had her own passport, so it was not a problem. She was born in the U.S., so she's a U.S. citizen. We got her a passport. I took her to the airport. I don't think I had ever cried before. But I did when I sent her back to China. Why? She was only seventy days old, [he cried] when I sent her back. But I don't have any money. I can't take care of her here. So many Fuzhounese are like this. To send a child away to grow up with grandparents in another country . . . it's very bitter. We are all working too. And to have a baby in the apartment making so much noise would disturb everyone. And my wife needed to go back to work too. Two daughters, a baby here and a one-year-old in China. I haven't seen a picture in a long time. They say she has a bad temperament so they can't get a picture of her. I want her to come back to America, but I don't know when we'll be able to work it out.

Lu Jianguo's story illustrates the way in which the Fuzhounese migration, spurred by economic restructuring in both China and the U.S. and facilitated by a vast and highly organized international human smuggling syndicate, has uprooted whole communities of people, dislocating them economically, culturally, and legally, and placing them in a receiving country for which they are unprepared and which is unprepared to incorporate them.

Amidst this dislocation, Fuzhounese immigrants are constructing and maintaining religious communities as one means of building supportive networks and activities, including religious networks and practices, and as a mode for negotiating their place in this complex and volatile global process. For many like Lu Jianguo, religious communities provide a safe haven, an island in a stormy sea. They are places to connect with family, friends, fellow villagers, and co-religionists, and to share news of jobs, housing lawyers, doctors, and reputable snakeheads. And they are places for these undocumented workers to reconnect to home—people, home communities, religious rituals, and even concepts of time, health, and knowledge.

Two Fuzhounese Religious Communities

The stories of the Daoist Temple of Heavenly Thanksgiving and the He Xian Jun Buddhist Temple reveal the complex roles these congregations play in the Fuzhounese migration process, in immigrant incorporation in the U.S., and in building networks that link religious communities in lower Manhattan and the lower Min River Valley outside Fuzhou, southeast China.

Daoist Temple of Heavenly Thanksgiving

In 1993 a group of seven immigrants from Chang'an and neighboring Dongqi established a temple in New York. Originally on Eldridge Street, in the spring of 1997 it moved a short distance away to Canal Street. Since its founding, the temple has served as a gathering spot for immigrants from the two villages and as a place for worship and ritual on the key days of the Chinese lunar calendar. By 1997, most of the original seven founders owned restaurants in the New York area, but they rotated responsibility for the temple operations. And in each of their restaurants there was also a small altar for the gods of the temple.

The New York temple took its religious inspiration from a temple established in 1985 in Dongqi. By 1995, with funds raised from 100 fellow villagers from Chang'an, several of the New York founders returned to Chang'an to build a third related Temple of Heavenly Thanksgiving there. With help from the first temple in Dongqi, construction began on a major temple complex hugging the hillside at the rear of Chang'an Village overlooking the Min River and the Pacific Ocean. Built on the site of an old Buddhist temple, this new structure rises steeply through five levels, each adorned with altars to the gods and configured in the same order as the miniaturized statues in the New York temple. From the highest landing the temple looks south over Chang'an Village, its newly constructed multi-story homes built with remittances sent from the U.S.

The religious community that is related to these temples reflects many of the characteristics of other Fuzhounese religious groups found in Chinatown. The Temple of Heavenly Thanksgiving in New York City clearly serves as a site in the immigrant journey for fellow believers. The leadership of the temple plays a role in the actual arrangements involved in the migration process. While serving as a ritual center, the temple is also equipped to assist immigrants in transit. On the main floor of the New York temple, behind the front room and altar, is a full kitchen. A set of stairs leads down to a basement level comprised of four smaller rooms filled with four to six beds each. These are used by fellow villagers passing through New York on their way to a network of restaurants spread from Virginia to Pennsylvania to Indiana to Michigan.

The temple serves as an important location for assisting the incorporation of new immigrants into the U.S. economy, connecting them to a network of restaurants owned by members. Although the temple's networks are highly stratified and new immigrants work as undocumented laborers for well below minimum wage, nevertheless, the social solidarity of the network provides off-the-books employment at wages far above what they could earn in China. At the same time, the workers' cheap labor enables the owners to reap a profit far above what they could earn if forced to employ U.S. citizens at the legal minimum wage or above. Thus, the Chinatown ethnic enclave extends beyond New York by means of the village and temple network that encompasses work locations scattered throughout the United States.

The Temple of Heavenly Thanksgiving also demonstrates the ways in which emerging Fuzhounese religious networks enable immigrants to contribute to and influence their home communities in China. While many immigrants interact with their sending community through remittances to build homes and support family members, participation in the Temple of Heavenly Thanksgiving allows members to contribute collectively to the larger social projects of their home village. Not only has significant money been invested in the construction of the home temple complex, but in 1999 the New York temple established a charitable foundation to engage in development and relief operations in the Chang'an and Dongqi areas as well as elsewhere in China.

Visits to the temples in New York, Dongqi, and Chang'an reveal the difficulties of maintaining religious networks that span towns, cities, and nations often half a world apart, particularly given the intense mobility of the migrant community. At times the temples have been empty because the leadership has gone elsewhere to work. At times internal conflicts have erupted over control of temples. As with the other religious communities considered in this study, the story of the Temple of Heavenly Thanksgiving reveals the inherent fragility of these nascent Fuzhounese institutions. Their leadership is constantly mobile and regularly reconstituted. They are unfamiliar with the United States and limited in their ability to establish networks of support there. Their attempts to bring together disparate elements of the immigrant community under broad organizational umbrellas often crumble.

Against the odds, however, both Master Lu's He Xian Jun Temple discussed below and the Temple of Heavenly Thanksgiving reflect the ability of local religious traditions, indigenous to the towns and villages of rural Fuzhou, to extend their reach and influence far and wide. In 1998 the Dongqi Village temple's spirit medium, a woman long engaged in fortune telling and dispensing herbal medicines and all manner of advice, immigrated with her husband to Indiana to open a takeout Chinese restaurant. Here she continued to serve as a spirit medium for the temple and its adherents. People with problems or questions, whether in China or in cities across the U.S., would call her in Indiana. Petitioners who could not afford to call would leave their questions on slips of paper on the temple altars in China or the U.S. so that temple leaders could call in for them. On the first and the fifteenth day of the lunar month, the medium would go into a trance and be possessed by one of the gods of the temple. Confirming her efficacy, the temple master in Dongqi claimed he could feel the god leaving the village to go to America to inhabit her. In Indiana, the spirit medium's husband posed the questions to the god inhabiting her, who would respond. The husband kept careful notes of the responses and afterward would return people's calls with the eagerly awaited answers.

In 1999, handwritten notes were still being placed on the altar of the temple on Canal Street in New York. But the sign above the front door had been changed and the people in charge of the temple were different. After several inquiries it became clear that one faction from the Chang'an temple had replaced another. This new faction had a spirit medium as well, but a different person, who was located in Illinois, not Indiana.

He Xian Jun Buddhist Temple

Master Lu, a short gruff man in his early sixties, established the small temple on Eldridge Street shortly after arriving illegally in 1985 from Fuqi Village east of Fuzhou. Fuqi Village lies on a hillside on the southern bank of the Min River. Out of 4,000 villagers, nearly 2,000 are now estimated to have made their way to or through New York. Fuqi's economy previously was built around farming and fishing; today this emigrant community relies primarily on remittances from villagers working in the U.S.

Master Lu is not uncharacteristic of local religious practitioners in both rural and urban China who incorporate a polytheistic blend of ritual and belief. For the ten years immediately preceding his migration to New York, Master Lu practiced his craft as a spirit medium in the towns and villages around his native Fuqi and on Langqi Island in the mouth of the Min River, home of his wife's family. What is unique about Master Lu is that he has transferred the central location of his practice from rural Fuqi to urban New York. At the same time he has built a direct connection to his hometown and maintained the local flavor of his work. Fuqi villagers visit him for advice in New York, just as they did back home. The deity, He Xian Jun, speaks to him in New York just as he did in China. Contributions from members have supported the temple in New York as well as the construction of a major temple complex in Fuqi.

The New York temple serves as both a ritual center and a community center for the people of Fuqi and surrounding areas. Festivities are held on the first and fifteenth of every month (Chinese lunar calendar) as well as three times a year in honor of Guan Yin. The largest gathering occurs at the Chinese New Year when many Fuzhounese working in restaurants across the country return to New York. Over 700 immigrants made the New Year's journey to Master Lu's temple in 2002.

The temple is named after He Xian Jun, a prominent Daoist deity in northern Fujian Province and the predominant local deity of Fuqi Village and surrounding areas. The association of a Daoist deity with an officially Buddhist temple reflects not only the integration of Buddhism, Daoism, and Chinese popular religious beliefs at the local level, but also the difficulty in using institutional religious frameworks to categorize the dynamic religious expressions of rural Chinese communities.

Master Lu has had an extremely intimate and personal relationship with the deity for over twenty-five years, a relationship which has not been lessened by the geographical distance between Fuqi Village in southeast China and Eldridge Street on the Lower East Side of Manhattan. In between festivals Master Lu receives visitors. They come to ask the god's advice about everything from business ventures to children's names to the potential success of petitions for political asylum. They come to pray for the health of sick relatives and to give thanks for safe passage across the ocean with snakeheads from China. He Xian Jun, who characteristically provides his adherents with dreams in response to their queries, is revered as a god of healing, who also resolves intractable problems. There is a steady stream of petitioners throughout the average day. Old friends drop in to say hello and show off a new grandson. Couples planning to be married come by to check the auspiciousness of their match or the date for their wedding. Sundays are busiest since many working Chinese have the day off. Master Lu intercedes on their behalf with He Xian Jun. The deity gives him a message or a vision to relay and interpret to the petitioners. At rare times He Xian Jun actually possesses Master Lu's body in order to communicate, but mostly the responses come in the form of dreams or visual images.

In an interview conducted in his New York temple one afternoon in September 1999, Master Lu traced his development from a poor rural youngster who gathered firewood to support his family on the banks of the Min River to his position as a ritual master of a religious community that spans the globe. In addition to providing the rich imagery of his life's journey, the interview reveals Master Lu's intimate relationship with the deity He Xian Jun and the religious framework he has constructed to give meaning to his life experience, particularly his immigrant experience.

> It was 1985. I found a snakehead in Tingjiang, across the river from Fuqi by boat. The price was $17,000 but I didn't give any money up front. Only after I got to America. If I didn't get here then I didn't have to pay. But when it was time to leave the country, I couldn't get out. When I got to Shanghai I couldn't get on the plane. I had a Chinese passport, but the smuggler hadn't gotten the right visa. I went

home to Fuqi and waited. When I finally did leave China I traveled from Shanghai to Japan. From Japan to Canada. From Canada to Ecuador. Ecuador to Mexico. From Mexico to Los Angeles. Los Angeles to New York. All on the plane except from Mexico to Los Angeles. In Mexico I climbed a mountain for an hour, then there was a small vehicle waiting for us to take us across the border. We all sat on that bus praying to He Xian Jun, "Protect us! Protect us!" I know some people who have been stopped at that customs checkpoint. One of my friends. So I was praying. In front of us they were searching a car. I was praying. But when we pulled up they just said, go through. We were so happy. There were five of us. One from Tingjiang, one from Min'an, two from Houyu and me. We were all praying. We just zoomed right through.

Since 1975 I had been doing this kind of work [with He Xian Jun]. In 1975 He Xian Jun had already come to inhabit my body. We didn't dare to do this work at home. It was still during the Cultural Revolution and religion was being repressed very intensely. I went to other places to work. Neighboring villages. Langqi Island. In my relatives' and friends' homes. Then I would go away. Sometimes they could pay me. Sometimes they just gave me rice or oil. Or people would come secretively to my home, just as guests. People would ask me to come if someone was sick, or if there were problems in the family: fights, divorce, family problems. I would try to make peace. People would introduce me, one to one to another.

These people helped me come up with the money when I got to New York. We already had a lot of people from Fuqi in New York at the time. In 1981-1982 there were already some that were smuggled out through Macau or Shanghai. They would go to Macau to "visit relatives" and then just keep on going to New York. I worked in a restaurant for two years. Every month I paid $1,000 back to the people who had loaned it to me.

Right when I got to America, He Xian Jun told me to open a temple. I told the god, since I borrowed other people's money, I'm embarrassed to just start a temple. After I've returned the money then I will do it. If I don't return the money people will say I'm lazy. But if I return the money I will be free to do anything. They can't say anything about it, regardless how little money I make. He Xian Jun told me in a dream to open this temple. And we had a conversation. He told me if you work in a restaurant it's too dirty. I can't get close to your body. The meat smells. Other smells. I was worried though. I was illegal. I didn't get my green card until after the 1989 amnesty. If I worked in the back of a restaurant, the police probably would not catch me. But if I opened a temple. What should I do? I asked the god. He said, "Don't worry. You won't get caught. No one will bother you." He told me where to open this temple too. Originally it was a little farther up on Eldridge Street. He told me to move here to this building. I said no, because it wasn't a very good neighborhood at the time. He said it was OK, nothing would happen to me. So I moved the temple here in 1993.

I told He Xian Jun that since my family was poor if I could get to America I promise to build a temple for him in Fuqi. I made that promise before I came. If he would send me to America and I could make some money the first thing I would do is build a temple in Fuqi for him. I do my work. He does his.

I didn't even know [I had the skill] myself. I just tried. If I got it right then I had the power. Like, is the baby going to be a boy or a girl. If I got it right, then I've got the power. Today you should go to such and such a place and do something. Did it work out? Yes? Then it works.

. . . If things didn't change why would people trust me? Why would they contribute to building the temple back home in China?

The He Xian Jun Temple in New York plays a key role in the lives of immigrants from Fuqi and neighboring villages as they seek to make sense of their new and often hostile environment and negotiate their difficult existence in New York City. The temple, with Master Lu as the centerpiece, serves as a site for the exchange of information among its adherents regarding jobs, housing, health care, and coping mechanisms for dealing with the struggles of daily life.

The temple and Master Lu also serve as an important link between New York and Fuqi. To honor his reciprocal pledge with He Xian Jun, Master Lu has orchestrated the construction of a beautiful temple complex on the hillside above Fuqi Village overlooking the Min River as it flows into the sea. With contributions of over $1,000,000 from adherents in New York, Master Lu has built a multi-leveled temple that dwarfs anything in the surrounding villages. Architectural drawings are prominently displayed inside the temple on Eldridge Street. A seven-story pagoda is the most recent addition and opened to great fanfare in September 2002, complete with rituals, parades, and speeches by local and provincial government authorities.

Master Lu returns to Fuqi Village at least once a year, usually in the spring. His brother has remained in Fuqi to manage the sprawling new temple complex. Master Lu's son is also there, living in the family's spacious new five-story home and waiting for his green card application to be processed. On his annual return visit to Fuqi, Master Lu conducts a month-long religious retreat for his followers. Hundreds of pilgrims from across the area visit Fuqi temple during this time. Monks from a large temple in Fuzhou City are hired to lead the rituals. The temple, like others throughout the region and across China, is playing a crucial role in revitalizing and reimagining Chinese religious life after a period of intense repression.

Master Lu also takes the occasions of his return visits to meet with local political and religious authorities. Despite living primarily in New York, he is recognized by the Changle Religious Affairs Bureau as a Buddhist monk and he retains membership on the Changle Buddhist Association Council. Back home in New York Master Lu proudly displays videos of his visits, the many pilgrims who attend the festivals, and the beautiful new temple buildings. The videos regularly play on the temple's VCR and are loaned out to adherents around the tri-state area, another span in the bridge between Fuqi and New York linking religious communities.

Fuzhounese Religious Communities and Transnationalism

One characteristic comes through in the two cases discussed above and in other religious communities considered in the larger study from which this material is drawn (Guest 2003). Fuzhounese religious communities in Chinatown exhibit a strong tendency toward building and sustaining transnational ties to communities at home in China. These linkages assist people both in the migration process and in their incorporation into the United States. They also channel resources back home, and they allow immigrants to build their prestige and project their presence in their home communities. For many undocumented Fuzhounese, participation in transnational activities happens because there are no other options. They are systematically marginalized in the U.S., discriminated against because of their economic skills, legal status, language, and even ethnicity. Participation in transnational activities allows them to build identities that transcend their dead-end jobs, their transient lifestyles, and their local marginalization.

Where do Fuzhounese religious communities fit into the discussion on transnationalism? In their book *Nations Unbound* (1994), Linda Basch, Nina Glick-Schiller, and Cristina Szanton Blanc pioneer the theoretical application of the concept of transnationalism. In one of their earliest formulations they write:

> We define "transnationalism" as the processes by which immigrants forge and sustain multi-stranded social relations that link together their societies of origin and settlement. We call these processes transnationalism to emphasize that many immigrants today build social fields that cross geographic, cultural, and political borders. Immigrants who develop and maintain multiple relationships—familial, economic, social, organizational, religious, and political—span borders we call "transmigrants." An essential element of transnationalism is the multiplicity of involvements that transmigrants sustain in both home and host societies. (1994:7)

Contemporary studies of U.S. immigrant communities have built upon and expanded Glick-Schiller's theorizing of transnationalism, examining the creation of transnational social fields (Mahler 1998), transnational migrant circuits (Rouse 1991), and the layering of transnationalisms from below, including everyday practices of individuals and groups, with transnationalisms from above, including global institutions and the state (Smith and Guarnizo 1998). Others have explored the question of what exactly is new about the patterns of transnationalism among the new immigrants (Foner 2000; Portes, et al. 1999). But as with much of the immigration literature, with a few recent exceptions (Brown 1991; McAlister 1998; Levitt 2001; Ebaugh and Chavetz 2002), work on transnationalism has consistently ignored the role of religious networks and communities in the migration process and the process of building and maintaining transnational social and economic ties.

Many studies of Chinese transnationalism (Ong and Nonini 1997; Ong 1999) focus primarily on middle class and economic elites who have the financial resources and legal status to live and work in multiple locations. For them, transnational identity is a byproduct of economic privilege. The vast majority of Fuzhounese immigrants do not fit this model. Some Fuzhounese who arrived prior to the 1986 or 1990 amnesties or who have successfully applied for U.S. political asylum may be able to participate in a more extensive set of transnational practices and identity building. They may have the legal status and financial stability to travel between New York and Fuzhou and engage in activities that span the two locations. But for the majority of Fuzhounese, their transnationalism is much more nascent, grassroots, and fragile; an ocean-borne transnationalism of the working poor, not the jet-set transnationalism of the elite. Unlike the transnational entities so often discussed that transcend the state, most Fuzhounese immigrants mobilize small-scale transnational networks from a position deep within and vulnerable to state structures. As workers, many of them undocumented, they are disciplined by economy and state alike. But beginning with their international migration utilizing the human smuggling networks, these immigrants find creative ways of overcoming the restrictions, borders, and boundaries of the state system and the local and global capitalist regime.

Transnational religious networks being established by Fuzhounese immigrants are independent, multi-faceted, decentralized, and opportunistic. Yet their influence spans the migration process between China and the U.S., the immigrant incorporation process, and the changing economic, political, social, and religious situation in Fuzhou. They expand our understanding of how transnational ties are built and maintained and their significance in immigrants' lives. Many Fuzhounese may not be able to travel back and forth between the U.S. and China. Their legal status in the U.S. and the Chinese governmental system may not allow many of them to participate politically in either place. But through social organizations such as religious communities and village and regional associations they do find means to participate across the Pacific.

In the case of the Daoist Temple of Heavenly Thanksgiving, for instance, the community at times plays a direct role in the migration process. The young man with his duffel bag clearly identified the Daoist temple as a way-station along the international journey between rural Chang'an and the U.S. Midwest. Members of the temple network help arrange passage with snakeheads, receive immigrants upon arrival in New York, and direct them to jobs awaiting them in a network of restaurants scattered across the Midwest and mid-Atlantic states. The temple foundation channels funds back to religious construction projects and relief efforts in Chang'an for which the contributors are given recognition. And the temple's spirit mediums allow marginalized immigrants to access homebound notions of spirituality, healing, and even epistemology.

Likewise, Master Lu's temple and other transnational religious networks have significantly increased immigrants' influence in the Fuzhou area. Perhaps the most visible signs are the large new religious structures that dot the Fuzhou countryside—ancestral halls, churches, and temples built with immigrant remittances. The newly constructed seven-story pagoda of the Fuqi He Xian Jun Temple towers over all other religious sites in the Min River Valley. Plaques line the temple and pagoda walls, engraved with the names of contributors and the amount of their gift, memorializing and immortalizing the gift and the giver regardless of their current country of residence or legal status. Underlying these material symbols is a revitalization of local ritual practices enabled by a relaxing of local government restrictions and fueled by significant international support from overseas Fuzhounese. Money and other material resources are flowing in, and despite the outmigration of significant numbers of rural constituents, religious programming in the area continues to expand thanks to remittances.

For Fuzhounese, this transnational participation may have many motivations. Interviews suggest that one powerful consideration is the ability of these marginalized struggling workers, many of whom are undocumented, to create alternative patterns of citizenship both in the U.S. and in China. Structurally excluded from full citizen participation both in the United States and China, through their transnational activities, circumscribed as they may be, Fuzhounese immigrants attempt to negotiate alternative strategies for participation and survival against the rigors of New York's ethnic enclave and the disciplining of the immigration laws of the state.

This study clearly demonstrates the significance of transnational religious networks established by Fuzhounese immigrants. Through these networks they seek to transcend regulated national boundaries and construct broader notions of citizenship and participation. They utilize their emerging transnational religious networks to articulate an alternative existence and identity in the face of the homogenizing influences of global capitalism and the U.S. labor market. Their participation in the life of their home communities—encouraged, facilitated, and rewarded through religious networks—assists in creating and enhancing a transnational identity which may in fact serve as an alternative to immigrant incorporation in the host society.

In addition, the religious community serves as a liminal space, a transitional place that bridges New York and China. It recreates physical surroundings, kinship and village networks, rituals, language, and food that recall life in China, and it reconnects its members to cultural and religious traditions back home. Yet it is in the midst of America. Religious communities allow Fuzhounese immigrants to imagine themselves differently in the midst of a hegemonic discourse which describes them in unflattering and dehumanizing terms.

On Guan Yin's birthday hundreds of recent immigrants from Fuqi Village leave their workplaces for lunch and make their way to Master Lu's temple on Eldridge Street. Exiting the temporal framework of American capitalism where the sweatshop clock keeps track of the grinding hours and number of garment pieces produced, the journey to Master Lu's temple transports these urban workers into an alternative notion of time and place. In the temple their lives are dominated not by the rhythms of the sewing machine and steam press, nor by fourteen-hour days and six-day work weeks, American holidays, customs, and the dense interactions of New York City. Inside the temple the familiar rituals connect them to the rhythms and pulses of home, to the Chinese lunar calendar, and to their rural roots. Re-evoked in these rituals are home-bound ways of conceptualizing health, morality, and fortune. The rituals also reconstitute and reterritorialize frameworks of self-understanding affirmed by the presence of old friends, fellow villagers, and talk of home. For a moment, the festival enables congregants to resist the dominant hegemony of time and place and provides them an opportunity to reconceptualize their lives and work, their past, present, and future.

Notes

1. The word "joss," meaning a Chinese idol or cult image, is not Chinese but derives from pidgin English based on the Portuguese or Latin *deus*, meaning "god" or "deity." A joss house was then a Chinese temple or shrine.

2. Respondents were selected at random from Chinese surnames in the Queens telephone directory (Min forthcoming).

References

Anbinder, Tylor. 2001. *Five Points*. New York: Free Press.

Basch, Linda, and Nina Glick-Schiller, et. al., eds. 1994. *Nations Unbound: Transnational Projects, Postcolonial Predicaments, and Deterritorialized Nation States.* Langhorne, PA: Gordon and Breach.

Brown, Karen McCarthy. 1991. *Mama Lola: A Vodou Priestess in Brooklyn*. Berkeley: University of California Press.

Chin, Charlie. 1995. "Chinatown." In *The Encyclopedia of New York City*, ed. Kenneth T. Jackson. New Haven: Yale University Press.

Ebaugh, Helen Rose, and Janet Saltzman Chafetz, eds. 2002. *Religion Across Borders*. Walnut Creek, CA: AltaMira Press.

Foner, Nancy. 2000. *From Ellis Island to JFK: New York's Two Great Waves of Immigration*. New Haven: Yale University Press.

Guest, Kenneth J. 2003. *God in Chinatown: Religion and Survival in New York's Evolving Immigrant Community*. New York: New York University Press.

Kwong, Peter. 1996. *The New Chinatown*. Rev. ed. New York: Hill and Wang.

———. 1997. *Forbidden Workers: Illegal Chinese Immigrants and Chinese Labor*. New York: New Press.

Levitt, Peggy. 2001. *The Transnational Villagers*. Berkeley: University of California Press.

Mahler, Sarah. 1998. "Theoretical and Empirical Contributions toward a Research Agenda for Transnationalism." In *Transnationalism from Below: Comparative Urban and Community Research*, vol. 6, ed. M. P. Smith and Luis Guarnizo. New Brunswick, NJ: Transaction Publishers.

McAlister, Elizabeth. 1998. "The Madonna of 115th Street Revisited: Vodou and Haitian Catholicism in the Age of Transnationalism." In *Gatherings in Diaspora: Religious Communities and the New Immigration*, ed. Stephen Warner and Judith G. Wittner. Philadelphia: Temple University Press.

Ong, Aihwa. 1999. *Flexible Citizenship: The Cultural Logistics of Transnationality*. Durham, NC: Duke University Press.

Ong, Aihwa, and Donald Nonini, eds. 1997. *Ungrounded Empires: The Cultural Politics of Modern Chinese Transnationalism*. New York: Routledge Press.

Portes, Alejandro, Luis Guarnizo, and Patricia Landolt. 1999. "Introduction: Pitfalls and Promise of an Emergent Research Field." *Ethnic and Racial Studies* 22(2):217-38.

Rouse, Roger. 1991. "Mexican Migration and the Social Space of Postmodernism." *Diaspora* 1:8-24.

Sangren, Steven P. 1987. *History and Magical Power in a Chinese Community*. Stanford: Stanford University Press.

Shahar, Meir, and Robert P. Weller, eds. 1996. *Unruly Gods: Divinity and Society in China*. Honolulu: University of Hawai'i Press.

Smith, M. P., and Luis Guarnizo, eds. 1998. *Transnationalism from Below: Comparative Urban and Community Research*. Vol. 6. New Brunswick, NJ: Transaction Publishers.

Weller, Robert P. 1987. *Unities and Diversities in Chinese Religion*. Seattle: University of Washington Press.

Yu, Renqiu. 1995. "Chinese." In *The Encyclopedia of New York City*, ed. Kenneth T. Jackson. New Haven: Yale University Press.

9

The Protestant Ethic and the Dis-Spirit of Vodou

Karen Richman

Introduction

Haitian Catholicism is a complex, syncretic blend of European and African-Creole religious ideologies and practices, centered around the material reality of spiritual affliction, sorcery, and magic. Until recently it was the religion of the vast majority of the approximately one million Haitians who settled in the United States. Within less than two decades of their arrival, however, the migrants have been increasingly disavowing Catholicism and identifying as evangelical Protestants. For Haitian migrants, conversion to the religion which has long signified Americanization unequivocally represents an appropriation of American capitalist culture. Yet underneath the modern, ascetic cloak worn by the new converts, spiritual healing, sorcery, and magic remain at the heart of their syncretic practices. This chapter explores the contexts and meanings of conversion in a transnational Haitian community. Their home is in western Haiti and their primary outpost is in South Florida. My ethnographic research spans these two sites.[1]

Everyday Transnationalism in Little River and its Diaspora

Ti Rivyè, or Little River, is a coastal hamlet in the plain of Léogane, in western Haiti. Little River is the moral and material anchor of a mobile, transnational community. Though people from Ti Rivyè are spread across Haiti, the Caribbean, North America, and France, the vast majority of their expatriate members live in Palm Beach, Broward, and St. Lucie counties, Florida. *Mayami* (Miami) is their term for this location, whose imaginary northern boundary is *Nouyòk* (New York), the primary destination point of earlier Haitian migrations to the United States. In 1979, young men from Little River started sailing to Miami in their own tiny, motorless, fishing boats, which they call "canoes" (*kanòt*). Attempts to cross the 700 miles of ocean increased, and more women joined the men, until 1982, when United States Coast Guard cutters ended the flow. Substantial efforts to reach Florida by sea did not resume until late 1991 to 1992, in response to the violent coup d'etat against the Aristide government.[2]

In addition to these brief, intense boat migrations, there has been continuous movement of Haitians into and within the county of Palm Beach. First is the stream coming from Little River (primarily by airplane), as the former "boat" migrants continue to sponsor the migrations of their family members who arrive by airplane with legal or quasi-legal visas in hand. Second is the movement of Little River migrants within South Florida, which parallels their changing labor incorporation. Alex Stepick's (1998) analysis of Haitian migrants' incorporation in the South Florida economy reveals that few industries offered employment to the Haitian "boat people." As a result, the new immigrants could find work only in the most wretched sector: migratory farmwork. They were based in Belle Glade, Immokalee, Fort Pierce, and other agricultural sites in Florida and worked on agribusiness farms along the middle East Coast during the summer. Most moved out of this irregular, low-paying, and dangerous work as soon as they could; some were pushed out by the agriculture industry itself, in retaliation for successful lawsuits filed against growers during the 1980s (Richman 1992b). By the early nineties, most of the Little River migrants had relocated to Palm Beach and Broward counties to work in the lower levels of the burgeoning industries of tourism, service, and health care (hotels, restaurants, theme parks, landscaping, construction, transportation, cleaning, and nursing homes.)

Their home anchor in Little River is a quasi-peasant village. The people of Little River eke out a livelihood through farming (primarily sugar cane), fishing, and marketing of the food. Yet, their main economic activities seem to be producing low-cost labor for export, consuming wage remittances and imported food, and reabsorbing migrants when their capacity to work elsewhere expires. Everyday discourse reproduces their consciousness as producers of mobile labor and consumers of migrants' remittances. Children grow up expecting one day to "leave in search of a livelihood for their family" (*chache lavi pou fanmi yo*). Mundane references in village discourse to members located "outside" (*deyò*) and "over there" (*lòt bo a*) further naturalize the reality of dispersal to South Florida, or Mayami, in particular.

From Mayami, the migrants remain intimately tied to their mooring in Little River. "Transmigrants" (Basch, Glick-Schiller, and Blanc-Szanton 1994) return when they can for vacation visits, religious and family celebrations, to seek therapy and recuperation, and for retirement. Since they can only travel infrequently, the migrants' residential concentration in Palm Beach and Broward Counties is an important aspect of their continued involvement with one another and with their home. Independent couriers who specialize "coming and going" (*va y vyen*) run personalized, efficient, and entirely unregulated "parcel services" between distinct villages and urban neighborhoods in Haiti and their migrant satellite sites abroad.

Members of this transnational community have long entrusted their money, correspondence, information, and gifts to the men and women who travel regularly between their host and home sites.[3]

One device has provided a particularly vital linkage across this transnational community: the portable radio and cassette recorder. For most Haitians, whose domination has long been reproduced by illiteracy in the colonial language, French, cassettes offer a way to "write" in their own beloved vernacular, Creole (Kreyòl). But even if people were literate, the tapes are far more congenial for extending their emphatically oral Creole aesthetic, one that prizes proverbs, figurative language, indirection, antiphony, and fluid shifting between speech and song. Corresponding by cassette has become so normal that the term "to write (a letter)" (*ekri*) means recording a cassette rather than the epistolary form. There is now a distinctive genre of cassette-discourse, including formulaic greetings and salutations. Both recording and listening to a cassette-letter are "performance events" (Bauman 1984; Richman 2002). The portable cassette-radio thus stands as an epitomizing symbol, that is, "a model of and a model for" this transnational society (Geertz 1973:93). The apparatus is likely to be prominently displayed in the migrants' Florida apartments. A "boom box" is likewise an appropriate gift to send home, especially with the price tag still conspicuously attached. The device radiates the vitality of the dispersed family's intimacy. As a symbol of conspicuous consumption—like any art object—the apparatus at the same time connotes the migrant's success abroad.

Multi-sited, transnational Haitian communities reach back two centuries, when Haitian families dispersed by the revolution prevailed upon trading vessels to help them stay in touch (Laguerre 1998). Migrants' innovative uses of instantaneous and inexpensive technologies of communication, travel, audio and video recording, and the circulation of money (by computer modems and human couriers alike) have intensified and eased these simultaneous involvements. The growing transnational consciousness of contemporary Haitians (both at home and abroad) was belatedly acknowledged and appropriated by Haitian political discourse after the fall of the Duvalier dictatorship.[4] Their transnational experience was validated and reformulated in the eloquent, stirring discourse of Father Jean-Bertrand Aristide, a liberation priest who became a presidential candidate in the first free elections of 1990 (Richman 1992a; Richman and Balan-Gaubert 2000). The campaign unfolded as much inside Haiti as in its diaspora as migrants simultaneously engaged in politics as immigrants and as transnationals, claiming political rights and obligations and practicing long-distance nationalism (Laguerre 1998, Glick-Schiller and Fouron 2001).

Aristide's landslide victory in 1990 culminated in the declaration of a nation-state without borders. Haiti now included, in addition to its nine internal provinces, an external Dixième Département, a Tenth Province, divided like the internal ones, into arrondissements and communes, with cabinet-level representation by the

"Minister of the Diaspora." (The Tenth Province is often referred to as simply "The Tenth"). This "deterritorialized" nation-state affirmed that many of its citizens must live outside the country, but it maneuvers to anchor them to the homeland and benefit thereby from return visits, remittances, and investments.

Religious ideologies, practices, and networks also span the transnational social spaces inhabited by Haitian communities. The ritual world of this transnational community stretches from Little River to South Florida. A new religious cosmography has emerged, criss-crossed by transnational spirits who, it is thought, can only be worshiped on the family land back home. Innovative uses of cassette recording connect distant kin in the deterritorialized ritual performance. Audio and, increasingly, video cassettes are transforming healing and religious rituals, so that they, too, take place across a vast transnational performance space. At rituals unfolding on family land back home, worshipers and spirits, who appear "in person" at ceremonies, personally address far-off migrants. Migrants who cannot personally attend the ritual can nonetheless participate vicariously in the rituals wherever they hear or see the tape (Richman 1992b).

Haitian Catholic priests follow the paths of the migrants to minister to Haitian communities in the diaspora, and Protestant pastors, trained in mission churches established by North Americans during the mid-late twentieth century, are completing the circle of their evangelist mission. They are remigrating to the "center," to set up satellite congregations of their (North American) mission churches in Haitian communities in the United States. These transnational networks, communications, and religious leaders have changed religious belief, identity, and practice mediating the ongoing experiences, relations, and incorporation of this mobile, transnational community.

The Contest for Souls in Palm Beach County

Among the Haitians of Palm Beach County today, self-identified Catholics and Protestants co-exist in a fluid system of religious pluralism. This flexibility of religious practice and association, the Protestants' hard-line stance notwithstanding, makes it difficult to measure their relative strength. Père Roland, who heads the Catholic parish in Delray Beach, home to the densest concentration of Haitians (about 17,000) in the county, estimated that in 2001, Protestants slightly outnumbered Catholics. Stepick (1998) estimated that 40 percent of Haitians in Little Haiti in Miami were Protestant.

The apparent early success of the Protestants in converting new members is in part due to the oversight of the Catholic Church. The tens of thousands of Haitians who arrived by boat in the early eighties and settled in towns of Belle Glade, Delray Beach, Fort Pierce, and Lake Worth were virtually invisible to the Catholic Church. The evangelical churches, on the other hand, responded swiftly to the new migrants' religious "needs." By the early 1990s they had repatriated portions of North American missions, now thoroughly Haitianized, from the Haitian periphery back to the North American core. Haitian pastors associated with North American missions in the Haitian countryside immigrated to the United States at the behest of their North American religious organizations. Sent to the denominations' seminaries in the United States, they were then helped to establish satellites of their "third world" mission churches in Palm Beach County (and elsewhere). The very qualities that propelled pastors' ascents in rural Haiti—literacy, a flexible, entrepreneurial bent and a charismatic style—proved equally valuable in the rapidly changing immigrant communities.

By contrast, the Catholic Church responded belatedly to the influx of Catholic Haitians into Palm Beach County between 1979 and 1981. The first Haitian priest settled in the area in 1987. Père Roland, a member of the Scalabrinian order dedicated to serving immigrant communities, moved from New York City, where he had been serving a Haitian community. He established Notre Dame, the first Haitian Catholic church in Delray Beach. A second Haitian church was established in the nineties in Fort Pierce, a town in the county of St. Lucie to the north with about the same population of Haitians as Delray Beach. The Catholic congregations in Belle Glade, Lake Worth, and West Palm Beach have recently hosted their own full-time Haitian Catholic priests, who use space in local Catholic churches.

Lacking access to a Haitian Catholic church, many Catholics who wanted to attend Christian services and worship in their own language began going to Haitian Protestant churches. Many remained Catholic; others inevitably converted. The belated establishment of Haitian Catholic churches largely reversed that pattern. As Père Roland told me, "We got them back." The church has added extra masses to accommodate the growing congregation of about 1,400 registered members (each representing about 5 family members), and it is currently undergoing expansion and renovation. The church hosts myriad religious and social clubs, as well as educational programs targeted at migrants' adjustment; some of the latter involve collaboration with local government agencies.

There are many Protestant congregations in Palm Beach County. Fissions are common. One Pentecostal church in Delray has allegedly segmented into four competing factions in the recent past. The congregations vary in size and autonomy. The Church of God (L'Eglise de Dieu) built an expansive new church in North West Palm Beach in 1994 and has about 250 member families. By contrast, a Baptist congregation on the southern border of West Palm Beach uses space in the rear of a large Baptist church (whose membership is white). This congregation has less than 50 members. The previous year, about half of its congregation broke away and started their own meetings. For the Pentecostal congregants, in particular, the church is the center of life outside of their (service) jobs. They spend long hours in church, including most evenings after work, part of Saturday, and most of Sunday. Those with young children take them along into the pews.

The Protestant congregations host myriad religious and musical groups, but, unlike the Catholic church in Delray Beach, offer few programs aimed at migrants' adjustment. Nonetheless, relations with church members are their primary social networks, through which they exchange food, loans, help, rides, job referrals, childcare, and other services. Their tightly knit Protestant social world separates them from both non-Haitians and unsaved Haitians. Their asceticism, prohibiting enjoyment of secular music, dance, drinking, and smoking, further estranges them from people outside their churches.

Catholicism, Colonialism, and Protestant Missionization in Haiti

Roman Catholicism was and remains the state religion of independent Haiti.[5] The Catholic Church was indigenized after independence in 1804, when French colonists and their priests fled the country. Haitians controlled their own church during the century-long political isolation that served as the metropole's punishment for Haitian slaves' successful challenge to colonialism and slavery. Toward the end of the century, however, as Haiti was reincorporated in the world order, authority over its church was returned to the Europeans. Indeed, Louis Joseph Janvier, who is regarded by some as the founder of the Haitian nationalist movement in the late nineteenth century, referred to the church as an oppressive colonial power and the key threat to Haiti's sovereignty. Janvier's vision for the establishment of Protestantism in Haiti was "of a severely Erastian kind, where the clergy, even in matters of doctrine, would be controlled by the temporal government" (Nicholls 1979:118).

In his 1883 treatise on Haiti's foreign affairs, Janvier argued that conversion to Protestantism would provide the requisite religious basis for capitalist economic development in the impoverished peasant nation. Janvier went so far as to claim that Protestantism was more suited to the African temperament than was Catholicism, and was in many parts of Africa a valuable means for introducing the population to Western culture. The Protestant, he wrote, "is thrifty and self-reliant, he does not waste his money on carnivals and other frivolities. Protestantism permits free discussion and encourages private initiative. . . . The Protestant is almost always a more practical worker and a better citizen than the Catholic," (cited in Nicholls 1979:118). Nonetheless, Janvier admitted that his vision amounted to little more than wishful thinking: "Le protestantisme ne serait jamais un danger pour Haïti et lui vaudrait l'affection des nations protestantes" (Janvier 1883:371).

Long before Protestantism "became a danger" in Haiti, it was ideologically linked to anti-colonialism and black nationalism. In the early twentieth century, and in the hands of Janvier's followers, the new discipline of Haitian ethnology completed (or mediated) the intellectual linkage between Protestantism and anti-colonialism. In the wake of the cultural imperialism and overt racism of the Occupation by the United States, which lasted from 1915 to 1934, ethnology responded to the need to assert an alternative, authentic national identity. Studies of the peasants' religion and folklore provided the material for promotion of an authentic Haitian identity located in peasant life and rooted in African culture. Jean

Price-Mars, who authored the first important text on the peasants' folklore, was Episcopalian. Yet he also extolled the evangelical Protestants, even though they opposed vodou even more strongly than the Catholic church and Protestants comprised the majority of the blatantly racist "colons en khaki," as Jacques Romain, a central member of the ethnological movement, termed the occupying force (Nicholls 1970:403,412). Haiti's incorporation as a United States neo-colony did not, however, immediately stimulate increased Protestant missionization either during the Occupation itself or after 1934.

North American Protestant missionization greatly intensified in the hemisphere generally, and in Haiti in particular, during the second half of the twentieth century. That period saw the consummation of many a happy union of a nationalist state with an apolitical Protestant mission. Seventy percent of the Protestant missions in Haiti in 1970 had been established in the preceding twenty years, and an estimated 20 percent of the population was Protestant (Conway 1978:165; Romain 1986:81). The champion of Protestantism in Haiti was President François Duvalier (1957-1971), the first pro-vodou, pro-peasant, black nationalist president, who claimed Janvier as his ideological mentor. Doctor François Duvalier, a medical doctor and ethnologist, was a central member of the ethnological group, and he authored or co-authored several studies of the peasant religion. The self-declared president-for-life developed a reputation not only for "practicing vodou" but also for incorporating the practices and priesthood in his ruthless politics. Duvalier appears to have fostered the myth of his promotion of vodou, which only bolstered outsiders' stereotypes of the exotic, mysterious religion. As Courlander and Bastien (1966:56) wryly observed, the fact that Duvalier fostered Protestantism, which opposes vodou even more strongly than the Catholic church ever did, demonstrates that "the relationship between Duvalier and religion should be viewed not as one of an individual to a faith, but rather it should be approached form the standpoint of the relations between church and state." Duvalier finally succeeded in breaking the power of the foreign-dominated Catholic Church. While he resorted to violence to crush the church, romancing North American evangelical Protestants was a more effective strategy. The Protestants could be depended upon to avoid involvement in political affairs as much as possible and meanwhile bring "development" into the country. By 1965, more than a third of the schools were run by Protestant missionaries. Duvalier received Oral Roberts at the palace in 1969 (Nicholls 1970:412).[6]

The expansion of Protestant missionization in Haiti since the seventies especially involved the growth of Pentecostal groups, which systematically covered the geography of the country and encompassed the poorest segments of the population. Charles-Poisset Romain (1986) credits the Pentecostals' early promotion of literacy in Creole vernacular, rather than the official language of French, with its "take-off" in rural Haiti. Romain claims that missionization was more intense in Haiti during the seventies than anywhere else in the hemisphere and that Haiti witnessed more proliferation of sects during that period than any other country. Fred

Conway (1978) noted that the missionary presence was so pervasive during the seventies that he, like almost all foreigners in rural Haiti, was taken for a Protestant missionary.

Romain's (1986) and Conway's (1978) studies of Protestantism in rural Haiti illuminate the religious landscape of rural Haiti during the decade which culminated with a massive exodus towards the "source" of progress.[7] Both studies demonstrate that evangelism oriented people toward North America. Conway's cultural exploration of local understandings of Protestant missionization describes an unequivocal linkage between the religion and an American dream. He (1978:193) argues convincingly that "missionary Protestantism in Haiti gives rise less to a 'Protestant ethic' of self-help than to the idea that the way to worldly success is identified with direct dependence on the foreign—North American—missionary." The discourse of villagers reaffirms Romain's (1986:159) assertion that the Protestant mission churches symbolized the hegemony of the Northern "mother country." They epitomized "progress." While pointing to Protestant missions, people told him, "the country is becoming more and more civilized" in contrast to the backwardness blamed on peasant vodou. Several converts frankly told Conway that their conversion was a contribution to "development" (Conway 1978:172). Vodou, by contrast, signified backwardness. Even when the church was established by Haitians and there was no American present, the religion signified a foreign, and specifically North American, culture.

Moreover, the Protestant churches signified American capital. According to Conway, villagers understood that Americans "needed" numbers of converts and they were willing to pay for them. No one benefitted more from their "needs" to build missions and count disciples than the pastors. The clergy was and is one of the few "jobs" for men in rural areas, and the field of candidates is vast. Romain comments that "tout protestant est à la fois pasteur et missionnaire" (Romain 1986:144). The success of the pastors reflects the convergence of the fluid, informal, lay, entrepreneurial character of the evangelical practice with local values regarding leadership and spiritual power, namely, diffuse leadership, charismatic, spontaneous power, and an intense distrust of authority and bureaucracies. The religion welcomes the man who aspires to have a congregation, begins by praying with two or three people, and eventually builds a congregation. The speech practice of addressing any male evangelical as "pastè" reinforces this assumption. Association with Protestant missions, and the implied opportunities of pastoring, signify upward mobility both figuratively and literally. For in addition to the social and economic boost of satisfying an American missionary organization's "needs" is the real possibility of a visa to the United States.

Indeed, the miracle of the visa to the United States, the fruit of mission sponsorship, is a frequent theme in pastors' narratives from the pulpits of Haitian churches in Palm Beach County today. One L'Eglise de Dieu pastor, for example, recounted during a sermon how, while working in a Haitian rural parish, Jesus instigated a rift between himself and his superiors. His exile propelled him toward Port-au-Prince and an encounter with a white American missionary. The missionary was establishing a new mission in another part of the countryside, and he invited the pastor to join him there. Then one day the American asked him, "Would you like to see the United States?" He soon found himself at the U.S. consulate with a visa in hand for the United States and eventually he became pastor of the Palm Beach County congregation.

What is Vodou? Is it Catholicism?

In Creole, the term *vodou* (*vodoun*) refers to a genre of ritual music and dance, performed in honor of a category of spirit. A legacy of the African cultural past, the term is the Fongbe (Benin) word for spirit. Over time, outsiders applied the term to refer to the religion as a whole, a usage widely accepted, though foreign to many in the countryside. Spirits are called *lwa* (pronounced like French *loi*). *Lwa* can be thought of as super (in the sense of all-too-human) human beings who are inherited through family lines among land-holding descent groups. Said to be from Ginen (Africa) and to dwell there still, they crystallize a deep historical memory of the violence and displacement of the African ancestors' past. Their iconography and naming blends African and European influences; some are based on Catholic saints, and many have African names. Indeed the term "saint" is used by some rather than the word *lwa*. A Haitian man explained to Alfred Métraux (1972), author of the classic text *Le Vaudou Haitiën*, many decades ago: "you have to be Catholic to serve your spirits (*lwa*)." Thus, despite official condemnation by the Catholic Church of practices oriented to the *lwa*, Catholicism is fundamental to serving one's *lwa*. All "feedings of the *lwa*" begin with substantial Catholic prayer, led by a lay priest. Attendance at mass and giving alms to beggars gathered at cathedrals are all requirements of serving one's *lwa*. Ritual action entails enthusiastic, spectacular, multimedia performance involving Catholic prayer (in French), drumming, singing (in Creole), dancing, visual art, parading, spirit possession-performance, and offerings of food, drink, toiletries, and animal sacrifice.

The symbolism of feeding encompasses all ritual discourse and performance. Significantly, the very term for worship is "to serve" (*sèvi*), as in to serve food. The personalities of *lwa* are differentiated by their particular tastes in food and drink. Additionally, a *lwa*'s displeasure is cast as hunger, and a ceremony is called a "feeding of the *lwa*." A successful "feeding" occurs when the spirit, having been enticed to journey all the way from Ginen, arrives personally to "party" with the family and to accept the lavish and copious offerings. The spirit's enjoyment of the music, dance, and food is an implicit signal that s/he has "let go" of the victim and/or agrees not to "take hold" of others, at least, not in the immediate future.

Scholarly and popular representations of the *lwa* or "saints" have created the inaccurate portrayal of universalistic, nature spirits. In fact, *lwa* are unique to each lineage (Murray 1984). Yet, they are also distinct from ancestors, who are worshiped in their own right and whose primary role, in virtue of their proximity to the other world, is to mediate relations between members of kin groups and their inherited *lwa*. Neither are the *lwa* nature gods. They do not wield powers to control air, land, or water. Their power is instead primarily confined to afflicting and protecting members of descent groups to whom they belong. They are the protagonists of a cult of affliction and healing. When *lwa* feel neglected or ignored by the heirs, as they often do in their remote home in Ginen, they retaliate by sending affliction, "seizing" heirs with somatic illness, misfortune, and property loss. Worship by the kin group is a collective effort to ward off illness by enticing the avenging spirits to "release" their victims and to prevent future attacks. Migrants do not escape the mobile *lwa*'s orbit. Indeed migrants are prime "choices" of avenging spirits and they are primary sponsors of rites taking place back home.

Haitian Catholics' overlapping, simultaneous practice of both Catholic and Afro-Creole devotions has puzzled outsiders, especially in the face of the church's representation of the two as moral and social opposites: Catholicism as the norm and vodou as the feared and exotic Other. Catholicism is associated with French culture and language, the local elite, and light skin, in contrast to the satanic superstitions of the poor, dark, non-literate majority. In reality, any given Catholic actor in Haiti falls within the continuum, some as "straight" Catholics (*Katolik fran*) who may know little or nothing of serving the spirits, and some as vodouists, and the vast middle living their lives in the middle going through the rites of passage of the Catholic church while simultaneously maintaining contact with vodou healers and the *lwa* (spirits), especially in times of crisis. People's involvement ranges from apathy (ignoring their spirits until a crisis looms), to those who are spectators at others' rituals but neither contribute nor worship (through prayer, song, dance), to self-described "sèvitè" (literally, "servants"). The last are often initiated into the ranks of a congregation headed by a professional *oungan* or *gangan* (priest) or *manbo* (priestess).

The practices of the contemporary Haitian Catholic Church further blur its separation from vodou. In a concerted effort to hold on to its wayward flock, the church consciously appropriates the captivating styles of vodou worship in its masses. Melodies that sound more like sacred songs for the *lwa* are sung in the pews, while a battery of vodou drums playing West-African derived rhythms accompanies them.

Moreover, this fluid, politicized Catholic-vodou religious culture has an ambiguous relationship to Haitian Protestantism. At least a third of Haitians identify as Protestant today, an effect of the post-war spread of North American evangelism throughout the hemisphere. Despite their short history in Haiti, however, the churches are deeply creolist, liturgies are in Creole, and there is a vast native-born clergy. And despite the assertive, separatist stance of the fundamentalists, Protestant practices are also blended ones. Their renunciatory rhetoric notwithstanding, they appropriate aspects of "the other." Underneath the modern, ascetic cloak worn by the new converts, spiritual healing, sorcery, and magic remain part of their syncretic practices.

Transnational Migrants and Their Transnational *Lwa*

Unlike Haitians in New York, who have established shrines to serve the *lwa* (Brown 1991), those in Palm Beach County have not endeavored to serve or feed their spirits in the host society setting.[8] Rather, the location of their ritual practice remains back home on the family land in Ti Rivyè, reinforcing a transnational orientation, as transmigrants remain morally, somatically, and spiritually anchored back home. Creative uses of cassette tape and video recorders have resulted in a reconfiguration of the boundaries of the ritual performance space, allowing migrants to continue to serve their spirits back home. When migrants cannot personally attend the services, they participate indirectly by listening to cassette tapes of the rituals. On these tapes the migrants hear not only the sounds of the performance itself—drumming, singing, prayers, and chatter—but also the voices of narrators describing what the listener cannot see: the flow of possessions, offerings, sacrifices, prayers, conversations, and so on. (The anthropologist was by no means the only one tape-recording the ceremonies.) Spirits possessing the bodies of ritual actors are not only aware of the recording devices, they often move to the recorder in order personally to address the absent migrant or migrants.

Although they are characterized as ancient, immutable symbols of "African" tradition, the *lwa* have shown that they can be most adaptable to changing conditions of global reproduction. With so many of their "children" now living and working "over there," the *lwa* are busier than ever. I once had the opportunity to interview a spirit about her protection of migrants. The female spirit was possessing a male ritual leader, who was conducting a healing rite for an absent migrant in the presence of the migrants' parents and me. The spirit, whose name is Ezili Dantò/Our Lady of Lourdes, said to us, "Every three days I am in Mayami. . . . I have to keep watch over everything that goes on. Mayami is where the core is." (*Tou le twa jou m Mayami. Fò m veye tout sa k pase. Se Mayami noyo a ye*). "Miami" is where most of the migrants from "her" Ti Rivyè village now reside. Like all of the spirits, whose movements are said to be like the wind, Ezili Dantò can instantly traverse these international boundaries. She meant by "watching over" her peripatetic dependents that, in return for "service" and "care," she would safeguard life, prevent accidents, and divert sorcerers' aggressions.

At the same time, the spirit implied that she would watch over migrants' abilities to alienate their labor and to accumulate savings (to be remitted to Haiti). Spirits are said to "protect" the migrants' productivity abroad. Consider how Ti Chini (Little Caterpillar), a Ti Rivyè migrant used the term protection with regard to his patron *lwa*: "I have my protection here. My protection won't abandon me in anything I could achieve, in anything I could get, it's there with me." Pepe, a ritual leader (*gangan ason*) in Ti Rivyè, explained to me how the *lwa* intervene in the lives of their emigrant "servitors." Rather than the term protection, Pepe favored words deriving from contract: "guaranty" (*garanti*) and "de-guaranty" (*degaranti*).

To illustrate the *lwa*'s guaranty, Pepe referred to the case of Lamèsi, a resident immigrant of the U.S. who not only contributed to the rituals for her *lwa* but also returned each year to attend them:

> There are (migrant) people like Lamèsi. She always returns to see how the annual service for the *lwa* is going. She sees how the work is going. It guaranties her. It supports her. It satisfies her. She knows that if she doesn't find anything today, tomorrow she'll find. She knows too that if she is employed, she won't be fired for any old reason. Instead of de-guarantying her, it always guaranties her little bonus even higher.

As long as an immigrant continues to "take care of" (*okipe*) her *lwa* in Ti Rivyè, the spirits may reciprocate by guarantying her employment opportunities in Mayami. The alternative, in Pepe's words, is the option of "de-guaranty." Pepe described how an emigrant might be de-guarantied by a *lwa*:

> If the person is in a job that pays $200 or $300 [a week], the *lwa* can make you lose your job. The *lwa* can make you sick so you'll never find work and you'll spend everything you saved. The *lwa* can also make you get into a car accident, lose your job, and make you an alcoholic so that you can never guaranty anything in that country.

To sum up how the mobile, transnational *lwa* intervene in the lives of migrants, then, the *lwa* reciprocate diligent "service" by protecting and guarantying their care-takers' *capacity* to produce in "Miami" and to reproduce, in the Marxian sense of self-replacement of persons and things, through the consumption of remittances by kin and *lwa* alike back in Haiti. The *lwa* take revenge for migrants' neglect by "thwarting" (*anpeche*) and de-guarantying the same.

Thus, spiritual affliction beliefs, ritual discourse, and performance symbolize and reinforce migrants' role as emissaries of their families' social, economic, and ritual interests. The social norm of generosity and giving to one's capacity influences the view of migrants as the kinsmen with the "biggest wrists" (*ponyèt*). Migrants are expected to contribute accordingly not just to their own but to their extended family's ever-increasing ritual and secular obligations. The sites where Haitian migrants work are now criss-crossed by mobile, transnational *lwa*. These spirits intervene by "holding" a recalcitrant migrant who can, but will not, take responsibility for his or her increased burden. Migrants are frequently the victims of vengeful spirits, which only an expiatory, healing rite performed by their home family, regardless of the migrant's absence, can assuage.

Migrants' Resistance and Conversion

Some Ti Rivyè migrants attribute their gradual, if modest, success in the host society to the positive interdependence between their home kin, the *lwa,* and themselves. Dutiful deployment of their "bigger wrists" for ritual expenditures on the family land in Ti Rivyè has resulted in an enhanced "guaranty" and "protection" of their productivity in the host society. Regular demonstrations of generosity to the spirits of their descent group have solidified their social relations and reputations across their transnational community.

But others have met disappointment as they struggle to survive in the lowest rungs of a hostile, discriminatory South Florida economy and, meanwhile, stay "healthy." In the background is the frustration of poverty. The migrants are not as successful as they hoped; their home families are still poor, remittances have been too meager to bring their families the hoped for mobility. The migrants' frustration is further linked to their perceptions that their families no longer look upon them as people but see them rather as insensate beasts of burden. They slave away in hostile, foreign countries for the sake of people who resent them for having left. Many migrants complained to me that their home relatives were lazy and just ate up their remittances rather than invested them. Since many in Mayami are still very poor and expect to recuperate and/or retire in Haiti, they are bitter and worried about their lack of economic security back home.

Migrants are turning to conversion to resist their perceived domination by home kin and their spirits. By converting, they take symbolic control of their remittances and the terms of their relationships with the home. They have rejected their *lwa*, withdrawn from the system of family ritual obligations, and joined Pentecostal churches. They blame the *lwa* for being useless to them, for colluding with their families who exploit them, for turning a blind eye to migrants in need, even though those migrants have sent money for rituals. One of the first of my friends from Ti Rivyè to use conversion as a means of rebellion against the system of kinship and ritual obligations was Little Caterpillar (Ti Chini), whose positive comments on the reciprocal dependence between migrants and *lwa* were cited above. Ti Chini had considered himself a loyal emissary for family and spirits alike. His family's alleged "wastes" of his remittances, his failure to get ahead and his spate of bad luck—injuries in an orange grove, a diagnosis of adult onset diabetes—despite all this sending thousands of dollars for ritual purposes—finally pushed him over the edge.

In 1992, he converted to Protestantism. Ti Chini is an eloquent master of Creole oratory. He is also non-literate. He and I thus correspond, as most Haitians do, by cassette tape. He sent me a cassette letter in Creole explaining his drastic action.

> Well, Karen, here is the reason why I converted. Regardless, I would have converted anyway. How could I be serving *lwa* for all of these problems to keep on happening to me in both the land of Miami and in the land of Haiti? Why? When a *lwa* needs to eat, I provide for him/her. If I'm [sitting] over here working these lousy jobs, and [my older brother, a ritual leader] Se Byen sends word that he's going to do such and such work in Haiti, like it or not, I have to send off $200 or $300.

Why? For the *lwa*. And then, after I've done all that work, who should have the biggest problems but me. Look how long I've been in another country working. I could just tell you, someone would think I must have something wrong with me, because whenever I have money in my hands, I don't know what to do with it.

Well I found out that for my part, there are no *lwa*. I can't say that for everyone there are no *lwa*. I wouldn't say to somebody else, "you don't have *lwa*." It's just me, myself, for my part—I hear I have *lwa*. There are no *lwa*. If I have *lwa*, I have thieving *lwa*. I have cheating *lwa*. I don't have *lwa*. Why is that? When someone takes three or four hundred dollars out of his/her pocket, takes that money, and finds a steer to buy with it to feed to the *lwa* or finds a pig to buy to feed to the *lwa*, the *lwa* must see that when you spend that money, they should take you in. That's what *lwa* means. When I'm in poverty, should I light a candle and say, "look how the *lwa* help me?" No. You [*lwa*] see my problem, and then I am worse off. . . . Things to do with the *lwa*, the only place where there are laws [homonym of spirit (*lwa*) in Creole] is in a court. For now, my *lwa* are in the hands of God. The *lwa* who are my companions—God is the one who is my companion. I am no longer involved with the *lwa*.

Why? I am standing here today. In one year alone, Karen, I sponsored a service at home. It cost me $1,500. I tell you up until the present I still owe [a man from Ti Rivyè]. I still haven't been able to pay off the money for that service. Does that mean you have *lwa*? For me to have done all those things for the *lwa*, for you to watch me borrowing to feed you, and slaving away at picking tree fruit to raise the money, well, as far as I'm concerned, there are no *lwa* anymore. My life is in God's hands. My life is in the hands of the Eternal. My life is not in the hands of the *lwa*. You understand? My life is in the hands of God. My life is not in the hands of the *lwa*. I remove myself from *lwa*. I remove myself from Satan. Now I am in the hands of God. All of my being is in the hands of the Eternal.

And that's why I converted, Karen. It has given me a respite.

It seems obvious that resistance to ritual exploitation, rather than firm conviction in the superiority of Protestant doctrine, was the reason Ti Chini converted to Protestantism. His periodic confirmations of confidence in the Protestant's God (and rejection of Satan) did not stand on their own; they were, instead, set against repudiations of his ungrateful, arrogant spirits. The tactical use of conversion to contest relations with the *lwa* and people who serve them is described in the literature on Haitian ritual practice. Alfred Métraux (1953b, 1972) noted the use of conversion as an act of revolt against *lwa* more than half a century ago, before the postwar expansion of Pentecostals in the country. Métraux explained how the act of conversion represented "a magic circle" of protection from attacks by *lwa* and sorcerers. He quoted what a Marbial person told him: "If you want the (*lwa*) to leave you in peace, become a Protestant." (Métraux 1972:351-352).

Another astute observer of the use of conversion as resistance was a Protestant theologian, Roger Dorsainville. He lamented that a "true conviction and profound commitment to be saved" were "rarely" the reason people converted. Rather, he stated, "Protestantism is pursued as a superior magical power, the pastor is like a more powerful sorcerer" (cited in Pressoir 1942:8).[9] The magic circle also protects the convert from very real fear of sorcery, a social weapon long used by peasants throughout the world to limit individual greed and enforce reciprocity. Among this community, there is a seemingly ubiquitous perception that those who dare to better themselves will inevitably be "killed for what they had." As economic emissaries, migrants are obvious targets for the envious.[10] As my friend Noufi, who migrated to South Florida from Ti Rivyè told me after her conversion in the mid-nineties, "as soon as you convert, nothing can harm you" (*depi ou konvèti, anyen pa ka fè ou*). Romain (1986:125) sums up the "délire du persécution" and the Protestant antidote to it.

> The common man fears his neighbor and usually harbors a feeling of distrust towards every expected competitor. This [proverb] well justifies the feeling of insecurity: From the time of Guinea [the very beginning] man has scorned his fellow man. . . . The Protestant exploits to its extreme this psyche of fear, offering the face of shelter and comportment of security.

The pragmatic use of conversion underscores the fluidity between these ritual options, the Protestant's militant rhetoric of renunciation notwithstanding. Fred Conway's (1978) ethnography of Protestants in a village near the southern town of Aux Cayes, conducted during a period of intense Pentecostal missionization, explores the logical bases of this fluidity. Conway found that Catholics (who may also serve spirits) tend to be tolerant of those who convert. The basis of their acquiescence is an understanding that conversion represents a personal adjustment in extreme circumstances. In spite of the Protestant's separatist rhetoric, conversion does not represent a wholesale rejection of their Catholic system of values.

> If conversion settles a problem an individual has with a family [*lwa*], that is not a family matter as long as the sèvis for the loua continue as before. Maintenance of good relations with the family *lwa* is the responsibility of the family as a whole rather than of the particular individuals of which the family is made up. Protestantism—even militant Pentecostalism—has not interfered with the general pattern of family ritual, which continues as before. This is a further indication that the "opposition" to Protestantism is more a creation of Protestantism than a deepseated reaction of Vodouists.

Insofar as both "religions" are systems of affliction and healing, many

Haitian immigrants take a pluralistic approach to the quest for therapy. An acute illness that has remained stubbornly resistant to the therapies of biomedical doctors and *gangan* alike may lead a Catholic to seek aid from a Protestant healer. The healer herself or himself, having exhausted her or his own spiritual resources, may even instruct a patient's desperate family to visit the local Protestant healer (Métraux 1972:352).[11] Thus when a similar dilemma beset my "god-relatives" in the compound where I lived, they turned to local Protestants for help. My god-child, "Matchstick," had been chronically ill for several years, despite the interventions of biomedical doctors, including a surgeon, and her paternal grandfather, a respected, senior *gangan*. When her maternal grandmother, who is Protestant, offered to "enter her in Protestantism," her paternal family willingly "gave her to them." Despite their prayers and the healing hands of a Protestant healer, she died in 2000 at age 16. Her father's family, my god-relatives, bear their in-laws no malice.

Incorporation and the Protestant Devil (or Ethic?)

Conversion is a strategy migrants have used to resist their perceived roles as exploited emissaries for kin and spirits. For some it is a temporary move. Ti Chini, for example, "backslid" into Catholicism (and serving *lwa*) after his Protestant protest achieved its effect. Yet others who may not have initially felt compelled by Protestant ideology are nonetheless appropriated by it and reoriented toward the Protestant ethic of individualism, saving, and abstinence. Max Weber (1992) argued that the Protestant's assertive, methodical, and sober behavior, tangible proof of the individual's elect status, is central to the religion's appeal and success. His analysis of the expansion of the Protestant ethic in the advance of capitalist culture in Europe centuries ago applies to the "developing" societies of the twentieth and twenty-first centuries. Métraux (1972:352) concluded that "No doubt it is the challenging attitude adopted by Protestants towards the [*lwa*] which has finally convinced the peasants that this religion confers upon its adepts a sort of supernatural immunity." Gerlach and Hine's (1968) pioneering study of Protestant expansion in Latin America anticipates the findings of many prominent scholars of the movement in the region (Sherman 1997; Chesnut 2003). "It is the certitude of the Pentecostal ideology which is its greatest strength" (Gerlach and Hine 1968:35).

The evangelicals teach this ideology in both subtle, metalinguistic ways and through more obvious means. Military metaphors of armies, fortresses, forces, and strength proliferate. One well-known Haitian sect calls itself a "celestial army." A rhetoric of progress, change, and advance articulates with the militant tone, while simultaneously invoking a principle that is central to capitalist culture. Though the Protestant discourse is in Creole, there is a distinct contrast between its language and that of sacred *lwa* songs. The latter situate the kin group as the social unit and interdependence between and among spirits and kin as core values. Instead, the discourse of Protestant hymns and sermons imagine an independent dyad of person and God. Moreover, possessive pronouns abound, a subtle lesson in individualism. Romain (1986:140-141) notes that "le protestant entretient une relation de personne à personne avec son Dieu. Le Christ est présenté comme 'mon rocher' 'ma forteresse,' 'mon asile protecteur' and 'mon recours dans la détresse.'" A further distinction has to do with the determination of meaning in the two sacred discourses. While the sacred *lwa* songs "throw" pithy, ambiguous, moral "points," whose underdetermined, oblique language is meant to be interpreted subjectively, the rhetoric of the hymns is unambiguously affirmative. They are literate and literal readings, telling you what they say and mean. This overdetermination of meaning in turn articulates with metaphors of armies, weaponry, soldiers.

Dorsainville's charge that converts valued their new faith for its superior magical power, and pastors for their skills as more powerful sorcerers (than priests or ritual leaders [*gangan*]), is echoed in sermons voiced in Palm Beach County Haitian churches today. The preachers captivate parishioners with *miraculous* stories of persons who converted and the next day discovered checks for $100,000 in their mailboxes. A sermon by one L'Eglise de Dieu pastor during an evening prayer service, for example, was a remarkably straightforward approbation of migrants' newfound liberation from the burdens of their former moral economy. The sermon, which he delivered in October 2000, had an indelible refrain. It was rendered in the oddly graceful mixture of Creole and English that typifies their speech: "Jezu, set *nou* free" (Jesus sets you free).

What did he mean by freedom? If he implied spiritual freedom, it was only in an indirect sense, as he continued to explain in Creole-English: "Free *de pwoblem ou*, free *de soufrans ou*, free *de dèt ou dwe yo*" (Free of your problems, free of your suffering, free of the debts you owe.) Jesus liberates you from your pecuniary obligations to send your wages back home. Jesus frees converts from the system of obligations tying them to their lineage, their spiritual legacy, and their inherited land. Fidelity to Jesus liberates you from your obligations to contribute to rituals back home, which are major mechanisms for sharing and redistributing resources among kin. The morality of hoarding is reconfigured. Now, it is good to keep the money in your own pocket.

> Haven't you noticed people who are working three jobs so they can send money back home to feed the devil? As long as you understand the Bible, your money will stay in your pocket [places his right hand on his right pants pocket]. You don't send it off; you go to the Win-Dixie with it. The Win-Dixie is beautiful [nice]. You can buy nice food for your children there.

What does he mean by "devil" *(dyab)*? The devil is the "other" in this righteous discourse, a diffuse, catch-all term for anything connoting the old religion. It confounds categories that people who serve the *lwa* carefully distinguish. The misuse of the term equates the anthropomorphic spirits of descent groups (*lwa*) who hail from the mythical time of Guinea (*Ginen*) with illicit powers manipulated by sorcerers. The term *dyab* in Creole, which derives from the French *diable*, retains the old French meanings. It is a symbolic representation of impersonal contracts forged between ambitious, antisocial individuals, and implicitly, a critique of the ethos of capitalism (which the early Protestants normalized). The devil is a power that you buy. Like a faceless wage laborer, it works for you, making money fast, like wild interest, or pure capital, which is distinguished from savings because it reproduces itself. But it is difficult to keep devils in check. They inevitably turn on their masters or their masters' progeny. Indeed, a contract is said to be made for a certain period of profit whose final payment is death.

It is important to understand that the pastor did not seek to deny the existence of *dyab*, rather he offered his faith as its most powerful antidote, a magic circle of protection. If you believe in Jesus, *dyab* cannot touch you. But this pastor's sermon was particularly focused on proving how a Protestant's faith could protect him or her from the financial costs of being afflicted or associated with *dyab*.

> The devil can't touch you as long as you know the Bible. There are people who have *zonbi* on them. [Zonbi are mobile powers manipulated by sorcerers and "sent on" victims.] They pay $2,500 to remove them. There was another man, the devil took him. The person who was treating him made him stand on all fours, as if he were a cow or a horse. [Bursts of laughter in the pews.] This is a serious thing, you know, don't laugh. They hit him; he bled. [More howls, and another admonishment not to laugh because it was real.] They put a bridle in his mouth, and injured his mouth, and made him walk around like that so the devil would leave him. But as long as you know Jesus, you don't have to do things like that. [Or underwrite others' treatments.]

Next, the pastor told the story of a destitute and desperate man who, like Jack of the Beanstalk fable, gave his last $100 to a group of Christians who were singing on a street corner. He instantly made $100,000, which conveniently had been earlier cited as the cost today of a college education for a child. Ironically, the preacher's central message appropriates the very same images that make *maji*, or buying *pwen*, serving *dyab*, illicit: individual ambition, money that grows by itself.

> The man didn't have anything. His children were hungry. He took his last $100 and was going to a store to buy food for his family. On the way he saw people gathered who were singing [hymns]. He gave them the $100. When he got back home, his wife asked him what he bought with the money. He told her, "we have to talk about something." He told her he gave the money away. She said, "WHAT?!?" The next day he received a check for $100,000.

The story ended here; there was no suggestion of how he should consume or distribute the riches. It is important to emphasize , therefore, that there is nothing akin to the moral discourse associated with serving the *lwa*, with its emphasis on sharing, giving to one's capacity, and reciprocity, and its incessant critique and containment of individualism and greed. The imagery, songs, and discourse associated with serving *lwa* are symbolic ways of keeping migrants tied to their homes. They are also means of critiquing and containing individualism, which are graphically symbolized in the imagery of *dyab*.

Ironically, the Protestants' discourse sacralizes instant rewards and private gain, the very means associated with immorality and sorcery. This Puritan devil is the very kind of sorcerer's power that the communal morality associated with *lwa* seeks to contain. But now it is cloaked and authorized through bodily practices of restraint: abstinence from secular music, dancing, drinking, and smoking, modesty in dress, and austerity in sexual relations, in other words, monogamous marriage within an autonomous nuclear family unit, unfettered by ties to lineages. As migrants resist their perceived exploitation by kin and *lwa* by turning away from this moral economy, they reorient themselves determinately toward the acquisitive spirit of the Protestant American dream. An "uplifting" song intoned at L'Eglise de Dieu prayer services captures this ethic. The first verse states, "Depi Jezi adopte mwen, mwen se yon milyonè" (Since Jesus adopted me, I am a millionaire).

Notes

1. The project builds upon ethnographic research I conducted in South Florida and in Western Haiti over the past two decades. I have amassed a rich body of detailed, longitudinal data on a single community, including patterns of settlement, household formation, work experiences, kinship relations, transnational linkages, political involvement, and religious affiliations and activities.

I first contacted migrants from Ti Rivyè in 1981, while working as an advocate for farmworkers on the Eastern Shore of Virginia. Informal anthropological research among the Haitian farmworkers, both on the Eastern Shore, where they spent summers, and in their base settlements in Palm Beach, St. Lucie, and Broward counties of Florida, led to the design of my dissertation project. My dissertation, based on bilateral research in a Léogane village and in South Florida, explored the ritual world of a single transnational community and was funded by funded by the Inter-American Foundation and Organization of American States. The project, carried out during the mid-eighties, was a community-based study, using qualitative ethnographic methods and substantial surveys of economic, land tenure, religious, kinship, and migration data. Between 1992 and 1995, I returned to South Florida as part of a team of researchers, headed by David Griffith, investigating inter-ethnic relations and migration incorporation among six ethnic groups in South Florida. The project, which involved an extensive survey as well as qualitative methods, was supported by National Science and Howard Heinz foundations. My current research on religious pluralism and conversion among Haitians in South Florida has entailed qualitative methods and participation in religious services. It was supported by the Social Science Research Council. Historical research and writing support in 2001 were provided by the Newberry Library.

2. People fleeing the violence of the coup d'etat against the Aristide government were also interdicted by the U.S. Coast Guard; most were summarily returned before even reach-

ing the United States.

3. The handling of money by these informal couriers casts doubt on the accuracy of official estimates of remittance transmission.

4. President Aristide was ousted in a military coup d'etat after barely eight months in office. A supporter of the brutal junta crystallized the extent of Aristide's ties to Haitian migrants when he told a *New York Times* journalist, "We don't want Aristide. Let him be the President of the Diaspora" (cited in Richman 1992a). The United States intervened in 1994, briefly restoring Aristide to the presidency. After sitting out one term, in keeping with a mandate against succession, he was re-elected to office in 2000.

5. The state recently officially recognized the Afro-Creole religion and Protestantism.

6. Fred Conway (1978:166-167) captures the paradox of the ethnologist-president's promotion of Protestantism: "For all his identification with Vodoun, François Duvalier might well be called the 'father of Protestantism' in Haiti. Duvalier's main potential opposition in the religious sphere was a Catholic Church dominated by foreigners. In his struggle with this adversary he enlisted both Vodoun and Protestantism in spite of the fact that the Protestants were more inimical to Vodoun than were Catholics. At a time when Duvalier was deliberately alienating foreign governments and foreign aid organizations, he welcomed Protestant missionaries, especially from the U.S. The Protestants drew people away from an allegiance to the Catholic church without themselves presenting a monolithic front to the government. Because the missionaries were competing with each other, fiercely at times, they were not in a position to oppose the government as a group."

7. Romain published a comprehensive sociology of Protestantism, "Le Protestantisme en Haïti." Fred Conway's (1978) dissertation is an ethnography of the plural religious life of a village near the southern town of Aux Cayes. Through his history of the establishment of various mission churches and the wry comments of the villagers who observed those projects, Conway depicts the mutual utilitarianism of American missionaries and Haitian pastors, with the missionaries' quantitative desire for more converts, and the Haitians' quest for American patronage, a decent job, prestige, and a visa to the United States.

8. Haitians serving their spirits in New York are nonetheless enjoined through spiritual affliction to return home occasionally as well. Karen McCarthy Brown describes how Mama Lola, a vodou priestess in New York, was punished by her spirits for pretending that serving them in New York would fulfill her ritual obligations. She recuperated by returning to her homeland to worship them.

9. *L'Evangile est aussi recherché comme un "ouanga" supérieur, le prédicateur est comme un bocor puissant.*

10. Indeed, some migrants avoid returning home for fear that they will be magically poisoned. Though they can be "hit" with poisonous powders anywhere in the world, and Ti Rivyè natives are believed to have been "hit" in Florida, the likelihood is believed to be far greater back home in Haiti.

11. Conway (1978:250) points out that since the therapy requires faith, conversion sometimes takes place while the patient is unconscious. In such moments of crisis, Protestants overlook the role of the individual's volition.

References

Appadurai, Arjun. 1990. "Disjuncture and Difference in the Global Cultural Economy." *Public Culture* 2 (2):1-24.

————. 1991. "Global Ethnoscapes: Notes and Queries for a Transnational Anthropology." In *Recapturing Anthropology*, ed. Richard Fox. Santa Fe: School of American Research Press.

Barry, Tom, Beth Wood, and Deb Preusch. 1984. *The Other Side of Paradise: Foreign Control in the Caribbean*. New York: Grove Press.

Basch, Linda, Nina Glick-Schiller, and Cristina Szanton-Blanc. 1994. *Nations Unbound: Transnational Projects and the Deterritorialized Nation-State*. New York: Gordon Breach.

Bauman, Richard. 1984. *Verbal Art as Performance*. Prospect Heights, IL: Waveland Press.

Brodwin, Paul. 1996. *Medicine and Morality in Haiti*. Cambridge: Cambridge University Press.

————. 2000. "Pentecostalism and the Production of Community in the Haitian Diaspora." Center For Latin American, Discussion Paper Series, No. 90. Milwaukee: University of Wisconsin-Milwaukee.

Brown, Karen McCarthy. 1987. "Alourdes: A Case Study of Moral Leadership in Haitian Vodou." In *Saints and Virtues*, ed. John Hawley. Berkeley: University of California Press.

————. 1991. *Mama Lola: A Vodou Priestess in New York*. Berkeley: University of California Press.

Bryce-Laporte, Roy. 1979. "The United States' Role in Caribbean Migration: Background to the Problem." In *Caribbean Immigration to the United States*, ed. Roy Bryce-Laporte and Delores Mortimer. Smithsonian Institution, Research Institute on Immigration and Ethnic Studies. Occasional Papers No. 1. Washington, D.C.

Chaney, Elsa. 1987. "The Context of Caribbean Migration." In *Caribbean Life in New York City: Sociocultural Dimensions*, ed. Constance Sutton and Elsa Chaney. New York: Center for Migration Studies.

Charles, Carolle. 1990. "Distinct Meanings of Blackness: Haitian Migrants in New York City." *Cimarrón* 2(3):129-138.

Chesnut, Andrew. 2003. *Competitive Spirits: Latin America's New Religious Economy*. New York: Oxford University Press.

Colas, Willem. 1981. "Canter." Recorded by Gemini All Stars de Ti Manno. Port-au-Prince: Audioteck, Jean-Claude Verdier, producer.

Conway, Frederick. 1978. "Pentecostalism in the Context of Haitian Religion and Health Practice." Ph.D. diss., American University.

Courlander, Harold, and Rémy Bastien. 1966. *Religion and Politics in Haiti*. Washington, D.C.: Institute for Cross-Cultural Studies.

D'Anticat, Edwige. 2000. *The Butterfly's Way: Readings from the Haitian Diaspora*. New York: Soho Press.

Geertz, Clifford. 1973. "Religion as a Cultural System." In *The Interpretation of Cultures: Selected Essays*. New York: Basic Books.

Gerlach, Luther, and Virginia Hine. 1968. "Five Factors Crucial to the Growth and Spread of a Modern Religious Movement." *Journal for the Scientific Study of Religion* 7:23-40.

Glick, Nina. 1975. "The Formation of a Haitian Ethnic Group." Ph.D. diss., Columbia University.

Glick-Schiller, Nina, and Georges Fouron. 2001. *Georges Woke Up Laughing*. Durham: Duke University Press.

Janvier, Louis Joseph. 1883. *La Republique d'Haiti et ses visiteurs: Un Peuple Noir devant les Peuples Blancs*. Paris: Editions Fardin.

Laguerre, Michel. 1984. *American Odyssey: Haitians in New York City*. Ithaca: Cornell University Press.

———. 1998. *Diasporic Citizenship: Haitian Americans in Transnational America*. New York: St. Martin's Press.

Larose, Serge. 1977. "The Meaning of Africa in Haitian Voodoo." In *Symbols and Sentiments: Cross-Cultural Studies in Symbolism*, ed. I. M. Lewis. London: Academic Press.

McAlister, Elizabeth. 1998. "Vodou and Catholicism in the Age of Transnationalism: The Madonna of 115th Street Revisited." In *Gatherings in Diaspora: Religious Communities and the New Immigration*, ed. R. Stephen Warner and Judith Wittner. Philadelphia: Temple University Press.

Métraux, Alfred. 1953a. "Médecine et Vodou en Haïti." *Acta Tropica* 10:28-68.

———. 1953b. "Vodou et Protesatantisme." *Revue de l'histoire des Religions* 144:198-216

———. 1972. *Voodoo in Haiti*. Translated by Hugo Charteris. New York: Schocken Books.

Mintz, Sidney. 1960. *Worker in the Cane*. New Haven: Yale University Press.

———. 1974. *Caribbean Transformations*. Chicago: Aldine.

Mittelberg, David, and Mary C. Waters. 1992. "The Process of Ethnogenesis among Haitian and Israeli Immigrants in the United States." *Ethnic and Racial Studies* 15(3):412-435.

Murray, Gerald. 1984. "Bon-Dieu and the Rites of Passage in Rural Haiti: Structural Determinants of Postcolonial Theology and Ritual." In *The Catholic Church and Religion in Latin America*, ed. Thomas C. Bruneau and Uli Locher. Montreal: McGill University.

Nicholls, David. 1970. "Politics and Religion in Haiti." *Canadian Journal of Political Science* 3:400-414.

———. 1979. *From Dessalines to Duvalier: Race, Colour, and National Independence in Haiti*. Cambridge: Cambridge University Press.

Peterson, Anna, Manuel Vásquez, and Philip Williams. 2001. "Christianity and Social Change in the Shadow of Globalization." In *Christianity, Social Change, and Globalization in the Americas,* ed. Anna Peterson, Manuel Vásquez, and Philip Williams. New Brunswick, NJ: Rutgers University Press.

Plummer, Brenda Gayle. 1988. *Haiti and the Great Powers, 1902-1915*. Baton Rouge: Louisiana University Press.

———. 1992. *Haiti and the United States: The Psychological Moment*. Athens: University of Georgia Press.

Portes, Alejandro, and Alex Stepick. 1993. *City on the Edge: The Transformation of Miami*. Berkeley: University of California Press.

Pressoir, Catts. 1942. "L'Etat Actuel des Missions Protestantes en Haïti." Conférence prononcée au Dimanche de la Bible, à L'église St. Paul. Le 13 Décembre (16 pages).

Price-Mars, Jean. 1983. *So Spoke the Uncle*. Translated by Magdaline Shannon. Washington, D.C.: Three Continents Press.

Richman, Karen. 1990. "Guarantying Migrants in the Core: Commissions of Gods, Descent Groups, and Ritual Leaders in a Transnational Haitian Community." *Cimarrón* 2(3):114-128.

———.1992a. "They Will Remember Me in the House: The *Pwen* of Haitian Transnational Migration." Ph.D. diss., University of Virginia.

————.1992b. "A *Lavalas* at Home/A *Lavalas* for Home: Inflections of Transnationalism in the Discourse of Haitian President Aristide." In *Towards a Transnational Perspective on Migration*, ed. Nina Glick-Schiller, Linda Basch, and Cristina Szanton-Blanc. New York: New York Academy of Sciences.

————. 2002. "Miami Money and the Home Gal." *Anthropology and Humanism* 7(2):1-14.

Richman, Karen with William Balan-Gaubert. 2000. "A Democracy of Words." *Journal of the Haitian Studies Association* 7(1):90-103.

Romain, Charles. 1986. *Le Protestantisme dans la Société Haïtien*. Port-au-Prince: Henri Deschamps.

Rouse Roger. 1991. "Mexican Migration and the Social Space of Postmodernism." *Diaspora* 1:8-23.

————. 1992. "Making Sense of Settlement: Class Transformation, Cultural Struggle, and Transnationalism among Mexican Migrants." In *Towards a Transnational Perspective on Migration*, eds. Nina Glick Schiller, Linda Basch, and Cristina Szanton-Blanc. New York: New York Academy of Sciences.

Sanders, Cheryl. 1996. *Saints in Exile: The Holiness Pentecostal Experience in African-American Religion and Culture*. New York: Oxford University Press.

Sherman, Amy. 1997. *The Soul of Development: Biblical Christianity and Economic Transformation in Guatemala*. New York: Oxford University Press.

Soto, Isa. 1987. "West Indian Child Fostering in Caribbean Life in New York City." In *Caribbean Life in New York City,* eds. Sutton, Constance, and Elsa Chaney. Staten Island: Center for Migration Studies.

Stepick, Alex. 1998. *Pride Against Prejudice: Haitians in the United States*. Boston: Allyn and Bacon.

Thompson, E. P. 1996. "Time, Work-Discipline, and Industrial Capitalism." *Past and Present* 38:56-97.

Toulis, Nicole. 1997. *Believing Identity: Pentecostalism and the Mediation of Jamaican Ethnicity and Gender in England*. Oxford: Berg

Tweed, Thomas A. 1997. *Our Lady of the Exile: Diasporic Religion at a Cuban Catholic Shrine in Miami*. New York and Oxford: Oxford University Press.

Weber, Max. (1905)1958. *The Protestant Ethic and the Spirit of Capitalism*. New York: Charles Scribner's Sons.

10

Structural and Cultural Hybrids
Religious Congregational Life and Public Participation of Mexicans in the New South

Marie Friedmann Marquardt

An Introduction

On the last Saturday in October 2000, I pulled my pointed witch hat and black wig out of the closet and prepared, once again, to cross the blurry line in field-based research between "observer" and "participant." I was on my way to the third-annual Halloween party at the Lutheran Church of *Sagrada Familia* in the Atlanta suburb of Doraville, Georgia. There, I would assume the role not of researcher, but of greeter: enticing small children into the fellowship hall turned house of horrors. By all accounts, the party was a great success, complete with an overabundance of candy. With more than fifty children and their parents present, this tiny church managed to draw as many children to its Halloween party as it does adults to Sunday worship. As often happens at Halloween parties, a few people arrived dressed in the same costume. In this case, the costume was not Harry Potter or one of the other popular characters of the year, but instead *la negra* (the black woman). Those who wore the costume explained to me that *la negra* is a character in the regional folklore of Guerrero, the Mexican state from which some in this congregation have recently migrated.

The next morning, I went to early morning mass at the *Misión Católica de Nuestra Señora de las Américas,* just around the corner from *Sagrada Familia.*[1] Since I arrived a few minutes late, the pews were full in this church that welcomes approximately 4,000 people to its Sunday masses, so I stood with dozens of other worshipers in the hallway. At this point, I was six months into an intensive phase of participant observation at both churches, so I was not surprised that while *Sagrada Familia* had been planning its Halloween fiesta for weeks, the *Misión Católica* made no mention of what its members view as a very "American" holiday.[2] Instead, volunteers and staff at the *Misión Católica* had constructed an elaborate altar for the Day of the Dead in a small room next to where I stood. The altar included framed photos of Oscar Romero (from El Salvador), César Chavez (a Mexican American), Padre Rutilio Grande (from El Salvador), and Monsignor Juan Gerardi (from Guatemala), and a sign that read (in Spanish) "This altar is dedicated to our martyrs who fought without arms for their brothers, for their people."

I begin with a description of these particular events to highlight a more general observation: The two churches undertook very different activities over the course of the weekend, yet both engaged in practices that shaped their participants' relationship to the host society. While *Sagrada Familia* introduced members to the customs and norms of the wider U.S. society and prepared them to be part of multicultural "America," the *Misión Católica* encouraged members to challenge U.S. customs and norms and assume a politicized pan-Latino identity. Furthermore, through these practices, participants in both churches symbolically forged and maintained ties to their place of origin. As a result, they formed new hybrids: At *Sagrada Familia* participants spliced a traditional U.S. practice with a regional Mexican variant, while those at the *Misión Católica* spliced a traditional Mexican practice with a politicized, pan-Latino variant.

Hybrid practices like these have important implications for our understanding of the role of immigrant religious institutions in the United States and, more specifically, in the U.S. South. These immigrant churches serve not simply as "refuge from America" (Warner 1993) by transposing artifacts and practices from place of origin to place of residence, nor do they simply assist immigrants in "becoming American" by embracing an ethnic identity with which to enter into multicultural United States society (Kurien 1998). Rather, such churches develop structural and cultural hybridity that affects both the internal functioning of immigrant religious organizations and also shapes the relationships that members of these churches will develop with their host society.[3] In this chapter, I offer a comparative case study of *Sagrada Familia Iglesia Luterana* and the *Misión Católica de Nuestra Señora de las Américas* to describe two trajectories along which immigrant religious organizations travel to promote the public participation of undocumented immigrants in the U.S. South, to clarify the structural and cultural configurations that give direction to these divergent trajectories, and to highlight how such configurations are shaped both by the local context in which immigrants now live and their ongoing connections to particular places of origin.

To understand the latter, I draw upon not only my research in Doraville and its local congregations, but also research I undertook in three Mexican *ranchos* from which church members have come.[4] I traveled to sending communities in the states of Oaxaca and Mexico to clarify how *Sagrada Familia* and the *Misión Católica* acted structurally both as local congregations and as sites on the multiple transnational circuits that linked their members to a range of localities of origin. To varying degrees, each church became a "defacto congregation" or an "affectively significant association under local and lay control" (Warner 1993).[5] The congregational form of religious association is generally understood as a strongly "American" institutional structure which immigrants assume upon their arrival in the United States. However, in these cases, each church simultaneously participated in the multiple, overlapping transnational migrant circuits (Rouse 1991) that connected their members to particular places of origin. These migrant circuits had an important religious component, as religious materials, practices, and values joined economic and social activities to establish and maintain relationships across national boundaries. As I describe below, for both churches, their status as one of many sites on members' transnational religious circuits shaped the structural form that the local religious organization took, even though neither church maintained extensive organizational-level transnational religious ties.[6]

My research in selected Mexican sending communities also helped me to understand that culturally, my case churches promoted particular forms of "ethnic" identity vis-à-vis the broader U.S. public and also transnational identities, which allowed their members to maintain ties to their place of origin. Again, these two cultural roles were interrelated, since encouraging the formation and maintenance of particular national identities helped the churches to shape their members' U.S. ethnic identities. More specifically, while both churches participated in multiple transnational circuits and encouraged the formation of transnational identities and "long distance nationalism" (Glick-Schiller and Fouron 2001), *Sagrada Familia* became a household for the "second family," where members were encouraged to adopt a multicultural identity as part of the broader U.S. society. By contrast, the *Misión Católica* served as a town square (*plaza del pueblo*) and shaped among its members a pan-Latino solidarity of resistance against that society. In so doing, I argue, the Catholic Mission became an alternative public space where members could develop strategies and identities for resisting discrimination, while the Lutheran Church became an alternative *to* public space, or a safe haven in which to learn the rules of engagement with the broader society.[7]

Mapping the Shifting Terrain of Doraville, Georgia

In the fall of 1999, as I was preparing to begin field research in Doraville, I visited the city's mayor to understand better the rapid and seemingly overwhelming change Doraville had undergone in recent decades. The mayor seemed well-suited to the task of providing historical perspective since he had been a member of the city commission since 1971 and mayor for seventeen years. In fact, his ancestors arrived in Doraville before its incorporation in 1871 and, according to local legend, the city was named for his grandmother, Dora (Barre and Barre

1995). As I sat across the desk from him in his neat, well-appointed office, staring toward the shelves behind him at the framed cover of *Hunting* magazine bearing his photo, I listened as the mayor described a Doraville frozen in time. He praised the city's commitment to providing recreational facilities and organizations for Doraville's youth, but failed to mention the city's prohibition of soccer, the most popular recreational activity for area Latinos, on its well-kept fields. He proudly touted Doraville's churches as the "most important places in the community," but when pressed to name which churches, he did not name the *Misión Católica de Nuestra Señora de las Américas*, which is the largest church in Doraville (by approximately 2,000 members) and visible from his office. Rather, the mayor named First Presbyterian Church, which was in the process of moving out of Doraville to make way for a Vietnamese congregation of the Salvation Army, and First Baptist Church. A few days later, the administrator of First Baptist explained to me that its membership had "really gone down because of the international people in the area" and that it managed to stay afloat financially by renting space to six immigrant nesting congregations.

How had the mayor failed to see such change? In the 1990s, Doraville's "Hispanic" population increased from 9.2 percent to 43.4 percent, making it one among many towns and cities in the southeastern United States experiencing an explosion in immigration from Mexico and other parts of Latin America.[8] During this decade, Doraville experienced a localization of the global as its homes, restaurants, and businesses filled with immigrants from throughout Asia and Latin America. Rather than becoming a Latino or Mexican *barrio,* Doraville became a multi-ethnic space, where Korean restaurants and *botánicas* stood side-by-side in shopping centers with names like Fiesta Latina and Asian Square, and where Cambodian refugees and Guatemalan undocumented immigrants lived next door to each other in garden-style apartments with names like Don Juan Duplexes. Participating in the post-Fordist shift from the manufacture of durable goods to the production of fleeting services (or, in geographic terms, from Rustbelt to Sunbelt), the city had deindustrialized and reindustrialized by replacing large-scale manufacturing with niche-market production of goods and services. And, as its neat suburban streets become increasingly chaotic, this peripheral Atlanta suburb rapidly subsumed into a sprawling, fragmented urban core. As a result, Doraville's identity shifted from that of a primarily Anglo, working-class suburb centered around the nearby General Motors manufacturing plant to that of a multi-ethnic, urbanized "edge city" (Garreau 1991) that relied on the tax base provided by hundreds of small businesses catering to "ethnic" clientele.

Nevertheless, in Doraville, as in other cities throughout the South, much stayed the same. As my interview with the mayor made clear, local power structures remained remarkably consistent, and long-time residents of Doraville and members of the city government often ignored and sometimes explicitly resisted the changes occurring around them. The result was a precarious juxtaposition of young, thriving immigrant communities with aging "old boy" networks of the Deep South. Pluralism was not to be taken for granted in Doraville, and this had clear implications for the divergent ways in which the city was conceptually mapped and spatially inhabited by its residents.

As Doraville's demography and economy shifted, the city's religious ecology also profoundly altered. In 2000, its churches were differentiated less along denominational lines than along the lines of ethnic and national identity. Doraville illustrated especially well R. Stephen Warner's claim that U.S. religious organizations provide a "free social space" in which solidarities and identities can be forged and maintained among similar people (Warner 1993). However, rather than being the foundation for a pluralist society, as Warner would claim, these churches seemed instead to be the spaces in which residents marked off Doraville's contested terrain. When I asked Doraville's long-time residents and recent immigrants what were the most important places in the city, I learned that while two contrasting maps had emerged in Doraville, both of these maps highlighted religious spaces as the most important places. Official cartographies (like the mayor's) mapped Doraville in ways that subtly—and sometimes explicitly—excluded the city's Latinos. Immigrants, though, altered the inhospitable terrain of Doraville by developing in their churches a "free social space" in which they could create places where they felt "at home."

Doraville's population was very diverse, but the largest proportion of immigrants had arrived directly from cities, small towns, and villages in Mexico. Many described their initial experience of attempting to navigate the city's unfamiliar terrain as one of disorientation. As one young woman from San Luis Potosí succinctly put it, her initial impressions of Doraville were "Very strange! Everything completely different from Mexico!" On these strange landscapes, a Mexican immigrant and long-time volunteer at the Catholic Mission explained, "The most basic thing that people need when they arrive—the thing they need first is orientation. . . . So how wonderful that we can tell them where to go, that we can offer them food or whatever for two or three days, some clothing." Throughout Metro-Atlanta, the Catholic Mission held a reputation for providing newcomers with a place in which to find their bearings. One employee of the Mission, himself a Mexican immigrant, explained, "from the time they set foot in Atlanta, just about from the time they show up at the airport, people are sent here. . . . I don't know how, but they show up here."

In 1995, Francisco had been such a newcomer. He was a construction worker who participated actively in the life of the Catholic Mission from the time of his arrival from Veracruz, Mexico. In our interview, during the fall of 2000, Francisco and his pregnant wife, Marta, described the constant fear and uncertainty that pervaded their lives in Doraville. As undocumented immigrants, they knew that, at any time, the lives they had worked so hard to build in Doraville could be cut short and they could be deported to Mexico. Such an event, though, would impact not only Francisco and Marta, but the families they supported back in Veracruz with the money they earned in Doraville. This uncertainty made even more important for Francisco and Marta the *Misión's* carving-out of a safe, comfortable space:

> Many changes have happened over the years. . . . For example, the people have begun to understand that [at the *Misión Católica*] we have a place where, where we can trust in someone, where we can be confident, where we can help each other. Also, during those times it really touched me to be able to participate in the thatching together (*techado*) of the community. Because everyone—I consider myself one among many who have participated with such vigor in creating what exists today. Now, it's a community that has three completely full masses on Sundays. It's because of this that the people, I think they feel, they feel so confident. Before, there were less Hispanics and they were a little more cautious—walking around, or gathering together in one place where we were able to feel OK. But now, there's been a really notable change.[9]

Francisco's description of "thatching together" the roof of the community is especially significant because it suggests that, beyond simply carving a safe space in the Doraville landscape and providing comfort and refuge, the Mission enacted practices that allowed its members to navigate confidently the terrain that surrounded the church. In other words, the Catholic Mission both made its members feel "at home" and provided them with resources to engage the "host" society.

The Lutheran Church of *Sagrada Familia* fulfilled a similar role for its members. Miguel and Olinda were a young couple in their early twenties at the time of our first interview in the summer of 2000, and they had been active lay members of the church since they began worshiping there a year prior. Miguel came to Atlanta from Acapulco, Mexico, after his mother relocated to the area from California. Besides his mother and brothers, who followed shortly after him, he knew no one in the city besides the men with whom he worked as a welder. When his girlfriend Olinda joined him in Atlanta a year later, they wanted to meet more people and become more involved in a community. They explained:

> (Olinda:) Well, in Mexico we always went to church and we wanted to attend a church here, too. And, well, to make friends, because we didn't know anyone. (Miguel breaks in:) We didn't know anyone and, you see, sometimes the neighbor that one has in the apartments is from another country or doesn't have the confidence to talk, doesn't have friends. In the years that I've lived here, I've never met my neighbor. See, the doors are always closed. Going from home to work and from work to home. So, a person feels lonely and we came to the church to look for—to get to know people.

For this couple, coming to church broke the familiar pattern of traveling to and from work without interacting with the people they encountered. It opened a "free social space" (Warner 1993) in which they could construct comfortable relationships and familiar places.

Feeling "at Home" in the New South: Space, Place, and Material Culture

The founding of the *Misión Católica de Nuestra Señora de las Américas* dates back to 1988, when a group of Mexican families joined together to rent an apartment in Doraville where they could house Latino immigrants to the area who had no other place to go. With the help of a local priest, they began gathering together for mass and offering a broader range of services, such as food, clothing, and emergency assistance. Such services were not provided to local immigrants by government agencies, because of their undocumented status, and they were still unavailable from local charitable organizations, which were not yet aware of immigrants' growing presence. Over the next three years, those who gathered to worship and serve in the apartment were joined by an increasing number of Latino Catholics in the area, forcing them to seek more space, first in a store basement and then in a warehouse. When they were evicted from the warehouse in 1990 by the fire department and city government, they took to the streets, meeting in parking lots and even in the middle of busy roads as a way to protest their treatment by local authorities. That year, Archbishop Eugene Marino joined them in a parking lot for their celebration of the Feast of Our Lady of Guadalupe, and he was so impressed by their vigor and organization that he vowed to find a space more appropriate for a "Hispanic Mission" in the Archdiocese of Atlanta. The *Misión Católica* was dedicated a year later, on the feast day of Our Lady of Guadalupe: December 12, 1991. As Fr. Richard Kieran, the priest originally responsible for the *Misión,* explained on the occasion of its dedication in 1991, "The people who come here have a sense of it being their home. Far from their native land, far from their family, it feels like a home away from home." (McInerny 1991). This "home away from home" was a large, drab warehouse, though, and members of the newly formed *Misión* immediately set to work making it a sacred space and a comfortable place.

Whereas the *Misión Católica* was created on the initiative of lay Catholics and emerged from public protest, *Sagrada Familia* was conceived jointly by Bishop Ron Warren and Pastor James Capers, the director of missions for the Southeastern Synod of the Evangelical Lutheran Church of America. *Sagrada Familia* was to be the Lutheran Church's first experiment with evangelization to the growing number of Latinos living within the boundaries of the synod. They invited a Panamanian immigrant to come to Doraville from the church he was pastoring in Houston. He and his Mexican American wife came to the Southeast somewhat reluctantly, having worked for two decades among established Mexican American communities in Texas, and they created *Sagrada Familia* as a mission of the Advent Lutheran Church in Doraville. Advent Church had a very small, aging Anglo congregation at the time of Pastor Rodrigo's arrival in April of 1998, but within less than a year, Advent Church dissolved and left the building entirely to the growing congregation of very recent Latin American immigrants. In the words of Miguel, who began worshiping at *Sagrada Familia* shortly after the arrival of the new pastor, "the most important thing, I think, was when the Americans moved away to another church and left us the church building—especially for the Hispanics." The first thing that members of *Sagrada Familia* did when the "Americans" left was rearrange the sanctuary and bring new items into it that made the church feel more like "home."

After carving out a space in Doraville that was its own, each church set about making such space into a place that felt like "home." Of course, a crucial element of this process was what anthropologist Karen McCarthy Brown calls "transposition": transferring the natal terrain onto the terrain of residence as a way to make those who feel "out of place" feel "in place" (1999). At both the *Misión Católica* and *Sagrada Familia*, members immediately began to transpose material artifacts and other familiar elements of the religious "terrain" of their places of origin into their newly created sacred spaces. For instance, at *Sagrada Familia* the silk flower arrangements lining the walls of the sanctuary were replaced with Mexican Stations of the Cross, and at the *Misión Católica*, the rear wall of the sanctuary was transformed into a colorful altar for the Virgin of Guadalupe. However, in the process of transposition, members of these churches did not simply reconstruct old worlds of meaning, but they instead created miniature border zones, "hybrid sites and spaces on the global landscape" (Nederveen Pieterse 1995) where new recombinations emerged. At the *Misión Católica* and *Sagrada Familia*, these new structural and cultural hybrids were anchored in, and emerged from, a particular place.

As they created a new sacred space, members of these churches also produced meaning, "anchoring a worldview in the world," classifying persons and orienting them in space and time (Chidester and Linenthal 1995:12). At the *Misión Católica* and *Sagrada Familia*, such processes included placement of and interaction with the material elements of religious life: the landscapes of sacred spaces, religious edifices, and religious artifacts. Colleen McDannell reminds us, "experiencing the physical dimension of religion helps to *bring about* religious values, norms, behaviors, and attitudes" (McDannell 1995:2). Thus, careful examination of the landscapes, structures, and material artifacts of each church offers a lens through which to see the range of hybrid forms immigrants constructed, the new worlds of meaning and their implications for immigrants' relationship to their new context.

La Misión Católica de Nuestra Señora de las Américas

When I met Luz Maria in 1999, she was an undocumented Mexican immigrant to Atlanta who cleaned homes for a living, but her vocation was the dozens of hours of volunteer work she did each week as the organizer of the *Misión Católica's* chapter of St. Vincent de Paul. Her dedication to this work had earned her the status of unofficial matriarch of the church. As we sat in the empty sanctuary of the *Misión* on a weekday afternoon (the only quiet place away from the daily hustle and bustle of the church), this founding member of the *Misión* explained to me why people feel "at home" there: "Here it feels like the town square (*plaza del pueblo*). We come, we get to know each other, we mingle with each other. We listen to the word of God, but we also develop friendships. . . . It's like a plaza, more or less, like a vision of a plaza where, where people from all countries encounter each other." Having spent time in the town squares of some Mexican communities from which members of her church had come, I understood precisely what Doña Maria meant: In many ways, this church bore little resemblance to churches in those communities. It was a warehouse, after all, and it also hosted a wide range of activities that would be highly unlikely to occur in a typical church in Mexican *ranchos*. Nevertheless, the *Misión* was very comfortable and familiar because it closely resembled another space (and associated set of practices) with which all Latin American immigrants would be familiar: the *plaza del pueblo*, or "town square," which generally stands adjacent to the local Catholic church.

The sanctuary of the *Misión Católica* was a large former warehouse with brown vinyl siding. The only clue that it was a place of worship was a statue of Our Lady of Guadalupe, the church's patroness, in one of two plate-glass windows on the building's exterior. The "Queen of Mexico and Empress of the Americas" overlooked the small parcel of land between the warehouse and the street, most of it paved with concrete. During the week this pavement was used as a parking lot, but on Sundays no cars were allowed to park there. Instead, the lot filled with people as men sold *paletas* (ice cream Popsicles) from pushcarts, vendors sold food and religious articles from stands, and music played from loudspeakers. The parking lot converted into the *plaza del pueblo*—the place to see and be seen. For most who worshiped at the mission, this was a familiar scene. In many of their *pueblos* and *ranchos* of origin, local parishes stood adjacent to the town square, and on Sunday afternoons after mass, vendors gathered to sell food and worshipers lingered to chat with their neighbors and family members.

The church building itself was an extension of this plaza, since it was not simply the site for sacramental functions like masses, as it was in the Mexican *ranchos* where I undertook research. Even on weekdays, the *Misión* was a center of activity in Doraville. Beyond undertaking its explicitly religious functions of hosting masses, religious processions, and religious education, the mission also hosted sports leagues, dances, parties, vocational training classes, English classes, social service and healthcare providers, and advocacy groups. In its early years, the mission was the only service provider in a city that lacked infrastructure for immigrant services and lacked government interest in providing much-needed health and social services to undocumented immigrants. Over time, some other churches and volunteer organizations began to offer limited services, but the mission remained the most important formal provider of services and informal gathering place in Doraville. On weekday evenings, hundreds of people came to the mission not only to participate in prayer or praise groups, but also to attend English and vocational training classes, find jobs through informal networks, get help filling out job applications, share information about housing and immigration issues, or simply hang out and drink coffee.

In 2001, almost three-fourths of those who gathered here were Mexican, joined by immigrants from all over the Americas.[10] This national diversity was matched by the socioeconomic, ethnic, and age diversity of the mission's members. However, the majority of those who worshiped at the *Misión Católica* shared in common a status as undocumented recent immigrants to the United States who maintained close ties to their place of origin. Seventy to eighty percent of the church's members were undocumented, and on average, members of the *Misión Católica* had arrived in the United States in 1993 and in Metro-Atlanta in 1995. More than half (57.7%) came directly to Georgia from their place of origin, while others arrived primarily by way of Texas and California. The vast majority of these immigrants (80.9%) maintained one very explicit form of transnational connection: the regular sending of economic remittances to their place of origin (Rees and Miller 2002).

The range of organizational roles the mission played for its relatively new, very fluid, and significantly transnational membership was made concrete and visible in the non-worship spaces of the building's interior. On Sunday mornings, worshipers made their way from the bustling town square outside the sanctuary through one of two pairs of glass double doors, as they headed toward the worship space at the rear of the building. Here, they were always greeted by volunteers, who shook their hands and said, "Welcome to our community, the *Misión Católica*." They were also greeted by a range of material artifacts, including shelves with informational flyers about everything from health issues to changes in immigration law and bulletin boards with posted announcements about rooms for rent, items for sale, and upcoming events both in the church and in the wider community. One of the most important activities of the mission was to provide services, informational materials, and a place for the informal exchange of information for recent immigrants to Metro-Atlanta. Like many contemporary immigrant churches throughout the United States, the *Misión Católica* assumed a congregational structure and a community center model of service delivery to members (Warner 1994; Ebaugh and Chafetz 2000). However, as we see below, such structures were not assumed simply as an adaptation to U.S. society, but rather as an affirmation of the many societies from which its members had come and to which they maintained close ties.

Connecting the reception areas to the sanctuary were two adjoining hallways. Worshipers often found themselves standing there during mass, since the sanctuary itself was too small to hold all who worshiped at the *Misión* on Sunday mornings. The way in which each hallway was adorned materialized the two forms of collective identity that the *Misión Católica* constantly negotiated. Lining the walls of one of these hallways were posters of Cesar Chavez, Mama Tingo (from the Dominican Republic), Padre Rutilio Grande, and Oscar Romero, as well as political posters (like one from the organization Rights Without Borders proclaiming, in Spanish, "No one is illegal"). Flanking the entrance to the sanctuary stood a human-sized paper-mache replica of the Statue of Liberty with a huge red question mark wrapped around its body. The youth made the statue for a protest at the Capitol in Washington, D.C., and it was used by the *Misión* in many other protest marches. These artifacts contributed to the mission's goal of building a hemispheric solidarity of resistance, providing support and advocacy for the newest immigrants to Metro-Atlanta.

In 2000, the pastoral council of the *Misión* wrote an *ideario* (ideology), which explained this solidarity and its sources:[11]

> Although we have lived through moments of tension, the community [of the Mission] has arrived at a sense that this Mission is our home. The simplicity of our building, the use of our own language, our confidence in interaction, our ability to listen to one another, the affectionate respect that we have for others and for our different cultures have all helped us to achieve this sense. The richness and diversity of our countries of origin teach us to accept, understand, and accompany one another, and not to leave each other alone to confront new situations of life and work. At the same time, we have discovered a great distance between the best things about our own traditions and ways of life and the values of this country. *These experiences lead us to continue as a community where we can be ourselves, as a place where we can be protected and feel a sense of belonging.*

At the *Misión*, the resources for maintaining distance from "the values of this country" came from the diverse values that members brought and sustained from their place of origin. In order to perpetuate a pan-Latino solidarity of resistance, the *Misión* also had to find ways to let its members "be ourselves" and respect and support "our different cultures." The *Misión* achieved this goal by developing and nurturing particular national identities and offering religious and non-religious resources for the creation and maintenance of ties to "home."

The second hallway leading to the sanctuary, covered as it was with maps of Latin American countries, made manifest this transnational facet of cultural identity. People often gathered around these maps, pointing out to others their "hometowns" or proudly describing the geography of their natal land. As one pastoral worker explained, "Because it's our lady of the Americas. . . . Father put the maps of the whole western hemisphere on the wall so that people would stand around them and talk, saying 'this is where I'm from.' So that's another important thing because it promotes conversation and community. It gets people talking." During my years as a participant observer there, I noted that maps were among the *Misión's* most prevalent material artifacts. When the mission organized relief efforts after natural disasters in El Salvador and Venezuela, volunteers painted huge maps of each country with its key cities and states to hang inside the sanctuary as a reminder for members to participate. These maps were the most explicit of many ways in which the mission nurtured immigrants' connections to their place of origin by "transposing" those places onto the mission's spaces (Brown 1999). In so doing, the *Misión* also worked to create "long distance nationalism" (Schiller 1999:99), "a claim to membership in a political community that stretches beyond the territorial borders of a homeland." Standing around talking about where they had come from not only allowed Hondurans to proudly describe their country to a Mexican, for example, but allowed Mexicans who shared little in common from their diverse places of origin (e.g., a young middle-class man from Mexico City and an elderly indigenous woman from Chiapas) to identify together as "Mexicans."

Especially for the Mexicans who worshiped at the *Misión*, local and regional identity tended to structure their relationships outside of the church. Many had enough friends and family in Metro-Atlanta from their place of origin that they created not "little Mexicos," but little "Michoacans" (a state) or little "Morelias" (a city) in Metro-Atlanta. For instance, one of the Mexican *ranchos* in which I conducted research, near the border between the states of Hidalgo and Mexico, had a tiny population of around 100 families, but so many members of those families lived in Metro-Atlanta that virtually every non-church social activity for members of this community living in Metro-Atlanta was with others from the *rancho*. These migrants were what Peggy Levitt identifies as "transnational villagers." They reside in Doraville, Georgia, but they established and maintained dense networks of relationship between Doraville and their sending community, which impacted their daily life to such a degree that they could be said to reside also in a "village" spanning across national boundaries (Levitt 2001:11-12). Nevertheless, at church, these families embraced their more general identity as Mexican. They used religious symbols like the Virgin of Guadalupe not only for personal, home-based devotions, but also to solidify that national identity, since this was the means of entering into "pan-Latino" solidarity under the auspices of the "Empress of the Americas."

The Virgin of Guadalupe was the patroness of the *Misión Católica de Nuestra Señora de las Américas,* and the church was named "The Catholic Mission of Our Lady of the Americas" in reference to the second half of her title as "Queen of Mexico and Empress of the Americas." She developed into Mexico's patroness over the course of centuries, but she became the patroness of the

Americas by papal decree in 1999 (Brading 2001), as part of a larger effort to unite Catholics throughout the hemisphere and reassert the primacy of Marian devotions. Like its patroness, the *Misión Católica* served at least three cultural and spiritual purposes. First, it nurtured and sustained individual devotional practices, providing a vehicle through which people of faith could offer praise and thanksgiving or fervent and sometimes desperate petitions to God, regardless of their place of origin, economic status, race, or ethnicity. Second, it shaped and supported among its members the formation of strong national identities. Third, it made these particular national identities into the constitutive elements of an emergent pan-Latino or hemispheric solidarity.

The artifacts used in the two worship spaces of the Catholic mission helped to achieve the delicate balance of identities that this church negotiated. On Sunday mornings, worshipers crowded the halls as they clamored toward the sanctuary, and the faux wood portable pews with red vinyl kneelers filled long before the mass began. This large, drab, rectangular room with linoleum floor and ceramic tile ceiling was enlivened a few years after the *Misión's* founding when the priest at the time, Father Carlos, decided to place flags along the bare white walls. Striving to promote the church's image as a gathering place for people from all parts of North, Central, and South America, he lined the walls with flags from every country in the Americas, each of which was identified by a small plaque bearing the country's name. Francisco, a Mexican from Veracruz, described the priest's decision to place national flags in the sanctuary:

> It is possibly the most important thing that Father was able to achieve, and that I don't think any other priest would have been able to do. See, the Mexicans have one set of customs, the Guatemalans have other customs, Cubans and all different types of people, we all have different customs. And what he did, I believe it was something that would have been the most difficult to do . . . He [put up the flags] so that we would all see one another as a community, we would all be one. This is what he was able to make us feel, that we are one . . . that we wouldn't see each other as Mexicans or as Cubans, but that we would see each other as brothers.

Although the space was always circumscribed in a way that solidified national identity to affirm a generalized pan-Latino identity (and the patroness's identity as "Empress of the Americas"), on special occasions the sacred geography of a country of origin was transposed onto the mission's worship space. For instance, on the Feast of Our Lady of Guadalupe, a large paper-mache sculpture of Tepeyac Hill (the site near Mexico City where the Virgin appeared to Juan Diego) was constructed in one corner of the sanctuary and huge murals hung behind the altar bearing images of the mountainous landscapes surrounding Tepeyac.[12] On other national feast days, members built small altars near the main altar with flowers, candles, and images of the particular Virgin being venerated on that day. On these national feast days, the *Misión Católica* became the place for Peruvians, Hondurans, Ecuadorians, or Dominicans (among others) to gather together from throughout Metro-Atlanta, affirm their shared national identity, and strengthen the transnational religious circuits they maintained with friends and family members who simultaneously celebrated the feast day in their place of origin.[13] Many of those who gathered at the *Misión* on these special occasions did not regularly attend the *Misión*, but instead made the church an occasional node on their particular transnational religious circuits. In other words, attending mass at the church on feast days became an important way for them to maintain close relationships of association with home.

The role of the mission as a site on transnational circuits also gave its feast-day celebrations a gender composition strikingly different from that of celebrations "at home." While more than 50 percent of participants at the *Misión's* celebrations of the Guadalupe feast were men in the two years that I participated, only about 15 to 20 percent of those gathered in the churches of Mexican sending communities where I attended feast-day celebrations were men. In Mexican sending communities, most men tended to gather outside in the town square during mass. Such a disparity suggests that feast-day celebrations in Doraville assumed a much broader significance than those in sending communities, religiously linking people to home who might not typically participate in formal religious activities. Furthermore, the overwhelming presence of men at the *Misión Católica* affirms that the church assumed an identity as town square, becoming a more comfortable gathering place for men than churches in Mexican sending communities.

Sagrada Familia Iglesia Luterana

Sagrada Familia was located around the corner from the *Misión Católica*, sandwiched between a McDonald's and a busy Asian shopping center on Buford Highway, the six-lane road that served as Doraville's central thoroughfare. It drew members form the same local population as the *Misión Católica*, but it was markedly different place. Most members described *Sagrada Familia* as a peaceful refuge. This had to do, in large part, with the landscapes surrounding the sanctuary. The lush lawn and mature shade trees provided the only green space for miles along a road lined with strip malls and gas stations. The sanctuary, set far back from the busy road, resembled a ranch-style suburban home or apartment with a well-kept yard more than a place of worship. One member explained, "I saw the sign that said 'Mass in Spanish,' but I had never gone because I thought it looked like a, like a house and nothing more." This church that so closely resembled a household in its physical layout also exhibited a household-like organization. As its name would suggest, and as its pastor and members explained to me, the congregation that gathered in this household was a "second family." One member explained, "In our church, everyone is like a brother . . . and the father knows us all."

Unlike the *Misión Católica*, where worshipers had to arrive very early if they wanted any hope of finding a place to sit in the sanctuary, *Sagrada Familia* seemed to encourage late arrival, and the pastor rarely began the *misa* within twenty minutes of its official starting time. Members took their time traveling down the concrete path that led across *Sagrada Familia's* deep lawn to the entryway of the church. As they entered the church, they often paused to hang jackets on coat racks and exchange greetings. As in many households, this entryway was filled with photographs, whose images revealed that the most important events offered by *Sagrada Familia* were not protest marches, vocational training classes, or big dances. Rather, they were Sunday dinners (potluck meals after mass), baptisms, first communions, confirmations, and retreats, Before and after Sunday services church members often gathered around these photos, sharing memories of certain events and commenting on how babies looked like one or another parent. These photographs created tangible evidence of the intimate relationships that had been formed in the congregation and also provided material with which to create new affective relationships as members gathered to discuss them.

Although the family structure of *Sagrada Familia* diverged significantly from the more explicitly congregational form of the *Misión Católica*, the organizational structure of both churches was largely shaped by the values and expectations that members brought from their places of origin as well as the demands of the local context. Like the *Misión Católica*, *Sagrada Familia* bore little resemblance to churches in members' places of origin but did assume a familiar, recognizable structure. Responding to the sometimes hostile and often unfriendly local environment, *Sagrada Familia*'s members worked to make the church a "haven in a heartless world" (de Tocqueville in Kimmel 2000:115), where affective relationships could be nurtured. However, this "family" was not an ideal-typical "American" nuclear family with somewhat egalitarian gender structures. Rather, it was a profoundly hierarchical and gender-segregated extended family. As the father in this family, Pastor Rodrigo assumed a traditional role of head of household. He represented the congregation to the outside world and made virtually all publicly recognized decisions about what would happen there. During the service, he often randomly assigned duties and responsibilities to church members, much like a father doling out chores. Meanwhile, his wife assumed a traditional maternal role (largely uncontested in this context), assuming responsibility for children's education, offering emotional support and advice to congregation members in crisis, and quietly assuring the smooth day-to-day functioning of the church.

In fact, the pastor largely abdicated his responsibility for the daily workings of the "domestic realm" that he controlled, in this case the church. He gave virtually all of the responsibility for administrative work and financial arrangements to his wife; he sometimes failed to attend scheduled events at the church and often came unprepared to those events he did attend. His wife and other lay members of the church (mostly female) were left to cobble together plans, which was sometimes difficult, but they were also left to form close affective relationships beyond the gaze and control of the "patriarch." The "domestic abdication" of the pastor and the resulting ability for members of the church to develop a somewhat congregational structure (even in a seemingly hierarchical church) emerged largely from the expectations that many members of this "family" brought with them about the structure of a family and, in particular, about how men's family roles are shaped by standards of "machismo." As Brusco rightly clarifies, machismo (as it is practiced) is less about patriarchy and male authority in the household than it is about men's virtual absence from the domestic sphere and lack of concern for domestic affairs (1995:80).

While members of *Sagrada Familia* universally accepted the authority of the pastor, they were unwilling to decry or challenge his frequent absence and sometimes irresponsible behavior as the church administrator, which precipitated occasional financial crises. Those members of *Sagrada Familia* who did lament the pastor's abdication of responsibility often explained that what appeared to be indifference on the part of other members toward this problem was actually an issue of the expectations that these members, and especially the Mexicans, had about men's participation in domestic life and about the ultimate authority of heads of household and church. As one non-Mexican member explained of the pastor, "He treated the congregation like children who couldn't take any responsibility and they just accepted it!" In fact, the situation was more complex than this: His non-participation in the daily workings of this "domestic" sphere created a space, like the spaces of many households in the Mexican sending communities where I lived during my research, in which women, in particular, could assume leadership roles without being conferred the associated titles or official recognition.

Sagrada Familia effectively functioned as a (disorganized) congregation with largely female leadership. Even though *Sagrada Familia* did not have a formal roster of members, a lay governing body, lay-led committees, or any of the other "ideal typical" elements of a congregation (Ebaugh and Chafetz 2000:347), it did exhibit one very important congregational tendency: People chose to worship together at *Sagrada Familia* because it was an "affectively significant association" (Warner 1993:1066), or a space in which intimate relationships were lovingly shaped among a group of people who voluntarily "gathered together religiously" (Warner and Wittner 1998). Just as the *Misión Católica*'s "town square" was a structure that members brought with them from their place of origin but that also altered its configuration to respond to a local context in which social services and informal public gathering places were severely lacking, *Sagrada Familia*'s household was a familiar structure for Mexican members that reconfigured to respond to the emotional and spiritual needs of persons living in an unfriendly and unwelcoming environment.

In most households, the second floor is a more intimate space than the first, and the act of climbing up the stairs to *Sagrada Familia's* upstairs sanctuary similarly encouraged intimacy. At the top of the stairs, the pastor's wife always waited to greet each person individually, welcome him or her, and offer a weekly bulletin. As they passed into the sanctuary, worshipers went by a small table on which was displayed a large elaborately illustrated English Bible flanked by framed photographs of Martin Luther King Jr. and Oscar Romero. Above this table hung a gilt cross with Latin inscription and next to the table stood a very small Mexican flag. In the quiet, half-full sanctuary, an eight-foot American flag often stood to the right of the altar and next to a brightly painted Salvadoran-style cross. Above the altar hung a crucifix, and sometimes behind it, placed among a row of tall white pilaster candles, was a devotional candle bearing the image of Our Lady of Guadalupe. Lining the walls of the sanctuary were framed prints representing the Stations of the Cross.

Like the *Misión Católica*, *Sagrada Familia* housed some key artifacts allowing for the transposition of, in this case, Mexican and Salvadoran places into its space. However, the primary way in which *Sagrada Familia* made its sanctuary a comfortable, familiar place for the immigrants who worshiped there was by making it resemble a Catholic church. A crucifix over the altar, Stations of the Cross, and images of the Virgin Mary are all uncommon in Lutheran churches. In this case, all of the immigrants who worshiped at *Sagrada Familia* were Catholics who found the church appealing because of its intimacy, but they were not willing to make a clean break with the Catholic traditions of their places of origin. Worshiping at *Sagrada Familia* did not require them to make this break. By making its space look and feel Catholic, *Sagrada Familia* created a comfortable and familiar place for its members and visitors. It also allowed many of them to make the church one node on the transnational religious circuits of devotion to the saints, baptisms, first communions, confirmations, and *quinceañeras* that closely linked their church members to friends and family back home.

In fact, more then half of the people who came to *Sagrada Familia* during the period in which I participated there were unaware that it was not a Catholic church. They initially came to *Sagrada Familia* seeking blessing for images of the Virgin of Guadalupe that they had brought from Mexico to grace their home altar, or they arrived looking for a place to baptize or confirm their child before the huge meal and party that would gather people in Doraville from the same "hometown" and their visiting relatives from Mexico. In the baptisms and first communions in which I participated, relatives from Mexico always came bearing gifts for the child and they returned to Mexico to distribute *recuerdos* (souvenirs) of the event for those who could not make the trip. These souvenirs served as material reminders of the religious rituals through which transnational linkages were established. From the perspective of family members back in Mexico, such linkages would have been impossible to maintain if their relatives had been baptizing or confirming a child in a non-Catholic church. In many Mexican sending communities, to be a non-Catholic meant to be a Pentecostal. Pentecostals generally lived as outcasts (or exiles, depending on one's point of view) in social worlds entirely separated from the larger society. *Sagrada Familia* could serve as a node on multiple transnational religious circuits, then, only if it could create a place that felt like "home" or, in other words, like a Catholic church.

Largely because it looked and felt Catholic, *Sagrada Familia*, like the Catholic Mission down the road, was a site for overlapping transnational religious circuits, and it assumed a family structure that was informed by the values and expectations that traveled along these circuits. The more active members of *Sagrada Familia* were aware that the church was not "Catholic," but they also appreciated the fact that it looked and felt Catholic, and they expressed little concern about (or knowledge of) the differences between a Catholic and a Lutheran church. However, for them, *Sagrada Familia* was not simply one of many sites on a transnational religious circuit connecting them to their place of origin, but instead a temporary substitute for the family that they left behind. Most active members of this church were newcomers to the area who did not have extended communities of friends and relatives in Doraville, and so they relied on each other to be a "second family." They had chosen to worship here, instead of at the *Misión Católica* around the corner, not for doctrinal or theological reasons but because of the ease with which they could form intimate relations with other members.

As they formed a second family, these active members of the congregation also gathered together to learn how to construct new, "American" identities that embraced the discourse of multiculturalism. For instance, church members often gathered in the fellowship hall after mass to share a meal together. On the Sunday after Thanksgiving in 2000, they planned a huge Thanksgiving feast. The week prior, Pastor Rodrigo had announced that each woman should bring a "typical" dish from her country of origin (men were exempted from bringing food, and single men were asked to bring simple items such as forks or drinks). The pastor and his wife would bring "turkey and pumpkin pie," since, in the words of the pastor, "it's not Thanksgiving without these!"

Such an example may seem mundane, but it illustrates that the building blocks of multicultural incorporation into U.S. society are shared national identities that must be constructed. What is a "Mexican" national dish, after all? In this case, *tamales* were chosen to do the work of representing Mexican national identity and using that identity to create ethnic (or hyphenated) Americans. Pastor Rodrigo, perhaps as a result of his long tenure in Houston, understood the formation of Mexican-American identity to be paramount for this community. Although Pastor Rodrigo brought with him from Houston a cultural commitment to shaping hyphenated Americans, he also allowed the church to assume a structure that would maintain members' loyalties and relationships to home. As a result, *Sagrada Familia* painted a more complex picture of multiculturalism than that described by theorists of transnationalism. As Schiller explains, "While the U.S. model of multiculturalism projects a culturally diverse society made up of multiple ethnic groups, it does not allow for long distance nationalism. The celebration of culture within multiculturalism is one of ancestral roots, not one of ongoing political relationships and loyalties." (Glick-Schiller and Fouron 2001). To the contrary, as both a household for the second family and a site of linkage for extended families across transnational circuits, *Sagrada Familia's* multiculturalism promoted incorporation into an imagined multicultural U.S. society that was sustained by membership in societies of origin. It thereby became a site of cultural and structural hybridity, where seemingly incommensurate structural and cultural forms, in fact, complemented and reinforced each other.[14]

The Politics of Hybridity: Immigrant Religion and Public Participation

Responding to their local context while also maintaining ties to their context of origin, members of *Sagrada Familia* and the *Misión Católica* created hybrid church structures and cultural identities. The *Misión Católica* became a church that more closely resembled a Mexican town square, where members gathered to both reinforce national identities and create a collective pan-Latino identity. *Sagrada Familia* developed into a family that was shaped by expectations of male "machismo." In this family, members gathered to both re-connect with home and established hyphenated identities with which to enter into multicultural U.S. society. What are the implications of such cultural and structural hybridity for political participation of immigrants to places like Doraville? I employ an approach to immigrant political participation that is not narrowly defined as issue-based activism, but rather examines the public function of religious organizations, the political identity of those who comprise them, and the resulting forms of religious participation in public life. With this approach, I argue that *Sagrada Familia* and the *Misión Católica* typify two key trajectories along which immigrant religious organizations travel toward promoting the public participation of undocumented immigrants. The first, traveled by the *Misión Católica*, creates structural and cultural forms that allow the church to serve as an alternative public, a parallel space to that from which its members have been excluded. In an alternative public space, immigrants promote interpretations of their identities and interests that challenge those assigned by the broader society. The second trajectory, traveled by the Lutheran Church of *Sagrada Familia*, creates structural and cultural forms that allow the church to serve as an alternative *to* public space, a safe haven in which members can learn the rules of engagement with the broader public, with the expectation of someday being invited to participate.

Misión Católica: Toward an Alternative Public Sphere

In Doraville, legitimate public spaces such as city parks and city commission meetings subtly or explicitly excluded some of those who resided within their boundaries, making the democratic ideal of one single public arena (distinct from both the state and the economy, in which "citizens" deliberate about their common concerns) seem the stuff of fantasy to the city's Latino newcomers. Many quickly recognized that in their "host" society, equal participation of all in one common public debate was not possible, and true discursive interaction required "contestation among a plurality of competing publics" (Fraser 1997:81). As it made space on the inhospitable landscapes of Doraville, the *Misión Católica* became an alternative public sphere, or an institutionalized setting in which a range of people could come together to form both shared opinions and shared identities (Fraser 1997; Habermas 1989). The *Misión Católica* functioned thus in at least three ways. First, it provided space and resources for "everyday forms of resistance to oppression and demoralization" (Higginbotham 1993:2) by offering a wide range of services and classes. Second, it offered resources for the formation of identities that challenged the label most commonly assigned to the mission's members: illegal immigrant. Third, and most explicitly, it collectively formulated oppositional interpretations of the values dominant in the larger public sphere.

As one *Misión Católica* member succinctly put it: "Here we simply try to protect and defend everyone. . . . Here in the Mission what we're doing is defending people, defending human beings." One important element of this defense was to establish alternative sources of identity formation. Instead of self-identifying as "illegal aliens," those who worshiped at the *Misión* embraced a broader identity as beloved by God and as willed by God to gather together in even the most inhospitable times and places. Beyond providing them with this alternative discourse of identity, the *Misión* provided its members with concrete practices of alternative identity formation. Many members of the mission spent their days as laborers, nannies, housekeepers, dishwashers, and landscapers, lacking authority and perhaps even public visibility. Yet, these same people spent their evenings preparing for big events like protests, deciding how to distribute aid to members of their community, teaching and taking classes, and making decisions about the fate of their community.

As they assumed a strong congregational form, they did so not to "become American" (Kurien 1998), but to challenge "American" values and the identities assigned to them by the "American" public. For instance, Oralia, a lay member of the *Misión* staff, offered an explanation of the importance of learning English at the *Misión* that challenged assumptions about the role of English acquisition for incorporation into U.S. culture: "Well, there has been discrimination, but . . . we have much more confidence to fight because now we are learning the language." For Oralia and the hundreds of others who crowded into English classes on weekday evenings at the *Misión,* learning the dominant language offered not only a way to get better jobs, but also a tool for critical engagement. Oralia explained, "People no longer say 'Oh, because I'm Hispanic, they're going to discriminate against me' or 'I can't do this.' Instead, we can fight with what we have and, if we want to succeed in the fight, we can do it."

Members of the *Misión Católica* indeed fought. They organized and participated in marches protesting hunger, immigration raids, and the School of the Americas, and honoring Martin Luther King and Oscar Romero. The *Misión* also created and circulated as petitions letters-to-the-editor for the prominent local newspaper, protesting U.S. immigration policy and supporting the expansion of guest-worker programs. Just as a particular image of God provided those who worshiped at the *Misión* with resources for formulating alternative identities, a certain interpretation of God's will and of the Gospel gave them the courage to challenge the broader public. When I asked Luz Maria, unofficial matriarch of the mission, about the question-mark-bearing Statue of Liberty described above, she explained:

> One time we went to protest at the capitol, when they were trying to pass a law that would be deleterious to us. . . . And they made a Statue of Liberty with a sign. And we took it there and we also walked in the march against hunger with this statue. . . . to make the people think. You know? That, so, yes, we are in a country of liberty, or, of justice. We were in the capital and a ton of people got together to protest that there be *true* justice.

Luz Maria's statement reveals how the mission provided space and resources to challenge the meanings assigned in the U.S. public to broadly held values like "justice" and "liberty." After creating this challenge, discursively and also materially in the form of the re-signified Statue of Liberty, members of the mission were prepared to enter the discursive arena. They did so critically, "to make people think." The *Misión* became what Nancy Fraser calls a "subaltern counterpublic": a "parallel discursive arena where members of subordinated social groups invent and circulate counter-discourses, which in turn permit them to formulate oppositional interpretations of their identities, interests, and needs" (1997:81).

Sagrada Familia: A Training Ground for Public Participation

Worshiping at *Sagrada Familia* encouraged an approach to political participation that diverged significantly from the contestatory approach outlined above. Ana, one of three adult sisters from San Luis Potosí, Mexico who have become very active members of the congregation, offered a typical and very pointed response to my question about political participation: "No, that's not something that the church is here to do. No, there are more important things that—more important because we're Hispanics and we need, more than anything, to learn how to get by here. And politics just doesn't benefit us." Rather than being an alternative public, *Sagrada Familia* served its members as an alternative *to* public space, or a "haven in a heartless world." The political work done there was the work expected of a family: First, *Sagrada Familia* mediated between the outside world and members of the congregation, helping out in times of need, providing emotional support and encouragement. Second, as Ana's response suggests, *Sagrada Familia* trained members for a more smooth incorporation into this outside world. In a family, this would be called socialization. In this case, it might more appropriately be called acculturation.

As the pastor envisioned it, *Sagrada Familia* served as a sort of training ground for entering the public-at-large. During worship services, Pastor Rodrigo prepared the children by teaching them the Pledge of Allegiance and encouraging them to speak English. He also encouraged their parents to learn English, interspersing it regularly into the worship service. (By contrast, at the *Misión Católica* the use of English during worship was strongly discouraged.) He encouraged parents to buy their children a Bible in English and he prayed that children would "acculturate to the U.S. and learn the ways of this country." He also upheld the possibility of achieving the "American dream." One week, in his sermon, the pastor explained to the parents that kids could achieve middle-class status through hard work: go to school, study hard, get an entry-level job and work hard, and you will move up. In addition, he used church activities such as Halloween parties and Thanksgiving dinners to introduce his congregation to U.S. customs and norms.

Pastor Rodrigo also sometimes used the pulpit to teach congregants about their rights, encouraging them to develop a strong voice against discrimination. For instance, one Sunday he explained to members of the congregation that, here in the United States, the Constitution and the Bill of Rights prevent the abuse of power. He explained that because of these, even undocumented persons have rights in this country. One right is that no one can enter one's house without a warrant. After explaining what a warrant was, he reminded the congregation "if anyone comes to your door—even a policeman—remind him that you are a member of this church and you know what your rights are!" In short, Pastor Rodrigo prepared members of his church to enter the broader public and to protect themselves in that public by knowing what their rights and responsibilities were, according to U.S. law. Rather than contesting the law, or contemporary perspectives on immigrants rights and responsibilities, Pastor Rodrigo taught them to understand these in order that they might participate more fully— and with less fear—in U.S. public life. Thus, much like members of the *Misión Católica*, those who worshiped at *Sagrada Familia* embraced an identity that allowed them to engage with the broader society. However, at *Sagrada Familia,* this engagement did not challenge, but rather embraced U.S. understandings of rights and responsibilities, justice, and liberty.

At *Sagrada Familia*, the pastor upheld the liberal ideal of a comprehensive public sphere: He encouraged members to participate in U.S. society by embracing the image of a "multicultural" United States, where people can "preserve their culture, customs, and identity yet be fully imbedded in an American mosaic" (Schiller, Basch, and Blanc 1995). This was somewhat problematic for two reasons. First, most of *Sagrada Familia's* members were undocumented immigrants who had been, and would continue to be, denied the opportunity for full participation in U.S. civic and political life.[15] Second, Doraville was a "host" society that was not pervaded with the discourse of multiculturalism and did not offer immigrant newcomers an opportunity to participate in local decision-making. Thus, the *Misión Católica* more adequately addressed the political needs of its members in relation to their particular context. As it assumed the role of alternative public, though, the *Misión Católica* lost the ability to effectively address another need of many newcomers to Doraville: the need to create intimate, affective relationships in a warm, comfortable setting. Some of those seeking such relationships left the *Misión Católica* to join *Sagrada Familia's* household.

Conclusion: Why Does Transnationalism Matter?

In the sociology of religion, the rapidly expanding field of religion and immigration has produced two volumes that are generally understood to have laid the foundations for future research agendas. Warner and Witter's *Gatherings in Diaspora: Religious Communities and the New Immigration* (1998) and Ebaugh and Chafetz's *Religion and the New Immigrants: Continuities and Adaptations in Immigrant Congregations* (2000) both survey a range of religious traditions and immigrant communities by using a well-established and rarely contested method in the sociology of religion: the congregational study (see Vasquez, this volume). In both volumes, the editors argue that, although the congregations they describe exhibit a range of characteristics, they broadly conform to patterns that Ebaugh and Chafetz call "cultural reproduction and structural change" (1999). In short, when the new immigrants "gather together religiously in the United States" they tend to assume new structural configurations, becoming more congregational and serving as community centers. However, the cultural work that they do tends to be the work of "reproducing ethnicity" (Ebaugh and Chafetz 2000) or re-creating identities by making taken-for-granted religious traditions key elements in the creation of ethnic identity (Warner 1993; Warner and Wittner 1998).

Such an approach, though, cannot make sense of the impact that transnational migration has on many immigrant religious organizations. Certainly not all new immigrants are transmigrants, and it may even be argued that the majority of immigrants are not (see Portes 2003). Yet, the vast majority of undocumented immigrants living in new receiving destinations such as Doraville appear to establish and maintain sufficiently dense relationships across national borders to merit scholarly attention to the impact of such relationships on congregational religious life.[16] As Stepick (this volume) argues, "we do not need to be told again that religion is a transnational force" but we do need to clarify the dimensions of transnational networks and practices. In this chapter, I contribute to this process of clarification, ironically perhaps, by promoting a theory of "fuzziness and mélange, cut-and-mix, crisscross and crossover" (Nederveen Pieterse 1995:55). In other words, I employ theories of hybridity to examine the structural and cultural impact that transnationalism has on two groups of Latinos that "gather together religiously" in Doraville, Georgia.

This comparative examination blurs the methodological boundaries of congregational studies, suggesting that how a researcher understands the structural and cultural work of congregations depends, in large part, on the vantage point assumed by that researcher. Structurally, hybridization means simultaneous engagement in multiple modes of organization (Nederveen Pieterse 1995:49) or the "emergence of new practices of social co-operation and competition" (Nederveen Pieterse 1995:64). From the vantage point of Doraville, these churches indeed appeared to be carving out local space to create clearly demarcated, tight-knit groups of people who gathered together religiously. Yet, from a *rancho* in Mexico, at the other end of a particular transnational circuit, and even from a household down the road, each church appeared to be one of many sites religiously linking immigrants to their place of origin. In other words, for many groups of transnational migrants, these churches were not the only locus of religious practice connecting Doraville to their city or town of origin, but they were one of many sites for such practices and they provided some of many resources through which transnational religious linkages were made. In addition to church-based religious activities, other practices, such as home-based devotional activities, *promesas*, and pilgrimage formed similarly important sites on these circuits.

These transnational circuits, though, were not peripheral to the internal workings of the churches, but instead provided the values and commitments that shaped the *Misión Católica* into a *plaza del pueblo* and *Sagrada Familia* into a particular kind of household. As each church assumed an organizational structure that drew upon a familiar social structure in sending communities, it also used this structure to respond to needs and concerns that arose as a result of the church's location in a particular receiving community. The *Misión Católica's* town square provided crucial social and health services, as well as informal gathering spaces, in a town that lacked these. *Sagrada Familia's* household provided intimacy and belonging in a local environment that was unwelcoming and sometimes hostile.

Cultural hybridization signifies "the ways in which forms become separated from existing practices and recombine with new forms in new practices" (Rowe and Schelling 1991:231) or "new translocal cultural expressions" (Nederveen Pieterse 1995:64). These two Doraville churches attracted very similar populations of Catholic, overwhelmingly undocumented, majority Mexican, very recent immigrants to the U.S. Southeast who maintained dense transnational connections to their place of origin. Yet, each church clearly shaped distinctive ethnic identities among its active members that encouraged particular kinds of engagement with the broader U.S. society. While the *Misión Católica's plaza del pueblo* shaped a pan-Latino solidarity of resistance among its members, *Sagrada Familia's* household promoted a multicultural identity of incorporation. As they created these ethnic identities, however, these churches also shaped national identities. Like ethnic identity, national identity was produced, not simply maintained, through processes that turned mundane objects like maps and *tamales* into sources of nationalist unity. Furthermore, each church balanced "long distance nationalism" with a particular attitude vis-à-vis the host society: The *Misión Católica* became an alternative public space where members developed a solidarity of resistance toward the public discourses from which its members were excluded, while *Sagrada* Familia became an alternative *to* public space, or a safe haven in which members could learn the rules of engagement with the broader society. As a result, each church developed a unique trajectory that led its members to engage in particular kinds of public participation: While the *Misión Católica* engaged in peace rallies and protests of INS raids, *Sagrada Familia* taught the Bill of Rights and the Pledge of Allegiance.

In her discussion of prevailing approaches in the contemporary sociology of religion, Nancy Ammerman comments, "The root of our problem with the either/or concepts with which we work is that we now live in a both/and world" (Ammerman 1997:213). My research confirms that immigrants and transmigrants in the U.S. South, indeed, live in a both/and world. The implications of my research for the study of immigrant religious groups in the United States are quite simple: If scholars hope to understand their world and structural and cultural configuration of religious organizations in that world, we must broaden our examination to include *both* the transnational circuits on which most of them live their lives *and* the ways in which they engage U.S. society. The difficulty with a both/and approach is that it can tend to lack clarity and specificity. To focus my examination more clearly, I have paid close attention to how immigrants engage the physical landscapes, structures, and material artifacts of a particular place to create specific structural and cultural forms. In so doing, I have employed one method that we can use to clarify the trajectories toward public participation that immigrant churches in the United States forge, as they "gather together religiously" (Warner and Wittner 1998) in local congregations while also religiously maintaining dense networks of relationships with home.

Notes

Selected portions of this chapter appeared in *Globalizing the Sacred: Religion Across the Americas.* (New Brunswick, NJ: Rutgers University Press).

1. *Misión Católica de Nuestra Señora de las Américas* translates to "Catholic Mission of Our Lady of the Americas." "Our Lady of the Americas" is another name for the Virgin of Guadalupe. *Sagrada Familia* is generally translated to "Holy Family" in English. Interestingly (and significantly for this case), "Holy Family" is an uncommon name for a Lutheran church, but a very typical name for a Catholic church.

2. Of course, Halloween is now celebrated in cities and towns throughout the world. The members of the *Misión* nevertheless consider the holiday to be a symbol of "American" culture, as do those at *Sagrada Familia*. In fact, during an English class that I taught on the morning of the party, many members of the church asked me (as an "expert" on "American culture") to explain the traditions of costumes and candy and to advise them on how to dress their children.

3. I use the term hybridity not to signify "a space betwixt and between two zones of purity" but instead as "the ongoing condition of all human cultures, which contain no zones of purity." Such an understanding of hybridity suggests that "instead of hybridity versus purity. . . . it is hybridity all the way down." Renato, Rosaldo "Introduction," in *Hybrid Cultures: Strategies for Entering and Leaving Modernity*, edited by N. G. Canclini (Minneapolis, MN: University of Minnesota Press, 1995).

4. *Ranchos* are very small towns in which the primary economic activity was once farming and/or ranching. Now, in the *ranchos* where I undertook research, migration to the U.S. and to large Mexican cities is a primary source of local income.

5. Significantly, both churches were organized as missions and had not yet established themselves as fully functioning parishes. Their mission status had contradictory impacts on the degree to which they could be congregational in form. On the one hand, being missions freed them, especially the Catholic church, from being structured as parishes delineated by geographical boundaries. Latinos were encouraged to come to both of these churches from throughout Metro-Atlanta as an alternative to going to their local church, which was unlikely to have a Spanish mass. On the other hand, their status as mission meant that they had not established many of the characteristic structural features of a congregation identified by Ebaugh and Chafetz (2000), such as a formal roster of membership or clergy selected by the local organization.

6. "Organizational-level transnational religious ties" would include formal relationships between these churches and churches in Latin American communities from which their members have come, such as relationships of economic assistance, exchange of priests or pastoral workers, or other formal ties. The *Misión Católica* did develop some informal organizational-level relationships with churches in sending communities, such

as the collection of funds during meetings of a charismatic prayer group to assist a return migrant in forming such a group in her home church.

7. The case study is based upon an ongoing research project in Doraville, Georgia. The data used for this chapter includes thirty brief interviews with pastors of Doraville's churches, ten interviews with community leaders in the city, thirty interviews with members of two Doraville churches, and approximately eighteen months of participant observation in those churches. The Doraville research was supplemented with six weeks of research in three Mexican sending communities, which included fifteen in-depth interviews with priests, pastoral workers, transnational migrants, and their family members.

The names of places in this chapter have not been changed, but I have used pseudonyms to protect the anonymity of church members, many of whom are undocumented immigrants to the United States. This research was supported by the Social Science Research Council. Also, a portion of the research comprised part of a project entitled "Responding to Community Crisis." This project, sponsored by the Lilly Endowment, was co-directed by Elizabeth Bounds and Nancy L. Eiesland, who have given permission for inclusion of materials here.

8. According to United States census data, Doraville's Hispanic/Latino population increased from 2.0% to 9.2% from 1980 to 1990 and from 9.2% to 43.4% between 1990 and 2000. In 2000, 30% of Doraville's population identified as "Mexican Origin," and 13% as "Asian." As the 2000 United States Census clearly illustrated, the most significant change in Latino population was in the Southeast, where six of the seven states that have experienced a more than 200% increase in Hispanic population from 1990 to 2000 are located (NC, SC, GA, AL, TN, AK). For more detail, see Cynthia A. Brewer and Trudy A. Suchan, *Mapping Census 2000: The Geography of U.S. Diversity.* Washington, DC: U.S. Government Printing Office, 2001.

9. Interview conducted in Spanish. This and subsequent quotes from interviews were translated by the author.

10. In March 2002, the Catholic Archdiocese of Atlanta published results of a survey of all of its churches offering Spanish masses, entitled "Quienes Somos? Que Necesitamos?: Needs Assessment of Hispanic in the Archdiocese of Atlanta" (Martha Woodson Rees and T. Danyael Miller). The authors found that 72.2% of participants at the *Misión Católica* were Mexican, 10.2% Central American, 6.3% Colombian, and 8.9% from other parts of South America.

11. This document, entitled "Ideology of our Mission and principles for our journey, prepared by our community during the institutional analysis" emerged as a result of an intensive institutional analysis, which included surveys of twenty groups within the *Misión* and a series of seven meetings over a four-month period in 1999 and 2000. Translation from Spanish by the author.

12. Interestingly, during my research in Mexican sending communities, I participated in three feast-day celebrations to honor the Virgin of Guadalupe, none of which featured images of the Mexican landscape, Mexican flags, or other nationalist imagery. Her taken-for-granted association with Mexican national identity had to be built (literally) when she was transposed to Doraville.

13. The Feast of Our Lady of Guadalupe each year was more complicated than these other national feast-day celebrations. Of course, thousands of Mexicans flocked to the *Misión Católica* on this day, filling not only the sanctuary and hallways, but the large

parking lot in front of the building. For many, if not most of them, this celebration was an opportunity to proclaim together "¡Viva México!" However, the *Misión* was careful to also promote the celebration as an affirmation of the diversity within this particular congregation whose patroness was the Virgin of Guadalupe, by bolstering the pan-Latino character of the Virgin. She was, after all, "Empress of the Americas" as well as "Queen of Mexico."

14. A similar observation has been made by Levitt, who argues that transnationalism and assimilation can be compatible, rather than contradictory processes (2001:5).

15. It was difficult to obtain a clear statistical portrait of the legal status of members of *Sagrada Familia*. In my own sample of interviewees, 70% were undocumented. Pastoral workers at both churches estimated that 80 to 90% of members were undocumented.

16. Ebaugh and Chafetz, recognizing this trend, subsequently directed a study of transnational religion that resulted in the volume *Religion across Borders: Transnational Immigrant Networks* (Walnut Creek, CA: AltaMira Press, 2002).

References

Ammerman, Nancy. 1997. "Organized Religion in a Voluntaristic Society." *Sociology of Religion* 58:203-215.

Barre, Laura, and Ken Barre. 1995. *The History of Doraville, Georgia*. Roswell, GA: Wolfe Publishing.

Brading, D. A. 2001. *Mexican Phoenix: Our Lady of Guadalupe: Image and Tradition Across Five Centuries*. Cambridge: Cambridge University Press.

Brown, Karen McCarthy. 1999. "Staying Grounded in a High-Rise Building: Ecological Dissonance and Ritual Accomodation in Haitian Vodou." In *Gods of the City*, ed. R. Orsi. Bloomington: Indiana University Press.

Brusco, Elizabeth E. 1995. *The Reformation of Machismo: Evangelical Conversion and Gender in Colombia*. Austin: University of Texas Press.

Chidester, David, and Edward T. Linenthal, eds. 1995. *American Sacred Space*. Bloomington: Indiana University Press.

Ebaugh, Helen Rose, and Janet Salzman Chafetz. 1999. "Agents for Cultural Reproduction and Social Change: The Ironic Role of Women in Immigrant Religious Institutions." *Social Forces* 78:585-613.

———. 2000. *Religion and the New Immigrants: Continuities and Adaptations*. Walnut Creek, CA: AltaMira Press.

———. 2002. *Religion Across Borders: Transnational Immigrant Networks*. Walnut Creek, CA: AltaMira Press.

Edgell, Penny. 2003. "Pathways to Innovation." Paper presented at the Louisville Institute Winter Seminar, January 17-18.

Fraser, Nancy. 1997. *Justice Interruptus: Critical Reflections on the 'Postsocialist' Condition*. New York: Routledge.

Garreau, Joel. 1991. *Edge City: Life on the New Frontier*. New York: Doubleday.

Glick-Schiller, Nina, and Georges Eugene Fouron. 2001. *Georges Woke Up Laughing: Long-Distance Nationalism and the Search for Home*. Durham, NC: Duke University Press.

Habermas, Jurgen. 1989. *The Structural Transformation of the Public Sphere: An Enquiry into the Category of Bourgeois Society.* Translated by T. Burger and F. Lawrence. Cambridge, MA: MIT Press.

Higginbotham, Evelyn Brooks. 1993. *Righteous Discontent: The Women's Movement in the Black Baptist Church, 1880-1920.* Cambridge, MA: Harvard University Press.

Kimmel, Michael S. 2000. *The Gendered Society.* New York: Oxford University Press.

Kurien, Prema. 1998. "Becoming American by Becoming Hindu: Indian Americans Take their Place at the Multicultural Table." In *Gatherings in Diaspora: Religious Communities and the New Immigration,* ed. R. S. Warner and J. Wittner. Philadelphia: Temple University Press.

Levitt, Peggy. 2001. *The Transnational Villagers.* Berkeley: University of California Press.

————. 2003. "'You Know, Abraham was Really the First Immigrant': Religion and Transnational Migration." *International Migration Review* 37:847-873.

McDannell, Colleen. 1995. *Material Christianity: Religion and Popular Culture in America.* New Haven: Yale University Press.

McInerny, Rita. 1991. "Hispanic Mission Serves Newcomers." *Georgia Bulletin* 12/5/1991.

Nederveen Pieterse, Jan. 1995. "Globalization as Hybridization." In *Global Modernities,* ed. M. Featherstone, Scott Lash, and R. Robertson. London: Sage.

Portes, Alejandro. 2003. "Conclusion: Theoretical Convergences and Empirical Evidence in the Stody of Transnationalism." *International Migration Review* 37:874-891.

Rees, Martha Woodson, and T. Danyael Miller. 2002. "Quienes Somos? Que Necesitamos?: Needs Assessment of Hispanics in the Archdiocese of Atlanta." Atlanta: Hispanic Apostolate of the Archdiocese of Atlanta.

Rouse, Roger. 1991. "Mexican Migration and the Social Space of Postmodernism." *Diaspora* 1(1):8-23.

Rowe, W., and Schelling, V. 1991. *Memory and Modernity: Popular Culture in Latin America.* London: Verso.

Schiller, Nina Glick. 1999. "Transmigrants and Nation-States: Something Old and Something New in the U.S. Immigrant Experience." In *The Handbook of International Migration: The American Experience,* ed. by C. Hirschman, P. Kasinitz, and J. DeWind. New York: Russell Sage Foundation.

Schiller, Nina Glick, Linda Basch, and Cristina Szanton Blanc. 1995. "From Immigrant to Transmigrant: Theorizing Transnational Migration." *Anthropological Quarterly* 68:48-63.

Soja, Edward W. 1995. "Postmodern Urbanization: The Six Restructurings of Los Angeles." In *Postmodern Cities and Spaces,* ed. S. Watson and K. Gibson. Cambridge, MA: Blackwell.

Vásquez, Manuel, and Marie Friedmann Marquardt. 2003. *Globalizing the Sacred: Religion Across the Americas.* New Brunswick, NJ: Rutgers University Press.

Warner, R. Stephen. 1993. "Work in Progress toward a New Paradigm for the Sociological Study of Religion in the United States." *American Journal of Sociology* 98:1044-93.

————. 1994. "The Place of the Congregation in the Contemporary Religious Configuration." In *American Congregations, Volume 2: New Perspectives in the Study of Congregations*, ed. J. P. Wind & J. W. Lewis. Chicago: University of Chicago Press.

Warner, R. Stephen, and Judith G. Wittner. 1998. *Gatherings in Diaspora: Religious Communities and the New Immigration*. Philadelphia: Temple University Press.

11

Historicizing and Materializing the Study of Religion
The Contribution of Migration Studies

Manuel A. Vásquez

This essay complements Alex Stepick's wide-ranging assessment of the impact of religion on migration studies. Coming from the other side of this relation of reciprocal determination, I would like to explore how taking the variable of migration seriously has affected the study of religion. I argue that recent shifts in migration patterns, which are closely connected with the current episode of globalization, are redefining the discipline of religion.

In the wake of the postmodern and postcolonial turns, it is now considered de rigueur to begin any academic exercise with a statement of one's own positionality. I come to migration studies as a religion scholar with a strong interest in the religious field in Latin America. My training is thus inflected by Cold War territorializations: especially by the U.S.'s "denial of coevalness" (Fabian 1983) with Latin America. By this I mean that the dominant paradigms in area studies have tended to see the U.S. and Latin America as existing in different times and spaces. The modernization paradigm, for example, imagined the U.S. as a developed, modern, Protestant, and democratic nation, while Latin America was considered an underdeveloped, traditional, and Catholic region, marked by authoritarianism. According to this paradigm, to achieve prosperity and democracy, Latin America had to follow the steps of the U.S. and other developed nations. One of the crucial steps entailed the replacement of the patrimonial, rural, and corporatist values enshrined in Latin America's Hispanic Catholic culture by Anglo-Saxon, Protestant values compatible with modern individualism, pluralism, scientific rationality, and entrepeneurialism.[1] In other words, modernization theory went hand-in-hand with the theory of secularization, the prediction of the gradual decline of religion's public significance and its increasing privatization and rationalization. Dependency theory, which emerged as an alternative to the modernization paradigm, while rightly critical of the latter's teleological assumptions (i.e., the reliance on a simplistic, ahistorical, and unilinear model of development), still locks the U.S. and Latin America in different spatial pockets, understood as center vs. periphery. Dependency theory certainly sees the U.S. and Latin America as historically linked, and this is the basis for the thesis on "the development of underdevelopment" (Frank 1969). However, dependency theory tends to give agency primarily to the United States, which is actively extracting surplus from a passive Latin America. The stark nature of these unequal structural relations also makes the study of culture (and, within it, religion) irrelevant. Since, according to dependency theory, Latin America's place in the world-system determines in the last instance what Latin Americans do, there is very little need to explore the creative and potentially transformative roles of Latin American cultures and religions.

The denial of coevalness in area studies has made it difficult to develop a truly hemispheric vision and to take religion seriously as a socio-political force. Much of my work, thus, has been an effort to challenge the spatio-temporal epistemologies implicit in area studies. Research in transnational and global Christian denominations and congregations has made me realize that one cannot understand what is taking place in Latin America without paying attention to on-going linkages with Latino communities in the U.S. When I asked people in small, rural Pentecostal churches in El Salvador how many had close relatives living in the U.S., invariably at least two-thirds raised their hands. By the same token, studying Peruvian Catholics in Paterson, New Jersey, I was immediately struck by the rich calendar of transnational fiestas and pilgrimages around El Señor de los Milagros, San Martín de Porres, El Señor de Qoyllur Ritti, and other rural saints, which transpose Peruvian sacred landscapes at the edge of New York City, the global city par excellence. As Roger Rouse (1991) puts it, in the time-space compression brought by the current episode of globalization, "it becomes increasingly difficult to delimit a singular national identity and a continuous history," and "the image of the center and periphery also [comes] under increasing strain," as the Third World implodes into the first and as core exhibits substantial "peripheralization." The result of these transformations is a "proliferation of border zones," zones of cross-fertilization and struggle that require a different kind of cognitive mapping than that provided by modernization, dependency theory, or even Wallerstein's world-system approach. Further, I would argue that religion plays a major role in the emerging border zones, marking difference and generating hybridity.

Given this trajectory and theoretical background, the reflections that follow stand at the intersection of the disciplines of religion and cultural, ethnic, area, and transnational and global studies. From this standpoint, I see five areas where migration studies have had a major impact in the study of religion.

I

Robert Orsi, whose work has focused on urban lived religion among immigrants, observed that among post-Vatican II Euro-American Catholics there has developed a "hegemony of the word over deed" that parallels the history of the academic study of religion. "To study religion in the United States today is to study texts. The briefest review of papers given at the meeting of the American Academy of Religion over the last two decades shows how few studies are empirically based. The written word, rather than engaged behavior studied in its place, are what occupies practitioners, and this resolutely textual orientation among American Catholics and scholars of religion both, is one the obstacles to the study of contemporary Catholicism" (Orsi 1994:142).

The hegemony of word over deed is not surprising, given that the study of religion began with biblical exegesis and attempts by Christian missionaries to translate the Gospel for their colonial subjects. Even an openly secular scholar like Max Müller, who wanted to detach the study of religion from its Judeo-Christian roots and declared that religion was "a disease of language," an erroneous transformation of "nomima" (names) into "numina" (transcendent beings) in the process of myth-making, felt that the study of religion should be centered around the great sacred texts. This focus on text, theology, and doctrine was reinforced by the whole genre of arm-chair sociology and anthropology.

Lest we consider this an anachronistic position, a disastrously quaint approach that we postmoderns have transcended (after all, Müller wrote in the 1880s and 1890s), one need only to turn to the work of Mircea Eliade, who arguably has done more than anyone else to establish the study of religion as an autonomous discipline. Eliade sought to define religion sui generis, challenging approaches that defined religion as purely derivative of deeper social, economic, or psychological processes. He, of course, had in mind the holy trilogy of Durkheim, Marx, and Freud. For Eliade, religion is fundamentally about the irreducible sacred, an ontological reality that gave rise to human time and space in *illo tempore*, at the beginning of times, out of chaos. The sacred expresses itself through foundational hierophanies, archetypal moments of revelation that human beings then endlessly retell through myth and re-enact through ritual. The task of the study of religion is to identify historical forms these archetypes take and to classify them cross-culturally.

According to Eliade, scholars in the West face a serious challenge in their efforts to develop a comparative history of religion. Because of the process of secularization, the West has lost touch with archetypal religious experiences and as a result we cannot grasp the full force of religion for what Eliade called the "archaic men." It is worth quoting him in full here: "The process of desacralization of human experience has sometimes arrived at hybrid forms of black magic and sheer travesty of religion. We do not refer to the countless 'little religions' that proliferate in all modern cities, to the pseudo-occult, neospiritualistic, or so called hermetic churches, sects, or schools; for all these phenomena still belong to the sphere of religion, even if they almost always present the aberrant aspects of pseudomorphs" (Eliade 1959:206). Although Eliade did not focus solely on the great sacred texts or on canonical doctrines, he still operated with a myth of origins, a logocentric regard that set a hierarchy between authentic originative experiences, which are expressed in the grand religious narratives, and today's "degenerate" religious practices.

A similar elitism is observed in the U.S. religious history. Until recently, to study religion in the U.S. was to study Protestantism, even when one made accommodations for Catholics and Jews in the melting pot, as Will Herberg (1960) did. And it was a particular strand of Protestantism with a focus on the ideas of the great religious men: the George Whitefields and the Lyman Beechers of the world.

The diversity of post-1965 migration, with large numbers of immigrants from Latin America, Asia, and Africa, working in tandem with social movements around identity (particularly race, gender, and national liberation) in the1960s, has been an arrow to the heart of this elitist perspective. For those of us who look at the religions of Latino migrants, it is precisely the "little religions" that matter. It is precisely the grassroots devotions, the syncretic rituals and beliefs that transgress the sacred-profane dichotomy, and the embodied and "emplaced" (in the sense of simultaneously creating and reflecting lived space) religious tropes, myths, and narratives that migrants perform in their day-to-day existence as they attempt to negotiate the perils of life in both their adopted country and the country of origin. Those of us studying religion and migration are primarily interested in what Orsi calls the "theologies of the street," or as Narayanan (2003) puts it, the "embodied cosmologies," which, while having their own logic and determinative power, are not necessarily articulated in standard written theological texts. Popular theologies and practices often exist at the margins of official orthodoxies and orthopraxis.

What Eliade deplored as hybrids, or "religious pseudomorphs," are in fact key to the revitalization of the religious fields worldwide, often at the very heart of the most secular societies. The revitalizations, of course, are not without contradictions, for institutions and ecclesial elites constantly attempt to normalize grassroots practices and beliefs and to impose orthodoxy. I do not want to give the impression that popular, lived religion is a free-floating reality outside of institutions or that institutions are always conservative. However, grassroots religious actors have a relative degree of autonomy that allows them to improvise and innovate. Attempts by elites to co-opt these actors are never fully successful, leading to yet more hybridity and heterogeneity. Thus, unintended effects of disciplinary practices are often the vehicle through which institutions generate change.

In sum, the diversity and rapidity of migration has challenged religious studies to abandon its exclusive focus on the unchanging truths of the great texts, to see these truths as historically constructed by subjects inflected by class, gender, and race, and other power dynamics. Migration studies have been instrumental in challenging the textual reductionism and the emphasis on religious elites, and thus on orthodoxy, at the core of religious studies. There is within the American Academy of Religion (AAR) a new focus on lived religions at the grassroots, on the contested nature of religious discursive and non-discursive practices that are often not of Judeo-Christian origin. For example, Narayaran, who served at the AAR's president, has recently called for a "decolonializing" of religious studies methodologies, which would shift

> our discussion in another direction; we can look at dances, temples, cities, alternative medical therapies, and so on and appreciate the embodied ways in which knowledge was transmitted in precolonial cultures and still continues to be transmitted in many diasporic realms. It is in and through these embodied narratives that identities are formed and homelands are imagined, re-created, and made secure, in nostalgia and in the present. The privileging of the written text and beliefs by dominant, hegemonic cultures has led to the marginalization of other ways of knowing, other sources of knowledge. By decolonizing methodologies, by dismantling the authority paradigms based on texts alone . . . we begin to explore the intersection of "globalization past" with "globalization present." (2003:516)

It would seem, thus, that Orsi's cries in the wilderness have been heard. In fact, a sign of the acceptance of Orsi's approach might be seen is his election as president of the AAR. The AAR has also recently voted to separate its annual meeting from the Society of Biblical Literature, partly in order to become more interdisciplinary. In addition, the *Journal of the Academy of Religion*, which is produced by AAR and is the discipline's flagship journal, has made a concerted effort to include voices from Latin America, Asia, and Africa. *JAAR* has received a substantial grant to hold a major conference entitled "Contesting Religion and Religions Contested: The Study of Religion in a Global Context."

Despite these visible changes, there are countervailing tendencies. Recently, there have been some high-profile attempts to "retheologize" religious studies. For example, John Milbank (1990), who is part of a larger theological movement called radical orthodoxy, condemns the social sciences as part of modernity's nihilist secular reason, which finally implodes with postmodernism. Theology would therefore do well to avoid reliance on social scientific epistemologies and methods. In fact, the bankruptcy of modern secular reason opens the way for the return of a pre-modern (Agustinian and Thomistic) theology anchored on God's mysterious and gratuitous revelations. The future direction of religious studies is thus very much contested. Yet it is clear that post-1965 migration has had a powerful impact on the discipline, redirecting its focus and reshaping its methodologies.

II

One of the key methodological aspects in religious studies that migration challenges is the excessive phenomenological and hermeneutic slant. In *Genealogies of Religion*, Talal Asad (1993) critiques the discipline of religion for universalizing a very Western definition of religion: religion as interiority. Such a definition assumes that individual identity is crystallized around a sovereign, unified, and fully intentional subjectivity. Religion then represents the essence of this subjectivity, its deepest beliefs, moods, and emotions. The strength of this approach, which was influenced by Max Weber's *verstehende* sociology, is as a good counter-point to crude materialism, for which religion is a mere ideological epiphenomenon. Nevertheless, the phenomenological-hermeneutic approach has become increasingly distorted by the "linguistic turn." Influenced by the semiotic culturalism of Clifford Geertz and by the deconstructionist idea that there is nothing outside the text, the phenomenological-hermeneutic approach has reduced religion to belief systems, to self-contained systems of signifiers, whose code we must break.

This exclusive focus on meaning and signification in religion has ignored the material, embodied, and place-making dimensions of religion. I am referring here to the ways in which religion helps carve out lived spaces ranging from architecture to the production of sacred artifacts to inculcation of a religious habitus in the body of the practitioner. As Marie Friedmann Marquardt shows in her article in this volume, religion often deals with the distribution of political and economic resources, the construction and management of bodies, buildings, and public spaces. Religion is also about "performance events," as our contributor Karen Richman demonstrates in the case of audio and videocassettes that circulate widely in the Haitian diaspora and make possible the creation of transnational ritual spaces.

Obviously, these material dimensions carry a symbolic component, just as any other set of practices does. However, the disciplining of bodies and transformation of spaces into places entail not just purely discursive practices. They are not simply texts, which we, as students of religion, must interpret and translate in an attempt to capture the inner life of the religious individual. We cannot treat home altars and garden shrines, or key rings, plastic glasses, or T-shirts bearing the pope's face—religious kitsch—in exactly the same way as we have traditionally approached written theology, sermons, or pastoral letters, as mere parts of a symbolic system that responds to universal existential plights like bafflement, moral evil, and physical suffering, as Geertzian anthropology would have it.[2] We are dealing here not just with mere emotive, symbolic, or cognitive expressions; they are physical artifacts created by individuals embedded in particular socio-historical realities, which simultaneously shape and are shaped by these cultural products.

Many religious practices among migrants highlight the material aspects of religion. The ubiquity of material religious practices comes to the fore in the study of transnational migration, because the latter is focused on everyday life. A focus on migration reveals for those of us who study religion the weaknesses of the phenomenological-hermeneutic approach: the failure to take power, domination, and resistance seriously. The phenomenological-hermeneutic approach fails to capture tensions like those between official and popular religions, between clerical elites and lay specialists. It fails to capture the internal tensions within immigrant groups, the fragmented ties, the use of religion to include and exclude, the attempts by state apparatuses in both sending and receiving countries to manage transnational populations and religious communities. The work of Thomas Douglas in this volume is illustrative on this point. He writes: "Churches, mutual assistance agencies, schools, and social welfare programs use their relationship with Cambodian immigrants to instill practices of self-discipline among these refugees in an effort to help them to adapt to American culture. These structures incorporate a capitalist logic that presents work and gainful employment as a moral issue through both their ideologies and their practices." In other words, religious institutions help to subjectivate, to use a Foucauldian word, Cambodian immigrants, rendering them as particular kinds of workers, consumers, and citizens. This argument parallels E. P. Thompson's (1966) study of the link between Methodism and incipient Fordist-Taylorist techniques of labor management in *The Making of the English Working Class* and Aihwa Ong's analysis of the role of Islam in regulating sexuality among factory women in Malaysia (1987).

In sum, migration pushes religion scholars to expand their focus beyond the Geertzian task of reconstructing webs of public meanings that express inner subjective states as individuals seek to respond to existential predicaments. It is also crucial to explore the multiple, fluid, and contradictory roles that religion plays in fostering domination and resistance, in mediating assimilation and affirmation of ethnicity, in constructing place and embodied identities. I see hopeful signs of a re-materialization of religious studies (which parallels the recovery of the notion of space in the disciplines of history and anthropology) in Tom Tweed's recent Deleuzian call to shift focus from "text to territory" (Tweed 2002). Other signs include the increasing interest on material and popular culture (McDannell 1995, Forbes and Mahan 2000), sacred architecture (Meyer 2001), pilgrimage (Eade and Sallnow 2000), territory (Gill 1998), and embodiment and performance (Narayanan 2003). Post-1965 migration, as part of the time-space compression accompanying the present episode of globalization, has played a key role in this re-materialization.

III

III

The third way in which migration has changed the study of religion has to do with the issue of secularization and pluralism. The secularization paradigm, which I would argue has been central to the identity of the social sciences, claimed in a nutshell that the significance of religion would decline with modernity's advance. As social complexity and differentiation, hallmarks of modernity, shatter the overarching sacred canopy that characterized pre-modern times, the place of religion is relativized. In a world disenchanted by science, religious narratives become delegitimized in the public sphere. Religion thus withdraws to the private sphere, where it becomes part of the moods and emotions that we described above.

It is clear that this teleological reading of the process of rationalization (the coming of the "iron cage") and the end of religion does not make sense of the contemporary scene. Rodney Stark and Roger Finke (2000), who have been among the key architects of the so-called New Paradigm in the sociology of religion, have a chapter in their latest book, *Acts of Faith*, entitled "Secularization RIP." There they quote Peter Berger, an earlier proponent of the secularization paradigm: "I think what I and most other sociologists of religion wrote in the 1960s about secularization was a mistake. Our underlying argument was that secularization and modernity go hand in hand. With more modernization comes more secularization. It wasn't a crazy theory. There was some evidence for it. But I think it's basically wrong. Most of the world today is certainly not secular. It's very religious" (1997:974).

Post-1965 immigration has played a major role in debunking the secularization paradigm. Migrants have brought to the U.S. a plurality of religious beliefs, practices, and forms of organization that have transformed and revitalized the religious field, at a time when mainline congregations have been steadily declining (Ebaugh and Chafetz 2000). As Stepick aptly puts it in his essay in this volume, "most immigrants missed Nietzsche's proclamation that God is dead." There is no question that the large influx of migrants of Latin American descent, for example, is transforming the U.S. Catholic Church, as Latinos spearhead the growth of a vibrant charismatic renewal movement. The fact that foundations such as Pew and Lilly have been sponsoring a wide array of studies on the impact of the new migration on mainline Christian churches is further proof of the important changes taking place in the U.S. religious field.

But it is not just in the U.S. that migration has transformed the religious field. Countries of origin have also been caught in transnational cycles of religious revitalization. Prima Kurien (1997), for instance, shows how Hindus in the U.S. have reworked their religious identities to participate in the American "multicultural table," while at the same time supporting Hindu fundamentalism in India. In this volume, Kenneth Guest demonstrates how Fuzhounese immigrants in the United States have fueled "the religious revival sweeping Fuzhou, as remittances flow back to build towering new religious edifices and fund the rapid revitalization and expansion of religious programming."

Berger (2001) argues that the secularization thesis is still useful if it is relativized. Secularization should not be seen as "the direct and inevitable result of modernity . . . not as the paradigmatic situation of religion in the contemporary world, but as one situation among others." For Berger, secularization still applies to Western and Central Europe and to a thin but influential slice of Western-trained intellectuals worldwide. The question, however, is whether increasing migration from Africa, the Caribbean, the Middle East, and Eastern Europe will eventually also transform the landscape of "Euro-secularity." Recent debates in France around the banning of overt religious symbols in public schools, which are thinly disguised attempts to regulate Islam, show that French secular republicanism can no longer be taken for granted but must be actively defended by the state.[3]

The notion that religious vitality is not opposed to religious pluralism is at the core of the New Paradigm (NP) proposed in 1993 by R. Stephen Warner in his now-classic article in the *American Journal of Sociology*. In this view, pluralism and competition do not spell the decline of religious vitality. Quite the contrary, lifting a page from Adam Smith, the NP holds that religious monopolies lead to a loss of vigor because they encourage laziness among religious producers. When religious producers face competition in unregulated markets, they are compelled to improve their products and make them distinctive in order to sustain or increase their clientele. In the process they simultaneously generate religious differentiation and vitality.

The NP is certainly not a monolith. There are multiple issues, methods, and voices involved in advancing it, some of them defending more explicitly a rational-choice approach to non-regulated religious markets. This is obviously not the place to discuss all the intricacies of the NP.[4] However, I want to call attention to the recent work of Christian Smith (1998), especially his so-called subcultural identity theory (SIT), which is one of the most sophisticated versions of the New Paradigm. This theory holds that the more highly differentiated a social setting, the more individuals need to define their identity. One of the key sources for this definition is religion. The more strict the religion is, the more it is in tension with the social setting and the more it will mark sharp boundaries and constitute cohesive identities. This is especially critical for people who have been dislocated by globalization. To quote Smith: "Religion survives and can thrive in a pluralistic, modern society by embedding itself in subcultures that offer satisfying morally orienting collective identities which provide adherents meaning and belonging" (1998:118).

Subcultural identity theory is an interesting approach, one that can help us understand, for example, the rapid growth of Pentecostalism in Latin America (among rural-urban migrants) and among U.S. Latinos, as they seek to negotiate anomie and marginalization through adherence to a "strong religion." However, subcultural identity theory does not provide a full account of the cultural dynamics of contemporary migration. SIT, like other versions of the New Paradigm, works with essentialized notions of identity, religion, and borders. It presupposes a unified subject who chooses, albeit with bounded rationality, one religious tradition to the exclusion of others. In other words, SIT equates identity with exclusionary difference, with the construction of static and clear borders. But as many of the contributors in this book argue, religious affiliations and practices are more fluid, polyvalent, and mixed than subcultural identity theory allows. Contemporary migration and globalization produce a dialectic of deterritorialization and reterritorialization that belie the claims of subcultural identity theory and other expressions of the New Paradigm. Here the work of Karen Richman in this volume is illustrative. She shows how the issue of boundaries is more complex than SIT proposes. Pentecostalism sets sharp boundaries between the elect and outside world, deemed as corrupt. This sectarian stand, the rupture with all human institutions, helps Haitian Pentecostal converts to break with what they perceive as the onerous transnational moral economy at the heart of folk Catholicism and vodou, with their plethora of saints and spirits (*lwa*) demanding expensive rituals in exchange for protection and favors. Moreover, Pentecostal Haitians can appropriate the disenchanted individualism of U.S. capitalist culture that may allow for some upward socio-economic mobility. In Richman's words: "migrants are turning to conversion to resist their perceived domination by home kin and their spirits, and to take control of their remittances and the terms of their relationships with the home. They have rejected their *lwa*, withdrawn from the system of family ritual obligations, and joined Pentecostal churches." Yet, Richman writes, the break with tradition is not wholesale. For "underneath the modern, ascetic cloak worn by the new converts, spiritual healing, sorcery, and magic remain at the heart of their syncretic practices." This fact leads Richman to affirm that among Haitians in Palm Beach County, "self-identified Catholics and Protestants co-exist in a fluid system of religious pluralism. This flexibility of religious practice and association, the Protestants' hard-line stance notwithstanding, makes it difficult to measure their relative strength."

A similar dynamic takes place within the Universal Church of the Kingdom of God (IURD), a controversial Brazilian neo-Pentecostal church that now has temples in far-flung places, including the United States, Nicaragua, Portugal, South Africa, and Mozambique. As a neo-Pentecostal church, the Universal Church does not shy away from adopting an unabashedly entrepreneurial ethos, which openly exchanges miracle cures and individual prosperity for monetary contributions. This calculative, means-ends rationality, however, exists side-by-side with the "pre-modern" belief in the devil, manifested as possessing spirits associated with Afro-Brazilian religions like *Umbanda*. Thus, in fighting *Umbanda* and establishing clear taboos around it, the Universal Church paradoxically ends up incorporating the Afro-Brazilian spiritual pantheon into its own cosmology and thus legitimating the existence of African-based religions. Scholars influenced by market approaches to religious choice hypothesize that, in taking on Afro-Brazilian spirits, the IURD simply demonstrates that its products are superior to those of African-based religions, since the latter only bring misery through the work of demonic agents. In contrast, the Holy Spirit defeats and expels these demons, opening the road to physical well-being and financial success. In other words, the Universal Church has skillfully packaged its religious products to "outsell" its "diasporan competitors" (Chesnut 2003:55-56). Nevertheless, both Richman's work and the case of the IURD indicate that religious pluralism is not only about competition and the drawing of sharp boundaries between self-standing products and affiliations. Religious pluralism does not necessarily operate under a univocal logic of clear winners and losers, but also works through a dynamics of symbiosis, exchange, and simultaneity. Thus the question remains: Can New Paradigm approaches account for the fluidity, cross-fertilization, and paradoxical nature of religious practice among Haitians in Florida and Haiti and in the Universal Church of the Kingdom of God?

In *Globalizing the Sacred*, Marie Marquardt and I argue that, for all its attention to complexity, the New Paradigm is a cluster of "provincial" theories modeled after the dominant, sectarian logic of the U.S. religious field (Vásquez and Marquardt 2003). In this field, the emphasis has been on doctrinal differences, on competition for the souls of the converted, and on establishing sharp boundaries and purity of identity, all of which have been the hallmark of the Protestant experience of religious pluralism. The multiplicity of religions involved in post-1965 migration again destabilizes this provincialism, showing that religion is not only about marking difference but also about hybridity, border-crossing, and transculturality. Thus, we agree with Ammerman

> that the context for [the] new paradigm is nothing less than the de-centering of modernism as our primary interpretive frame. Modern frames assumed functional differentiation, individualism, and rationalism as "the way things are." Modern frames looked for bureaucratically organized institutions with clear lists of members and tasks. Modern frames looked for a clear line between rational, this worldly, action and action guided by any other form of wisdom. Modern frames looked for the individualized "meaning system" that would be carved out of differentiation and pluralism. I hesitate to invoke the word postmodern, given all its baggage, but it seems to me a useful concept here. The root of our problem with the either/or concepts with which we work is that we now live in a both/and world. (Ammerman 1997)

We need a "hermeneutics of hybridity" (Orsi 1997:11) to complement and critique the "hermeneutics of differentiation" at the heart of the New Paradigm and Subcultural Identity Theory.

IV

This takes me to the fourth point I want to make. The critique of the attempt to universalize the U.S. model, to establish it as the new paradigm to understand religion today, also challenges the recent focus in the sociology of religion on congregations. I want to make clear from the outset that I am not discounting the fruitfulness of congregational studies, especially when they are done with care, as in the cases of Nancy Ammerman (1997) or Penny Becker (1999). By focusing on "what new ethnic and immigrant groups [are] *doing together religiously* in the United States, and what manner of religious institutions they [are] developing *of, by, and for themselves*" (Warner 1997:9), congregational studies have helped us to shift our attention away from the great sacred texts and the theologies of elites toward a more textured understanding of grassroots practices and institutions. Congregational studies have also moved us away from the exhausted focus on denominations. Furthermore, the emphasis in congregational studies on agency and the role of religious creativity in the production of multiple identities is right in line with the points I have made above.

The problem emerges when congregationalism is used to reinforce the claim of American exceptionalism and to deny the coevalness of the immigrants' societies of origin. In a recent article in the *American Sociological Review*, Yang and Ebaugh (2001) build on Warner (1994) to hypothesize that migrants "transplant their traditional religious institutions in their new land" by, among other things, "adopting the congregational form in organizational structure and ritual," which characterizes American Protestantism. And, since 60 percent of Americans identify as Protestants, this process amounts to organizational assimilation or Americanization. This hypothesis seems prima facie straightforward and it can be tested against qualitative and quantitative studies of immigrant religious practices and institutions. However, there is a crypto-normativism behind "congregationalism." The assumption is that congregationalism as "the official norm" is unique to American religion. In contrast, the societies of origin are characterized as being dominated by tradition and religious monopolies. As Yang and Ebaugh put it: "In the countries from which the new immigrants migrated, people tend to be born into a religion that has been the tradition for generations for the nation or ethnic group. In contrast, there is less social pressure in America to adhere to a particular religion or any religion at all—alternatives to traditional religion are many and easily accessible." Implicit in this distinction between the U.S. and the Other—the countries from which new immigrants come—are the dichotomies between mechanical and organic solidarity, *Gemeinschaft* and *Gesellschaft*, and between tradition and modernity, which have disabled modern social science. Post-colonial historian Dipesh Chakrabarty (2000) has offered a powerful critique of these dichotomies, seeing them as devices to invent a hegemonic Euro-centric history. In the specific case under discussion, the adoption of congregationalism as a process of Americanization of immigrant religion assumes a positive valence because, in contrast to "denominational hierarchies [in their home countries], congregationalism focuses on the local community . . . which includes the increased voluntary participation of members in religious functions," a strong lay leadership, and a multitude of social, ritual, and spiritual functions (Yang and Ebaugh 2001).

I have several problems with this particular reading of congregation. For one thing, it tends to deny that societies of origin are differentiated and pluralistic. They are also "hot societies," as anthropologists would say, where change takes place, where religion is contested, not of a single cloth. Like the United States, immigrants' societies of origin are embedded in global processes that produce disjunctures and tensions. That is the whole point about transnational scholarship's critique of "methodological nationalism," the naturalization of the self-contained nation-state as the key unit of analysis in the social sciences (Wimmer and Glick Schiller 2003). The intense and sustained back and forth movement of peoples, goods, capital, and ideas creates transnational fields of social action that make it increasingly difficult to claim national uniqueness. In these back-and-forth exchanges, immigrants may already bring "congregational" resources from their countries of origin. In Latin America, for example, the experiences of liberation theology and base Christian communities have helped open and strengthen civic life at a time of precarious democratic transition.[5] Central American immigrants, in particular, have brought these participatory experiences to the U.S., transforming the hierarchical tendencies that Irish and Italian American Catholicism developed in response to its minority status. In this case, "Latin American" practices produce, as Marquardt shows in her essay here, "counter-publics" that challenge assimilation into a hegemonic way of being Catholic in the U.S.

By the same token, scholars like David Martin (1990) have argued that evangelical Christianity, which is growing rapidly in Latin America, is also fostering voluntarism, reciprocity, and "peaceability." I have seen Latino churches, many of them recently founded offshoots of indigenous churches, retool these values to deal with problems more specific to the U.S. such as drug addiction and gang violence among second-generation youths. In this case, the congregational practices were already there; they are not the product of crossing the U.S. border. They have merely become reconfigured to deal with changing conditions in the U.S.

The danger behind the use of congregationalism to mark the distinctiveness of the American religious field lies not only in denying that immigrant religions carry anti-structural elements, but also of ignoring power dynamics that crisscross congregations. Himanee Gupta (n.d.), for example, argues that while temples, with all the structures and services associated with congregationalism, have allowed to immigrants from India to establish their place in the American multicultural scene, they have also become spaces for the "hardening of an Indian-American identity along a Hindu line," defined primarily by upper-caste, upper-middle-class Brahmins. In this context, the pluralism that existed in India becomes "standardized," homogenized under an Orientalist conception of Hinduism for U.S. consumption. As Gupta writes,

> In India, Hindus make up eighty-five percent of the population. Nevertheless, temples compete for spiritual space with mosques, gurdwaras, and houses of worship from numerous other faiths. In urban colonies of New Delhi, for instance, it is not unusual to be awakened at dawn by a clamor of religious noise: the clanging of temple bells, the singing of hymns, the muezzin calling to prayer. By contrast, in the United States, where Indians make up less than one percent of the population, the cacophony of religious noise within this community is effectively silenced by the majority Hindus who dominate, numerically and economically.

In this volume, Derek Chang demonstrates that there is a link between the construction of America as an exceptional Christian nation and racial identity among immigrants. In seeking to minister to a growing number of Chinese immigrants in the late nineteenth century, the American Home Baptist Mission Society deployed a vision of a racially inclusive and egalitarian Christian nation, while almost simultaneously narrowing the spectrum of religious and cultural differences in order to remake Chinese immigrants and African Americans in the image of white, "middle-class" citizens. For her part, Danielle Brune Sigler discovers a very interesting counter-discourse in the figure of Cape Verdean immigrant preacher Charles Manuel "Sweet Daddy" Grace. Grace saw America not as the Promised Land, but a god-forsaken foreign land in need of evangelization. Thus, he derived his authority by emphasizing his status as an outsider. He then became the exception against a profane America. I have heard a similar narrative from a Brazilian Baptist pastor in South Florida who tells members of his congregation not to feel inferior about their undocumented status. They are here as part of God's plan to save this nation. Their migration here is part of a cosmic struggle between good and evil, notwithstanding what the U.S. Bureau of Citizenship and Immigration Services has to say.

Let me be provocative here: Just as we have disclosed the contradictory ways in which religion has been implicated in the construction of nationhood, I believe that it is time to explore how U.S. sociology of religion has contributed to the invention and reproduction of American exceptionalism. To what extent is the rhetoric of congregationalism not just describing social and historical saliences but also reinforcing the prescriptive view of America as the "city upon the hill" and the secular notion of the American Dream?

Methodologically, the sociology of immigrant congregations has a more serious limitation. Congregations are just one aspect (and in some cases not the most salient one) of the complex interactions among religion, everyday life, and the micropolitics of identity among immigrants. Put in other words, not everything that immigrants "do together religiously" has to do with visible, culturally homogenous religious groups. Public religious life for immigrants is not just about "local, face-to-face religious assemblies," to use Warner's definition of congregation. In a collaborative study of transnational migration, religious life, and identity among three Latino groups in Florida, one of the groups we are studying is Mexican agricultural workers in Immokalee, a poor rural town in south Florida. There we have found a plethora of religious organizations, from the Catholic Church, which has been strongly supportive of the rural workers' union, to Pentecostal churches of various sizes (Assemblies of God as well as storefront churches founded by migrant pastors from Mexico) to Jehovah's Witnesses. As we study these congregational forms, the work of Warner, Ammerman, and Ebaugh and associates definitely resonates. Nevertheless, we have found that churches and other collective organizations only reach a small portion of the immigrants. Because of their instability, mobility (these workers follow the agricultural seasons traveling upstate, even traveling up the East Coast and to the Midwest), dispersion and marginalization (they live in remote dilapidated trailers), they are only very loosely connected to any form of local assembly, including voluntary religious associations. In fact, because of the material and spatial conditions that Mexican immigrants in Immokalee encounter, they express and experience religion in spontaneous, though frequent and very powerful, ways, in their homes, workplaces, and in the schools their children attend. The practices involved here are not mere "private devotions," for they are often mediated by fluid informal networks of lay religious specialists, from *curanderas* (healers) to *rezadoras* (prayer specialists) and *espiritualistas*, who work in the large gaps left by religious institutions.[6] These religious practices involve shared but contested moral economies where symbolic and material goods are exchanged between the dead and the living (patron saints and their devotees, for example), and between religious specialists and their shifting "clientele."

Contrary to what to Yang and Ebaugh would expect, among Mexican immigrants in Immokalee there is a movement away from congregationalism. The radical experience of being undocumented and disenfranchised, of having to work from dawn to dusk and being afraid of police and other institutions, makes the Mexican migrants in Immokalee less likely to adopt congregational structures and rituals. Ironically, some of them were more engaged in community-based congregations in Oaxaca, Guerrero, or Chiapas than in rural Florida. In his chapter in this volume, Ken Guest observes a similar dynamic among Chinese immigrants in New York. Precarious social conditions and class stratification within their ethnic enclaves make it difficult for Fuzhounese immigrants to reproduce in New York the level of involvement in collective religious life they sustained in China.

Could it be that developing a robust congregational life requires a high volume and intensity of social interactions, both of which can be found among established immigrant communities in large cities but often not among recently arrived migrant groups or in sprawling rural fields? In this sense, the stress on congregations among recent works on religion and immigration is perhaps due to the fact that most research has hitherto concentrated on the large "gateway cities." And here we cannot deny the impact of funding agencies like the Lilly Endowment and Pew Charitable Trusts, which in generously supporting our research, have shaped our agendas. At least in the case of U.S. Latinos, the focus on the traditional gateway cities provides only a partial view of the dynamics of religion and the new migration, for, as the census shows, the fastest-growing Latino populations are in non-conventional places like suburbs and mid-size cities in the South and Midwest (Brewer and Suchan 2001).

Nevertheless, even in the congregation-rich context of big immigrant cities, our preliminary findings in rural Florida resonate. Pyong Gap Min has found that, while Hindus in Queens attend their temple a few times a year "to celebrate important religious holidays or to get rituals performed for their children and other family member," they maintain ethnicity "by practicing Hindu religious faith and rituals at home." This leads to the conclusion that Hinduism is not a congregation-oriented religion. More than reflecting an Americanization (the tendency toward congregationalism), the practices of the Korean and Hindu immigrants Pyong Gap studied "reflect their practices in their home countries."

It is too early to pass summary judgment on the congregational approach. If it is relativized and stripped of normative and teleological assumptions, as the secularization and the assimilation paradigms have been, the congregational approach will likely continue to yield valuable insights into the ways in which religious organizations mediate the formation of collective identities among immigrants.[7] Perhaps rather than assuming that congregationalism is the natural (or desirable) outcome of migration to the U.S., we should ask under what conditions is the development of congregational structures more or less likely. More importantly, how are age-old congregational morphologies changing in response to recent migration patterns? We cannot ignore the history of religious disestablishment and sectarianism in the U.S. and the tax codes and legal frameworks that delimit the ways in which immigrants can practice their religions. Nevertheless, responses by immigrants are diverse and complex, not simply reducible to an automatic acculturation. Immigrant responses, in turn, affect the U.S. religious field, leading to new forms of organization, belief, and practice that often challenge our traditional nation-bound methodologies. As Marquardt puts it in her contribution in this volume, "churches develop structural and cultural hybridity that affects both the internal functioning of immigrant religious organizations and also shapes the relationships that members of these churches will develop with their host society."

In any case, it is necessary to augment congregational approaches with analyses of ways in which lived religion is intertwined with the politics of daily life, analyses that explore the "diffuse" but not less intense or valid religious life of immigrants beyond visible assemblies and well-organized, territorially bound associations. To carry out this task we need to embed congregations in their larger context. Using concepts such as "religious ecologies" and "religious districts," some scholars have begun to examine the ways in which congregations shape and respond to their immediate social environment, transforming in the process intra-congregational relations in a given locality (Eiesland 2000; McRoberts 2003). These approaches, helpful as they are, have to be deepened and extended by crafting new in-depth methods that allow us to explore religion as it is lived in kitchens, clinics, social service centers, plazas, bars, restaurants, and other quotidian sites. We also need to embed personal and local religious life within translocal flows, networks, and itineraries. For these networks and flows crisscross self and locality, linking them with regional, national, transnational, and global processes. In particular, the concept of networks, which has had a long and distinguished career in migration studies (Bretell 2000), can be very useful for studying emerging religious morphologies at the crossroads of multiple spatio-temporal scales. However, as Vertovec (2003:647) rightly warns, network analysis can be highly abstract, falling into a "structural determinism" that fails to acknowledge "questions of cultural content and agency." It is important, thus, to see religious and migrant networks not as rigid, totalizing structures but rather as flexible, open-ended, and co-adaptive webs (Taylor 2001). Religious networks are not primarily mathematical models but negotiated phenomenological realities: meaning is not just another commodity that circulates alongside social capital but is constitutive of the networks themselves. For example, the location of an individual in particular networks shapes and is shaped by his/her sense of place and belonging and by his/her habitus, which allows him/her to "invent within limits," to create discourses, tastes, and practices that fit that location (Bourdieu 1984).

If we are to map out the interplay of local and translocal religious phenomena, our methods will have to be more refined at both the micro and macro levels. At the micro levels, we will need more longitudinal studies, requiring lengthy and close involvement in the day-to-day lives of our informants. Such studies would involve not just traditional field techniques such as participant observation, focus groups, and in-depth interviews, but also the collection of detailed oral histories of physical and spiritual migration, and the use of projective social-psychological tests to evoke memories and other cognitive and moral maps from our informants. At the macro level, we will have to take care to embed everyday life in regional, national, transnational, and global processes that de- and re-territorialize it. These processes invariably represent a complex mixture of socio-economic, political, and cultural dynamics.

V

I have saved the most difficult point for last, since it goes to the very core of the discipline of religious studies. In their essay in this volume, Susan Sered and

Ronald Nakasone dramatize the provincialism of our understandings of religion among immigrants when they critique the

> lack of fit between what Americans commonly understand to be relig-
> ion and the understandings and practices of many non-American and
> newly American populations. In the United States religion is gener-
> ally seen as a discrete segment of life of the individual and the com-
> munity. Religion is understood as having to do with notions of God
> or gods—notions that we generally speak of people "believing in" or
> "adhering to," and religion is practiced in the context of an identifi-
> able congregation of some sort—usually in the sense of a "faith based
> organization" that people "join" or "belong to."

Does this suggest that we should give up the category of religion altogether? And would that not mean the end of religious studies as a relatively coherent discipline? As Durkheim argued in his *Rules for Sociological Method*, a discipline must have, above all, a circumscribed object of study.

It is undeniable that the category of religion and the discipline attached to it have been "manufactured" under particular socio-historical conditions that included acts of physical and symbolic violence perpetrated by missionaries, administrators, explorers, and other colonialist actors (Chidester 1996). The latter provided the "data" out of which arm-chair sociologists, anthropologists, and Orientalists built *Religionswissenschaft*. The work of these scholars, in turn, served colonial administrations to exert "biopower," to borrow from Foucault, that is, to manage native populations. In light of the intertwining of discourses on religion and power, some scholars of religion have begun to challenge the un-critical use of the category of religion. The category can be used to characterize anything from anthropophagy to Marxism or faith in the invisible hand of the market. In view of this indeterminacy, Willi Braun (2000) argues that "religion" is "substantively empty . . . infinitely fillable with aeolian qualities." Jonathan Z. Smith (1982) goes further, claiming that "there is no data for religion. Religion is solely the creation of the scholar's study. It is created for the scholar's analytic purposes by his imaginative acts of comparison and generalization. Religion has no independent existence apart from the academy. For this reason, the student of religion, and most particularly, the historian of religion, must be relentlessly self-conscious. Indeed, this self-consciousness constitutes his primary expertise, his foremost object of study."

I do not agree with Braun's and Smith's radical nominalism—the no-tion that religion is merely a label. However, I believe that they are right to call our attention to the constructed and contingent nature of the category of religion. Recognition that the category of religion is manufactured, however, should not lead us to conclude that there is no religion as such. For what the academy has normalized as religion, as an object with certain stable attributes, has had a pow-erful impact outside the academy, shaping the ways in which individuals live their daily lives and construct identities. For example, Gill (1987) has shown how the figure of "Mother Earth" came to be considered as central to all Native American traditions as part of a process whereby scholars constructed a single, homogenous Native American worldview out of diverse and complex religious practices. In this process, Native Americans were not passive receptacles of European desires; rather, they appropriated the figure and molded her according to their needs for survival and resistance. This is why Gill claims that Mother Earth's "existence stems primarily from two creative groups: scholars and Indians." Gill's work resonates with Nakasone's and Sered's, as they show how Euro-Christian definitions of religion affect relations between Okinawans and U.S. government agencies.

In response to Nakasone and Sered's challenge, I would argue that eliminating the category of religion would not solve the problem, any more than abandoning other constructed categories like culture, community, and nation would render the social sciences contradiction-free. Nakasone and Sered try to bypass the limitations of the category of religion by replacing it with "spirituality." According to them, "'Spirituality' is preferable to 'religion' when speaking of the Okinawan faith tradition. Derived from the Latin 'religio,' a bond between humanity and the gods, 'religion' implies a belief in a transcendental being who created and guides the universe. Such a definition . . . [does not] apply to the faith tradition of the Okinawan people. In contrast, 'spiritual' and 'spirituality' referring to the non-material inner core where a person is open to the transcendental and touches ultimate reality, is more appropriate." With this shift, Nakasone and Sered try to offer a more flexible term that does not devalue Okinawan ritual practices and subject them to discrimination by U.S. government agencies.

However, substituting spirituality for religion runs the risk of re-inscribing the Protestant "subjectivist" bias in religious studies, the bias that sees "religion" as an essential "non-material inner core" that has to do with ultimate reality. To understand ritual transformation among Okinawan and other immigrant communities we cannot rely on a universal, a priori definition of religion or spirituality. Rather, I would suggest that we be attentive to ways in which local, grassroots, official, national, and transnational actors continuously and creatively construct, transgress, and appropriate the boundaries between specific religious and non-religious practices and discourses. These multiple situated perspectives (which often lead to contested canons, traditions, and orthodoxies), in interplay with the researcher's own positionality, determine religious studies' proper subject matter. In Nakasone and Sered's case, it would be interesting to explore how Okinawans appropriate and confront Euro-Christian definitions of religion and how their "spirituality" is transformed as they negotiate power differentials.

Religion is thus a heuristic category, one that has to prove its usefulness for understanding the historical ways in which individuals constitute themselves as subjects and through which they engage in "place-making." As Jonathan Z. Smith puts it (1978:291), religion "is the quest, within the bounds of the human, historical condition, for the power to manipulate and negotiate one's 'situation' so as to have 'space' in which to meaningfully dwell. . . . What we study when we study religion is the variety of attempts to map, construct and inhabit such positions of power [i.e., over the natural and social environment] through the use of myths, rituals and experiences of transformation."

In exposing religion scholars to protean, transnational, and hybrid religious expressions, post-1965 immigration has heightened our awareness that the category of religion is always contingent and open to contestation, that its universal application and current usefulness should not be taken for granted. At the very least, contemporary migration forces us to historicize the notion of religion, construct a genealogy of its descent, show its limitations as part of a regime of knowledge, and detach it from its current hegemonic uses.

VI

I have been describing how the study of religion has been transformed by recent trends in migration. However, this is a two-way street. Alex Stepick addresses the other side of the relation between migration and religion in his chapter. Without being redundant, I would like to stress that religion also plays a determinative role. For example, religious institutions shape the morphology of migration by providing transnational networks which generate, concentrate, and distribute social capital among individuals and localities. However, the role of religion goes beyond these material and institutional aspects, which have been the traditional focus of the migration studies. Religion is also central in the "work of imagination," to quote Appadurai (1996), among immigrants. Religion helps immigrants imagine their homelands in diaspora and inscribe their memories and worldviews into the physical landscape and built environment. In addition, religion regenerates and re-centers selves challenged by the migration process, producing new habituses, introducing new forms of collective and individual identity, and new understandings of citizenship, locality, and community. Although these processes are "imagined," they are not inconsequential; they have tangible effects on space, time, and the body.

Here, we are back to the phenomenological and hermeneutic dimensions of religion, which the Euro-centric discipline of religious studies has delineated so well. The dimensions of meaning, signification, and textuality are still very useful, if they are properly historicized and embedded in various power grids involving, among other things, economics, institutional politics, geography, ecology, and technological change. In fact, in recent years we have seen outstanding examples of the recovery of the phenomenology and hermeneutics of religion through critical contextualization and interdisciplinary work. In the area of migration and religion, we can cite the examples of Tweed (1998), Brown (1999), Orsi (1999), McAlister (1997), Mahler (2001), and Levitt (2003). Their work and that collected in this volume show the promise of a cross-fertilization between religion and migration studies.

Notes

1. For current examples of this thesis see Berger 2002 and Huntington 2004.

2. Interestingly, Richman reads cassette-letters among Haitians as "models for and models of," following Geertzian holistic symbolism. Alternatively, one could read these cultural artifacts as "commodities" with particular "lives," with modes of production, circulation, and appropriation (Appadurai 1986). This alternative approach would allow her to understand better the tight interaction among power, context, material culture, and religious praxis in the Haitian diaspora.

3. Of course, the French "headscarf affair," which has had analogues in other European countries such as the Netherlands, Germany, and Italy, is more complex. According to Terray (2004:120), the affair is rooted in two realities: "Firstly, there is the 'breakdown of integration' as it affects France's 5,000,000-plus Muslim community: segregated cities, irreducible pockets of misery and unemployment, ghetto schools, educational failure, discrimination in the job and housing markets, workplace racism. . . . Secondly: the slowdown or stagnation of any equalization of the sexes. Since its victories of the 1970s on contraception and abortion, the women's movement has made scant progress." The second reality explains the obsession with Muslim girls' self-presentation, an obsession that simultaneously reflects and obscures persistent sexual inequality in the West.

4. See Vásquez and Marquardt 2003 for an extended discussion of the New Paradigm and rational choice theories.

5. Base Christian communities are small neighborhood-based groups in which poor people come together to read the Bible and Catholic social thought and to apply them to their everyday life. Base communities emerged out of Vatican II reforms, which enhanced the role of the laity in the Catholic Church. In many countries in Latin America, such as Nicaragua, Brazil, El Salvador, and Peru, base communities have contributed to the process of democratization by encouraging the development of grassroots leadership and voice among disenfranchised sectors of the population. See Levine 1993.

6. I should note here the gendered dimension of these religious networks, with women often playing a protagonist role. Among Mexicans in Immokalee, the majority of whom are young men, women are very often "empowered" extra-congregationally.

7. See Alba and Nee 2003 for a reformulation of the assimilation paradigm away from the linear, generation-driven model toward one that proposes differential non-linear outcomes mediated by the strategies of immigrants, levels of transnationalism, and the contexts of reception.

References

Alba, Richard, and Victor Nee. 2003. *Remaking the American Mainstream: Assimilation and Contemporary Immigration*. Cambridge, MA: Harvard University Press.

Appadurai, Arjun. 1986. *The Social Life of Things: Commodities in Cultural Perspective*. Cambridge: Cambridge University Press.

———. 1996. *Modernity at Large: Cultural Dimensions of Globalization*. Minneapolis: University of Minnesota Press.

Asad, Talal. 1993. *Genealogies of Religion*. Baltimore: Johns Hopkins University Press.

Ammerman, Nancy. 1997. *Congregation and Community*. New Brunswick, NJ: Rutgers University Press.

Becker, Penny Edgell. 1999. *Congregations in Conflict: Cultural Models of Local Religious Life*. Cambridge: Cambridge University Press.

Berger, Peter. 1997. "Epistemological Modesty: An Interview with Peter Berger." *Christian Century* 114 (October 29): 972-75, 978.

———. 2001. "Reflections on the Sociology of Religion Today." *Sociology of Religion* 62(4): 443-454.

———. 2002. "Introduction. The Cultural Dynamics of Globalization." In *Many Globalizations: Cultural Diversity in the Contemporary World,* ed. Peter L. Berger and Samuel P. Huntington. Oxford: Oxford University Press.

Bourdieu, Pierre. 1984. *Distinction: A Social Critique of the Judgement of Taste*. Cambridge, MA: Harvard University Press.

Braun, Willi. 2000. "Religion." In *Guide to the Study of Religion*, ed. Willi Braun and Russell McCutcheon. London: Cassell.

Brettell, Caroline. 2000. "Theorizing Migration in Anthropology: The Social Construction of Networks, Identities, Communities, and Globalscapes." In *Migration Theory: Talking Across Disciplines*, eds. Caroline Brettell and James Hollifield. New York: Rutledge.

Brewer, Cynthia, and Trudy Suchan. 2001. *Mapping Census 2000: The Geography of U.S. Diversity*. Washington, DC: U.S. Government Printing Office.

Brown, Karen McCarthy. 1999. "Staying Grounded in a High-Rise Building: Ecological Dissonance and Ritual Accommodation in Haitian Vodou." In *Gods of the City*, ed. Robert Orsi. Bloomington: University of Indiana Press.

Chakrabarty, Dipesh. 2000. *Provincializing Europe: Post-colonial Thought and Historical Difference*. Princeton: Princeton University Press.

Chesnut, R. Andrew. 2003. *Competitive Spirits: Latin America's New Religious Economy*. Oxford: Oxford University Press.

Chidester, David. 1996. *Savage Systems: Colonialism and Comparative Religion in Southern Africa*. Charlottesville: University of Virginia Press.

Eade, John, and Michael Sallnow. 2000. *Contesting the Sacred: The Anthropology of Christian Pilgrimage*. Urbana: University of Illinois Press.

Eiesland, Nancy. 2000. *A Particular Place: Urban Restructuring and Religious Ecology in a Southern Exurb*. New Brunswick, NJ: Rutgers University Press.

Ebaugh, Helen Rose, and Janet Chafetz. 2000. *Religion and the New Immigrants: Continuities and Adaptations in Immigrant Congregations*. Walnut Creek, CA: AltaMira Press.

Eliade, Mircea. 1959. *The Sacred and the Profane: The Nature of Religion*. New York: Harcourt Brace Jovanovich.

Fabian, Johannes. 1983. *Time and the Other: How Anthropology Makes Its Object*. New York: Columbia University Press.

Forbes, Bruce, and Jeffrey Mahan, eds. 2000. *Religion and Popular Culture in America*. Berkeley: University of California Press.

Frank, Andre Gunder. 1969. *Latin America: Underdevelopment or Revolution*. New York: Monthly Review Press.

Gill, Sam. 1987. *Mother Earth: An American Story*. Chicago: University of Chicago Press.

——. 1998. "Territory." In *Critical Terms for Religious Studies*, ed. Mark C. Taylor. Chicago: University of Chicago Press.

Gupta, Himanee. n.d.. "Staking a Claim on American-ness: Hindu Temples in the United States." Unpublished manuscript.

Herberg, Will. 1960. *Protestant, Catholic, Jew: Essays in American Religious Sociology*. Garden City, NY: Doubleday.

Huntington, Samuel. 2004. *Who Are We? The Challenges to America's National Identity*. New York: Simon & Shuster.

Kurien, Prima. 1997. "Becoming American by Becoming Hindu: Indian Americans Take their Place at the Multicultural Table." In *Gatherings in Diaspora: Religious Communities and the New Immigration*, ed. R. Stephen Warner and Judith Wittner. Philadelphia: Temple University Press.

Levine, Daniel. 1992. *Popular Voices in Latin American Catholicism*. Princeton: Princeton University Press.

Levitt, Peggy. 2003. "'You Know, Abraham was Really the First Immigrant': Religion and Transnational Migration." *International Migration Review* 37(3): 847-873.

Mahler, Sarah. 2001. "Bringing Religion to a Transnational Perspective: Clarifications and Initial Ideas on the Viability of the Framework." Presentation at the University of Florida, April 2.

Martin, David. 1990. *Tongues of Fire: The Explosion of Protestantism in Latin America*. Oxford: Blackwell.

McAlister, Liza. 1997. "The Madonna of 115th Street Revisited: Vodou and Haitian Catholicism in the Age of Transnationalism." In *Gatherings in Diaspora: Religious Communities and the New Immigration*, ed. R. Stephen Warner and Judith Wittner. Philadelphia: Temple University Press.

McDannell, Colleen. 1995. *Material Christianity: Religion and Popular Culture in America*. New Heaven: Yale University Press.

McRoberts, Omar. 2003. *Church and Community in a Black Urban Neighborhood*. Chicago: University of Chicago Press.

Meyer, Jeffrey. 2001. *Myths in Stone: Religious Dimensions of Washington, DC*. Berkeley: University of California Press.

Milbank, John. 1990. *Theology and Social Theory: Beyond Secular Reason*. Cambridge: Blackwell.

Narayanan. Vasudha. 2003. "Embodied Cosmologies: Sights of Piety, Sights of Power" *Journal of the American Academy of Religion* 71(3):495-520.

Ong, Aihwa. 1987. *Spirits of Resistance and Capitalist Discipline: Factory Women in Malaysia*. Albany: State University of New York Press.

Orsi, Robert. 1994. "'Have You Ever Prayed to Saint Jude?': Reflections on Fieldwork in Catholic Chicago." In *Reimagining Denominationalism: Interpretive Essays*, ed. Robert B. Mullin and Russell E. Richey. New York: Oxford University Press.

————. 1997. "Everyday Miracles: The Study of Lived Religion." In *Lived Religion in America*, ed. David D. Hall. Princeton: Princeton University Press.

————. 1999. "Introduction: Crossing the City Line." In *Gods of the City*, ed. Robert Orsi. Bloomington: University of Indiana Press.

Rouse, Roger. 1991. "Mexican Migration and the Social Space of Postmodernism." *Diaspora* 1:8-24.

Smith, Christian. 1998. *American Evangelicalism: Embattled and Thriving*. Chicago: University of Chicago Press.

Smith, Jonathan Z. 1978. *Map is Not Territory: Studies in the History of Religion*. Chicago: University of Chicago Press

————. 1982. *Imagining Religion: From Babylon to Jonestown*. Chicago: University of Chicago Press.

Stark, Rodney, and Roger Fink. 2000. *Acts of Faith: Explaining the Human Side of Religion*. Berkeley: University of California Press.

Taylor, Mark C. 2001. *The Moment of Complexity: Emerging Network Culture*. Chicago: University of Chicago Press.

Terray, Emmanuel. 2004. "Headscarf Hysteria." *New Left Review* 26(March-April):118-127.

Thompson, E. P. 1966 *The Making of the English Working Class*. New York: Vintage Books.

Tweed, Thomas. 1998. *Our Lady of the Exile: Diasporic Religion at a Cuban Catholic Shrine in Miami*. New York: Oxford University Press.

————. 2002. "On Moving Across: Translocative Religion and the Interpreter's Position." *Journal of the American Academy of Religion* 70(2):253-277.

Vásquez, Manuel A., and Marie Friedmann Marquardt. 2003. *Globalizing the Sacred: Religion Across the Americas*. New Brunswick, NJ: Rutgers University Press.

Vertovec, Steven. 2003. "Migration and Other Modes of Transnationalism: Towards Conceptual Cross-Fertilization." *International Migration Review* 37(3):641-665.

Warner, R. Stephen. 1993. "Work in Progress Toward a New Paradigm for the Sociological Study of Religion in the United States." *American Journal of Sociology* 98:1044-1093.

————. 1994. "The Place of the Congregation in the American Religious Configuration." In *American Congregations*, vol 2, ed. James P. Wind and James W. Lewis. Chicago: University of Chicago Press.

————. 1997. "Immigration and Religious Communities in the United States." In *Gatherings in Diaspora: Religious Communities and the New Immigration*, ed. R. Stephen Warner and Judith Wittner. Philadelphia: Temple University Press.

Wimmer, Andreas, and Nina Glick Schiller. 2003. "Methodological Nationalism, the Social Sciences, and the Study of Migration: An Essay in Historical Epistemology." *International Migration Review* 37(3):576-610.

Yang, Fenggang, and Helen Rose Ebaugh. 2001. "Transformations in New Immigrant Religions and their Global Implications." *American Sociological Review* 66:269-288.

Index

About the Contributors

Danielle Brune Sigler received her Ph.D. in American Studies from the University of Texas, Austin in 2002. She is a participant in IUPUI's Center for Study of Religion and American Culture Young Scholars Program. She contributed an essay to the anthology *Race, Nation, and Religion in the Americas* (Oxford University Press, 2004), and her book *Sweet Daddy Grace: The Man and His Ministry* is forthcoming from the University of Massachusetts Press.

Derek Chang is assistant professor of History and Asian American Studies at Cornell University. He received his Ph.D. in History at Duke University in 2002. He recently contributed an essay to the anthology *Race, Nation, and Religion in the Americas* (Oxford University Press, 2004). He is currently completing a manuscript entitled, "Converting Race, Transforming the Nation: Evangelical Christianity and the Problem of Diversity in Late-Nineteenth Century America," about African American and Chinese interactions with the American Baptist Home Mission Society.

Thomas J. Douglas received his Ph.D. in Anthropology at the University of California, Irvine and currently holds lecturer positions in the Department of Anthropology at both the University of California, Irvine and California State University, Long Beach. His research has focused on Cambodian immigrant communities in both Long Beach, California and Seattle, Washington. He has contributed an essay to the anthology *Revealing the Sacred in Asian and Pacific America* (Routledge 2003) and also contributed to the anthology *Religion and Healing in America* (Oxford 2004).

Kenneth J. Guest is assistant professor of Anthropology at Baruch College, City University of New York. He is the author of *God in Chinatown: Religion and Survival in New York's Evolving Immigrant Community* (NYU Press, 2003) and other articles about Chinese immigration and religion. Guest received his B.A. from Columbia University in East Asian Studies, an M.A. in Religious Studies from Union Theological Seminary in New York, and his Ph.D. in Anthropology from the City University of New York.

Jennifer Holdaway is Program Officer for the International Migration Program of the Social Science Research Council.

Karen Leonard, Professor of Anthropology and Asian American Studies at the University of California, Irvine, holds a Ph.D. in History from the University of Wisconsin. Her research interests are interdisciplinary and comparative, ranging from the socio-economic history and anthropology of South Asia and the analysis of caste, ethnicity, and gender to Asian-Americans in the United States. Her publications include, *Social History of an Indian Caste: the Kayasths of Hyderabad* (University of California Press, 1978), *Making Ethnic Choices: California's Punjabi Mexican Americans* (Temple, 1992), and *South Asian Americans* (Greenwood Press, 1997). Currently, she is working on personal and national identities in the diaspora of Hyderabadi emigrants from India after 1948, a cross-national comparative project being carried out in Hyderabad, Pakistan, the United Kingdom, Canada, the United States, Australia, and the Gulf States of the Middle East. Her most recent book is the bibliographic essay, *Muslims in the United States: The State of Research* (Russell Sage Foundation, 2003).

Marie Friedmann Marquardt is a postdoctoral research fellow at Emory University, where she received her Ph.D. in spring 2004. She is co-author, with Manuel A. Vásquez, of *Globalizing the Sacred: Religion across the Americas* (Rutgers University Press, 2003).

Pyong Gap Min is professor of Sociology at Queens College and the Graduate Center of the City University of New York. His areas of research interest are immigration, ethnic identity, ethnic business, religion, and gender issues, with a special focus on Asian Americans. He is the author of three books, including *Caught in the Middle: Korean Communities in New York and Los Angeles* (1996), the winner of two national book awards. He is the editor or co-editor of five books, including *The Second Generation: Ethnic Identity among Asian Americans* (2002) and *Mass Migration to the United States: Classical and Contemporary Periods* (2002).

Ronald Y. Nakasone, Buddhist cleric, ethicist, and calligrapher, offers reflections on bioethical and other modern dilemmas at a variety of international and national forums and publications. "Religious Views on Biotechnology, Buddhism" in the *Encyclopedia of Ethical, Legal, and Policy Issues in Biotechnology* (Wiley 2000, 2002 online edition) the doctrine of *pratityasamutapada* crystallizes the basis for his thoughts. Of Okinawan ancestry, he edited *The Okinawan Experience* (Dharma Cloud Publishers, 1996) and *Okinawan Diaspora* (University of Hawai'i Press, 2002). He has exhibited in Japan, China, Hawai'i, and the continental U.S.A. The Mobile, Alabama Museum of Art recently purchased two of his works for its permanent collection.

Karen Richman is a cultural anthropologist and an assistant professor in the Department of Anthropology at University of Notre Dame. She is the author of the book and compact disc *Migration and Vodou* (University Press of Florida, 2005). Her research over the past two decades has spanned Haiti and Haitian immigrants in the United States, focusing in particular on a single community in Western Haiti and its satellites in South Florida. Her work has especially engaged issues of religious change and ritual practices in relation to sustained transnational migration, aesthetic and rhetorical performance, gender relations and political mobilization.

Susan Sered, Senior Research Associate at Suffolk University's Center for Women's Health and Human Rights, is the author of six books and dozens of articles spanning the fields of medical anthropology, religious studies, and gender studies. Before coming to Suffolk, Sered directed the Religion, Health and Healing Initiative at Harvard University's Center for the Study of World Religions, and served as Associate Professor of Anthropology at Bar Ilan University in Israel. Sered's publications include *Sick & Out of Luck: Uninsured in America* (University of California Press, forthcoming), *Religion and Healing in America* (Oxford University Press, 2004), and *Priestess, Mother, Sacred Sister: Religions Dominated by Women* (Oxford University Press, 1994).

Alex Stepick, Professor of Anthropology and Sociology and Director, Immigration and Ethnicity Institute, Florida International University in Miami, received his B.A. in Anthropology at the University of California at Santa Cruz, and his Ph.D. in Social Sciences at the University of California at Irvine. Dr. Stepick has been conducting research on the impact of immigration on Miami for the past 20 years. His co-authored book, *City on the Edge*, on how immigration has changed Miami, won the Robert Park Award for the best book in Urban Sociology and the Anthony Leeds Award for the best book in Urban Anthropology. His most recent book, *This Land is Our Land*, published by University of California Press, has been described as providing a "new framework for understanding immigration and interethnic relations." The American Anthropological Association and the Society for Applied Anthropology awarded him the Margaret Mead Award for his work with Haitian refugees. He has received grants from all the major scientific research institutions, including the largest grant ever in Cultural Anthropology from the National Science Foundation. He recently served a National Academy of Sciences Committee on Immigrant Children and Health and on the Cultural Anthropology Panel of the National Science Foundation. The Pew Charitable Trusts recently funded him to be principal investigator on a major grant to examine immigration, religion, and civic engagement in Miami.

Manuel Vásquez holds a Ph.D. in Religion from Temple University. His publications include, *The Brazilian Popular Church and the Crisis of Modernity* (Cambridge University Press, 1998), *Christianity, Social Change, and Globalization in the Americas* (Rutgers University Press, 2001), which he co-edited with Anna L. Peterson and Philip J. Williams, and *Globalizing the Sacred: Religion Across the Americas* (Rutgers University Press, 2003), co-authored with Marie Friedmann Marquardt. Currently, Vásquez is preparing a special volume of *Latin American Perspectives* focusing on religion and identity. He is also co-directing a study on lived religion, space, and power among Brazilian, Mexican, and Guatemalan immigrants in Florida, supported by the Ford Foundation.